DEARNE VALLEY
COMMUNITIES AN

Dave Fordham

Acknowledgements

The author would like to thank the following for their assistance in compiling this work: John Ambler, Colin J Bowes, Giles Brearley, Michael Brearley, Brian Brownsword, Steve Butler, Barrie Dalby, Peter Davies, Maureen Dossor, Noman Ellis, Dave Fernie, Richard Fordham, John Fordham, Paul Fox, Cory Garner, Gordon Harriman, Geoffrey Hutchinson, John Law, Christine Leveridge, Barry Lockwood, Geoff Lumb, Andrew McGarrigle, Duncan McPake, Diane Pinder, John Petch, John Ryan, Chris Sharp, Paul Stebbing, Robin Tooley, Joan Ulley, Chris Veasey, Paul Walters, Andrew Warnes, Geoff Warnes, and the staff of Barnsley Archives, Doncaster Archives, Rotherham Archives and Sheffield Archives. Acknowledgment is also extended to Doncaster Local Studies Library for allowing access to contemporary newspaper records from *The Doncaster Gazette* and *The Doncaster Chronicle;* the University of Birmingham Library and The National Coal Mining Museum for England Library for viewing their holdings of *The Colliery Guardian, The Iron & Coal Trades Review and The Mining Journal*. I would like to especially thank the Maurice Dobson Museum & Heritage Centre, Peter Davies, Norman Ellis, Paul Fox, Andrew McGarrigle, John Ryan, Chris Sharp and Geoff Warnes for viewing their Dearne Valley photographic and ephemera collections and generously loaning material for use in this publication. Finally, acknowledgement is extended to the early postcard photographers whose work has been used to illustrate this publication: John Crowther-Cox, Edgar Scrivens and James Simonton. Finally, my appreciation is extended to all those who have contributed memories and photographs. Unless otherwise credited, all illustrations featured in this publication are from the author's collection and all attempts to attribute copyright have been made and apologies are extended to anyone omitted from the acknowledgements.

All rights reserved. No part of this publication may be reproduced, stored in a retrieval system, or transmitted, in any form or by any means, electronic, mechanical, photocopying, recording, or otherwise without written permission of the author.

Published by Fedj-el-Adoum Publishing, Email: Fedj-el-Adoum@Outlook.com
© Dave Fordham 2017

ISBN 9780956286482 First Edition 2017

This book is dedicated to the Dearne Valley Miners and their families and to the memory of local historians Norman Ellis (1920-2016) and Geoff Warnes (1936-2015)

Above: Following a number of disasters at British collieries and the death of 1,099 men in the Courrières Colliery explosion in France in 1906, a Royal Commision was established into working practices at British Coal Mines. This resulted in the publication of the 1911 Mines Act which introduced legislation for the complusory establishment of Mines Rescue Stations. However, the Wath Mines Rescue Station had already been established in 1908 by a number of local pits and housed 140 men trained in rescue techniques. This postcard features the Manvers Main No 1 Rescue Team displaying their breathing apparatus and equipment and is one of a series of views depicting the various rescue teams based at the station.

Colour Section

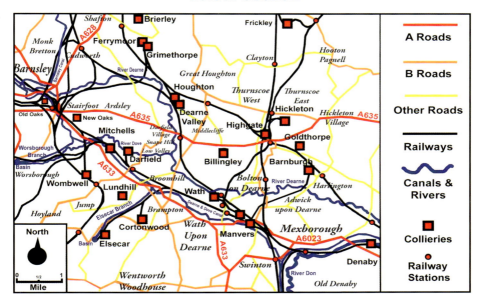

Above: Simplified map of the Dearne Valley (c1930), showing the roads, railways, canals and pits plus some of the places mentioned in the text.
Below: Yorkshire Coalfield Map showing the Dearne Valley Colliery Royalties, the position of the Pits, Coke Ovens and the Roads and Railways serving the district c1922. *(Business Statistics Co Ltd)*

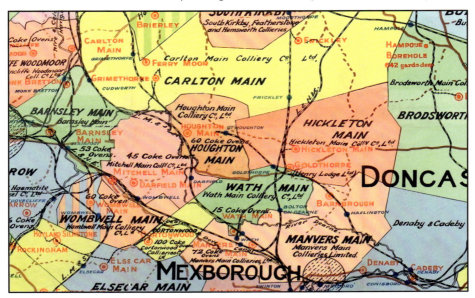

Above: All collieries had to lease the rights to mine coal from the local landowners and this illustration depicts a typical map accompanying a colliery lease document. This plan dates from c1925 and shows the land in the Brampton Bierlow and West Melton areas (shaded pink and yellow) under which the Barnsley, Parkgate, Swallow Wood and all other coal seams had been leased by the Ellis Charity Trustees to the Cortonwood Colliery Company Ltd. The colliery company purchased the land for the pit site from the trustees together with land for the company housing settlement on Knoll Beck Lane known as Concrete Cottages. Most of the surrounding fields in the area were owned by Earl Fitzwilliam of Wentworth Woodhouse. *(Reproduced with the consent of Rotherham Metropolitan Borough Council Archives & Local Studies Service, Reference 63-B/6/20/11).*

Below: Darfield Main Colliery was sunk to the Barnsley seam in 1856 and produced coal for 130 years from 1860 to 1989. This Plan shows workings (shaded pink) in the Beamshaw seam which was abandoned on 14 July 1981. *(Maurice Dobson Museum & Heritage Centre)*

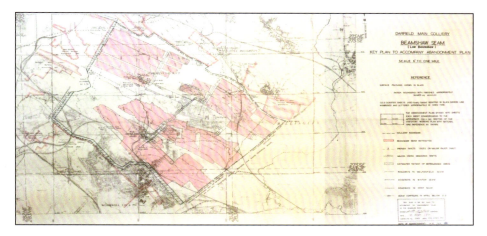

Below: Most pits produced enormous quantities of waste material which was tipped to form 'black mountains' which characterised mining districts. This 1978 photograph shows the 'extension dumping frame aerial ropeway' at Darfield Main Colliery which was used to convey the unwanted spoil to the tipping site. This was developed by the NCB following the restructuring of the pit in 1955. Note the buckets conveyed by the pylons on the right, the upturned example having disgorged its contents before returning to the coal preparation plant from which it will be filled with spoil. *(Maurice Dobson Museum & Heritage Centre)*

Above: Manvers Main Colliery was sunk in 1867 and gained its name from Sydney Pierrepoint, the third Earl Manvers, who owned the Adwick-upon-Dearne estate. The colliery became the home of the NCB South Yorkshire Area headquarters which published a series of information cards for all the pits within its division. This example, probably issued sometime in the 1970s, shows the Number 4 shaft which was sunk to the Parkgate seam in 1900. The shaft was enclosed in a steel and concrete collar to form an air lock. The structure left of centre is the exhaust to the Waddle Engineering ventilating fan.

Below: This postcard from c1905 was produced by John Crowther Cox of Rotherham and features a fine study of the original wooden headgears, engine houses and chimneys at Manvers No 1 Pit dating from the late 1860s/early 1870s. The wooden headgear above No 1 Shaft is on the right with the much smaller wooden headgear of No 1A shaft on the left. Canal barges in the foreground are being loaded with coal. The first two fatalities at the pit were probably two of the shaft sinkers, Thomas Smith, 26 and H Pashley, 30, who were killed whilst drilling an explosive charge in No 1 shaft. By 1950, 112 men and boys had been killed in accidents at Manvers Main Colliery.

Below: On 21, 22 & 23 July 1994, the production company *Lullaby Tunnel* staged the Dearne Valley Opera, based on "The Day the Earth Trembled- the story of the Barnburgh Pit Disaster". It was staged against the backdrop of Hickleton Main Colliery's magnificent No 3 headgear (installed in 1921) and played to audiences of 1,500 every night. It was the largest open-air community opera ever to have been staged in this country at the time. *(Peter Davies)*

Below: Since the closure of the pits, the local communities of the Dearne Valley have commemorated their contribution to the economic development of the country through the production of coal. Many of the colliery sites feature winding wheels (**Left:** Barnburgh) or Memorials to those who died in the quest of coal (**Right** Hickleton, in Thurnscoe Park). *(Peter Davies)*.

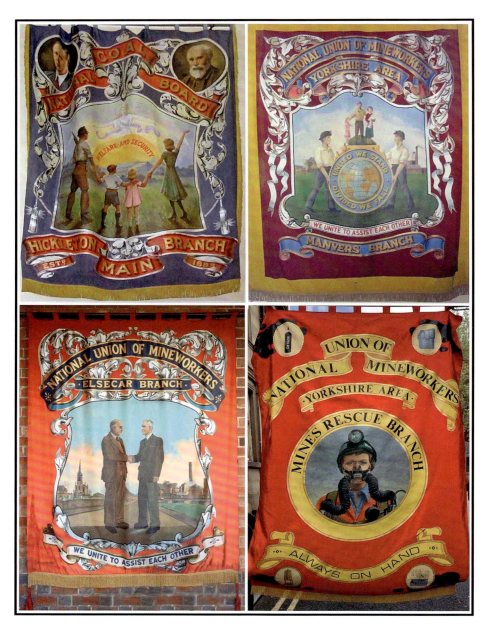

Above: These wonderful colourful banners were a feature of most pit union branches and the Dearne Valley was no exception. **Upper Left:** Hickleton Main Branch *(Peter Davies)*. **Upper Right:** Manvers Branch. *(Peter Davies)* **Lower Left:** Elsecar Branch (currently on display at Elsecar Heritage Railway Station) **Lower Right:** Mines Rescue Branch

Below: Following the 1919 Housing Act, local authorities took advantage of government loans and subsidies to provide council housing and various layout plans were commissioned. This plan of the proposed future developments at Middlecliffe is by Hemsworth Rural District Council. The Little Houghton No 1 Scheme, a development of 30 houses, was completed in 1924 with the building of George Street and John Street. This scheme included eight Type A houses – arranged in blocks of four with a living room, scullery and downstairs bathroom. However, the Little Houghton No 2 Scheme was far more ambitious and was originally planned to include 102 semi-detached houses (shown shaded red). However, only 50 of these houses were built on Charles Street and Mary Street. The reason for the failure to complete this scheme is unclear - possibly the 1926 General Strike and the fluctuations in the fortunes of the mining industry reduced the need for housing. The plans were drafted by W T Lynam, engineer and surveyor, around 1924. *(Reproduced with the consent of Barnsley Metropolitan Borough Council Archives Reference SY/9/RD13/8R)*

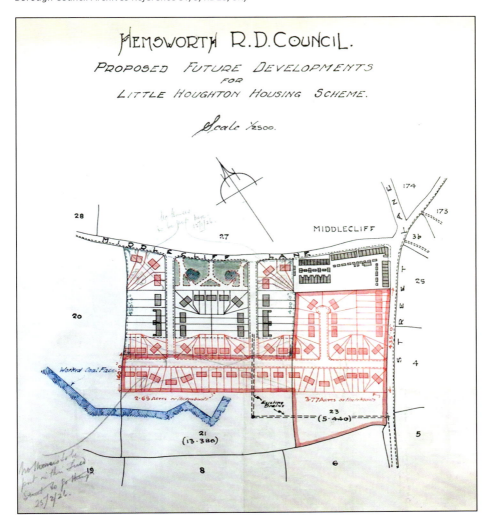

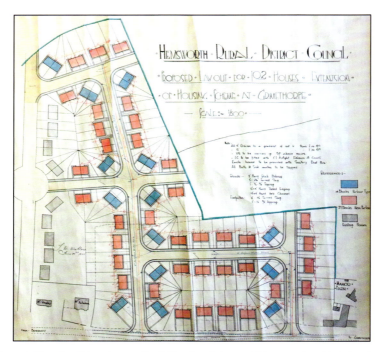

Above: Layout Plan for Grimethorpe No 3 Housing Scheme. This was the third development by Hemsworth Rural District Council at Grimethorpe and featured a development of 102 semi-detached houses provided in 1925. The houses were laid out on Park Road, Park Avenue, Willow Dene Road, Clifton Road & Brierley Road and the plans were prepared by J W Waller on 22 June 1925. **Below:** The houses forming the Grimethorpe No 3 Scheme were built to two distinct types: 28 Type B Parlour Houses (Left) and 74 Type C Non-Parlour houses (Right). The Type B houses were provided with a parlour, living room and scullery downstairs and a bathroom and three bedrooms upstairs. However, the Type C houses differed in that the configuration on the ground floor consisted of a large living room, a scullery and a bathroom downstairs– the idea being that miners coming off shift could head straight for the bathroom without trailing dirty clothes through the rest of the house. *(Reproduced with the consent of Barnsley Metropolitan Borough Council Archives Reference SY/9/RD13/7R).*

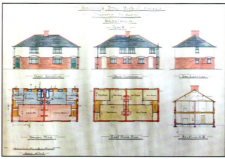

Below: The 266 houses which formed Thurnscoe Urban District Council's 'Thurnscoe Housing Number 2 Scheme' were built under the 1923 Housing Act and were designed by Corby Hall & Sons, Architects and Surveyors of Leeds - who drafted these hand-drawn linen plans featuring two of the four designs. The new estate was prepared and executed with great care and the houses were built to a far superior standard than those provided earlier. *(Thurnscoe Local History Group)*

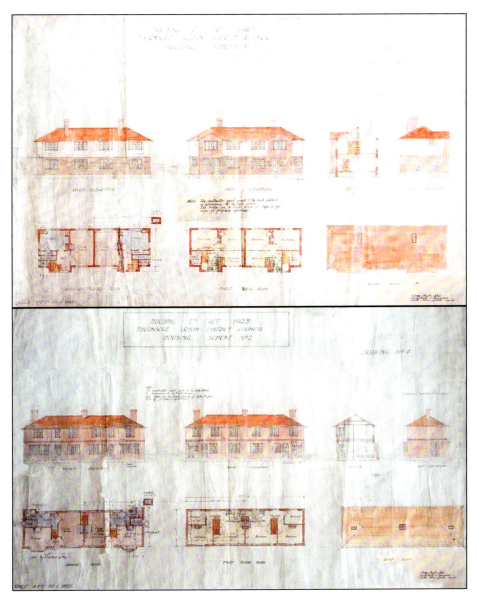

Above: A splendid postcard of one of the five motor buses purchased by Barnsley & District in 1913. This vehicle, a Leyland S8, with seating capacity for 27 passengers, was registered HE 10 and received fleet number 3. It is shown outside the Goldthorpe Hotel, ready for the return trip to Barnsley. The Barnsley to Goldthorpe service commenced on 3 May 1913. *(Norman Ellis Collection)*

Below: Ninety years later, sister vehicle HE 12 was discovered being used as a chalet on a farm in Newark and was purchased by Mike Sutcliffe and restored to roadworthy condition. HE 12 was entered in the 2006 Historical Commercial Vehicle Society's London to Brighton run, and was awarded the Outright *Concours d'Elegance* Winner. It is shown here at the Leyland Society's visit to National Tramway Museum on 13 July 2008, complete with Grimethorpe destination.

Above: Not many people can claim 51 years of service with a single company. However, conductor Diane Pinder started at Yorkshire Traction's Doncaster depot on a snowy 10 January 1966 and her first duty was shadowing clippie Mabel Wood operating a duplicate journey from Barnburgh to Doncaster. She would often work with driver Gordon Harriman, on the '*Donny-Mex*', (service 222 from Barnsley to Doncaster passing through the Dearne Valley). Diane is shown here in 1972 in front of JHE 639E, a 1967 Leyland Atlantean. With the declining use of conductors, Diane passed her bus driving test on 26 June 1981 and in 2008 transferred from Doncaster to Rawmarsh depot. At the time of writing she often drives Service 22X (Rotherham – Manvers- Barnsley). *(Gordon Harriman)*

Previous Illustration: The Dennis Dart bus was a popular purchase by Yorkshire Traction during the 1990s and this example is registered N110 CET and numbered 450 in the fleet. The vehicle was originally delivered new in 1995 to the Yorkshire Terrier subsidiary in Sheffield, passing back to the parent company a few years later. It is seen here in 2005 on Brierley Road in Grimethorpe operating service 37 to 'Red City' - a development of Hemsworth Urban District Council houses, finished in red brick, hence the name. The houses behind form part of the 'seaside' estate which were refurbished rather than demolished. The vehicle subsequently saw further service with Eastonways of Kent.

Below: A publicity postcard issued by Dan Smith during the interwar period and published by photographer R J Short of Wombwell. During 1932 and 1933 there was extensive flooding in the River Dearne and Dove valleys and this may date to this time. The postcard depicts Dan Smith's bus (registration WE 7314) travelling along Station Road in Low Valley near the New Station Inn. The origins of the vehicle are a mystery as it is absent from any of the published fleet histories.

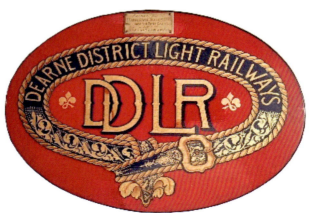

Opposite: On the closure of the Dearne District Light Railway, this hand painted wooden panel bearing the DDLR insignia was presented to Mark Lane Nokes. The brass plaque reads: *Presented to Mark Lane Nokes JP who drove the first car 14/7/24 and the last car 30/8/33*. Many years later the author purchased it on an internet auction site from a dealer in Canada. How this presentation panel ended up in Canada is a mystery. A Mark Nokes was a landlord of the Butchers Arms in Thurnscoe – did our man later emigrate from Thurnscoe to Canada? Whatever, it is nice to bring this unique piece of local history back to South Yorkshire.

Upper Left: Burrows 83 (HGC 280) was a 1946 Daimler CWA6 with Duple H30/26R bodywork, acquired from London Transport in 1953. The company sent it for rebodying in 1957 to extend its life and it returned with Burlingham H33/28RD bodywork. The vehicle passed to Yorkshire Traction on 22 October 1966 which sold the vehicle. This splendid view of No 83 has been recorded outside the company's Jubilee petrol station in Wombwell High Street. *(Geoff Lumb)*

Upper Right: Photographed outside the Dearneways depot in Goldthorpe High Street is fleet number 49 (MWO 146), a 1954 Leyland Leopard with Burlingham 44 seat bodywork acquired by the company in 1964 from John Bass of Fleckney, Leicestershire. *(Norman Ellis Collection)*

Lower Left: Mexborough & Swinton Trolleybus JWW376 is pictured in 1960 at the Adwick Clock terminus in Mexborough. The vehicle was sold to Bradford Corporation and rebodied as a double decker trolleybus with seating capacity for 68 passengers. It is currently housed at The Trolleybus Museum at Sandtoft but is not normally on display. *(Geoff Warnes)*

Lower Right: This publicity photograph appeared on the back of the Sheffield & Rotherham timetable issued by SYPTE in 1985 and shows one of the three Leyland DAB 67 seat articulated coaches purchased to operate former Dearneways service X91. The vehicle is 2012 (registered C112 HDT) and shown passing beneath the notoriously low and narrow Midland Railway bridge at Wath. The bridge was removed around 1990 following the closure of the railway. *(SYPTE 1985 Timetable)*

Below: A montage of Dearne Valley bus timetables, flyers and leaflets from the previous 100 years.

CONTENTS

Colour Section

Part 1 Dearne Valley Collieries

Introduction and Geographical Background
Early Mining prior to 1853:
    Around Elsecar.
    Around Worsbrough
Mining in the Dearne Valley from 1853:
    Lundhill Colliery 1853-1895
    Wombwell Main Colliery 1853-1969
    Darfield Main Colliery 1856-1989
    Manvers Main Colliery 1867-1988
    Mitchell's Main Colliery 1871-1956
    Cortonwood Colliery 1872-1985
    Wath Main Colliery 1873-1988
    Houghton Main Colliery 1873-1993
    Hickleton Main Colliery 1892-1988
    Grimethorpe Colliery 1894-1992
    Elsecar Main Colliery 1905-1983
    Barnburgh Main Colliery 1912-1989
Mining the Shafton seam:
    Brierley Colliery
    Ferrymoor Colliery
    Dearne Valley Drift Mine
    Billingley Drift Mine
    Highgate Colliery
    Goldthorpe Colliery 1909-1994

Part 2 Dearne Valley Communities

    Introduction
    Bolton-upon-Dearne
    Brampton Bierlow
    Broomhill
    Darfield, Snape Hill & Low Valley
    Elsecar, Hemingfield & Jump
    Goldthorpe & Highgate
    Great Houghton & Middlecliffe
    Grimethorpe
    Swinton
    Thurnscoe
    Wath-upon-Dearne
    Wombwell

Part 3 Dearne Valley Transport

The Road Network.
The Dearne & Dove Canal.
The Arrival of the Railways.
    Early Wagonways
    The Midland Railway
    The South Yorkshire Railway
    The Swinton & Knottingley Railway
    The Hull & Barnsley Railway
    The Midland Railway (Sheffield Line)
    Dearne Valley Railway
    Wath Concentration Yard
    Railway Reorganisation in the 1920s
    Industrial and Colliery Railways
    British Rail
    Privatised Railways
Public Transport
    Yorkshire Traction
    Mexborough & Swinton
    Dearne District Light Railways
    Independent Bus Operators:
    Burrows of Wombwell
    Camplejohns of Darfield
    Darfield Bus Operators Association
    Dearneways of Goldthorpe
    Larratt Pepper of Thurnscoe
    The Deregulated Market

Part 4 Conclusion

Table of Colliery Openings & Closures
Table of Mining Memorials & Pit Wheels
Glossary
Bibliography

Part 1 Dearne Valley Collieries

Introduction and Geographical Background

For most of the 19th and 20th centuries, the Dearne Valley was synonymous with coal mining, although the last deep coal pit ceased operation in 1994 with the closure of Goldthorpe Colliery. Open cast mining continued for a further few years, but since the start of the 21st century, most of the visible signs of the industry have been demolished, leaving a legacy of former colliery villages and communities, disused railway lines and landscaped spoil heaps - with new industries and retail parks occupying the former pit sites.

Although the River Dearne rises high on the moors above Birdsedge in West Yorkshire, before following a course south-eastwards towards Barnsley, the term 'Dearne Valley' has been traditionally used to designate the lower course of the river between Barnsley and the river's confluence with the River Don near Mexborough. Many of the settlements in this area have the suffix 'Dearne' appended to their place names, for example Wath-upon-Dearne, Adwick-upon-Dearne and Bolton-upon-Dearne. The lower Dearne Valley, located between the towns of Barnsley, Rotherham and Doncaster, and forming part of the larger East Midlands and Yorkshire Coalfield, proved to be a region rich in coal with several quality seams waiting to be exploited to power the furnaces of the industrial revolution.

The Dearne Valley is located on rock strata forming the Coal Measures, a series of rock layers deposited during the Carboniferous Period, a geological era of time dating to approximately 300-320 million years ago. Despite its name, the Coal Measures contain very little coal, consisting mostly of alternating layers of sandstone, mudstones and clays (the latter ideal for brick making), with occasional ironstone layers and around 30 coal seams. These seams vary in thickness and quality: some are relatively thin and of little interest, but around twelve seams have commercial potential, including the famous 'Barnsley Bed', a high-quality coal seam up to 10 feet thick.

Approximately 320 million years ago, the area forming the British Isles was a very different place to how it appears today. Originally occupying a location to the south of the equator in the hot and steamy tropics, the region was covered by a vast forested plain with numerous swamps, lakes and lagoons, traversed by a series of large river systems. Dead trees and vegetation accumulated in the swamps and their remains decayed into peat; layers of mud were laid down in the lakes and lagoons and the rivers deposited sand in their channels, and across the whole area during times of flood. Repeated cycles of deposition coupled with the continual subsidence of earlier sediments led to the accumulation of a great thickness of unconsolidated material which, over time and now buried at great depths and under the influences of intense heat and pressure, was transformed into the rocks that form the Coal Measures. During this process, peat was transformed into coal, sand into sandstone and mud became clay.

Earth movements (resulting from plate tectonics and continental drift) saw the British Isles gradually move northwards during the succeeding 300 million years to occupy its current location in the northern hemisphere. Uplift and erosion of younger rocks brought the Coal Measures of the Dearne Valley towards the surface. Due to a gentle downward tilting of the rock strata towards the east or northeast, coal seams exposed at the surface in the west of the region become buried at greater depths as one proceeds in an eastwards direction. The coal seams are usually named after their place of outcrop. Thus, the Silkstone seam is found at the surface around the village of Silkstone to the west of Barnsley before dipping eastwards beneath that town. Similarly, the Barnsley seam outcrops near the town of that name, before dipping in an eastwards direction beneath the younger strata of the Dearne Valley. At Wombwell the Barnsley seam is located around 250 yards beneath the surface. Further down the valley at Wath the same seam is encountered at a depth of 350 yards. Further towards the east, the seam is encountered at even greater depths, around 750 yards beneath the town of Doncaster and over 900 yards below the town of Thorne.

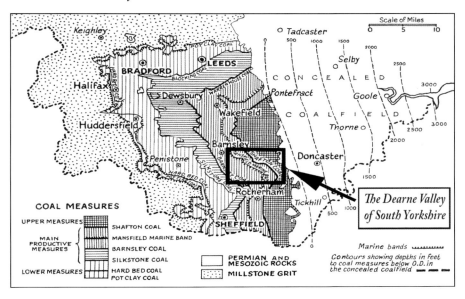

Above: Geological Map of the Yorkshire Coalfield highlighting the Dearne Valley region. See the Colour Section at the start of the book for a Dearne Valley Location Map and Colliery Royalty Map.

Prior to 1800, the Dearne Valley was largely rural in nature with very little signs of industry. It is known that the Romans worked the coal along the surface outcrops and during the mediaeval period the monks of Monk Bretton Priory and Nostell Priory also mined coal. In 1161, the monks of Kirkstead Abbey were working the Parkgate seam near Thorpe Hesley, and elsewhere there was some mining activity along the outcrop of the major coal seams; however, these operations were on a small scale and principally involved the opening out of small quarries, or the sinking of small bell pits and shallow shafts, together with drifts or tunnels into the hillside to access the coal seams. However, the total output from these early operations was insignificant, the coal being sold and consumed in the immediate vicinity. At the time, there was no canal or railway network and coal, being a bulky product, was very expensive to transport long distances via the roads of the day. The large London market, requiring vast amounts of coal, was out of reach for the land-locked Dearne Valley. Yet, at the dawn of the industrial revolution and with increasing advances in engineering and mining technology, this was about to change. Development of new pits was initially simulated by the opening of the Dearne & Dove Canal in 1800, followed by a dramatic boom following the opening of the South Yorkshire Railway in 1850.

Before 1850, the villages of the Dearne Valley were agricultural in nature and several of the settlements were mentioned in the Doomsday Survey of 1086. Many of the villages were located above flood plain of the Dearne Valley and consisted of stone built cottages clustered around a village church. Examples are numerous and include Darfield, Thurnscoe, Wombwell, Wath-upon-Dearne, Bolton-on-Dearne, Adwick-upon-Dearne and Mexborough. The agricultural land between these settlements was largely in the hands of the local landed gentry and the tenanted farms provided most of the work for the local population.

Prominent amongst the local landowners was Earl Fitzwilliam of Wentworth Woodhouse who had extensive estates at Swinton, Wath, Elsecar, Brampton Bierlow, Wombwell, Great Houghton and Billingley and who owned 19,164 acres throughout the West Riding in 1873. Other prominent landowners included: Frederick Vernon-Wentworth of Wentworth Castle near Barnsley with 5,111 acres; William Smelter Cadman of Ballifield Hall near Sheffield – owner of 1,476 acres in Wath and Bolton; the Reverend Thornley Taylor of Dodworth who owned the manor of Thurnscoe; his brother Francis Howard Taylor who resided at Middlewood Hall in Darfield; the Earl of Halifax of Hickleton Hall - who owned extensive lands in Thurnscoe, Goldthorpe and Bolton; the Foljambe family of Osberton Hall near Worksop - owner of the 4,000 acre Brierley and Grimethorpe estate; Earl Manvers of Thoresby Hall with 1,300 acres at Wath and Mexborough; Major Marmaduke Nesfield Wright – owner of the Little Houghton estate; and the trustees of the George Ellis Charity of Brampton Bierlow. There were also numerous minor landowners together with the Church of England which leased the coal beneath the church and village glebe land through the Ecclesiastical Commissioners.

Widespread practice was for potential colliery promotors to approach landowners for the granting of a mining lease. This the landowners were more than willing to do, as coal royalties could provide a significant and increasing proportion of estate incomes. Once a coal lease had been signed and sealed, colliery promotors were liable for an annual rent plus an acreage rent which typically amounted to £275 per acre, equivalent to 6d per ton of coal. Landowners were also due a royalty on every brick produced at the colliery brickworks plus a wayleave rent on coal beneath the estates of other owners which was brought to surface on shafts located on their land. Therefore, coal royalties provided extensive payments and by 1925, Earl Fitzwilliam was the third highest beneficiary of coal royalties in the country, behind the Marquis of Londonderry who dominated the County Durham coalfield and Lord Rhondda of South Wales.

Typically, small groups of industrialists and promotors would sign a deed of partnership to form a private coal company to secure a mining lease. To make a colliery pay, several adjoining leases would be required to form the colliery royalty, anything from around 500 acres in the west to 5,000 acres in the eastern areas where the coal seams were at their deepest. The promotors of the new venture then engaged local mining engineering companies to organise the difficult job of sinking the shafts and developing the underground workings. Surface buildings would need to be constructed and equipped with headgears, winding engines, boiler houses, chimneys, coal screens and ventilation fans, together with the purchase of a fleet of railway wagons ready to transport the coal over the national railway network. All this expenditure was occurred before a single piece of coal could be sold; therefore, the promotors had to be men of financial means, preferably with experience in the coal trade and, perhaps most importantly, having shrewd business acumen. Despite the upfront cost borne by the members of the partnership, the potential vast profits to be made from the marketing of coal inevitably made the venture worthwhile.

Above: Acting almost as a giant parody of the traditional northern back to back house, Wentworth Woodhouse is formed from two houses built together. The earlier brick built house was built by Thomas Watson-Wentworth, first Marquis of Rockingham in 1725. Shortly afterwards in 1734 work commenced on the eastern extension, an entirely new and much larger stone house built back to back with the earlier building. At 606 feet in length, the new East front is said to have the largest façade in Europe. In 1783, William Fitzwilliam, the fourth Earl Fitzwilliam, inherited the Watson-Wentworth estates, making him one of the largest landowners in the country; shortly afterwards he initiated the industrialisation of Dearne Valley by promoting the Dearne & Dove Canal and developing several small collieries at Elsecar. During the Second World War, the Ministry of Health attempted to requisition the house, but to prevent this, the seventh Earl Fitzwilliam tried to donate the property to the National Trust, who declined to accept it. Consequently, Lady Mabel Fitzwilliam signed a deal with the West Riding County Council leasing most the building to the Lady Mabel Teaching Training College whilst retaining a suite of 40 rooms as living quarters. Two sets of death duties in the 1940s and the nationalisation of the family's coal mining interests greatly reduced the wealth of the Fitzwilliams and most of the contents of the house were dispersed by auction - the famous life size study of the race horse *Whistlejacket* by George Stubbs now hangs in the National Gallery in London. In 1979, the tenth Earl Fitzwilliam died without issue and the family trustees, with extensive estates elsewhere (including 80,000 acres at Malton in North Yorkshire and 50,000 acres at Milton Hall near Peterborough) decided to dispose of Wentworth Woodhouse whilst retaining the surrounding 15,000-acre estate. In 1988, the college closed allowing the sale to proceed the following year and the house passed to pharmaceutical industrialist Wensley Haydon-Baille who started a restoration plan. However, the house then passed to architect Clifford Newbold in 1998 who continued the restoration programme and opened some of the rooms to the public. Following the death of Clifford Newbold, the house was offered for sale in 2015 and on 27 March 2017 the Wentworth Woodhouse Preservation Trust purchased the property and 83 acres and secured its future on behalf of the nation. The purchase price of £7,000,000 included donations from Fitzwilliam family members and a £3,500,000 grant from the National Heritage Memorial Fund. The Wentworth Woodhouse Preservation Trust hope to raise £42,000,000 in funds to repair the house and open it to the public. Due to the immense length of the eastern façade, it is difficult to successfully capture it in a single photograph and this example by Edgar Scrivens from 1910 features cattle grazing on the east lawn in front of the house, an area which would later be subject to open cast coal mining. The impressive length of the eastern façade has increased in recent times due to the formation of cracks in the building attributed to mining subsidence.

Once the partnership had secured the mining leases and established the capital to develop a pit, a name was selected for the new venture. This was typically called after a nearby locality or occasionally after the major landowner – examples of the latter include Manvers Main Colliery in the Dearne Valley and Monckton Main Colliery and Wharncliffe Colliery in the Barnsley area. The suffix 'Main' was appended to the colliery name, indicating that the pit had the privilege of extracting the main seam: the Barnsley bed, one of the most famous coal seams in the world.

The sinking of a new colliery was very capital intensive. Initially attracted to the western areas where the seams were at their shallowest and thus cheaper to extract, new colliery promotors had to later look to undeveloped coalfields further to the east where the seams were deeper and therefore higher amounts of capital were required. Deeper seams meant that larger royalties would be required to make a substantial and sustained profit. Where possible, private partnerships looked to remain in control, thus ensuring that profits were shared with as few people as possible. However, the establishment of The Limited Liability Act in 1855 was increasingly seen as a beneficial method of raising finance.

By registering a limited liability company, the members of the partnership would no longer need to raise the initial outlay itself; instead. A set amount of capital was calculated to cover construction and developmental costs which would form the shares of the company. The original members of the partnership could therefore remain in control and receive salaries as the directors of the new company as well as having the first option to subscribe for shares in the capital, with the remainder offered to the public. The disadvantage of this scheme was that, during periods of prosperity, a dividend would be payable to all shareholders; therefore, the original partnership would end up sharing the profits with others. The advantage was that any further expansion and development or the sinking of new shafts could be easily undertaken by increasing the capital the company by issuing additional shares, thus sharing the risk with outside shareholders. In time, most of the private colliery companies of the Dearne Valley converted to limited liability companies.

Once the shafts had been sunk and the mine was equipped and ready for production, the task of engaging a workforce would be undertaken and new colliery settlements were constructed, typically in rows of red brick terraces, starkly contrasting with the mellow sandstone cottages of the older villages. Many men came from the local area as coal mining was a relatively well paid occupation compared to the average wage for agricultural work. However, this only provided a limited supply of labour, and therefore recruitment was encouraged from throughout the country, especially from the older coalfields, where the collieries, staffed by a skilled workforce, were facing declining coal reserves and closure. Many migrants came to the Dearne Valley from the rest of Yorkshire and the West Midlands counties during the 1850s, 1860s and 1870s. Others came from London, Wales and Ireland with a representation from most counties, thus contributing to a considerable mixture of local and regional accents and contributing to a major increase in population.

There were several waves of migration into the Dearne Valley, each helping to dramatically boost population levels and reflecting the prosperous economic climate of the time. The first phase occurred with the initial opening of the earlier pits between 1855 and 1875. A recession in the coal industry followed, after which a second phase of migration occurred in the 1890s with the opening of additional collieries following the coal boom of 1889-91. The Boer War boom in the early years of the 20th century brought another influx of workers and this boom and the war years that followed generated considerable profits for the private colliery companies. In the early 1920s, a post-war boom brought more men to the area, as several of the pits were now exploiting their deeper reserves and sinking additional shafts, together with the development of a new group of collieries which were extracting the shallow Shafton seam.

On 1 January 1947, known as vesting day, the government nationalised the mining industry the National Coal Board (NCB) was established. The NCB acquired 958 collieries (employing 800,000 miners) and formerly owned by around 800 different private colliery companies and they paid out £164,660,000 in compensation. The NCB also inherited colliery owned coke ovens, brickworks and power stations and 140,000 houses, and became the country's largest landowner acquiring numerous colliery farms and 200,000 acres of land. In the 1950s, another post-war boom in the mining industry was reflected with considerable NCB investment in the South Yorkshire Coalfield which brought a wave of mainly Scottish families displaced by the closure of their own pits north of the border and local population levels reached their maximum. Following the Miner's Strike and the closure of the remaining Dearne Valley pits, some people have moved from the area causing a drop in the population in the 1990s. However, a final phase of migration, this time international, has recently occurred in the 21st century, particularly from 2005-2015, as workers from Eastern European countries have moved to the Dearne Valley, many working in factories and warehouses constructed on the former colliery sites.

Above: The River Dearne and the 'Dearne Valley Alps'. This photograph was taken around 1977 from the meadows at the bottom of Dearne Road in Bolton-on-Dearne and shows the swollen waters of the river and the snow dusted mountains of the Dearne Valley Alps – the colliery spoil heaps established at Manvers Main Colliery following the installation of the largest coal preparation plant in Europe in 1956. The pylons support the aerial ropeways for tipping waste material. The Dearne Valley was once noted for its mountains of spoil, known variously as muck stacks, spoil heaps, pit tips or slag heaps. *(Peter Davies)*

In the early days at least, there was the potential to earn considerable sums of money. But this had to be balanced by the terrible safety record in the pits, particularly prior to the formation of the NCB. Major explosions and accidents made the headlines, but numerous individual deaths and injuries occurred, frequently caused by roof falls or from accidents with coal tubs. Records of fatalities at the Dearne Valley pits are unfortunately far from complete, and it would be a fitting achievement to establish a national database of all those who lost their lives whilst working in the pursuit of coal.

The railway network, chiefly concerned with the transport of coal, saw passenger trains as an afterthought and railway stations were few. This gap in a growing market was served by public transport operations, provided by motor bus operators, tram operating companies (Barnsley & District Traction and Mexborough & Swinton Traction) and four local councils who joined together to operate a street tramway under the name Dearne District Light Railway. In time, the tramways faced increasing competition from charabancs and motor buses, provided by a multitude of independent operators as well as from the expanding Yorkshire Traction Company which was renamed from Barnsley & District Traction in 1928.

Today, with coal mining now a memory, the Dearne Valley has seen a total transformation over the past 200 years, from a quiet agricultural backwater, through rapid exploitation of its coal reserves and a spectacular increase in population, followed by an equally rapid decline in the industry with the people of the towns and villages suddenly facing economic hardship through reduced employment opportunities. This has been partially addressed with the construction of new industrial units, offices, retail parks, warehouse distribution and call centres on many of the former colliery sites. Even tourism is now a growth industry, with the development of Elsecar Heritage Centre and Old Moor Nature Reserve being two notable examples.

Early Mining around Elsecar prior to 1853.

In the Dearne Valley, the earliest mining operations had become centred around areas where the coal seams were at their shallowest, for example in the Barnsley area and in the upper reaches of the two tributary valleys; the River Dove at Worsborough and the Knoll Beck at Elsecar. At the latter, Earl Fitzwilliam's Elsecar Old Colliery, consisting of a collection of eight shallow pits, had commenced production in 1750. However, these were relatively small scale operations until the opening of the Dearne & Dove Canal provided a tremendous stimulus to trade. Coal, which previously could only find markets in the local vicinity, could now be exported to the rest of the country via the canal and river network.

At Elsecar, on the estate of Earl Fitzwilliam of Wentworth Woodhouse, coal pits were subsequently sunk along the line of the Elsecar canal branch, many owned and operated by Earl Fitzwilliam's Collieries. In 1795, Elsecar New Colliery opened, complete with the installation of a technological marvel of the day, a 'Newcomen beam engine', an atmospheric steam engine designed to pump water out of the colliery and drain the surrounding coal workings. This major advance in mining engineering had the effect of lowering the water table, thus enabling easier mining operations. The Newcomen beam engine operated continuously from 1795 until 1928 when it was replaced by electrically operated pumps. The engine presently remains in situ, restored to full working order, and scheduled as an Ancient Monument by the Government, the only surviving Newcomen engine in its original location and now forming one of the attractions of the Elsecar Heritage Centre.

Engineering advances like the installation of the Newcomen beam engine, further stimulated mining in the area and in 1837 Jump Pit opened, and, in 1840, Elsecar Low Colliery was sunk at Hemingfield, complete with its own canal basin and loading staithes on the Dearne & Dove canal. Around this time Elsecar New Colliery was renamed Elsecar Mid Colliery and Elsecar Old Colliery was renamed Elsecar High Colliery. In 1853 Elsecar Mid Colliery was replaced with the new shafts of Simon Wood Colliery. An undated newspaper report (possibly c1865) lists the five collieries worked by Earl Fitzwilliam as Lord's Pit, Jump, Upper, Top Wood and Hemingfield – Lord's pit, Upper pit and Top Wood possibly being alternative names for Elsecar Mid, Elsecar High and Simon Wood respectively. In 1903 Simon Wood Colliery ceased operation and was replaced with Elsecar Main Colliery, a huge operation sunk by Earl Fitzwilliam's Collieries Ltd to exploit the deeper seams throughout the area as the Barnsley seam was now mostly worked out in the Elsecar region.

Elsecar canal basin was served by an inclined tramway from 1840 which connected the basin with Milton Ironworks. The Ironworks were worked under lease from Earl Fitzwilliam by iron masters Walker & Company of Rotherham from 1795, extracting the Tankersley Ironstone seam from within the Coal Measures. The Milton Ironworks passed through other hands before coming under the control of William and George Dawes from 1849 and they also took possession of the nearby Elsecar Foundry. Further west from the top of the incline, a horse drawn wagonway continued westwards to Lidgett Colliery around two miles from the canal basin. The incline and wagonway rails were laid on stone sleeper blocks with wagons loaded with coal and pig iron being winched by rope down the incline to the canal basin. Another incline connected the canal basin with Earl Fitzwilliam's Jump Pit before continuing to the Hoyland Silkstone Colliery, one mile away at Platts Common.

The arrival of the South Yorkshire Railway in 1850 with its terminus next to the canal basin further stimulated trade to this developing industrial region and together with its iron foundries, coal mines and engineering workshops, Elsecar developed into an important industrial centre, largely controlled by Earl Fitzwilliam who lived a short distance away at Wentworth Woodhouse. To house his workforce at Elsecar, Earl Fitzwilliam created a model industrial settlement, with cottages, workshops, schools, shops, places of worship and facilities for the employees on his estate.

Further east along the canal branch, the land passed out of the influence of Earl Fitzwilliam and pits were developed by other colliery proprietors. New Brampton Colliery or Rainborough Colliery opened in 1819 some distance to the south of the canal near Westfield Road in Brampton Bierlow. In 1838, a small pit by the name of Cortwood (not to be confused with the much larger and later Cortonwood Colliery) was sunk on a location just to the south of the canal. Cortwood pit was also served by a short railway branch from the South Yorkshire Railway. It changed its name to Willow Main Colliery in the 1870s to avoid confusion with its larger neighbour and was shown as disused on the 1892 Ordnance Survey 1:1250 map. The site of Willow Main Colliery was subsequently buried beneath the spoil heaps of Cortonwood Colliery. On the northern side of the canal branch directly opposite Cortonwood Colliery, Lundhill Colliery was sunk in 1853.

Early Mining around Worsbrough prior to 1853

In a similar nature to Elsecar, Worsbrough also developed as a centre of industry clustered around the canal basin and along the branch of the Dearne & Dove Canal. The major landowners of the area were William Elmhirst of Ouslethwaite Hall (owner of 433 acres in 1873), the Martin-Edmunds family of Worsbrough Hall (owner of 1,462 acres in 1873) and a much larger estate belonging to Frederick William Thomas Vernon-Wentworth of Wentworth Castle, Stainborough (owner of 5,111 acres in 1873).

At Worsbrough Bridge, a watermill had been recorded in the Domesday survey of 1086, and there were small scale mining operations, together with iron works and blast furnaces exploiting the Tankersley and Silkstone iron seams in the Coal Measures. However, it was the opening of the canal basin in 1804 that lead to the industrialisation of the area with the establishment of a centre for industry which in addition to coal mining, included the Dearne & Dove Steelworks, the Dearne & Dove Saw Mills, Wood Brothers Glassworks, Worsbrough Furnace, Worsbrough Chemical Works and Worsbrough Dale Powder Mills

From the canal basin, a wagonway opened around 1820 to Rockley Pit and Rockley Furnace over two miles away whilst an inclined tramway headed south from Park Staithe to the small pits being worked in Worsbrough Park by Messrs Cooper & Company. In 1834, the Darley Main Colliery was sunk by G J Jarratt of Elmfield House, Doncaster. Mr Jarratt was joined in this venture by Mr Jeffcock of Sheffield and their colliery was connected to the canal basin by a short tramway. Located at the head of the canal basin was Martins Main Colliery, operated by the Martin-Edmunds family. In 1807, Joseph Mitchell was born at nearby Swaithe Hall and he served his apprenticeship at the Milton Ironworks in Elsecar before returning to Worsbrough where he established the Worsbrough Foundry. He turned his attention to coal mining and purchased Bell Ing Colliery and opened a new pit, California Colliery, both clustered around the canal basin.

The arrival of the South Yorkshire Railway in 1855 further stimulated the coal industry and on 19 October 1854, Joseph Mitchell signed a deed of partnership with Charles Bartholomew of Rotherham and John Tyas of Barnsley to establish the Edmunds Main Colliery at Worsbrough Dale to the south of the canal. The name was taken from the old Edmunds family of Worsbrough Hall and the coal was leased from local landowners: Augusta Marcia Martin and Frederick Vernon-Wentworth. Edmunds Main Colliery was ideally situated to export coal via the Dearne & Dove Canal and the South Yorkshire Railway. Mitchell, Bartholomew and Tyas opened a second colliery, Swaithe Main in 1857, located not far from Joseph Mitchell's residence at Swaithe Hall and the new pit was ideally located between the Dearne & Dove Canal and the South Yorkshire Railway. The establishment of Edmunds Main and Swaithe Main were necessary due to declining coal reserves in Joseph Mitchell's earlier pits at Worsbrough basin which quickly exhausted their seams and when the 1892 1:2500 Ordnances Survey map was published only Martins Main Colliery was shown on the map and this was marked as disused.

However, Worsbrough continued as a mining district following the sinking of Barrow Colliery on 4 June 1873. This was the property of the Barrow Haematite Company Ltd who were looking to secure its own supply of coking coal for their works in Barrow-in-Furness. Production commenced in 1876 from the Parkgate, Thorncliffe and Silkstone seams. A new colliery community of around 300 houses was constructed for the workforce at Worsbrough Bridge. The new settlement was known as New England and consisted of Arthur, William,

Thomas, Robert, Edmund, James, John, George & Charles Streets. New England was demolished in the 1970s and Barrow Colliery worked its last shift on 17 May 1985.

One saddening aspect shared by many of the pits of the Elsecar and Worsbrough area was their terrible safety record as several of the collieries were affected by a series of disastrous explosions resulting in the loss of many lives. Whereas, individual deaths and accidents were a common occurrence and were of course a disaster to friends and relatives of the individual concerned, they received little publicity. However, larger death tolls caused by major disasters had a devastating effect on the local community, sometimes wiping out three generations of a family and removing the male members from the households of entire streets. Such disasters attracted national media attention and were usually followed by the establishment of a relief fund to pay subsistence to wives and children of the victims.

The main cause of many pit disasters was the explosive ignition of methane. The Barnsley coal seam is notorious for releasing highly flammable gas emissions. This, coupled with the inadequate ventilation of the pits at the time and the use of naked flames for illumination caused several horrific explosions. On 24 January 1849, 75 men died at Darley Main; 10 died at Elsecar Low on 22 December 1852 and six men sinking the shafts at Lundhill Colliery died in an explosion on 22 August 1854. This was followed by an explosion on 19 February 1857 at Lundhill Colliery which killed 189 miners and left 90 widows and 220 fatherless children. At the time the Lundhill pit disaster was the greatest loss of life at any colliery in the country. On 8 December 1862, 59 men died in the Edmunds Main disaster, whilst the Swaithe Main disaster claimed 143 deaths on 6 December 1875.

Above Left: Elsecar Canal Basin captured on a postcard by Edgar Scrivens c1908. On the left are the derelict buildings forming Simon Wood Colliery which ceased production in 1903. Note the circular ventilating fan house. On the right are the replacement buildings of Elsecar Main Colliery where shaft sinking commenced in 1905. *(John Ryan Collection)*

Above Right: When J Semley of Worsbrough Bridge produced this postcard of Worsbrough Canal Basin, the canal was already a shadow of its former self, with barge traffic having ceased in 1906 with the abandonment of the Worsbrough branch. On the right is Cawker Row and a railway staithe from the Rockley wagonway. The site of Martins Main Colliery was on the left in front of the properties of Marriot's Square, with Bell Ing Colliery behind. *(Chris Sharp / Old Barnsley)*

Mining in the Dearne Valley from 1853

From around 1853, the Dearne Valley coalfield was rapidly and extensively developed with the mining frontier moving in an eastwards and north-eastwards direction as colliery promotors sought to exploit the vast profits to be made from extracting the Barnsley coal seam This sudden charge forward was caused by several factors:

- The industrialisation of the country;
- The development of the canal and railway network;
- Advances in mining technology;
- Introduction of methods of raising financial capital.

By the beginning of the second half of the 19th century, the British Empire was thriving on a steam powered industrial revolution, fuelled by the nation's ample coal reserves. Coal drove the factories of industry and was consumed in vast quantities throughout the country. Nearly every small town had its own gas works, generating gas from coal, and larger towns had their own power station for the generation of electricity, with both gas and electricity being consumed by industry and increasing amounts used domestically. The distillation of coal into its by-products generated tar and chemicals for the chemical industry and the production of coke from slack (small pieces of coal) found a ready market in the steel industry. The rapidly growing railway network was powered by coal-consuming steam locomotives which transported fuel to home markets and to ports for export throughout the British Empire and to other world markets, conveyed across the high seas in coal powered steam ships. By the end of the 19th century, Britain had become the leading exporter of coal in the world. Domestically, most household fires changed from wood to coal, with coal generated gas and electricity being supplied to the increasing number of homes.

The canal and especially the railway network had opened the previously land locked coalfields and London, at the time the largest city in the world, was a huge market for coal. Colliery companies and promotors realised that large profits were to be made by the mining, transporting and selling of coal. This in turn promoted the development of mining technology which enabled mining to be carried out at greater depths. The installation of steam powered twin cylinder horizontal winding engines enabled larger quantities of coal to be raised at the pit shaft whilst steam powered ventilation fans enabled safe mining operations to be carried out at increasing distances from the shaft bottom.

All this, of course, required capital. Previously, coal mines had been largely owned by wealthy landowners, or were in the hands of consortiums of entrepreneurs and promotors or individuals, usually local businessmen who formed private coal companies to obtain leases from landowners. Initially these private coal companies were controlled by industrialists who would use their own money to sink the pits and share the profits between themselves. However, the establishment of the Limited Liability Act in 1855 and the Joint Stock Companies Act of 1856 created easier ways of raising finance. Over the following decades most of the new private coal companies would convert to limited liability companies, and by the start of the twentieth century, when the massive pits of the Doncaster Coalfield were sunk to exploit the Barnsley seam to the east of the Dearne Valley, limited liability companies were the norm, many of them controlled by interests from outside of Yorkshire.

However, in 1853, with the canal and most of the railway network now in place throughout the Dearne Valley, coal working started on an industrial scale and the countryside in the area was carved up into huge coal royalties. A succession of deep pits was sunk to the Barnsley seam at Lundhill, Wombwell, Darfield, Manvers, Mitchells, Cortonwood, Wath, Houghton, Hickleton, Grimethorpe, Elsecar and Barnburgh and most of these went on to have lives of around 100 years, producing countless millions of tons of coal. Most of the new collieries all followed a similar pattern, with a difficult sinking through the water bearing strata of the Oaks and Woolley Edge Rocks, followed by the successful working of the Barnsley seam, initially by hand and with the use of ponies. Increasing mechanisation in the 1920s and 1930s followed, coupled with the sinking to deeper seams to replace falling output from the Barnsley seam. Around 1910, a second generation of smaller pits was sunk along the northern edge of the Dearne Valley to develop the Shafton seam at a shallow depth at Brierley, Ferrymoor, Little Houghton (Dearne Valley Drift), Highgate and Goldthorpe together with the Billingley Drift Mine in 1951. In the following pages the first generation of deep pits are described in chronological order followed by the second generation of shallow pits, described in order from west to east.

Below: Manvers Main Colliery was one of the largest pits established in the Dearne Valley following the development of the railway network. Sinking operations commenced in 1867 with No 1 and No 1A shafts and in 1875 No 2 Shaft was sunk, all three to the Barnsley seam. In 1900, No 3 and No 4 shafts were sunk to the Parkgate seam. In 1912, No 5 and No 6 were sunk at nearby Barnburgh and by 1923, the whole complex was employing 5,084 men who produced 1,500,000 tons of coal. The company continually invested in the site and this 1931 postcard by Edgar Scrivens shows the newly rebuilt No 1 and No 4 headgears (centre and right). The colliery closed in 1988, with the Barnburgh site following in 1989 and the coking plant in 1990. *(Norman Ellis Collection)*

The Dearne Valley Collieries

Lundhill Colliery (1853-1895)

Lundhill Colliery (sometimes referred to as Lund Hill Colliery) was formed by a syndicate headed by William Taylor Junior of Redbrook near Barnsley, a linen and bleach manufacturer. The partnership traded as a private company under the name of Taylor & Company and later as the Lund Hill Coal Company. The business also included Thomas Galland of Brampton Bierlow, Edward Simpson of Wakefield and William Stewart of Wakefield - the last two associated with the Wakefield soap manufacturers Hodgson & Simpson. Other shareholders included Mr Greaves of Manchester, Robert Dymond of Barnsley, William Henry Crossley of Maltby and Charles Simpson of Ackworth. Early records are unclear and it is unsure whether some of the later partners had succeeded earlier members, were shareholders from the start, or had joined later. Also unclear is the exact division of capital, although it was recorded that William Stewart loaned the company £21,000, possibly for reconstruction costs following the terrible explosion of 1857.

In the early 1850s, William Taylor Junior leased an area of the Barnsley coal seam at Hemingfield near Wombwell from several landowners and the leases were transferred to the Lund Hill Coal Company. These leases were signed with Sir George Wombwell, James Wilson Rimmington-Wilson, the Trustees of the George Ellis Charity, John Swift and W & J Johnson. A coalfield of around 400-500 acres had been secured forming a block of land between the Dearne and Dove Canal's Elsecar branch to the south and Hough Lane to the north. A site for the new colliery was chosen not far from the canal and a railway connection was made with the nearby South Yorkshire Railway (Elsecar Branch) and coal loading staithes were constructed on the canal.

On 22 March 1853, a ceremony was held to record the cutting of the first sods. Three shafts around 40 yards apart were sunk: No 1 downcast was sunk to a depth of 77 yards and was used as a water pumping shaft. No 2 shaft (11 feet in diameter) and No 3 shaft (9 feet in dimeter) were sunk to the Barnsley seam. The first sod above the No 2 downcast or drawing shaft was cut by William Taylor and the first sod above the No 3 upcast or cupola ventilation shaft was cut by Mr Greaves. Wooden headgear was erected above both shafts and was used for sinking purposes. The sinking operations, under the direction of contractor and master sinker John Jepson, did not proceed smoothly. Water flowed into the shafts from the surrounding rock strata and this required pumping out. In the base of the shafts, during the sinking operations, a borehole was drilled to the Barnsley seam to estimate the depth to the coal. On 22 August 1854, when the shafts were around 80 yards deep, six of the shaft sinkers died in an explosion caused by the ignition of methane issuing from the borehole. The force of the blast was so intense that one of the unfortunate shaft sinkers was blown out of the top of the shaft and the wooden headgear was destroyed.

At the inquest, a verdict of accidental death was recorded for the six victims. The headgear was repaired and shaft sinking continued. The Barnsley seam was finally encountered at a depth of 217 yards in early 1855 and underground workings commenced with the first coal drawn on 14 April 1855. On 27 December 1855, all the surplus sinking equipment and plant were sold at auction. Men were recruited from the local area to work at the pit under the management of Joseph Coe of Hemingfield, the head steward. To house some of the workforce, the colliery company constructed a terrace of 53 houses nearby named Lundhill Row, with the bricks provided from the small colliery brickworks. The houses of Lundhill Row were provided with privies to the rear and a stone built barn was converted for use as a Wesleyan Methodist Chapel. There was no school but the community was provided with a large public house, named the Lundhill Tavern.

Coal was initially cut by the pillar and stall method, due to the relatively shallow depth, and ventilation was provided by a furnace at the base of the No 3 upcast shaft. This arrangement was known as a furnace or 'cupola' shaft and involved the controlled burning of coal at the base of the upcast shaft, with the warm air rising and being expelled from the shaft top. This created a ventilation circuit, in that cool air was drawn down the downcast shaft and through the underground workings to replenish the air consumed by the furnace at the base of the shaft. It may seem extraordinary by today's standards to have a fire burning in a coal mine with all its flammable gas emissions, but this was widespread practice at the time.

By 1856, the colliery was one of the largest and deepest in South Yorkshire and employed around 300 men and boys, the latter working at the pit from the age of 11 upwards. The Mines Act of 1842 prohibited the use of all girls plus boys under the age of 10 from working underground. The Act resulted from the Huskar Colliery disaster near Silkstone in 1838 when 26 children drowned in the underground workings - 11 girls aged 8 to 16 and 15 boys aged 9 to 12. Queen Victoria ordered a public inquiry and established a Royal Commission to consider the use of child labour in the mining industry, resulting in the publication of the Mines Act in 1842. However, it wasn't until the establishment of the 1911 Mines Act when boys under the age of 14 were prohibited from working underground. The 1911 Mines Act also established an 8-hour day and ordered all colliery owners to provide Mines Rescue Stations equipped with dedicated rescue teams.

At Lundhill (and many other collieries in the Dearne Valley) many boys were employed to open and close ventilation doors or used as pony handlers; these animals hauled coal tubs of 10 cwt capacity from the coal faces to the shaft for winding to the surface, returning with empty tubs to the men working at the coal face. The empty tubs were then hand-loaded with coal cut by men known as hewers or colliers. The coal was worked on the advancing face method where a series of alternating blocks or stalls of coal were worked first, with other groups working the remaining pillars of coal shortly afterwards. These workers were then surrounded by the gas filled gob (areas of worked out coal) on three sides; this method of coal working was notoriously difficult to efficiently ventilate. At the surface, coal handling facilities were somewhat primitive, coal passing through a simple screening building before loading into railway wagons for dispatch via the South Yorkshire Railway or into barges on the Dearne & Dove Canal.

On Thursday 19 February 1857, Lundhill Colliery experienced a terrible explosion that killed 189 men and boys, the worst disaster in British coal mining history up to that date. Around 220 men and boys were in the pit having stopped work for their snap break when an explosion ripped through the underground workings in the Barnsley seam. The blast was so violent that the winding cage was blown into the headgear and flames leapt 100 feet into the air from the cupola shaft. A search and rescue party immediately assembled to extinguishing the flames, open the workings and recover the bodies. News of the disaster spread throughout the area and the national newspapers and magazines of the day dispatched reporters and artists to the pit to draw scenes of the explosion for publication. The disaster created 90 widows and 220 orphans. It was not until 22 April 1857, once the mine had been flooded and drained that work recovering the bodies began with the last body finally recovered on 16 July. The inquest returned a verdict of accidental death from an explosion of carburetted hydrogen. Once again, the colliery company were exonerated of any blame although there was criticism of the mining and ventilation methods and recommendations were made to cease the use of candles and naked flames in the pit and introduce safety lamps. A relief fund was established to provide for the dependents which raised £10,676 with the colliery company donating £500. Several of the boys killed in the disaster were only 10 or 11 years old and included brothers Ezra and John Illingworth, both aged 10 (possibly twins) and their 32-year-old father William Illingworth.

Above Left: Extract from the Ordnance Survey 1:2500 map of 1892 showing Lundhill Colliery, Lundhill Row and Lundhill Staithes. The colliery was connected to the South Yorkshire Railway by a branch line which crossed the Dearne & Dove Canal on Intake Bridge where there were also staithes for the loading of coal onto barges. On 19 February 2007, to mark the 150th anniversary of the Lundhill disaster, a new memorial was unveiled adjacent to the club house of the Wombwell Hillies Golf Course overlooking the site of the former colliery. The memorial was created by the Wombwell Heritage Group and the Lundhill Memorial Project with funding of £10,000 awarded from the Heritage Lottery Fund.
Above Right: This illustration appeared in the 28 February 1837 issue of the London Illustrated News and shows the crowds gathered at the site of the Lundhill explosion. The No 2 shaft is on the left and the No 3 shaft on the right. The disaster attracted widespread and sometimes sensational coverage in the national press and thousands of people travelled to the pit to view the scene. Most of the victims were buried in four mass graves in Darfield Church yard. Two years later a memorial to the victims, in the form of an obelisk, was placed there.

Following the 1857 disaster, the colliery was reopened under the supervision of Mr Beaumont a Barnsley mining engineer. An underground drift was constructed to carry foul air away instead of allowing it to pass over the cupola furnace. The ventilation of the underground workings, so criticised in the inquest, was vastly improved and by 1858 the colliery was re-opened for production with coal now worked by the advancing longwall method, a much safer form of working. The repairs had been carried out at a cost of £20,000, possibly covered by the loan of £21,000 forwarded by William Stewart. It seems almost callous by today's standards that the colliery should reopen after such a calamitous loss of life; however, this may have been welcomed by the remaining workforce at the time as the explosion had thrown them all out of work.

Five years after the explosion, the colliery company exhibited a section of the Barnsley seam at the 1862 London Exhibition. By 1874, 550 men and boys were employed and several of the shallower seams were developed to replace falling output in the Barnsley seam. Faces were opened out in the Kent's Thick, Swallow Wood, Meltonfield, and Abdy seams. Compared to other Dearne Valley collieries, the Lundhill royalty was relatively small and, unlike their neighbours at Wombwell Main and Cortonwood, the colliery company lacked the capital to sink new shafts to exploit the deeper seams.

To the south, the Lundhill fault, a geological fault running approximately under the line of the Dearne & Dove Canal, was designated as a natural boundary with the neighbouring workings of Cortonwood Colliery. On 12 December 1885, 15 acres of coal to the south of the fault were subleased to Cortonwood Colliery including coal in the Low Wombwell, Wombwell Close and Cliffe Field areas in Brampton Bierlow. By now the Lundhill partnership consisted of Edward and Charles Simpson, William Crossley and William Stewart. In 1893, 350 men and boys were working at the pit when the decision was made to sell the operation to the Wombwell Main Company Ltd. In 1895, the Lundhill royalty was added to that of Wombwell Main Colliery, increasing the latter's royalty to around 1,800 acres, the deeper seams being worked from the Wombwell shafts. Many of the workforce transferred to Wombwell Main and the new owners took possession of the houses on Lundhill Row. In 1901, Lundhill Row housed nearly 300 people and a Sunday school had subsequently opened in the Methodist Church.

The surface buildings at the pit were dismantled and the shafts were filled; the site had been cleared by 1903 when the Ordnance Survey 1:2500 map was published, although adjacent to Lundhill Staithe, a pumping station, was retained to 'dewater' the Barnsley seam workings in the surrounding area. By 1930 this pumping station had been closed, presumably because the Barnsley seam had now been worked out in the neighbouring pits. Around 1970, Lundhill Row and the chapel were demolished and the war memorial plaque from the old chapel was removed to St Mary's Church in Wombwell. Subsequent landscaping of the area has seen the opening of the Wombwell Hillies Golf Club and the capped Lundhill shafts remain adjacent to the fairways. The Lundhill Tavern, now trading as The Tavern, remains open at the time of writing in an isolated site surrounded by fields with no signs of there ever having been a colliery which claimed the lives of 257 men during its short existence. Now the only noise comes that breaks the peaceful surroundings of Lundhill comes from traffic on the nearby A6195 Dearne Valley Parkway.

Wombwell Main Colliery (1853-1969)

Above: A superb study of Wombwell Main Colliery issued as a postcard by Lamb of Barnsley. The horse and cart belonging to the Barnsley British Co-operative Society Ltd and is delivering pop to the pit, a welcome refreshment for the miners coming off shift. Note the wooden headgear above No 1 shaft (with No 2 shaft visible beyond with the colliery offices to the right. *(Chris Sharp / Old Barnsley)*

One of the largest Dearne Valley pits to open in the second half of the nineteenth century was Wombwell Main Colliery. The Wombwell estate was owned by Sir George Wombwell, who married into the Fauconberg family in 1791, inheriting the Newburgh Priory estate in 1825. Having previously lived at Wombwell Hall, he made Newburgh Priory his family home and settled on his 12,000-acre estate near Coxwold in North Yorkshire. Around 1850, the Darley Main Colliery Company (owners of Darley Main Colliery at Worsbrough Dale) sank a trial borehole near Wombwell Woods. The borehole successfully intercepted the Barnsley seam but they decided not to proceed with developing a new pit on the grounds of unsatisfactory geological conditions. However, their activities in the area were noticed by other colliery speculators, promoters who perhaps had more experience and who were prepared to take the risk of developing the coalfield.

Thus, on 20 August 1853, Sir Henry Herbert Wombwell signed a Deed of Assignment for his 1,007 acre Wombwell estate (which included 350 acres forming Wombwell Woods) with Charles Bartholomew of Doncaster, granting the latter the option to exploit all the coal and other minerals from beneath the estate for a period of 100 years - although the formal mining lease was not signed until 19 November 1855 following the death of Sir George Wombwell. Charles Bartholomew was manager of the River Don Navigation Company and engineer to the South Yorkshire Railway, a new railway presently under construction in the area, and he represented a syndicate looking to develop a new pit at Wombwell, with the output dispatched via the new South Yorkshire Railway which would obviously benefit from the carriage of the coal.

Other members of the partnership included Samuel Roberts, Edmund Baxter and Robert Baxter. Samuel Roberts was a Sheffield cutler and the Baxter brothers of Doncaster were director and lawyer to the South Yorkshire Railway. With the deed of assignment in place, the new consortium selected a site for the sinking of two shafts at the western end of Summer Lane along an unnamed track subsequently given the name Pit Lane, approximately a mile from the centre of Wombwell and near the hamlet of Smithley. The new pit site was in a depression in the land enabling easy access by a short spur from the South Yorkshire Railway's Aldham Junction to Woodburn Junction branch which was currently under construction.

The method of shaft sinking required the use of temporary headgears and temporary steam powered winding engines to raise the spoil from the shafts. To fuel the steam engines, a small 'gin pit' was opened in Wombwell Wood to supply a poor-quality coal from a minor seam for use in sinking purposes. A brickworks was opened adjacent to the pit to supply bricks to line the 12-foot diameter shafts and to construct the surface buildings; the first sods above the site of the shafts were cut on 8 December 1853. The No 1 downcast shaft (south shaft) and No 2 upcast shaft (north shaft) were positioned 40 yards apart and they reached the Barnsley seam at a depth of 224 yards on 28 October 1854. The seam was 7 feet 6 inches in thickness and of exceptional quality, believed to contain the finest coal in the country. This was confirmed in 1862 when the colliery mounted an exhibition of their "Wombwell Hards – best Barnsley coal" at the London Exhibition; it was awarded a Gold Medal.

On 1 January 1855, the promoters named their new business the Wombwell Main Coal Company and began trading immediately. The temporary headgear and winding engines were removed and replaced with permanent wooden headgears above both shafts, served by permanent winding engines manufactured by John Musgrave & Sons of Bolton, Lancashire. The winding engines were serviced by eight Lancashire boilers to generate steam power and the smoke exhausted through the large pit chimney. Screen buildings and sidings were laid out on the South Yorkshire Railway and the pit was nearly ready to work.

The original Deed of Assignment had stated that a shaft pillar 125 yards in radius must remain in place to protect the surface buildings from subsidence, a shaft pillar essentially being a circular disc of unworked coal. However, through the shaft pillar, headings were tunnelled to open out faces in the western rise side workings and the eastern dip side workings, so called because the gentle dip of the Barnsley seam from west to east. Ventilation for the underground workings was provided by a furnace or cupola shaft attached to the No 2 shaft, the air drawn upwards by the furnace having been previously sucked down the No 1 shaft and circulated through the underground workings, thus replenishing stale air with fresh air. To operate the colliery, men were recruited from the older coalfields of the country, possibly persuaded to transfer to the new venture by the fact that the colliery company were providing their own accommodation in the form of a new settlement of terraced cottages nearby. This new development took its name from the pit and was known as Wombwell Main.

Most of the coal was mined by advancing longwall faces, with groups of men working in stalls along the face, removing the coal by pick and shovel and supporting the roof with pit props. The area removed behind the workers was allowed to collapse in a controlled manner into the void as the face advanced. Coal was hand-loaded into iron tubs, which were then hauled by pit pony or by two underground haulage lines to the pit bottom. The coal tubs were raised in the cage up the shafts for sorting into various grades for dispatch to customers via the South Yorkshire Railway. The colliery was an immediate success and from 1853-1856 recorded a small profit of £6,755 despite all the start-up expenses. However, a major underground fire in 1862 caused the closure of the colliery and the pit recorded a loss during 1862 and 1863 as the fire had cost £24,000 to extinguish. This was a calamity for the workforce as they were thrown out of work and had to seek work elsewhere. However, by the end of 1863 the colliery re-opened and the men were re-employed and production began to steadily increase.

On 7 April 1865, the Wombwell Main Company Ltd was registered with a capital of £120,000 to acquire the business from the original promotors. The entire share capital of the new company was provided by the original owners who thus retained control. Charles Bartholomew and Samuel Roberts each subscribed for £40,000 in shares and the two Baxter brothers each subscribed for £20,000 in shares. There then followed a period of prosperity with the company recording a huge profit of £78,719 in 1873. By this time Wombwell Main was averaging an output of 1,000 tons of coal per day under Mr Blythe the manager and agent, and the *Mining Journal* stated that the pit was "one of the finest collieries in South Yorkshire". A considerable tonnage was sent to London via the South Yorkshire Railway to Doncaster and the main Great Northern Railway mine to the capital, whilst every day a coal train was dispatched to Grimsby Docks where the continental coal merchant Henry Josse organised its export throughout the world.

In the 1870s and 1880s, the company sought to consolidate its position in the area. Sir Henry Herbert Wombwell had mortgaged his Wombwell estate and chose to dispose of it to Frederick Vernon-Wentworth of Wentworth Castle, whilst retaining the mining royalties. However, through a complex of transactions, it appears that the colliery company and Charles Bartholomew purchased the freehold of the estate, with Frederick Vernon-Wentworth acquiring certain 'Lord of the Manor' rights. Thus, the Wombwell Main Colliery Ltd now became the owner of 1,007 acres, which included several farms, ideal for providing grain and fodder to supply the many pit ponies that worked underground. On 10 September 1870, the capital of the company was increased to £155,000 to provide funds for future expansion.

Further land was leased from adjoining land owners in the Wombwell area and this included: the 198 acre Aldham House Estate belonging to the executors of the late Robert Dowson Rylar of Hull; 139 acres owned by the Rimington-Wilson family of Broomhead Hall, Sheffield; 130 acres leased from Sir Theodore Francis Brickman, who held the Baronetcy of Monk Bretton; 96 acres sub-leased from the neighbouring Mitchell Main Colliery Company and which could be more easily worked from the Wombwell shafts and 260 acres leased from smaller land owners. This produced a total royalty of around 1,830 acres, a figure which included the neighbouring Lundhill Colliery royalty beneath which the company intended to work the deeper seams.

The Barnsley seam had been worked very successfully since the 1862 fire; it was remarkably easy to work being almost completely free of geological faults and output had been sustained at a healthy and profitable 350,000 tons per year. In 1874, around 720 men and boys were working at the pit. In 1876, the *Midland and Northern Coal & Iron Trades Gazette* stated that "the best wages in the district are paid at Wombwell Main". However, looking to the future and with no possibility of acquiring adjoining royalties due to the development of neighbouring collieries, the directors chose to bring forward plans to exploit the deeper seams beneath their 1,830 acres.

In 1884, a third shaft located 70 yards to the west of No 1 shaft was sunk to the Parkgate and Silkstone seams. The No 3 shaft was 12 ½ feet in diameter and reached the Parkgate seam at a depth of 475 yards and the Silkstone seam at a depth of 581 yards; in 1893 the No 1 shaft was deepened to the Parkgate level with the new No 3 shaft becoming the upcast shaft for the Parkgate workings. In 1895, the adjoining royalty belonging to the Lundhill Colliery was acquired. This pit had worked out its Barnsley seam royalty and was closed by the new owners, although the 53 cottages of Lund Hill Row were retained to house Wombwell Main miners. In 1895, Charles Bartholomew, the original promoter of the colliery, passed away and he was succeeded on the board of directors by his son Charles William Bartholomew.

Above Left: Wombwell Main's No 3 shaft is on the left and No 1 shaft is on the right on this postcard by John Crowther Cox dating to 1905. *(Norman Ellis Collection)*
Above Right: A similar view captured around 15 years later by Edgar Scrivens and featuring the newly completed coal preparation plant and washery together with its distinctive funnel shaped settling tank.

The development of the Parkgate seam required the reorganisation of the surface workings. The depth of the seam required the installation of a powerful steam driven fan to ventilate all the underground workings and in 1895, the old cupola shaft was filled in when furnace ventilation ceased. A new winding engine and winding engine house was installed at No 3 shaft. A new screens building was constructed to sort and grade the coal, together with the installation of a new haulage unit and air compressor plus the installation of electrical machinery to provide power for lighting on the surface and underground. On their visits underground to inspect the new seam and tour the operations, Charles Bartholomew and Samuel Roberts rode upon a specially converted truck which was hand propelled by the miners. The development of the coking plant coincided with the opening of a second railway outlet when the Midland Railway Sheffield to Barnsley line passed adjacent to the colliery. The development of the deeper seams at the pit saw the need for additional men who were accommodated in new houses built near Wombwell and in 1896 the workforce totalled 1,160 men and boys.

The Parkgate seam was opened out and worked very successfully. However, compared to the Barnsley seam, it produced more 'slack' or small coal, for which there was no market. To handle the slack coal, a battery of 90 'beehive' coking ovens was built to convert the slack into coke for selling to the steel industry. The Parkgate seam was initially worked by hand but the company were looking to introduce mechanisation. In 1901, the Dunsil seam, lying a few yards below the Barnsley seam horizon was worked and mechanised coal cutters were employed in this seam, although coal was still loaded by hand into tubs at the coal face. The opening out of new seams required the construction of a large coal washery in 1912 and this was installed by Simon Carves Ltd and had a capacity of 75 tons per hour. Increasing amounts of waste material were now being produced because of the use of mechanised coal cutting. Consequently, an aerial ropeway was installed northwards from the washery to a tipping point adjacent to the nearby hamlet of Smithley. Eventually the spoil heap would grow to cover part of Smithley Lane causing the road to be diverted to the north.

The production of coke had proved to be a profitable side business and in 1912 the old Beehive ovens were replaced by a battery of 50 modern Simon Carves Ltd coking ovens. The share capital of the company was increased to £300,000 on 20 July 1915. Some shares were issued to the public but most of the capital was supplied by the issuing of a share bonus to the three main shareholding families who received one free share being for every share held. From 1919, the coking and by-product plant was operated by a wholly owned subsidiary, the Wombwell Coke & Bye-Product Company Ltd, operating with a share capital of £200,000.

Above Left: Edgar Scrivens has captured Wombwell Main Colliery in its setting c1920, with from left to right: No 3 shaft sunk in 1884 with its newly completed coal preparation plant; the smaller No 2 shaft and prominent No 1 shaft. The bridge on the right carries the Midland Railway's Barnsley to Sheffield line across Pit Lane. One of the first fatalities at the pit was recorded on 14 July 1859: Richard Gledhill was killed by a fall of coal from the roof. Records, are incomplete, but by 1950 at least 45 men and boys had lost their lives whilst working at the pit.
Above Right: The By-Product Plant and Coking Works as depicted on a postcard from 1920 issued by Edgar Scrivens. The central bunker was supplied with coal transported along conveyor belts from No 3 shaft and fed a battery of coke ovens on the right, with exhaust gases expelled via the tall chimney. Coke and by-product plants often proved to be a very profitable side line at many pits in the Dearne Valley

War time coal production had ensured the generation of substantial profits for the company with £104,791 being recorded in 1916 (and even more in 1920 when the profits totalled £178,595), whilst workforce totals had now reached 1,668 men. As well as its investment in the coking subsidiary, the company also owned £4,987 in shares in the nearby Cortonwood Colliery Company and £800 in the Sheffield & South Yorkshire Navigation Company. In 1920, its freehold land was valued at £10,008, its farms at £10,243 and its fleet of private owner railway wagons £9,093. Despite these impressive financial records, it is only fair to say that the coal trade has always suffered from periods of economic depression, and losses were recorded in 1895, 1896, 1903-5 and during 1926, the year of the General strike. Following the General Strike, the workforce of the pit numbered 1,400, but in 1924 before the strike, the highest ever employment total of 1,717 was recorded.
In 1935, the Wombwell Coking and By-Product Company together with the coking operations of Barrow Barnsley Main Collieries Ltd were restructured into a new company titled the Barnsley & District Coking Company Ltd, of which Wombwell Main held 33.3% of the share

capital. A new coking works was opened at Blacker Hill to replace the separate facilities at Barrow, Barnsley and Wombwell which were all closed. Coal for this new plant was supplied from Wombwell Main Colliery by means of a new 2,400-yard-long aerial ropeway conveyed through Wombwell Woods from the pit to the new operation. By 1932, the whole of the Parkgate seam was machine cut at the coal face with coal loaded onto conveyors powered by air compressors; thus 100% of the output was mechanically obtained. The colliery was also working the Silkstone seam and had developed workings in the Beamshaw seam at a depth of 105 yards, the Fenton seam at a depth of 480 yards and the Thorncliffe seam at a depth of 520 yards. The Barnsley seam had been exhausted around the turn of the century and the workings in the Silkstone seam were nearing exhaustion.

In 1940 pithead baths with capacity for 1,200 men were opened by the Miners Welfare Scheme. During the Second World War, the pit was working five seams: Winter, Beamshaw, Fenton, Thorncliffe and Parkgate, although reserves in this last seam were nearing exhaustion. On 1 January 1947, the colliery transferred into the ownership of the National Coal Board and that year its 1,300 employees produced 315,000 tons of coal that year. During its life as a private company, the colliery had been managed by four generations of the Bartholomew and Roberts families and the Wombwell Main Company Ltd was subsequently wound up on 8 July 1958. Of the £300,000 capital of the company, the Bartholomew family held £127,740 and Sir Samuel and Martha Roberts held £88,820, with another £40,000 held by the Cleyfield Company Ltd of which Sir Samuel Roberts was chairman.

Under nationalised ownership, one of the first improvements was the replacement of the three wooden headgears above the shafts with steel headgears in 1948. However, the NCB was reluctant to fund future investments in the pit as the narrow diameter shafts restricted the ventilation. Nevertheless, some improvements were commissioned with the full-scale introduction of mechanised coal cutting and loading at all the five seams, coupled with the introduction of underground diesel locomotives hauling one ton capacity mine car trucks from the coal faces to the pit bottom. Production stabilised around 250,000-300,000 tons per year, although the workforce had declined to below 1,000 by 1955.

In 1966, coal production started in the Kent's Thin seam and Kent's Thick seam, accessed from drifts in the Beamshaw horizon. However, with the Parkgate seam now exhausted, concern was expressed at the lack of quality in these replacement seams due to their high levels of dirt which required extra processing time - hence the colliery was now becoming unprofitable. With limited and inferior quality reserves left the NCB consequently opted to close the pit with effect from 23 May 1969 after 116 years of operation. Most of the workforce of 670 transferred to neighbouring pits although some older men were made redundant. The colliery site and the adjoining miners housing were demolished in the early 1970s and the spoil heap landscaped and the whole area restored to agricultural and grazing use. Today, with wildlife filled hedges and cattle grazing in the fields covering the sight, and with no surrounding housing developments, it is hard to imagine that this was once the scene of a bustling colliery, the only clue being the name Pit Lane and the large green mound of the former muck stack.

Left: Dismantling of Wombwell Main colliery occurred in 1971 and this photograph depicts demolition of the coal preparation plant adjacent to No 3 shaft. Note the distinctive funnel shaped concrete settling tank also depicted in one of the earlier illustrations. *(Norman Ellis Collection)*

Below: This paper scroll was presented to the employees in 1947 following the transfer of the Wombwell Main Company to the NCB. During private ownership, the colliery had remained in the hands of four generations of the Bartholomew and Roberts families. *(Norman Ellis Collection)*

THE
Wombwell Main Co. Ltd.
1853 — 1946

ABOUT the 20th August, 1853, it was decided by Mr. Charles Bartholomew and Mr. Samuel Roberts to sink a shaft to the Barnsley Thick Seam of coal at Wombwell, and start a concern which became known as The Wombwell Main Co. Ltd. . . .

These two families, by personal contact, have directed the affairs of this Colliery during the whole of the 93 years of its existence, up to the nationalisation of the Coal Industry on 1st January, 1947. . . . . .

The present Directors hope that the successful results achieved by the team work of the Board of Directors, Officials, Staff and Men together with the atmosphere of mutual affection and respect will not easily be forgotten. . . . .

To this end we present you with this momento and wish you good luck and success for whatever may lie ahead.

Samuel Roberts
Chairman of Directors.

James Bartholomew
Vice-Chairman of Directors.

Peter G. Roberts
Managing Director.

Ch Bartholomew
Director.

Charles Bartholomew, Esq.

C. W. Bartholomew, Esq.

Major James Bartholomew, M.B.E.

C. E. Bartholomew, Esq.

Samuel Roberts, Esq.

The Rt. Hon Sir Samuel Roberts, Bart. P.C.

Sir Samuel Roberts, Bart.

Major P. G. Roberts, M.P.

Darfield Main Colliery (1856-1989)

Contemporary with the development of Wombwell Main Colliery, another partnership of colliery promoters was targeting the Wombwell area, keen to exploit the new rail links to the capital via the South Yorkshire Railway to Doncaster and the Great Northern Railway onwards to London. In the 1850s a consortium of West Yorkshire industrialists headed by George Pearson looked to open a new pit on the 375-acre estate of Charles & Henry Harvey, occupying the low-lying area between Darfield and Wombwell known as Low Valley, or simply 'the valley'. The Harvey family were involved in linen manufacture and in 1841 they were resident in Pitt Street, Low Valley, the street name probably derived from a clay pit rather than a coal pit. The Harvey family later moved to Park House at Ardsley, and became colliery house owners - as the Denaby Main Colliery mortgaged 162 houses at Denaby Main to Charles Harvey for £9,000 in 1890.

George Pearson was a railway building contractor and mining engineer based in Tanshelf near Pontefract. He had formed a partnership with London coal merchant John Buckingham Pope and railway contractor John Woodhouse to open the West Riding Colliery at Altofts near Wakefield. This Partnership would later trade as Pope & Pearson Ltd from 1874. George Pearson was now turning his attention to exploit the new coal markets of the Dearne Valley, firstly at Darfield and secondly (in conjunction with John Buckingham Pope) at Denaby Main Colliery once the Darfield enterprise had been established.

A site for a new colliery at Low Valley was selected and an option to take a mining lease for the Barnsley seam was signed with Charles Harvey. The pit site was located on Netherwood Hall Lane near Netherwood Corn Mill on the River Dove and not far from the South Yorkshire Railway, and, in 1856, work on sinking the shafts began. Although the new site was nearer to Wombwell than Darfield, the name Wombwell Main Colliery had already been taken by Charles Bartholomew so the promoters christened the new pit Darfield Main Colliery, after Darfield, a village located atop a hill a mile away to the north-east, and the new company traded as the Darfield Main Coal Company. The site was already connected to the South Yorkshire Railway by a branch line to the Darfield Clay Works. From here the single-track line continued north-eastwards via Low Valley Farm, possibly in the form of a wagonway, to a sandstone colliery near Wood Hall Lane. The pit site was therefore ideally located by a pre-existing branch line which was utilised to bring sinking plant and machinery to the location.

The option to mine coal beneath the 375 acre Harvey estate was finally converted into a mining lease on 28 May 1867 with royalty payments being made at the rate of £250 per acre. To increase the size of the royalty other leases were signed with adjacent landowners. These included 50 acres subleased from the Wombwell Main Company (an outlying portion of the Wombwell estate for which they had purchased the freehold); the executors of George Hawson and Thomas Hoyland; and 16 acres beneath fields in Low Valley owned by the trustees of the Wombwell Town Land Charity. The company also purchased the freehold of land belonging to several minor landowners in the Low Valley area.

Two shafts were sunk: No 1 downcast at a diameter of 11 feet; and No 2 upcast with a diameter of 10 feet. Almost immediately problems were experienced from influxes of water from the Oaks Rock and Woolley Edge Rock, a thick band of water-logged and fissured sandstones. This caused sinking operations to be delayed whilst the shafts were lined with cast-iron tubbing to a depth of 55 yards through the water bearing strata. Once this lengthy delay had been overcome, it was a relatively straight forward operation to continue sinking the shafts to the Barnsley seam. This was finally completed in 1860 at a depth of 330 yards and the seam was nearly 8 feet thick. Several other coal seams with commercial potential were encountered during the sinking operations including the 3-foot-thick Meltonfield Coal at 150 yards; the Winter seam 2 ½ feet thick at 165 yards; the Beamshaw seam 3 feet thick at 220 yards and the Kents Thick seam, a 3 ½ foot thick seam at a depth of 270 yards.

Two wooden headgears were erected above the shafts connected to two winding engines installed by Bradley & Craven Ltd of Wakefield. These would raise the double deck pit cages which could carry four tubs of coal on each draw. Steam was raised by a series of 9 Lancashire boilers and exhaust emissions were despatched via the large brick pit chimney. Ventilation of the underground workings was provided by a furnace at the base of the cupola shaft – this was essentially a chimney within the upcast No 2 shaft. The furnace drew fresh air down the downcast shaft, through the workings, before expelling the air via the cupola shaft. It was reported that the pit had cost £50,000 to develop and it was now ready to commence production. Men and boys were recruited from the local area and from the older coalfields particularly from Staffordshire to work at the new pit and a sizeable proportion of Irish immigrants also settled in the area. The colliery employed the services of Paul Roper of Bilston in Staffordshire, a recruitment agent who brought many families from the Black Country of the West Midlands to start a new life in Darfield.

Above: A postcard from c1905 showing Darfield Main Colliery from the south with the No 1 headgear central and the smaller No 2 headgear on the right. A colliery owned shunting engine is moving private owner wagons around the pit yard. These include a Darfield example on the far right and a wagon from Mitchells Main beneath the somewhat ramshackle wooden gantry. *(Norman Ellis Collection)*

The colliery was worked by advancing longwall faces in the Barnsley seam. Coal was hand-filled into iron tubs which were then drawn by pit ponies to the main haulage roads. Endless rope haulage then conveyed the full tubs to the pit bottom for raising to the surface. Probably the first fatality at the pit was recorded on 18 April 1861, when Joseph Taylor, a boy working on the surface, was killed in a terrible accident when he was drawn over the pulley wheel in the headgear. By 1950 at least 59 men and boys had been killed in accidents at the colliery.

On Sunday 13 October 1872, a disastrous fire broke out in the underground workings at the pit, caused by the rupturing of the cast iron tubbing in No 2 shaft which allowed water to spill down the shaft. This caused the air flow to become reversed resulting in the flames from the furnace to be drawn through the underground workings, firing the coal in the process. Flames leapt up the No 1 downcast shaft into the night sky, incinerating the wooden headgear and most of the surface buildings. Fortunately, nobody was working in the pit at the time, although 45 pit ponies, stabled underground, sadly lost their lives. Through the efforts of the Barnsley Fire Brigade, the fire was extinguished although the damage was extensive, which had the effect of throwing the 500 men and boys employed at the pit out of work for a year. The colliery was intentionally flooded for a period of six months as a precaution.

The management spent around £100,000 to reopen the colliery, which included the reorganisation of the underground workings, the construction of a new screens building and the installation of a steel lattice headgear above the downcast shaft. The furnace ventilation was replaced by a steam powered fan at the surface, a much safer way of providing ventilation, especially in a pit working a gassy coal seam like the Barnsley seam. After thirteen months of repairs the workforce was re-engaged, no doubt somewhat relieved at the prospect of finally being back at work after suffering over a year of hardship, and, by 1874, 400 men and boys had been re-employed.

Following the pit reconstruction during 1872/3, further leases were carried out to extend the royalty northwards into the Darfield area. A lease was signed on 1 October 1877 at a royalty of £280 per acre for the Barnsley seam beneath 55 acres of land belonging to the Masters, Fellows & Scholars of Trinity College, Cambridge, who owned land at Snape Hill. Other landowners included 75 acres leased from James Rimmington-Wilson of Broomhead Hall and 88 acres leased from the Vicar of Darfield Church. Finally, a lease was signed with Earl Fitzwilliam who owned Wombwell Ings, a series of flood meadows near the confluence of the River Dove and River Dearne. Together with additional smaller leases and freehold purchases this brought up the total royalty to around 1,000 acres. However, the Darfield Main royalty was now surrounded by other pits with no room for further expansion. To the south was Wombwell Main Colliery; the area to the east was leased by Cortonwood Colliery and Wath Main Colliery and bounded by the Lundhill Fault; Houghton Main Colliery had secured all the land to the north; whilst to the west, the rival Mitchell Main Colliery was rapidly developing. Consequently, Darfield Main settled down to produce around 250,000 tons of coal per year with a workforce of 750.

George Pearson died at the end of 1880 leaving a small fortune of £160,000, not a bad achievement for an illiterate man who often signed his name with an X. His descendants and the other partners continued to run the colliery but it subsequently passed into receivership, possibly due to the expenses incurred in re-equipping the pit after the disastrous fire in 1872.

In early 1894, the Darfield Main Coal Company, now employing a workforce of 949, was sold by the receivers for the sum of £44,500 to its rival next door, the Mitchell Main Colliery Company Ltd. This company were looking to expand their coal mining interests, firstly by the purchase of Darfield Main Colliery and secondly with the sinking of a new pit at

Grimethorpe, and it was stated at the Grimethorpe Colliery sod cutting ceremony that the enlarged Mitchell Company royalty, including Darfield and Grimethorpe would produce over 1,000,000 tons of coal per year.

Above: Darfield Main Colliery from the north as captured on this Haigh Brothers postcard from c1910, with No 2 shaft on the left and No 1 shaft on the right. The large brick chimney is supported by a series of metal hoops for strength; the smaller chimneys belong to the Darfield Clay Works. These were operated by James Gooddy but in 1895 they passed into the ownership of the South Yorkshire Sanitary Tube Works. *(Andrew McGarrigle Collection)*

By 1910, the Barnsley seam was nearing exhaustion so plans were drawn up to sink a third shaft at Darfield. The new owners were looking to exploit additional seams to replace the declining output from the Barnsley seam. It was proposed that the deeper seams beneath the Barnsley seam level within the combined Mitchell/Darfield royalty would be brought up through the Mitchell Main shafts and the shallower seams would be raised at the Darfield shafts. Consequently, in 1913, work started on sinking No 3 Shaft at Darfield Main. This was a much larger shaft, being 21 feet in diameter, and was sunk to the Thorncliffe seam at a depth of 623 yards, to act as an upcast shaft for the deeper workings at Mitchell Main and improve the ventilation. From this shaft workings were opened in the Meltonfield seam, Beamshaw seam, Swallow Wood seam, Lidgett seam, Flockton seam and Fenton seams. Work on sinking the No 3 shaft was delayed by the outbreak of the First World War, but it was eventually completed by 1917. The 1911 Coal Mines Act had forbidden the construction of wooden headgears; therefore, a large steel headgear was erected above the new shaft, dwarfing the headgear at the other two shafts.

In 1925, when the workforce totalled 1,236, Shipley Collieries Ltd acquired Darfield Main Colliery when they purchased a controlling interest in the Mitchell Main Colliery Company. The new owners commissioned a report in 1931 into the future of the combined operation.

This report proposed the closing of Darfield Main with all coal being raised at the Mitchell Main shafts, with the Darfield shafts being retained only to act as ventilation and for water pumping purposes. However, these plans were not acted on, possibly due to the severe downturn in the economic climate at the time. Collieries were allocated a fixed standard tonnage by the government; therefore a higher standard tonnage could be obtained by working a greater number of shafts and Darfield remained operational. For a long time, colliery spoil had been tipped into the abandoned clay pits of the adjacent brickworks to the east but in 1931 the brick works ceased operation. Consequently, the colliery now claimed this area for the proposed 'Darfield Muck Stack' formed by tipping spoil from an 'extension dumping frame aerial ropeway'. The new muck stack started to grow to a considerable height, the large grey artificial mountain eventually towering over the houses on nearby Pit Lane. In 1936, it was reported that the muck stack was ablaze, and smouldering pit tips were often a common occurrence at the time.

Above: Darfield Main Colliery was sometimes known as Low Valley Colliery, as can be seen from the caption on this postcard published by Doncaster Rotophoto Company in 1922, taken from Pit Lane. The wooden No 1 headgear is on the left (with the smaller No 2 headgear obscured) and the newly completed No 3 headgear on the right. The new gantry carried coal to the land sale yard and spoil across Pit Lane. Note the stacks of wooden pit props, imported from Scandinavia and used in vast quantities underground.

In 1943, coal winding at No 2 shaft ceased and its original wooden headgear was dismantled. On Vesting Day in 1947, 926 Darfield miners transferred to the new National Coal Board having produced 280,000 tons the previous year. The NCB decided to immediately implement a complete reconstruction of Darfield Main and this work was completed by 1954, with the aim of raising all the output at Darfield and closing the Mitchell Main site where there was no room for expansion. At Darfield Main, new electrically driven winding engines replacing the old steam winding engines at No 1 and No 3 shafts were installed. The surface buildings were rebuilt, including pithead baths with a capacity for 1,300 men which opened on 23 July 1955. A large coal preparation plant was constructed and equipped to handle an output of 500,000 tons per year, the output produced from longwall faces with all coal machine cut and loaded. From the coal preparation plant a new extension dumping frame aerial ropeway was installed to take the spoil to a new tipping site half a mile to the west. The River Dove now passed between the conical spoil heaps of Darfield Main and Mitchell Main, with the old Darfield Muck Stack now derelict, the whole forming a substantial blot on the landscape.

In 1956 with the closure of Mitchell Main, the workforce at Darfield increased to 1,478 and by 1958, 472,000 tons of coal were being produced. In 1960, an 8-ton capacity skip was installed in No 3 shaft replacing the use of coal tubs for raising coal. Coupled with the introduction of mechanised coal cutting and haulage conveyors, this had the effect of increasing output to around 450,000 tons per year throughout the 1960s from the Meltonfield, Winter and Beamshaw seams. The derelict pre-war muck stack near Low Valley remained an eye sore for several years but was subsequently removed, possibly for use in road building schemes.

However, coal production subsequently declined to around 320,000 tons in 1975 when retreating face mining methods were introduced into new workings in the Kent's Thick seam which had been developed to replace the earlier exhausted seams. In the early 1980s a major investment saw both shafts deepened to the Silkstone seam at a depth of 695 yards and it was further proposed to extract this seam from beneath the neighbouring Houghton Main and Cortonwood Colliery areas, with coal brought to the surface at Grimethorpe Colliery's new Barnsley South Side Complex, where a huge coal preparation plant designed to handle the output from several neighbouring pits had been completed.

For a time, the two retreat mining faces in the Silkstone seam were highly efficient and incredibly productive and in 1986 Darfield was officially merged with Houghton Main Colliery. The following year over 1,000,000 tons of coal were produced from the Silkstone seam by the Darfield/Houghton combined mine. However, the rapidly declining markets for Silkstone coal saw the pit finally close in July 1989 although the Houghton Main operations within the Silkstone seam remained for a few more years. Darfield Main had been operational since 1860, and had produced coal for a period of 130 years before final closure.

The surface buildings were subsequently demolished and the shafts filled in and capped. The post war spoil heap was reprofiled and landscaped and is now occupied by fields with the top planted with trees. For several years, the derelict pit site remained undeveloped, although the surrounding area was landscaped and trees planted. Finally, on September 2012, a new school opened on the pit site replacing the secondary schools in Wombwell and Darfield. The new school was named Netherwood Advanced Learning Centre, taking its name from Netherwood Hall, which stood adjacent to the pit. The site of the colliery now lies beneath the school car park and children play on the sports fields where once above their heads were millions of tons of spoil forming the Darfield 'muck stack' on fire in the 1930s. An unusual survivor at the time of writing, nearly 20 years after closure, is the roundabout sign at the western end of the A633 Wombwell bypass which still indicates the way to Darfield Colliery.

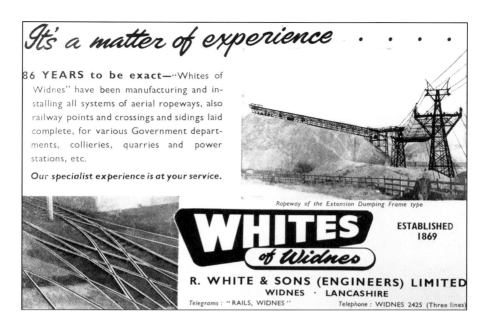

Ropeway of the Extension Dumping Frame type

Above: This advertisement for R Whites & Sons (Engineers) Limited features the newly installed 'Extension Dumping Frame' aerial ropeway (top right) installed at Darfield Main Colliery in the 1950s (See Colour Section at the front of the book). There were two main types of aerial ropeways used for the disposal of colliery waste. The extension dumping frame type, as its name suggests, could be easily extended, both at an inclined angle and along the horizontal, as the spoil heap grew and was fed by continuous buckets of spoil conveyed by the pylons in the foreground. The second type was a known as the 'Pylon Supported Aerial Flight' and typically used at pits producing massive quantities of waste material. A series of tall pylons were erected over the proposed tipping site, and buckets were conveyed along an aerial rope, tipping the contents from a great height at various stages, thus forming a series of conical mounds. These aerial ropeways and their man-made mountains of black colliery spoil, frequently on fire and smouldering away, became a common sight throughout the Dearne Valley. However, in later years, both types of aerial flight were replaced by simple covered conveyor belts and waste material was spread and compacted by heavy plant machinery and the tip profiles were lowered and smoothed and subsequently grassed over. The advertisement appeared in the publication *National Coal Board: The first ten years. (Author Collection)*

Manvers Main Colliery (1867-1988)

Sydney William Herbert Pierrepont, the third Earl Manvers, lived at Thoresby Hall in Nottinghamshire, which formed one of the famous Dukerie estates within Sherwood Forest and his family had inherited the Adwick-upon-Dearne estate in 1707. This was a largely agricultural estate which included arable land between Wath and Mexborough including Spring Well Farm, High Wood Farm, Adwick Lodge Farm plus the Manvers Arms public house in the small village of Adwick-upon-Dearne.

During the mid-1860s, Earl Manvers leased the coal beneath his Adwick-upon-Dearne estate to a consortioum of colliery promotors who intended to develop a pit between Wath and Mexborough. The new partnership was headed by four Newcastle colliery proprietors: James Morrison (who subsequently developed Houghton Main Colliery); William Hunter, William Hutchinson and Hilton Philipson. The partnership also included Henry Tennant of York (general manager of the North Eastern Railway); together with significant Sheffield industrialists: Alfred Allott - an accountant and colliery proprietor; George Hague, of the Midland Ironworks and David Davy of Davy Brothers Ltd. Messrs Morrison, Hunter, Philipson, Tennant and Allott were already trading together as the Renishaw Ironworks under the name of Appleby & Company. The Renishaw Ironworks were located to the south of Sheffield just over the border into Derbyshire where they also operated a small colliery at Cottam near Barlborough. With the experience gained from this operation they were looking to develop a colliery at Wath-upon-Dearne on a much larger scale. The partnership had leased 1,050 acres of coal and they had purchased an additional 290 acres of freehold land from Earl Manvers giving them a royalty of 1,340 acres.

The proposed new venture would trade under the name of Manvers Main Colliery Company in honour of Earl Manvers and two sites around 650 yards apart were chosen for the sinking of three shafts. Both sites had excellent transport links, being located adjacent to the Midland Railway, the South Yorkshire Railway (now trading as the Manchester Sheffield & Linconhsire Railway) and the Dearne & Dove Canal. On 21 May 1867, a small ceremony was held to mark the cutting of the first sods at the southeastern site, known as No 1 pit, located between the former South Yorkshire Railway and the Dearne & Dove Canal. Two shafts, both 13 feet in diameter, were sunk to the Barnsley seam. These were the No 1 downcast shaft and the No 1A air shaft or upcast shaft. Both shafts were lined with iron tubbing to a depth of 52 yards to make a watertight seal to stem the flow of water from the fissured and permeable sandstones forming the Oaks Rock. The cast iron segments had been maufactured in Sheffield and conveyed to the Manvers site along the canal. Beneath the 52 yard level, the shafts were lined with bricks produced in a small brickworks opened on a site near the junction of Doncaster Road and Golden Smithies Lane. Clay from this brick pit was mixed with 'spavin' obtained from the sinking operations, spavin being an unusual mining phrase for clay seams found beneath coal seams in the rock strata.

The Barnsley seam was reached in both shafts at the end of 1869 at a depth of 276 yards and was 8 ½ feet in thickness. The seam conisited of the upper part, an excellent steam coal known as the 'Barnsley Hards', and the lower part, which was marketed as' Barnsley Softs'. Other coal seams were interesected during sinking: these were the Newhill, Wath Wood, Abdy, Kent's Thin and Kent's Thick. Above No 1 shaft a large wooden headgear 75 feet high was erected coupled to a 100 horse power steam powered winding engine manufactured by Black Hawthorne & Company of Gateshead. No 1 cast was equipped with a double deck cage for winding 4 coal tubs, with each draw taking 30 seconds to raise the cage to the surface.

The wooden headgear above No 1A upcast shaft was much smaller. It wasn't the intention to wind coal from this shaft and hence it didn't require such a strong and substantial headgear, as it was only used for manriding purposes and so was equipped with a small steam powered winding engine installed by Robey & Company of Lincoln. The No 1A shaft was used for ventilating the underground workings. Intitally a ventilation furnace was installed but this was replaced by a steam powered Guibal ventilation fan in 1872. Steam raising power was provided by a suite of Lancashire boilers and a coal screening plant was erected by Qualter Hall & Company of Barnsley.

Men were recuited from the local area and the older coalfields of the country to work at the new pit and coal prodction commenced in 1870 when underground longwall faces were opened out. Coal was hand loaded into tubs which were then hauled by one of the pit's 40 ponies to the main roadways. From here steam powered endless rope haulage conveyed the coal tubs to No 1 shaft for winding to the surface. Above ground, the coal was sorted in the screens building which extended over sidings on the adjoining railway to the north and over the canal to the south. The whole of the colliery surface plant was laid out by George Hague and Mr Gomersall the engineering manager. George Hague died in 1871 in an accident at a railway station and he was succeded in the partnership by his son Ernest Hague.

By the time the *Mining Journal* paid a visit to the colliery in 1872, it was believed to have the highest coal output in Yorkshire and the 500 men and boys employed at the pit produced 1,000 tons of coal per day earning collectively £700 per week in wages. The *Mining Journal* also noticed that the surface buildings were still being erected which included the colliery offices and a pick sharpening shop, where the men could purchase their coal picks and shovels and have them sharpened, as the colliery company surprisingly did not provide these implements! By 1874, the workforce on the books amnounted to 600 men and boys.

With No 1 pit now producing coal, attention was turned to a second site 650 yards to the northwest located between the Midland Railway and the South Yorkshire Railway. This site was given the name Manvers Main Colliery No 2 pit, although it was sometimes referred to as New Manvers, with the No 1 pit gaining the name Old Manvers. At the second site, a single shaft 14 feet in diameter was sunk in 1875 reaching the Barnsley seam at a depth of 280 yards in 1877. This shaft was designated as the No 3 downcast shaft for ventilation purposes and was equipped with a 75 feet high wooden headgear and a winding engine installed by Davy Brothers of Sheffield. Steam raising was provided by a group of Lancashire boilers and coal was handled by a coal screening building constructed over a short branch line from the Midland Railway. The undergound workings between the two sites were linked to form a ventilation circuit.

The development of Manvers Main No 2 pit had continued despite the death of another member of the original partnership when William Hutchinson passed away and in 1876 Alfred Allott was declared bankrupt. The remaining members of the Manvers partnership sought to extend their royalty and secured a lease for the coal beneath Earl Fitzwilliam's Swinton estate. Numerous other smaller landowners in the Wath, Swinton and Mexborough areas sold or leased the coal beneath their land to the colliery company, thus enlarging the royalty to 3,000 acres. In 1880, a small battery of Beehive coking ovens opened adjacent to Manvers Main No 2 Pit, the first phase of what would become a very succesful side line in the production of coke and by-products. During this period output was approaching 500,000 tons per year from the two sites and an area of housing was constructed at Nash Row along Doncaster Road for the workforce.

In 1896, 1,076 men and boys were employed at the No 1 pit and 1,032 were employed at the No 2 pit, a total workforce of 2,108, with production approaching 650,000 tons of coal annually. Aware that the colliery had been very sucessful because of its high output and that reserves in the Barnsley seam were rapidly declining because of this, the company decided to exploit the deeper seams beneath their royalty. To provide finance for this expansion, the original partnership was reconstituted as the Manvers Main Colliery Company Ltd on 31 Januray 1888 with a capital of £420,000 provided by the partners. However, the depression in the coal trade during the mid 1890s saw these plans postponed and further capital was required for the sinking of additional shafts to the deeper seams and for enlarging the royalty. Consequently, on 21 February 1899 the Manvers Main Collieries Ltd was registered with a capital of £500,000 and shares in the new company were issued to the public. David Davy was appointed Chairman and Ernest Hague was appointed Managing Director.

Above: Manvers No 2 Pit was located 650 yards north west of No 1 Pit and is pictured here in this postcard dating from c1920 by Edgar Scrivens. The steel headgear above No 3 shaft (left) dates from 1900 and the wooden headgear above No 2 shaft (centre) dates from 1875. The coking plant is on the right which consisted of 50 coking ovens.

With capital in place two new shafts were sunk to the Parkgate seam in 1900. The No 3 dowcast shaft was 14 feet in diameter and positioned adjacent to No 2 shaft at Manvers Main No 2 Pit. The No 4 upcast shaft was 16 feet in diameter and positioned at Manvers Main No 1 Pit, but this time to the north of the South Yorkshire Railway and linked to No 1 shaft by a gantry across the railway line which also carried the coal to the screens building for processing. The Parkgate seam, measuring over 5 feet in thickness, was intersected at a depth of 554 yards in 1904. Above the shafts, steel headgears 72 feet high were erected by the Grange Iron Company of Durham and steam powered winding engines were installed by Markham & Company of Chesterfield - both shafts wound double deck cages.

The first few years of the new century were extremely profitable for Manvers Main Collieries Ltd. In its first year of trading a massive dividend of 35% was paid out to shareholders and £80,791 profit was recorded the following year. During the rest of the decade dividends of 20% and 25% were common, representing a tremendous return for the investors. The pit was producing around 1,000,000 tons of coal per year from the Barnsley and Parkgate seams, entirely hand loaded into coal tubs and hauled by 300 pit ponies. Feed for the ponies and hay for the underground stables were grown on the fields of High Wood Farm and Adwick Lodge Farm. To handle the enlarged output, a Baum coal washery was installed at No 2 pit by Simon Carves Ltd in 1910.

The directors of the colliery company were looking to extend their royalty and develop another pit and on 20 September 1906 they commenced negotiations for the 2,000 acre Barnburgh estate owned by the Trustees under the will of Andrew Montague of High Melton Hall. This new lease would enlarge the Manvers royalty to approximately 5,000 acres and they proposed to sink another pair of shafts at Barnburgh where they hoped to operate a colliery with an annual output of 1,000,000 tons per year, employing 3,000 men. The shafts at Barnburgh were to be numbered No 5 and No 6, continuing the sequential numbering of the Manvers shafts. It was hoped to find the Barnsley seam at a depth of 550 yards and the Parkgate seam at a depth of 800 yards. In 1915 the capital of the company was increased to £500,000 to pay for the development of Barnburgh Colliery and shortly afterwards existing shareholders enjoyed a 40% share bonus when the capital of the company was increased to £700,000 with the issuing of £200,000 new shares to exisiting shareholders, who received two free shares for every five shares owned.

Despite the outbreak of the First World War, production remained high and by 1917, 1,017 men were employed at No 1 Pit and 2,140 at No 2 pit. During this time, the colliery company kept modernising the pits and the original wooden headgear above the No 1 shaft was replaced with a modern steel lattice headgear installed by Redpath Brown & Company of Edinburgh, complete with pulley wheels 16 feet in diameter. In 1919 gas was supplied to the Wath & Bolton Gas works and the Swinton & Mexborough Gas works and a new brick yard was opened adjacent to Bolton Road with a production capacity of 10,000 bricks per day. The increased expenditure required at the colliery saw the issuing of an additional £300,000 in shares to the general public, enlarging the capital of the company to £1,000,000.

In 1923 the directors of the Manvers Main Collieries Ltd were headed by George Charles Davy of Alderwasley Hall, Matlock as Chairman (who had replaced his father David Davy); David Hague of the Hotel Russell, London as Managing Director (the son of Ernest Hague); F C Hunter of Exmouth in Devon; W S Hunter of Gilling Castle in Yorkshire; Hylton Phillipson and his son Hylton Ralph Murray Phillipson, of Stobo Castle in Scotland. The general manager was Arthur Thomas Thomson, a local man who lived at Woodside in Wath-upon-Dearne. They oversaw a workforce of 5,084: 3,882 of whom worked underground and 1,202 of whom worked on the surface; these produced 1,500,000 tons from the three pits owned by the company. In 1923 pithead baths with accomodation for 2,897 men were provided at No 2 Pit by the Miner's Welfare Fund, one of the first such installations in the country.

In 1924, the capital of the company was increased again from £1,000,000 to £1,300,000 to cover further developments and the building of houses. That year an overland railway connection was established with Barnburgh Colliery with the intention that all the coal produced at the latter would be brought to the washery at Manvers Main No 2 pit for processing. In 1925 insets were made in the No 1, 1A & 2 shafts into the Meltonfield seam at a depth of 121 yards. This seam was 4 feet thick and known informally as the bright seam. Rather than working with the traditional advancing longwall faces, it was proposed to operate more efficient retreating longwall mining methods with the introduction of mechanised coal cutting and loading. By 1929, 1,314 men were employed at No 1 pit, 2,592 at No 2 Pit and 2,298 at Barnburgh, a total of 6,204 employees who produced 1,673,000 tons of coal that year. The introduction of coal washing and mechanised mining operations meant that more waste material was produced. This was conveyed along the private railway towards Barnburgh Colliery where it was tipped from side tipping wagons by extending railway branches onto a tipping site on Bolton Common.

Modernisation continued throughout the 1930s following the establishment of an electrical connection with the Doncaster Collieries Association main electrical ring. Underground haulage was converted to electric power in 1931 and a new electrically driven Sirocco ventilation fan was installed at No 1A shaft and a replacement steel lattice headgear was erected above No 4 shaft, replacing the earlier steel headgear. A Simon Carves Ltd Baum coal washery with a capacity of 140 tons per hour was installed adjacent to No 4 shaft. The introduction of the nationally imposed quota system to stem over production had caused operations to cease in the Meltonfield seam in 1930 but these were restarted in 1935. On Saturday 25 September 1936 pithead baths with accomodation for 2,500 men were opened at the No 1 pit, provided by the Miners Welfare Fund at a cost of £27,000 and with accomodation for 2,500 men.

Above Left: The chimneys of Manvers Main No 1 Pit are reflected in the still waters of the Dearne & Dove Canal in this postcard view by an anonymous photographer dating from c1905 and taken from Doncaster Road. No 4 headgear is on the left and No 1 headgear is on the right. The colliery community of Nash Row was located to the left of the picture.
Above Right: Edgar Scrivens has captured a fine study of the new steel headgear at No 1 shaft in 1920. This was installed during the First World War and replaced the original wooden headgear. The steel headgear above No 4 shaft on the right dates from 1900 and has been encased in a collar to create an upwards draught to assist with the ventilation of the underground workings.

During the 1930s attention was focussed on renewing the coking operations and the old Koppers and Simon Carves ovens were shut down in 1932, being replaced with a battery of 30 Simon Carves Otto Regenerative Ovens which were opened during a ceremony on Monday 18 September 1933 when the wives of Oliphant James Phillipson and Hylton Ralph Phillipson cut the ribbon and turned on the gas. Simon Carves Ltd then entertained the party to lunch at the Danum Hotel in Doncaster. Oliphant Phillipson was now the manging director of the colliery company with Mr F C Hunter as Chairman.

In May 1942, the Barnsley seam was finally exhausted after 72 years and production commenced in the Haigh Moor seam at a depth of 347 yards. This seam was 4 ½ feet thick and elsewhere in the Dearne Valley was known as the Swallow Wood seam. Operations also commenced in the Winter Seam at a depth of 150 yards and accessed from drifts in the Meltonfield seam horizon. In 1944 drifts were driven down from the Parkgate seam to access the Silkstone seam at a depth of 648 yards. Despite the depression of the 1930s and the effects of the Second World War in the 1940s, Manvers Main Collieries Ltd continued to record substantial profits. On 1 February 1945 the company purchased Kilnhurst Colliery and its adjoining brickworks from the United Steel Company of Sheffield. Kilnhurst Colliery was mining the coal to the south of Swinton and it was hoped to combine the operations following the end of the Second World War. In 1945 the original wooden headgear at No 2 shaft was replaced with a steel headgear and winding of coal in 8 ton skips was introduced in this shaft, replacing the need for the raising of individual coal tubs.

In its last year of independent operation the Manvers shafts produced 910,000 tons of coal and employed 2,873 men and the Barnburgh shafts produced 775,000 tons of coal and employed 2,299 men, a total production of 1,685,000 tons of coal by the workforce of 5,172. Consequently, with the formation of the NCB in 1947, the Manvers operation was considered one of the jewels in the crown of the new nationalised mining industry. The Manvers Main Collieries Ltd received £2,364,500 for its colliery and by-product operations and was finally wound up on 25 September 1952 following the closure of the brickworks.

In 1949 the NCB embarked on a £6.5 million scheme to centralise production at Manvers Main Colliery by forming the Manvers Main Combined Mine where coal from four collieries would be handled in a new coal preparation plant. It was proposed to tunnel new underground links to Wath Main and Kilnhurst Collieries to raise their output at the Manvers No 2 and No 3 shafts with Barnburgh Colliery coal delivered by the surface railway as before. As part of this scheme the old No 1 shaft would be dismantled and No 4 shaft adapted for the man-riding purposes and new 1,500 horse power GEC electric winding engines installed at No 2 and No 3 shafts.

In 1950, work commenced on constructing the Manvers Combined Mine, designed to handle an output of 12,000 tons per day or 3,225,000 tons per year. The whole scheme was expected to take six years to construct and involved the introduction of skip winding at all the Manvers shafts from which coal was transported by conveyors to the Central Coal Preparation Plant which was built on Low Common to the north of the Midland Railway. This structure was huge, the largest coal preparation plant in Europe and consisted of three separate washeries; the whole plant straddled 18 railway sidings from which coal could be loaded into railway wagons passing underneath for transport to new power stations being developed by the Central Electricty Generating Board. Several miles of railway sidings were laid out to accommodate the numerous trains of wagons waiting to load at the plant.

The coal preparation plant produced 1,500 tons of dirt per day for disposal. A new tipping site was purchased on the flood plain of the River Dearne to the north. Two aerial ropeways were constructed to handle the dirt disposal. Unlike traditional aerial ropeways with their continuous stream of buckets, the new operation at Manvers featured a single large capacity skip on each aerial ropeway, the ropeway itself being suspended at great height from tall pylons. The skips were loaded from loading hoppers at the coal preparation plant and when full, they were then vertically hoisted to the level of the ropeway, before passing along it for tipping at various points, leading to the formation of a series of mountainous cones of spoil material, nicknamed the 'Dearne Valley Alps'. In 1957, its first year of operation, the coal preparation plant handled a massive 2,944,000 tons of coal. Of this 1,054,000 was contributed from Manvers Main, 1,036,000 tons from Barnburgh Colliery, 555,000 tons from Wath Main Colliery and 299,000 tons from Kilnhurst Colliery.

As well as reconstructing the coal preparation side of the business, the NCB also invested £9,000,000 in modernising the coking plant, and, in 1953 the NCB commissioned the largest carbonisation plant in the country at Manvers Main Colliery, replacing the coking ovens that had opened 20 years earlier. Simon Carves Ltd installed five batteries of coking ovens totalling 66 in number and designed to produce 3,000 tons of coke per day, designated for industrial use in steelworks in Sheffield and Scunthorpe. The plant also produced tar, ammonia, benzol and methane gas for the local gas works. The coke works included one of the tallest chimneys in the country and the whole complex opened in 1958. The coking plant, with its gas flares lighting up the night sky, and the distinctive smell of coke and tar production was certainly a memorable sight.

Above:. Manvers Main was famous for its huge coking plant which was completed in 1958 by Simon Carves Ltd and was the largest carbonising plant operated by the NCB. Coke production on the site had commenced in 1880 and in 1906 the original battery of beehive coking ovens was demolished and replaced with a battery of 36 Kopper regenerative ovens to handle the slack produced from the Parkgate seam. In 1912, the coking operation was increased with the installation of 14 Simon Carves Ltd Waste Heat Ovens. The coking plant was renewed in 1933 and replaced with the plant pictured above 20 years later. The new works included 66 coking ovens housed in five batteries. The coking plant closed in 1990 ending 110 years of coke maufacturing on the site. *(Paul Walters / Walters Worldwide Photography)*

From its heydey at the end of the 1950s, the coal preparation plant continued to handle impressive amounts of coal although it never reached its full potential. In 1964, output had declined to 2,259,000 tons of which 758,000 tons were produced from the Manvers workings, and, in 1975, output had declined to 1,466,000 tons of coal of which only 445,000 were produced from the Manvers workings, attributed to declining reserves in the remaining coal seams. Concern was mounting over the growing spoil heaps as the waste material wasn't being compacted properly so in the mid-1970s a new covered conveyor belt transported dirt disposal across Bolton Road to a new tipping area on Wath and Billingley Ings. Waste material was now spread by a fleet of Euclid Trucks Company spreaders and scrapers and a long but low spoil heap was created heading westwards towards Darfield.

On 27 March 1967 the new NCB area South Yorkshire headquarters was opened on Golden Smithies Lane and a training centre was developed which included the recreation of underground roadways. In 1985 an open day was held at the training centre and the author, an impressionable young boy at the time, was fascinated by the proceedings but somewhat dismayed when his helium filled balloon burst loudly in one of the training tunnels startling many of the other visitors. However, things improved with the highlight of the day being the chance to sit in the cabin of one of the huge Caterpillar wheeled loading shovels!

In January 1986, Wath, Manvers and Kilnhurst Collieries merged to form the Manvers Complex, forming Manvers West, Manvers Central and Manvers South respectively, working coal in the Silkstone, Haigh Moor and Newhill seams. However, during the period from 1983 to 1988 which included the Miners Strike, losses of £54,000,000 were recorded and British Coal opted to close the colliery on 25 March 1988. Wath Main Colliery had already closed the previous year and Kilnhurst Colliery had closed on 26 February 1988. Most of the remaining men at Manvers Colliery accepted an enhanced redundancy package although some transferred to other colleiries. Barnburgh Colliery finally closed on 16 June 1989 with the coking plant following in 1990.

The closure of Wath, Manvers and Barnburgh Colleiries and the removal of the Wath Marshalling yard left what was described as 'the largest area of dereliction in Europe'. Demolition and site clearance followed in the early1990s but for several years the area remained undeveloped as the remaining assets of British Coal were privatised. However, the formation of English Partnerships and the Dearne Valley Partnership together with the injection of local authority, national governement and European Union funds saw the transformation of the area with the construction of new roads, industrial units, housing and customer service centres, with the Dearne Valley College opening on the site towards the end of the 1990s. The spoil heaps have been reclaimed and planted with trees and in 1998 a new wetlands and visitor centre was opened by the RSPB at Old Moor Farm. Today, ornothologists scan the lakes and wetlands, all beneath the wooded backdrop of the former Manvers Complex spoil heap. The Manvers Main shafts numbers 1, 1A and 4 are now concealed beneath an industrial park. However the capped shaft plugs at No 2 and No 3 shafts are visible from Manvers Way, the shaft markers having been decorated by artistic designs as a memorial to the colliery. Near Dearne Valley College stands the Manvers War Memorial, honouring the 206 employees who gave their during the First World War.

Mitchell's Main Colliery (1871-1956)

Joseph Mitchell (1807-1876) was a self-made man who had been influential in developing the industries of the Worsbrough area, establishing the Dearne Steel Works and an iron foundry by the canal basin before turning his attention to coal mining. He purchased and re-opened Bell Ing Colliery near Worsbrough Dale in 1851 and opened the nearby California Colliery, named after the great Californian Gold Rush of 1848. He then focused his operations by developing pits further down the River Dove valley by forming a partnership with Charles Bartholomew of Doncaster and John Tyas of Barnsley. The new syndicate successfully opened Edmunds Main Colliery in 1854 followed by Swaithe Main Colliery in 1860. The success of these undertakings caused Joseph Mitchell to seek a much larger royalty nearer Wombwell and in the mid-1860s he began to secure coal leases in the area. At this time, he was living in nearby Swaithe Hall with his sons Joseph Junior and John, but after his death, the family moved to Bolton Hall in Bolton-on-Dearne.

To develop his new venture near Wombwell, Joseph Mitchell signed a partnership with Monsieur Josse and Monsieur Worms. Herve Henri Andre Josse was originally born in France but had moved to Barnoldby-le-Beck near Grimsby, operating a coal exporting business from Grimsby Docks. On 4 May 1871, he received British nationality and became known as Henry Josse. Monsieur Worms was the largest continental coal importer with operations in Paris, Lyons, Geneva and Peru, and he imported 1,000,000 tons of English coal per year. Joseph Mitchell was already familiar with Henry Josse who had handled coal exports from Swaithe Main Colliery and it seems that he was keen to tap into the growing export market to the continent and South America, using the expertise of his French business partners to help achieve his aims.

In 1868, Joseph Mitchell purchased a 32-acre site from the Manchester, Sheffield & Lincolnshire Railway near Aldham Bridge, a site conveniently located between the railway line and the Dearne & Dove Canal, forming an ideal location for a new colliery. The first coal lease was signed on 1 July 1866, securing the 166 acres beneath the Netherwood Hall estate in Wombwell belonging to Harry Garland. This was followed by 50 acres sub-leased from the neighbouring Wombwell Main Company on 1 January 1867; 16 acres leased from the Trustees of the Wombwell Town Land Charity on 1 April 1869; 112 acres leased from James Wilson Rimmington-Wilson of Broomhead Hall, Sheffield on 1 January 1871 and 29 acres leased from Mrs Garland on 1 July 1871. Additionally, 27 acres belonging to Joseph Mitchell's son John were leased on 1 July 1871. The coal was typically leased beneath these estates on a royalty of £300/acre.

In August 1871, sinking commenced of a pair of shafts both 13 ½ feet in diameter, the No 1 downcast and No 2 upcast shaft, and the sinking work was carried out by James Beaumont, the Barnsley mining engineer. The shafts were positioned on a NW/SE axis, parallel to the Dearne and Dove Canal. Sinking operations were immediately delayed by inrushes of water from the fractured Woolley Edge Rock, the same band of porous and waterlogged sandstone that had caused so much trouble at Darfield Main Colliery a few years earlier. To overcome the water incursions, the shafts were lined with cast iron tubbing to a depth of 132 yards. This expensive remedial work delayed the sinking operations but in September 1875 the sinking team discovered the Barnsley seam at a depth of 307 yards. To celebrate the discovery of the 7 ½ foot thick seam, the French Tricolour flag was raised and flown from the top of the headgears at the pit and the new operation was named Mitchell's Main Colliery.

57. MITCHELL'S MAIN COLLIERY, WOMBWELL.

Above: The Rotherham based postcard publisher John Crowther Cox has captured a scene on the Dearne & Dove Canal at Mitchells Main Colliery c1905. In the far distance a barge is being loaded with coal whilst in the centre another vessel is possibly delivering imported wooden pit props before taking its place at the coal staithe for loading. The effects of mining subsidence on the canal are apparent: the barge remaining in the centre of the canal and unable to reach the bankside. On the right washing had been hung out to dry in the yards of Pit Cottages whilst on the left the gable end of the terraces of Myers Street can be seen which formed part of the mining settlement of Mitchell Main or Mitchell's Terrace. *(Norman Ellis Collection).*

As sinking was being undertaken, the surface buildings, plant and machinery were provided by Henry Josse. Two large wooden headgears were installed above the shafts coupled to steam powered winding engines. Both shafts were equipped for raising coal, with a triple deck cage used in No 1 shaft which could raise 6 tubs of coal at a time and a double deck cage accommodating 4 tubs of coal installed in No 2 shaft. Ventilation was provided by a steam powered fan on the surface; the promotors - no doubt aware of the recent fire at nearby Darfield Main Colliery caused by the older method of ventilation by underground furnace - were not wishing to suffer from any fires in their new pit. On 14 February 1874, the first death at the colliery occurred when James Denford, a brick maker's assistant, died in an accident on the surface. The boy was only 13 when he fell into the brick making apparatus forming the pugmill machinery. By 1950, at least 38 men and boys had died at the pit.

By 1875, it was estimated that it had cost £121,000 to sink and equip Mitchell Main Colliery which was now ready to start production. Miners were recruited to work at the pit, possibly with the attraction of a company owned house being provided for them and their family at a new housing development to the south of the canal and named 'Mitchell Main' after the colliery. Groups of men worked in various stalls along the longwall faces, hand filling tubs of coal which were then hauled by pony to the main roadways, whereupon the tubs were hauled by an endless rope to the pit bottom for transfer to the shafts. At the surface, the coal was sorted in the screens buildings and most of the output was exported via the adjacent South

Yorkshire Railway to Grimsby Docks, although some of it was despatched by barges on the adjacent canal.

In January 1876 Joseph Mitchell died, apparently from the shock of the recent horrific explosion at Swaithe Main Colliery. This had occurred on 6 December 1875 resulting in the deaths of 143 men, and was under the management of his son John Mitchell at the time. Following his death, coal production continued at Mitchell's Main Colliery with Joseph Mitchell Junior now in charge. However, towards the end of the 1870s and into the early 1880s, the coal trade suffered from a severe economic depression. Consequently, the promotors offered new pit for sale on 25 October 1882. Bidding opened at £10,000 but only reached £21,500 with a bid from corn factor Thomas Wilkinson, when the property was withdrawn from auction. The partners then decided to restructure the concern as a limited liability company to provide a more secure financial footing and in 1883 they registered the business as the Mitchell Main Colliery Company Ltd.

The new directors of the concern were Joseph Mitchell Junior (Manging Director), Henry Josse and William Mauve, the latter possibly having purchased Monsieur Worm's share. The new company was registered with a capital of £32,000 in £100 shares with the aim of purchasing the colliery from the former partnership together with the London coal merchanting business formerly belonging to Joseph Mitchell and in 1884 the colliery produced 231,712 tons of coal. The new company began to immediately secure additional coal leases from the surrounding land owners to ensure the future of the pit. Coal was leased beneath 89 acres of land belonging to Francis Howard Taylor of Middlewood Hall, Darfield; 110 acres of land in the area belonging to the Bishop of Llandaff, Wales; 186 acres beneath the Tyers Hall estate belonging to Sir John Dodson (Lord Monk Bretton); a further 123 acres from Francis Howard Taylor (No 2 Lease) and 180 acres belonging to Earl Fitzwilliam, the latter signed on 1 January 1895. In addition to these large acreages, coal belonging to numerous smaller landowners was either leased or purchased outright.

In the 1890s, the company purchased Netherwood Hall from Arthur Garland, the son of Harry Garland who had originally leased the coal beneath the estate to the colliery company. Netherwood Hall was initially used as a residence for one of the members of the Mitchell family and later became the colliery pit offices and the home of John Halmshaw, the general manager, although around 1925 the building became a Miners Welfare Club and Institute.

The 1890s were a boom time for the coal trade and Joseph Mitchell Junior was looking to expand the company's activities. In 1891, the capital of the company was raised to £119,700 to fund the new developments, a complete turnaround considering the pit was unsuccessfully offered for sale only nine years earlier. By 1893, 650 men and boys were on the books and, in 1894, the Darfield Main Coal Company was purchased from its liquidators for £44,500. The combined Mitchell and Darfield Barnsley seam royalty now totalled 2,326 acres and 905 men and boys were now working at Mitchell Main Colliery. The new combined royalty now bordered Charles Cammell & Company's New Oaks Colliery to the northwest, Wombwell Main Colliery to the southwest, Wath Main Colliery to the southeast and Houghton Main Colliery to the northeast. However, to the north was the vast untapped coalfield at Grimethorpe, containing millions of tons in unworked Barnsley seam coal lying beneath the Grimethorpe and Brierley estates belonging to Francis John Savile Foljambe of Osberton Hall near Worksop.

On 21 January 1893, the Mitchell Main Colliery Company signed a lease with Francis Foljambe to develop a new pit beneath this 4,000-acre estate, under the subsidiary name of the Grimethorpe Coal Company. Shaft sinking commenced in 1894 but in 1896 the Grimethorpe venture was sold to the Yorkshire & Derbyshire Coal & Iron Company Ltd of Carlton near Barnsley. The Mitchell Main Colliery lacked the resources and expertise to complete the development of this huge new pit and were suffering from expensive shaft remedial work to counteract the influx of water. They therefore chose to sell the new venture, the sale enabling them to consolidate their operations at Mitchell Main and Darfield Main by exploiting the deeper coal reserves. It was decided to restructure the operations and raise all the deeper seams beneath the Barnsley level at Mitchell Main and all the shallower seams at Darfield Main and in 1895 the two pits produced 605,020 tons of coal.

On 18 April 1895 Joseph Mitchell Junior died at his residence at Bolton Hall at the age of 54. He had successfully overseen the early development of Mitchell Main Colliery following the death of his father in 1876. He was succeeded in the business by his sons Thomas Mitchell and Joseph Mitchell who had been trained as civil and mining engineers and colliery managers. This Joseph Mitchell was the third generation of the Mitchell family to bear the same Christian name.

On 21 December 1898, work commenced on deepening the No 1 shaft to the Parkgate seam. On 12 June 1899, this seam was encountered at a depth of 585 yards. Work on deepening No 2 shaft commenced on 3 January 1900 and was completed on 5 June that year and headings were made into the Parkgate seams to open out advancing longwall faces. The Parkgate seam was four feet in thickness and provided a quality coking coal, ideal to serve a proposed new coke works. The surface plant was re-equipped to handle the raising of coal from a much greater depth. New Winding engines and 10 Lancashire boilers were installed together with a huge new pit chimney in 1903. In 1906, the wooden headgears were replaced with steel lattice headgears and new screens buildings were erected to handle the increased output. A new powerful steam powered ventilation fan was installed by Waddle Engineering & Fan Company of Llanelli.

A field to the south of Bradbury Balk Lane was purchased from James Rimmington-Wilson for the site of the new coking plant and by 1907 a battery of 40 coking ovens had been installed by Simon-Carves Ltd. These ovens were supplied from a large coal bunker which was fed by an aerial ropeway which conveyed coal from the colliery across Bradbury Balk Lane to the coking plant. The workforce had increased to 1,118 by 1905 and by 1917, 1,718 men were working at Mitchell Main and the coke works. War time profits enabled the company to issue a 100% share bonus in 1919 when the existing shareholders received a free share for every share held, doubling the capital of the company to £239,400.

In 1925, the Mitchell family decided to retire from the coal industry and their controlling interest was sold to Shipley Collieries Ltd of Derbyshire, although as part of the deal John Mitchell gained a seat on the board of the parent company. A new chairman was appointed, Robert Claytor, with his fellow Shipley directors, Edgar Goss and Joseph Fletcher, joining the Mitchell Main board of directors. The new management continued to develop the Mitchell and Darfield pits. In 1927, 1,800 men were employed producing 336,333 tons of coal at Mitchell Main and 1,011 men producing 191,583 tons at Darfield Main, possibly the highest yearly production figures recorded to date. The new management improved the screens and colliery dirt disposal; the latter was now conveyed to an area north of the Great Central

Railway where two extension dumping frame aerial ropeways created two large conical mountains of spoil.

Upper Left: Despite the caption reading Mitchell's Main Colliery, this view depicts the new coking plant which was supplied by coal transported along the aerial ropeway to the bunker in the centre. The battery of coke ovens is situated behind the pylon with the chemical works on the right. This postcard was issued c1908 by Regina Press of Doncaster.
Upper Right: Postcard publisher Edgar Scrivens recorded this view of the Coking Plant and Chemical Works in 1908. The Dearne & Dove canal is lower right and the chimneys at Darfield Main Colliery can be seen in the distance to the left of the pylon. As both pits were located quite close together, Mitchells Main and Darfield Main always enjoyed a healthy rivalry until 1895 when Mitchells Main purchased its neighbour.
Lower Left: The Dearne & Dove Canal separated Mitchell's Main Colliery from the Aldham Glass Bottle Works. In 1872, Messrs Dickinson and Hammerton started the Aldham Glass Bottle Works Company and in 1895 the business was acquired by George and Joshua Redfearn of the Old Mill Glassworks in Barnsley. The site specialised in the production of glass bottles including the famous Codd pop bottle. The Aldham Glass Works closed in 1946 when production was transferred to a new site near Monk Bretton. *(Norman Ellis Collection).*
Lower Right: This postcard, produced c1925 by Edgar Scrivens, shows some of the improvements at Mitchells Main Colliery, including the new steel headgear installed in 1906 which replaced the original wooden headgear. No 2 upcast shaft is on the left and No 1 downcast shaft is on the right. Both postcards were issued by Edgar Scrivens in 1908 and 1925 respectively. *(John Ryan Collection).*

The Great Depression in the 1930s hit the pit hard and the workforce dropped from 1,800 to 1,299 men working coal in the Parkgate, Fenton, Swallow Wood and Silkstone seams, the last at a depth of 690 yards. In 1936, the colliery only recorded a small profit of £4,500 and proposals were put forward for raising the entire output at Darfield Main and closing Mitchells Main Colliery. However, these plans were postponed because of the war.

On Vesting Day in 1947, 852 men worked at Mitchell Main. Following nationalisation, the National Coal Board carried out an assessment of the operations at Mitchell and Darfield Main. Concern was expressed at the inadequacy of the site at Mitchell Main. There was little room for any future expansion and the surface buildings were in poor condition, there was also inadequate ventilation to the underground workings due to the small diameter shafts. Consequently, it was decided to close Mitchell Main and raise all the output from the three shafts at Darfield Main. In its final year of operation, 852 men were employed producing 235,000 tons of coal and on 25 July 1956, the workforce transferred to Darfield Main Colliery.

The surface buildings were soon demolished although the shafts were retained as the Mitchell Pumping Shafts, draining the underground workings. By 1962, most of the site had been cleared and the two conical muck stacks had been lowered and reprofiled and planted with fir trees. In the 1970s, the colliery houses of Mitchell's Terrace were demolished and in the 1980s a new industrial estate opened on the site of the colliery, glassworks and Mitchell's Terrace. The new road created to access the industrial estate was given the name Mitchell Road. The Mitchell Pumping Shafts were removed following the closure of Darfield Main Colliery in 1989 and finally capped in March 1994. In 1985, the new A633 Wombwell by-pass was opened. The western end of this road was named Mitchell's Way in honour of the Mitchell family and the trade they had brought to the Wombwell area.

Above: Colliery surfaces often had a cluttered appearance, and Mitchells Man Colliery is no different, as can be seen on this c1910 postcard by Haigh Brothers of Barnsley.

Wath Main Colliery (1873-1988)

Wath-upon-Dearne, once the home to the poet James Montgomery, was once a handsome and aristocratic village because its number of fine Georgian properties and was well known in the district as 'the Queen of Villages'. However, the development of Manvers Main and Wath Main transformed the village into a new and prosperous small town. The success of Manvers Main Colliery tempted a group of nine colliery speculators to secure the leases on the unworked coalfield to the north of Wath-upon-Dearne in the early 1870s and on 12 December 1872, a deed of covenant was signed between:

John Waring of Rotherham, colliery proprietor;
Joseph Waring of Barnsley, colliery proprietor;
George Shaw of Sheffield, colliery proprietor;
George Kenyon of Linthwaite, colliery proprietor;
William Sellars of Rawmarsh, colliery manager;
Charles Coking of Wath, merchant;
John Darcy Peech of Wentworth, veterinary surgeon;
James Crawshaw of Hoyland Nether, Corn Miller;
Benjamin Walter Sellars of Rawmarsh, Mining Engineer.

The deed stated that "the above entered into a partnership for the working and getting of the Barnsley Thick Bed of coal in lands in Wath and Bolton and now held by them under lease and agreements for lease under the firm of the Wath-upon-Dearne Main Colliery Company". The capital of the partnership was £45,500, with the first three named promotors contributing £7,000 each, with £3,500 being subscribed from each of the six remaining partners.

Of the above, John and Joseph Waring had developed Carr House Colliery near Rotherham (in partnership with George Hague and George Rhodes of Rotherham and Mr Harvey of Barnsley) mining the coal beneath land belonging to Earl Fitzwilliam in the 1850s and in 1864 the Waring brothers leased 1,000 acres of minerals lying beneath the estate of George Savile Foljambe of Aldwarke Hall near Rotherham, sinking Aldwarke Main Colliery. The Waring brothers had also made an unsuccessful attempt to sink a pit to the Barnsley seam at Denaby Main near Mexborough. In 1873, they sold Carr House and Aldwarke Collieries to the Sheffield steel makers John Brown & Company Ltd. George Shaw of High Hazels Hall in Darnall near Sheffield, was a member of a partnership operating Newhill Colliery in Wath-upon-Dearne, a small pit extracting the shallow Wath Wood coal seam from beneath the estate of John Henry Payne of Newhill Hall. The Reverend George Kenyon was a partner in a small-scale mining operation in the Huddersfield area. William and Benjamin Sellars were working Greasborough Colliery having undertaken a coal lease beneath the estate of Earl Fitzwilliam. Charles Coking was a chemist and seed merchant who also ran Wath Post Office. John Darcy Peech was a veterinary surgeon with no previously known connections to the mining industry and James Crawshaw was a corn miller from Hoyland, again with no previously known connections to the mining industry.

The partnership had acquired leases from numerous landowners in the Bolton-on-Dearne area. These included Joseph Mitchell Junior of Bolton Hall, a rival colliery promoter involved with Mitchells Main Colliery near Wombwell; Sir Charles Wood (Viscount Halifax) of Hickleton Hall; Earl Fitzwilliam, owner of Bolton Ings, Billingley Ings, Old Moor Farm and Carr Head fields; William John Smelter Cadman of Handsworth Grange near Sheffield, who had extensive land holdings in Wath and Bolton; Robert Charles Otter of Royston Manor,

Clayworth and Sir Theodore Brinckman of Monk Bretton. Together with freehold lands purchased by the partnership, this gave a total royalty of around 1,500 acres.

A site on the southern edge of the new royalty was chosen between the Midland Railway and South Yorkshire Railway and connections were made to both lines. Work started on sinking two shafts at the start of 1873 but was abandoned soon afterwards due to a massive influx of water from the porous sandstones of the Woolley Edge Rock. Consequently, two new shafts were started nearby next to the Midland Railway. With knowledge of expected water problems, the promotors decided to line the new shafts with cast iron tubbing to a depth of 96 yards from the surface to form a water tight seal through the permeable sandstones. To facilitate shaft sinking, two permanent wooden headgears 52 feet high were constructed over each shaft. There were two shafts, each 14 feet in diameter and positioned around 60 yards apart: the No 1 downcast shaft and the No 2 upcast shaft. Initially the colliery didn't have its own brickworks so bricks were imported via the railway network for constructing the surface buildings and lining the shafts from below the 96-yard marker to the level of the Barnsley seam. This seam was intersected at the end of 1876 at a depth of 346 yards and was 8 ½ feet thick. The shafts were equipped with steam powered winding engines installed by Clayton Goodfellow & Company of Blackburn and both shafts were equipped for coal winding. The downcast shaft was equipped with a triple deck cage holding two 10 cwt tubs of coal per deck. The upcast shaft was equipped with a double deck cage with a capacity of four 10 cwt tubs of coal. Therefore, both shafts could raise 100 cwt of coal with each draw of the winding engines. A steam powered 'Guibal' style ventilation fan was installed at the top of the upcast shaft; this had been manufactured by the colliery company themselves and was 28 feet in diameter. The surface buildings were completed with 17 Lancashire boilers for steam raising and a tall brick chimney, together with a coal screening building installed by Qualter Hall & Company of Barnsley. A battery of 64 beehive coking ovens was provided to carbonise the output of slack coal.

Men were recruited to the colliery although production did not start until 1879 three years after finding coal; the reason for this delay is unknown. Speculation maybe, but perhaps the partners needed to raise further capital to equip the underground workings. Perhaps additional problems with water incursions had to be first overcome. Perhaps the economics of a forthcoming trade depression meant that the pit was unprofitable to work. Perhaps the death of John Waring on 24 September 1876 led to a delay in establishing control of the colliery between the remaining partners. There is even the possibility that the colliery company found it difficult to recruit workers due to the recent opening of other pits in the area and they did not have the attraction of offering company owned housing. Whatever, from 1879, operations eventually commenced using the pillar and stall method, where pillars of coal were left to support the roof. Coal was extracted from the stalls and hand loaded into tubs which were then pulled by pony and endless rope haulage to the pit bottom. However, pillar and stall working was rather inefficient, as around half the coal was left in place and from 1891, traditional advancing longwall faces were opened and the colliery eventually developed a 750-yard-long longwall face in the Barnsley seam.

In 1893, a depression in the coal trade caused the colliery companies to impose a 25% pay cut on their workforce. This was rejected by the Miners Federation of Great Britain and the men withdrew their labour and went on strike, whereupon the colliery companies locked them out and a bitter and acrimonious national dispute followed, leading to acts of rioting and civil disturbances. At the nearby Thorncliffe pits belonging to Newton Chambers of Chapeltown, the owners brought in Scottish labour to work the colliery and occupy the company owned homes of the striking men. Rioting took place around Westwood Rows in Chapeltown and soldiers were billeted in the area to keep the peace. The disturbances spread throughout the Dearne Valley leading to angry mobs of striking miners descending on the pit gates where they were met with police guards deployed by the colliery owners. On 4 September, there were disturbances at neighbouring Manvers Main Colliery where property was damaged and the colliery officials injured.

On 6 September 1893, Wath Main Colliery was wrecked and the offices were set on fire. The following day, proceedings reached a head when rioting at Lord Masham's Ackton Hall Colliery near Pontefract saw the reading of the Riot Act following which the military opened fire on the striking miners, killing three men and injuring many others. Following this terrible event, the strike was settled by Government intervention, the first time in which the government had become involved in an industrial dispute. In November, the miners agreed to return to work and the government agreed to establish a Conciliation Board. In July 1894, the colliery owners asked the Conciliation Board for an immediate 10% reduction in miners' wages and in January 1896 the colliery owners called for another 10% wage reduction. The rioting miners at Wath that had been apprehended on 6 September 1893 were tried at Leeds Assizes Court on 20 September 1893, when 14 men were acquitted and 7 others were sentenced to prison for terms varying from 1 to 15 months.

At Wath Main Colliery, the pit buildings were subsequently rebuilt at a cost of £7,000 following the disturbances and most of the men were re-engaged, albeit on lower wages. To increase the colliery's output, drifts were made in 1896 from the Barnsley seam to the Swallow Wood Seam at a depth of 408 yards. This seam was nearly five feet in thickness and the coal was wound in the upcast shaft with Barnsley seam coal wound in the downcast shaft. Electrical lighting was installed underground and a new Schiele ventilation fan replaced the original colliery constructed fan. By the end of that year, the colliery was employing 986 men and boys who produced around 500,000 tons of coal, or 1,500 tons of coal per day from the two seams with George Shaw running the operation as Manging Director. By this time, Hickleton Main Colliery was operational to the north, Manvers Main Colliery to the east, Cortonwood Colliery to the south and Darfield Main Colliery to the west. To avoid the encroaching of workings into adjoining royalties, boundary agreements were drawn up between Wath Main Colliery and its neighbours. In 1894, the royalty was enlarged with the purchase of the Barnsley bed beneath land in Billingley owned by J & J Charlesworths Ltd - the Wakefield colliery proprietors who owned Kilnhurst Colliery - and who had previously mined the Shafton seam at Billingley in the 1830s.

On 1 June 1900, the Wath Main Colliery Company Ltd was registered with a capital of £137,500 to acquire the operation and adopt an agreement with George Shaw to carry out the colliery business. The subscribers to the new company included George Shaw; Matthew Lodge of Rotherham, a retired grocer; Thomas Waring, a Castleford grocer and presumably related to the Waring brothers; David Nicholson, a Wath Solicitor; Horace Nash a Barnsley mining engineer; Thomas Shaw, a Rotherham pottery manufacturer.

In 1902, the colliery was connected to a new railway outlet with the opening of the Wath Branch of the Hull & Barnsley Railway and over the following years the new company gradually implemented a programme of improvements. The old Beehive coking ovens were replaced with 30 Huessener Patent coking ovens and in 1907 Simon Carves Ltd installed a modern Baum type coal washery with a capacity of 50 tons per hour, with a 75 ton per hour extension added 6 years later. The By-product plant was complemented with the erection of six Simon Carves coking ovens in 1912 to produce tar, benzol, methane and sulphate of ammonia. By 1909 Coningsby Phillips had been appointed as the general manager, having previously served as undermanager at Maltby Colliery.

Above Left: From the village of Wath to the south, Moor Road led to Wath Colliery where Edgar Scrivens recorded this view of the pit in 1908, featuring a group of miners about to report for work. The two identical taller chimneys were attached to the two winding engine houses whilst the smaller square sectioned chimney was part of the pit's coking plant which included a batch of Beehive coke ovens installed in the 1890s.
Above Right: A postcard from a similar date published by Hawley of Hillsborough but viewed from the north with the Midland Railway in the foreground. In the sidings are private owner wagons belonging to Manvers Main, Wath Main and coal exporters William Brothers (Hull) Ltd.

In 1912 work started on deepening both shafts to the Parkgate seam and in 1915 this seam was reached at a depth of 609 yards and was found to be 4 ½ feet thick. The Parkgate seam was developed to replace declining output in the Barnsley seam and made excellent coking coal. Longwall faces were developed in the Parkgate seam and additional men were recruited to work at the pit. By 1917, the workforce totalled 1,847, despite the outbreak of the First World War. Increasing output meant increasing amounts of spoil, and this was tipped to the west, parallel with the Midland Railway. Tipping railways were driven at a gradual gradient to the end of the spoil heap and as this grew, the railways were extended westwards. A colliery brickworks was opened at Ingsfield Lane in Bolton-on-Dearne to provide bricks for a new development of colliery housing. War time profits were extensive and in 1917 a 100% share bonus was issued where the shareholders were rewarded with one free share for every share held, thus doubling the capital of the company to £275,000. In 1923, both shafts were deepened to the Silkstone seam at a depth of 697 yards. This seam was four feet in thickness and of excellent quality. By now the workforce totalled 2,346 men working four seams at the pit and, on Saturday 23 October 1923, one of the first pithead baths to be installed in the country was opened at the colliery. The original winding engine at No 1 shaft was no longer fit to raise coal from such great depths; therefore in 1928 an unusual vertical winding engine was fitted by Bradley & Craven of Wakefield. This unique piece of engineering was installed due to the limited amounts of surface space and was housed in a large reinforced concrete structure; it was one of only three such engines ever to have been installed at a British colliery.

Improvements at Wath Main Colliery continued throughout the 1930s. The by-product plant had been enhanced by the addition of five Simon Carves Ltd regenerative coking ovens in 1929 and a further 15 were installed in 1937. A fifth coal seam was developed when operation in the Meltonfield seam was accessed from insets in the shafts at a depth of 177 yards with the coal being dispatched down a staple shaft to the Barnsley horizon for winding; and, by 1933, coal cutters and mechanical haulage had been installed in all the faces. The introduction of full mechanisation resulted in a reduction of the workforce which had dropped to 2,122 in 1937. In 1940, a profit of £35,178 was recorded and the following a year a dividend of 6.5% was paid to shareholders. Operations in the Barnsley seam were exhausted in 1944 and the seam was abandoned after 65 years of production. At nationalisation in 1947, 2,000 men transferred to the NCB and 495,000 tons of coal were produced that year.

Following nationalisation, rumours circulated that the pit was set to close with the coal extracted from neighbouring collieries - the coking ovens had been partly closed in 1946 with coking operations fully ceasing in 1956. However, in 1950, the NCB decided to implement the Manvers Main Combined Mine Reconstruction Scheme with the output from Wath, Barnburgh and Kilnhurst Collieries being transferred to a huge new coal preparation plant at Manvers Main for processing. It was proposed to keep winding coal from the Parkgate, Silkstone and Swallow Wood seams at the Wath shafts. However, coal from the shallower Meltonfield seams and proposed workings in the 5 ½ feet thick Newhill seam at a depth of 300 yards would be transferred to Manvers Main for winding. A 1,400-yard-long underground tunnel was driven between the two pits and coal from the Meltonfield and Newhill seams was hauled by underground diesel locomotives to new skip winding facilities at Manvers Main.

In 1952, the Parkgate seam was abandoned, followed by the Swallow Wood seam two years later. The coal preparation plant at Wath was subsequently demolished although new electric winding engines were installed at both shafts. From 1954 operations were concentrated in the Meltonfield seam and in 1956, a workforce of 1,536 men produced 573,000 tons of coal, all sent to the Manvers shaft for winding to the surface. In 1957, the Newhill seam was developed and mining operations in both the Newhill and Meltonfield seams were fully mechanised. In 1964, the pit employed 1,405 men who produced 470,000 tons of coal. Coal output remained at this level throughout the 1960s but had declined to 430,000 tons by 1978 when 800 men were employed at the pit. In 1970, the wooden headgear above No 1 shaft was replaced with steel headgear, having been one of only two surviving wooden headgears in the country.

Following the Miners' Strike, the pit officially merged with Manvers Main Colliery from 1 January 1986 and was renamed Manvers Complex West. However, that year the colliery recorded losses of £6,000,000 and the pit was placed in the NCB's Colliery Review Procedure. The workforce of 345 voted to accept closure and the mine closed on 23 January 1987 after a life of 114 years. Some of the men accepted a redundancy package and the remainder transferred to other South Yorkshire collieries. The shafts remained operational until the final closure of the Manvers Main Complex on 25 March 1988. Following demolition, the area formed part of the largest zone of dereliction in Europe during the early 1990s, but the site was subsequently landscaped towards the end of the decade. A new lake and country park was constructed to the south of the pit together with a memorial to the men who had worked in the colliery. This formed part of a feature that detailed the rock strata and the nearby Wath Marshalling Yard and was accessed by a new footbridge across the A6195. The shafts were capped and now remain hidden in the vegetation between the lakeside and a new golf course to the north. During its life, Wath Main Colliery was a relatively safe pit to work in, although by 1950, 29 men and boys had died in accidents whilst working at the pit. The worst individual tragedy occurred on 24 February 1930 when an explosion of fire damp killed seven men and injured two others. One of the first recorded fatalities was on 28 December 1881 when Eli Davis, aged 30, was struck down by a fall of coal from the roof whilst manoeuvring coal tubs, the man sadly taking 20 days to die from his injuries.

Above: Edgar Scrivens published this postcard c1908 featuring the pit yard with two of the colliery company's internal industrial locomotives which may have been housed in the engine shed in the centre. The wooden headgears and coal screening plants are visible on the right.

Below: When Wath Main Colliery closed for its annual holidays, the pit ponies who were brought to the surface to spend the week grazing in a nearby field. All too soon, they would be required to work underground again – that's if the ostler could successfully round them up first!

Houghton Main Colliery (1873-1993)

The manor of Little Houghton was owned by Charles Booth Elmsall Wright of Bolton Hall, in Bolton-by-Bowland near Settle in the Yorkshire Dales. It consisted of 802 acres of arable and pastureland near the River Dearne to the north of Darfield and comprised Edderthorpe Farm, Beech House Farm, Manor Farm, Park Farm, Colliery Farm and Mill Farm with its adjacent watermill.

On 1 January 1873, a lease was signed for the Barnsley seam for a period of 60 years beneath the manor of Little Houghton with a partnership of four colliery promotors. The partnership was headed by James Morrison, William Hunter, Alfred Allott and Alfred Davy. James Morrison was a colliery proprietor from Newcastle and William Hunter was a colliery proprietor from County Durham. Alfred Allott was an accountant and colliery proprietor from Sheffield. Alfred Davy was a practical and consulting engineer having formerly established Davy Brothers Ltd of Sheffield. Messrs Morrison, Hunter and Allott plus the brother of Alfred Davy had been members of a partnership which had recently developed Manvers Main Colliery and they were looking to open another colliery in the area. In 1875, the partnership was incorporated as the Houghton Main Colliery Company Ltd with a capital of £100,000 subscribed equally by the four partners.

The partnership subsequently enlarged their Houghton royalty by signing leases with Earl Fitzwilliam for the coal beneath his 700 acre Great Houghton estate and his 360 acre Billingley estate; James Wilson Rimington Wilson of Broomhead Hall for the coal beneath his 100-acre Crook House estate; and with Richard Monckton Milnes of Fryston Hall near Castleford, owner of 175 acres forming the manor of Great Houghton. Richard Milnes was created Lord Houghton and his son became the Earl of Crewe in 1895. Together with coal leases signed with smaller landowners and freehold purchases made by the partnership, this created a royalty of 2,500 acres of prime Barnsley coal.

In 1873, a site was purchased from Charles Wright for a proposed colliery adjacent to the Midland Railway at Little Houghton and work commenced on sinking a pair of shafts both 14 feet in diameter and positioned 40 yards apart. The No 1 shaft was designated as the downcast shaft and the No 2 shaft was the upcast shaft. Sidings were created with the adjacent railway to bring machinery and materials to the site and a small clay pit and brick works was opened to provide bricks for lining the shafts and constructing the surface buildings. Water incursions from the sandstones forming the Woolley Edge and Oaks Rocks plagued the shaft sinking operations, as was the case at many of the other pits in the Dearne Valley. To overcome this the shafts were lined with cast iron tubbing to a depth of 150 yards from the surface.

The water problems proved especially troublesome but, eventually after five years of shaft sinking, the Barnsley seam was reached at a depth of 516 yards on 1 February 1878. The seam was of exceptional quality and measured eight feet in thickness. Two steel lattice headgear 65 feet high were erected over each shaft. The No 1 shaft was equipped with a Davy Brothers Ltd of Sheffield steam powered winding engine whilst Bradley & Craven Ltd of Wakefield provided a similar steam powered winding engine at No 2 shaft. Steam raising was provided by a suite of Lancashire boilers and a steam powered Guibal ventilation fan was installed at the upcast shaft. The permanent headgear had been used to sink the shafts and on completion each shaft was equipped for coal winding; the No 1 shaft had a triple deck cage with capacity for 6 x 12 cwt coal tubs and No 2 shaft had a double deck cage holding 4 x 12 cwt coal tubs.

Thus 120 cwt or 6 tons of coal could be raised with each draw of the shafts. On the surface the coal was sorted and graded in the screens building for dispatching into wagons in the railway sidings.

Men were recruited to work the colliery, many from Staffordshire, and most of the initial workforce was housed at Snape Hill in Darfield, some distance away. As at neighbouring collieries, advancing longwall faces were opened out in the Barnsley seam. Men worked in small groups along the stalls of the coal face, hand cutting the coal with picks and hand loading the coal with shovels into tubs. Ponies then hauled the tubs along the face to the main roadways at either end of the coal face, from which the tubs were attached to an endless rope for hauling to the pit bottom. To provide feed and bedding for the ponies in the underground stables, the colliery company took up leases on some of the nearby farms. John Scott Elliott was appointed as the first pit manager and John Jarratt as engineering manager.

In 1876 Alfred Allott was declared bankrupt and then, at some time afterwards, the two leading members in the partnership, James Morrison and William Hunter, passed away. They were replaced on the board of directors by their sons Martin Morrison of Faceby Manor near Middlesbrough and Charles Edward Hunter of Selaby Park, Darlington. The colliery continued to expand its output and in 1884 it produced 291,408 tons of coal.

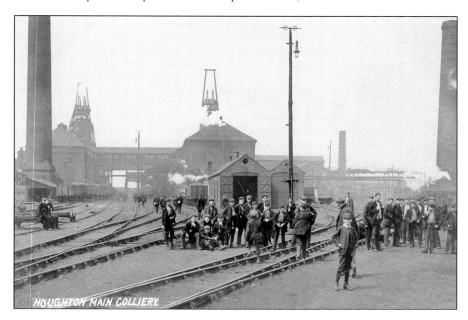

Above: A superbly atmospheric postcard dating from c1905 featuring men and boys waiting to go down the pit at Houghton Main Colliery, each one wearing pit boots or clogs and a flat cap. This photograph was taken before the 1911 Mines Act which prohibited the use of boys under the age of 14 from working in the mining industry and the lad on the right looks very young. Perhaps he was employed on surface duties. Perhaps he was used to open and close trap doors underground or lead the pit ponies hauling coal tubs. Whatever, it is still remarkable that the use of child labour in the pits seems to have been permitted well into the 20th century.

On 30 December 1886, a terrible winding accident occurred at the pit killing 10 men. The men were coming off shift and ascending in the upper deck of the cage and being wound up the No 1 shaft when the engineman working in the winding engine house was knocked temporarily unconscious by a piece of falling wood. The rising cage continued to ascend into the headgear above at high speed. The force of the impact smashed the cage winding safety mechanism and caused the steel winding rope to snap and detach from the cage. Consequently, the cage then plummeted down the shaft, smashing through the wooden boards at the pit bottom and into the sump, 526 yards below, killing the ten men inside the cage instantly.

The men killed included Joseph Walker and his two sons, Samuel and Charles; James Hardcastle and his son Alvin; Joseph Pearson and his son Joseph Junior; Edward Baxter; William Mannion and William Barton, the latter a 17-year-old pony driver from Snape Hill. Allen Beresford, the winding engineman, was charged with manslaughter but was acquitted at a hearing at Leeds Assizes Court. A granite memorial to the ten men was erected in Darfield churchyard on 12 November 1887 and 125 years after the disaster, the restored memorial was unveiled at service at the church which included a stirring performance by the Houghton Main Male Voice Choir.

At the time of the disaster, the pit employed 690 men and boys who returned to work after the winding cage had been repaired, having been thrown out of work by the effects of the incident. The colliery erected a battery of beehive coking ovens to carbonise the slack for sale to the steel industry. Ten years later the colliery employed 1,060 men who produced around 400,000 tons of coal. In the mid-1890s, the colliery drew up boundary lines with the Mitchell Main Colliery Company to the south and west who were the owners of Mitchell Main and Darfield Main Collieries and who were developing a new pit at Grimethorpe. A boundary line was also drawn up to the east with the Hickleton Main Colliery Company who were developing a large pit on the estates of the Reverend Thornely Taylor and the Earl of Halifax. In 1892, 377,988 tons of coal were produced and this figure had increased to 588,252 tons three years later.

At the start of 1900, Martin Morrison died and the colliery company was restructured as the Houghton Main Colliery Company Ltd with a capital of £250,000 formed by an agreement between the original colliery company, Charles Edward Hunter and the executors of Martin Morrison. The capital was subscribed by Charles Edward Hunter of Selaby Park; J Johansson of London; W S Hunter of Aldwark Manor, Easingwold; Newton Charles Ogle of Kirkley Hall, Northumberland; R W Cooper of Newcastle; Charles Perkins of Middleton, Bedford, and Roland Phillipson of Tynemouth. The registered offices of the new colliery company were at 34 Grey Street, Newcastle.

It was always beneficial to have a second or third railway outlet from a colliery to keep transport costs down. In 1892 a branch line from Stairfoot to the pit was opened by the Great Central Railway and Charles Edward Hunter was one of several local colliery promotors who initiated the Dearne Valley Railway. This line opened in stages from 1902 and created new markets as it fed into the Lancashire & Yorkshire Railway's network throughout West Yorkshire and Lancashire. By 1904 it was reported that the colliery was producing 3,000 tons of coal per day, or around 750,000 tons per year, and, the following year, 1,513 men were employed at the pit under the supervision of the colliery manager, John Brass, who lived at New Hall in Ardsley.

However, by 1909 reserves in the Barnsley seam were beginning to decline. Therefore, the colliery company decided to exploit the Meltonfield and Parkgate seams and approached the local landowners to grant leases for these seams. Insets in the shafts were made at a depth of 347 yards to access the Meltonfield seam from which coal was lowered down a staple shaft to the Barnsley horizon for winding to the surface. Increased ventilation of the two seams was required and thus the original Guibal fan at the upcast shaft was replaced with a much larger steam powered fan installed by the Waddle Engineering & Fan Company of Llanelli. In 1917, the old Beehive ovens were replaced with the installation of 50 Otto Waste Heat ovens. The by-product plant also produced tar, sulphate of ammonia, benzol and methane gas. During 1918, the colliery produced 424,525 tons of coal from the Meltonfield and Barnsley seams. This was substantially less than the figure achieved 10 years earlier, even though the pit now employed 2,176 men.

Above Left: W Stables, a Darfield photographer, issued this postcard view of the pit from the north in c1905 during a period of change to its ancillary operations. The remains of the brick kilns are in the foreground with the chimneys of the Beehive ovens on the left. In 1917, new coking ovens were built on this site. *(John Ryan Collection)*

Above Right: A postcard study featuring the pit yard viewed from the west c1910. The original steel headgears date from c1875 with No 1 downcast shaft on the left and No 2 upcast shaft on the right. Vast quantities of pit props have been off-loaded from the Midland Railway wagons whilst those on the left annotated L Y belong to the Lancashire & Yorkshire Railway and will have travelled along the Dearne Valley Railway to the pit. *(John Ryan Collection).*

In 1920, the capital of the colliery company was doubled to £500,000 with the issuing of £250,000 in shares to the public. It was intended that the revenue raised would pay for more surface buildings, the deepening of the No 2 shaft and the sinking of a third shaft to the Parkgate seam. Work on this project had commenced the previous year and in 1921 this seam was intersected in the No 2 shaft at a depth of 776 yards. A staple shaft was installed to wind the Parkgate coal to the Barnsley horizon for raising to the surface. A new reinforced concrete headgear was installed at No 2 shaft and new screens and coal washing equipment were installed on the surface, together with a large extension dumping frame aerial ropeway to tip the waste material on the fields between Little Houghton and Great Houghton.

In 1925 when the pit was employing 2,523 men, work started on the sinking of the 20 feet diameter No 3 shaft to the Parkgate seam. This was equipped with a new Markham & Company of Chesterfield winding engine and a reinforced ferro-concrete headgear and hempstead were constructed on the surface. To counteract the water incursions, the shaft was lined with concrete and sunk using the cementation process, where liquid cement is pumped into the surrounding rocks to stem the flow of water It was intended that the new shaft would increase the colliery output by 50% to 1,200,000 tons per year. However, sinking operations were carried out sporadically due to the uncertain trade conditions of the time, and it wasn't until 1940 that the shaft was completed when it entered the Thorncliffe seam at a depth of 818 yards.

In 1927, the pit had been connected into the Carlton Main Collieries electrical supply ring and could draw electricity from the power station at Frickley Colliery and the coking plant was enhanced the following year with the opening of 10 Simon Carves Ltd Otto Regenerative Ovens. On 24 January 1931, Emmanuel Shinwell, Government Secretary for Mines, opened new pithead baths with accommodation for 2,016 men constructed by the Miners Welfare Fund at a cost of £25,000. Mechanised coal cutting was introduced to the Meltonfield and Parkgate seams and the Beamshaw seam was being accessed at a depth of 406 yards, being dropped down one of the staple shafts to the Barnsley horizon for winding to the surface. By 1935 the colliery was working the Meltonfield, Beamshaw, Barnsley and Parkgate seams which together produced 773.076 tons. That year the colliery company recorded a profit of £28,883 and paid a dividend of 5%. By 1938, trading conditions had substantially improved and the colliery produced 802,949 tons and recorded a profit of £107,971. The capital of the company was increased to £700,000 by the issuing of £200,000 in shares to the public.

In 1947, when the pit passed into NCB ownership, the workforce of 2,636 produced 820,000 tons of coal. On 30 June 1953, the Houghton Main Colliery Company Ltd was formally wound up. The NCB decided to modernise the colliery and introduce mechanised coal cutting and loading in all the seams. In 1950, the inefficient coking plant was closed and the Barnsley seam was finally abandoned after 72 years of operation. The NCB decided to merge Houghton Main and Grimethorpe Collieries with the long-term plan being for all coal to be raised at the Grimethorpe shafts, with the Houghton Main shafts used for man-riding purposes; underground tunnels were driven between the two collieries at two levels along which coal was transported by diesel locomotives.

However, before this long-term plan was implemented a modernisation scheme was implemented at the colliery with the introduction of mechanised coal cutting and haulage to the pit bottoms. Skip winding facilities were installed in No 1 and No 3 shafts and the ventilation was re-organised so that No 1 and No 2 shafts became the downcast and No 3 became the upcast. During this phase of reconstruction production dropped to 640,000 tons in 1951 when the pit employed a workforce of 2,323. During 1961, the original steel headgear at No 2 shaft was dismantled and replaced with a ferro-concrete Koepe winding tower equipped with an overhead electric winding engine fitted by David Brown Ltd of Huddersfield equipped with a 850 horsepower Metropolitan Vickers electric motor. At No 1 shaft a new electrical winding engine was installed by Robey & Company of Lincoln.

In 1963, the underground connection was finally made with Grimethorpe Colliery in the Parkgate horizon and coal from this seam was wound at Grimethorpe. In 1964, the workforce of 1,672 produced 569,000 tons. In 1967, a pair of drifts was driven from the Parkgate level to access the Thorncliffe seam at a depth of 818 yards and the Silkstone seam at a depth of 939 yards. It was proposed to work the Silkstone seam first via fully mechanised retreat mining operations. The scheme was very successful and by 1975 output had increased to 972,000 tons, all of it now wound at the Grimethorpe shafts.

On 16 July 1977, Houghton Main Colliery held an open day to celebrate its centenary. A £16,000,000 project was announced to access 43,000,000 tons of reserves in the Dunsil seam at a depth of 520 yards. This would be extracted by mechanised mining methods using conventional advancing longwall faces and was expect to produce around 500,000 tons of coal per year, extending the life of the colliery into the 21st century. As part of this project, the Dunsil coal would be brought to the surface at Houghton Main for washing and processing in a new coal preparation plant complete with a rapid loading bunker for the loading of Merry-Go-Round trains to convey the coal to Central Electricity Generating Board Power Stations. The new coal preparation plant would also handle the output from Dearne Valley Colliery and a new overhead covered conveyor was constructed. Spoil from the coal preparation plant was tipped on a new site near Grimethorpe Colliery and the scheme came online in 1980. In 1982 the colliery produced 1,077,000 tons of coal from the Dunsil, Fenton, Thorncliffe and Silkstone seams.

In 1984 Houghton Main and Grimethorpe were formally combined and became part of the Barnsley Area South Side Project. In 1986, Darfield Main Colliery joined the combined mine and in 1988 the Houghton Main division produced over 1,000,000 tons of coal. However, the pit was performing below its potential and substantial losses were made over the following years despite the high output. In October 1992, British Coal announced the closure of 31 collieries with the loss of 30,000 jobs including the closure of Houghton Main Colliery. The pit ceased production on 30 October 1992 with formal closure following on 30 April 1993. With the impending privatisation of British Coal Corporation, the government offered Grimethorpe and Houghton Main to the private sector in September 1993 but there were no buyers and the colliery closed with the loss of 440 jobs.

An attempt was made to preserve the surface buildings due to the unique architecture of the three remaining shafts: the No 1 shaft with its original 1870s steel headgear, the No 2 shaft with its reinforced concrete headgear from 1920 and the No 3 shaft with its distinctive vertical concrete tower. However, the initiative was unfortunately unsuccessful and the surface buildings were subsequently demolished and the shafts filled in and capped, and for several years the site remained derelict. In the mid-1990s there was some reworking of the later colliery spoil heap and open cast operations were carried out on land between Houghton Main and Grimethorpe collieries to extract the Shafton seam. On 24 August 1995 one of the pit wheels was mounted near the former entrance to the colliery as a memorial to all the men and boys who were killed during the life of the colliery and to all miners and their families who had suffered hardship and grief in their pursuit of coal. Records are far from complete, but by 1950 at least 38 men and boys had died whilst working at the pit, including W Fletcher, a boy of 15, who died on 25 August 1881 when he was crushed between coal tubs, and J McGrath, a man aged 72, who died on 21 July 1898, when he was also crushed by coal tubs.

In 2003, a new road, following the course of the Midland Railway track bed opened between Middlecliffe and Grimethorpe. A new roundabout was also opened bearing the name Houghton Main Colliery roundabout with the intention of enhancing the road network to encourage new business to the former colliery sites, so far with limited success, as the only new development has been a large warehouse currently operated by ASOS / XPO Logistics. However, the pit wheel serves as a memorial to those who worked at the pit and in 2011 the 'ten men' memorial was restored by the Friends of Darfield Churchyard and the name of Houghton Main lives on through the performances of the Houghton Main Male Voice Choir.

Above Left: The distinctive No 3 headgear was constructed from reinforced concrete and work started in 1925 but it wasn't completed until 1940. In 1934, nine feet high red neon letters spelling out HOUGHTON were positioned on the top of the No 3 engine house and were visible from the windows of passing trains on the Midland Railway.

Above Right: The No 3 headgear was rebuilt in 1961 and equipped with a Koepe winding tower. The empty shell is pictured here in 1994, a couple of seconds after the explosive charges were fired causing the headgear to come crashing to the ground. *(Peter Davies)*

Above: This colliery spoil heap, known as 'the big black mountain of Houghton', dominated the view from Darfield. It was 300 feet high when captured in this photograph by K W Buckley in 1956. The spoil heap was reclaimed in 1982 by the South Yorkshire County Council, reprofiled, grassed over and used as pasture land. Houghton Main Colliery is to the left. *(Maurice Dobson Museum & Heritage Centre)*

Cortonwood Colliery (1873-1985)

Brampton Bierlow is located between Wath and Wombwell and one of its former notable residents was Dr George Ellis who lived in Brampton Hall. George Ellis was a generous benefactor to the parish and in 1711, the year before he died, he established a trust to provide for the education of children in the area. Under his will and the actions of the seven Trustees of George Ellis's Charity, several schools were constructed, with funding coming from the rental proceeds of his Brampton estate. The Ellis Trust helped to establish Brampton The Ellis Church of England Primary School (sic) and The Ellis Church of England Primary School at Hemingfield. The trust still supports education in the locality some 300 years later.

Coal mining had been occurring in the area since 1486 and during the 18th century there were several small pits in the region adjacent to Melton Green and West Melton and at New Brampton and Rainborough. Along the small valley of the Knoll Beck stream were Greenland's pit and Cortwood Colliery. The latter was renamed Willow Main Colliery and was large enough to have a railway connection with the Elsecar branch of the South Yorkshire Railway. However, these pits were working the Meltonfield seam at a shallow depth, their output was relatively small and the Barnsley seam remained unworked at depth. Most of the land in Brampton Bierlow was owned by the Trustees of the George Ellis Charity and Earl Fitzwilliam and in the early 1850s, a consortium of colliery promoters approached the landholders with proposals to work the Barnsley seam beneath the Brampton area.

On 2 January 1854, a lease was signed by the Trustees of the George Ellis Charity and Charles Bartholomew, Robert Baxter, Samuel Roberts and Robert Dymond for the right to work the Barnsley seam for 99 years beneath the 191 acres owned by the Trustees for a royalty of £240/acre. On 10 April 1854, the same four gentlemen signed a lease for the Barnsley seam beneath 218 acres of Brampton lands belonging to Earl Fitzwilliam, although Earl Fitzwilliam secured a higher royalty of £275/acre. Nevertheless, this brought together a total royalty of 409 acres which would form the basis of the proposed Brampton coalfield.

However, the promoters did not immediately proceed with the development of a colliery. This was because they had already secured the much larger Wombwell estate royalty and they decided to focus their attention on developing Wombwell Main Colliery. Although they were liable for annual rental payments on their Brampton coalfield, by securing the leases they had effectively barred rival industrialists from developing the adjacent area. This arrangement remained in force for 18 years until the initial promoters decided to sell the coalfield to a new partnership trading as the Brampton Colliery Company.

The Brampton Colliery Company was formed on 12 July 1872 by a group of seven industrialists: Henry Davis Pochin, Benjamin Whitworth MP, John Devonshire Ellis, James Holden, William Pochin, Thomas Whitworth and Edward Pochin. Henry Davis Pochin represented a consortium of Manchester business men, rich with profits gained from the cotton and chemical industry, who wished to invest in new limited liability companies in the coal and iron industry. Together they founded the Staveley Coal & Iron Company Ltd of Chesterfield; the Sheepbridge Coal & Iron Company Ltd of Chesterfield; John Brown & Company Ltd of Sheffield; the Tredegar Coal & Iron Company Ltd of South Wales and Bolckow Vaughan & Company Ltd of Middlesbrough. The Brampton Colliery Company was the next project. Henry Pochin was also Liberal MP for Stafford and when not involved with his industrial activities he was a keen gardener. In 1877, he purchased the 80 acre Bodnant estate in North Wales to develop his gardening interests during his retirement. In 1877, his daughter Laura married Charles McLaren, the future Baron Aberconway, who would later inherit Bodnant. The property was gifted to the National Trust in 1949.

The Brampton Colliery Company had a capital of £50,000 and the partners paid a deposit of £18,000 for the two leases with the balance of the sale to be paid by the new company once they had started producing coal. A site for their new colliery on the northern edge of the royalty, adjacent to the Dearne & Dove Canal and the Elsecar Branch of the South Yorkshire Railway, was purchased from the Trustees of the George Ellis Charity. This site was not far from Willow Main Colliery and just across the canal from Lundhill Colliery, the latter already working the Barnsley seam.

In October 1873 work commenced on sinking two shafts on what was titled Cortonwood Colliery. The name had caused some confusion because there was a Cortwood Colliery located on Cortwood Lane but this had become known as Willow Main Colliery. Whether this name change was effected by the new concern wishing to claim the name is unknown and the same applies to the reason for the change in spelling from Cortwood to Cortonwood. Whatever, the No 1 downcast shaft and No 2 upcast shafts were sunk on the new site for Cortonwood Colliery. No 1 shaft was 20 feet in diameter and named the Whitworth Shaft after one of the promotors. No 2 shaft was smaller in width at 15 feet in diameter. Both shafts were lined with iron tubbing for the first 70 yards to protect them from water issuing from porous sandstones and the old Willow Main Colliery Meltonfield coal seam workings. Beneath this depth, the shafts were traditionally brick lined and in March 1875 both shafts encountered the Barnsley seam at a depth of 212 yards, the seam being 8 feet thick and of excellent quality. Other seams passed during the sinking operation were the Meltonfield at a depth of 40 yards, the Abdy at 70 yards, The Kent's Thin at 106 yards and the Kent's Thick at 144 yards.

During sinking operations work was undertaken in laying out the surface buildings. A brickworks was opened on the site for supplying the bricks required for construction of the buildings and lining the shafts. Two pitch pine wooden headgears supported 15 feet diameter pulley wheels supplied by Qualter Hall & Company of Barnsley, who also constructed the coal screening building. Two 84 horse power winding engines and 6 Lancashire boilers were supplied by W J & J Garforth of Duckinfield. A 45 feet high pit chimney exhausted smoke from the boilers. Underground ventilation was provided by a Schiele's patent steam powered fan at the No 2 shaft. The double deck shaft cage at No 1 shaft could accommodate 8 x 12 ½ cwt tubs of coal, enabling 100 cwt of coal to be raised with each draw of the winding engine. No 2 shaft was equipped for winding men and materials.

In 1876, the colliery was equipped and ready to start production from the highly lucrative Barnsley seam. Men and their families were recruited from the area to work at the pit, possibly persuaded by the provision of a company house in a new community of 106 newly built cottages, together with a new pit school. These were provided in a new settlement named Concrete Cottages. Coal working was by the establishment of advancing longwall faces, with groups of men working in stalls or stints, hewing coal with picks and hand loading it with shovels into the iron tubs. These were then hauled by pit pony to the main underground roadways from which endless rope haulage conveyed the tubs to the pit bottom.

In 1877, the Brampton Colliery Company was reconstituted as The Cortonwood Collieries Company Ltd with a share capital of £250,000. Of this £140,000 was subscribed equally by the seven original partners and the balance was offered as shares to the public. During this time output was 1,500 tons of coal per day and a battery of beehive coke ovens was constructed to supply the steel industry. On 19 October 1883, the company was reconstituted as the Cortonwood Collieries Ltd and the capital was reduced to £175,000, presumably as this figure had been sufficient to develop the pit. With other colliery companies signing up leases with landowners throughout the Dearne Valley, the Cortonwood Collieries Company decided to consolidate its positon by acquiring leases from adjacent landowners in the 1880s to bring up its royalty to around 1,000 acres.

Above Left: Although of poorer quality, this c1905 postcard of the headgear and screens at Cortonwood Colliery is included for its rarity value. The No 2 upcast headgear on the left had already been replaced with a new steel headgear whilst the original wooden No 1 downcast headgear on the right awaits a similar fate. A rake of the colliery company's private owner wagons is fully loaded with coal ready for market. *(Norman Ellis Collection)*
Above Right: This c1925 postcard by Edgar Scrivens was taken from the footpath leading to the pit from Westfield Road and shows the colliery in its rural surroundings with Wombwell Woods on the horizon. The structure on the far left is a wooden water cooling tower, a common feature on colliery sites at the time, and the coking plant is prominent on the right.

Leases were signed with Henry Payne of Newhill Hall; the trustees of the Poor Houses and Lands of Brampton Bierlow; Frank Wever; Philip McAdam; George Nicholson; Joseph Carnley; Alice Sutton; Anthony Mundella; Heaton Cadman (owner of Wath Ings); Henry Briggs; Mrs Johnson's Trustees; the Vicars of Wath Parish Church and Bolton-upon-Dearne Church; and with other minor landholders. Sub leases were also acquired from beneath parcels of land in the area leased to Wombwell Main Company and the Lundhill Coal Company. Additionally, the company purchased the coal beneath various other smaller landowners to enlarge their royalty, including Emily Cash's Broomhill estate, Edwin Casson, J N Terry of Wombwell and the trustees of Joseph Mitchell. However, it wasn't all one way traffic as the colliery company had no intention of working the shallow Meltonfield seam and 5 acres of this seam beneath land purchased from Edwin Casson was sold to the Willow Main Colliery Company for £600 on 30 June 1887.

By 1890 the Cortonwood royalty was surrounded by other colliery royalties and boundary lines were drawn up with neighbouring pits. To the north, the Lundhill colliery had been acquired by the Wombwell Main Company and a geological fault named the Lundhill Fault formed a natural boundary, the fault following approximately the line of the canal. In 1893, the Willow Main Colliery Company went into liquidation and its assets were acquired by Cortonwood Colliery which now employed 850 men and boys. To the west mining activities were controlled by Earl Fitzwilliam's Elsecar Collieries. To the south was the Manvers Main Colliery royalty whilst to the east was Wath Main Colliery. Conscious of their small royalty of around 1,000 acres and the fact that the Barnsley seam was being rapidly worked out, the directors decided to deepen the shafts to exploit the Parkgate and Silkstone seams, thus prolonging the life of the colliery, and negotiations with landowners commenced to obtain coal leases for the deeper seams.

By 1900, the first generation of directors had now been succeeded by a new generation, which included Frank Pochin as Chairman succeeding his father Henry Pochin; Frank's brother in law Charles McLaren as Managing Director; Robert Henry Clayton succeeding James Holden; Sir Charles Ellis succeeding John Devonshire Ellis; and Henry McLaren, the grandson of Henry Pochin. Several of these directors also served on the board of the Sheffield Steelmakers, John Brown & Company, who were developing their own collieries elsewhere in South Yorkshire at Aldwarke, Rotherham Main, Silverwood and Rossington Main.

In 1904 work started on deepening the shafts to the Parkgate seam and replacing the original wooden headgears with steel headgears. However, in December, a disastrous underground fire broke out in the Barnsley seam workings. Fortunately, nobody was working in the pit at the time, however, the fire had the effect of throwing the workforce out of work. By the following year 347 men had been re-employed in the Barnsley seam and work recommenced on deepening the shafts. By 1907, despite the aftermath of the fire, output had increased to 600 tons per day, although this was still half of what was achieved during the 1880s. In February 1907, the Parkgate seam was intersected at a depth of 481 yards. It was found to be 5 ½ feet thick and believed to be the finest in the district. No 1 shaft would continue to wind Barnsley seam coal whilst the Parkgate seam coal was wound from No 2 shaft.

To handle the increased output the surface buildings were reconstructed and the old beehive coking ovens were dismantled. The Parkgate seam contained a greater amount of friable small coal or slack, which could be carbonised and sold to the steel industry. Consequently, on 8 February 1909 the colliery company signed an agreement with the Humboldt Engineering Works of Cologne in Germany to provide a battery of 50 modern Koppers Regenerative By-Product Coking Ovens, a coal crushing plant, a 'Baum' washery, a coal bunker and new screens, together with new Lancashire boilers and extensive railway sidings. The colliery manager was now J E Chambers who was the son of William Chambers, the managing director of Denaby & Cadeby Main Collieries Ltd.

The coking plant was an immediate success and in 1912 an additional batch of 50 Koppers ovens was installed. Waste material from the pit and coking plant was tipped on the former Willow Main Colliery site. Coal production by now had exceeded the pre-1904 fire total and the workforce was back to strength. The colliery was about to enter a period of incredible prosperity. During 1913 Cortonwood Collieries recorded a profit of £94,835. Most of this profit was issued as a 50% share bonus payment to shareholders of the original £175,000 capital who received one free bonus share for every two single shares held. This had the effect of increasing the capital of the company by £87,500 from £175,000 to £262,500.

In 1916 workings were made into the Swallow Wood seam at a depth of 270 yards which was transported to the Barnsley horizon for winding to the surface; by the following year the workforce had reached 1,440. War time profits were incredibly high with £133,689 being recorded in 1916. To celebrate, another share bonus was distributed to shareholders at a rate of 25%, thus increasing the capital from £262,500 to £328,125. Profits during 1917 were £92,687 which was celebrated with payment of a healthy dividend to the shareholders and a £1000 bonus to each of the directors.

Following the end of the First World War, a subsidiary company under the name of The Nerquis Colliery Company Ltd was established in 1919 to work a small coalfield in North Wales. Nearer home, a joint venture was formed in 1923 with Bolckow Vaughan of Middlesbrough to open a new pit at Upton between Doncaster and Pontefract. In 1923, Cortonwood Colliery employed 1,738 men and with the Barnsley seam having been exhausted two years earlier, it was decided to develop the Silkstone seam. This would provide work for an additional 400 men and in 1925 work commenced on deepening the shafts. To house the workforce required to mine the Silkstone seam, the colliery company commissioned the Housing & Town Planning Trust to construct 60 houses on Knoll Beck Avenue and the Industrial Housing Association to provided 318 houses on Knoll Beck Lane, with additional houses provided later by Rotherham Rural District Council.

In 1925, the 43rd annual report of the Cortonwood Collieries Ltd was published. Profit that year had only been £10,643 and no dividend was paid to shareholders. This reduced profit was due to a decline in the coal price and losses recorded at the coking and by-products operations due to a fall in the price of coke. The report reveals that the company now owned 157 houses with contracts signed for more houses and that they also owned 1,010 private owner wagons. They held the entire £29,915 capital of the Nerquis Colliery Company, £181,054 in the Upton Colliery Company and £62,572 in shares in the Industrial Housing Association in exchange for the latter constructing the new colliery village. They also owned the Bulls Head Inn at Brampton which was leased to Whitworth's Wath Brewery for £315. Income from farms owned by the company on their freehold land and cottage rentals to the workforce raised £1,006. The company hoped that the forthcoming exploitation of the Silkstone seam would help to return the annual profit to much higher levels.

In 1927, the Silkstone seam was intercepted at a depth of 575 yards and the it measured 2 feet 8 inches in thickness and provided excellent coking coal. Longwall faces were opened in the seam and mechanisation was introduced, with machine cutting at the coal face, although the coal was still hand filled into tubs and hauled to the pit bottom. Nevertheless, output was around 500,000 tons that year. Employment at the pit now totalled 2,348, the highest figure ever recorded. However, the Wall Street Crash of 1929 saw a collapse in the price of coal and by 1931 the workforce had reduced to 1,795.

On 9 December 1932, a methane explosion in the Silkstone seam killed four men instantly and seriously wounded four others who later died from their injuries. A Disaster Fund was established to raise money for the families of the dead men and it closed on 27 February 1933 having raised £1,334. The first half of the decade saw widespread hardship throughout the Dearne Valley. The national government had imposed a standard tonnage quota on every colliery to limit production, which in turn held down profits. To make Cortonwood colliery more profitable, the small Nerquis Colliery in North Wales was closed and its standard tonnage added to that of Cortonwood.

Despite the depression of the 1930s, the sale of coke and by-products had proved more profitable than the sale of coal. Therefore in 1936 the colliery company decided to invest £90,000 in a new battery of efficient coking ovens. The 100 Koppers ovens dating from 1909 and 1912 were dismantled and replaced by 23 Koppers Gas Circulating Regenerative Ovens with a production capacity of 130,000 tons of coal per year. The new ovens and an improving economic situation enabled a profit of £46,162 to be made during 1939, no doubt assisted by the disposal of the colliery company's share in Upton Colliery to Dorman Long & Company of Middlesbrough. To celebrate a dividend of 2.5% was paid to shareholders, still a long way from the 50% share bonus dividend paid in 1913. During the 1930s an extension dumping frame aerial ropeway was installed at a new tipping site and the colliery spoil heap gradually grew in height, eventually covering the fields to the north of Smithy Bridge Lane.

In 1941, reserves in the Parkgate seam were exhausted and the seam was abandoned with production concentrating on the Silkstone and Swallow Wood seams. With the outbreak of the Second World War, the government had abandoned the quota system and encouraged maximum coal production, although this was hampered by a lack of a skilled workforce as many men had left the industry to enlist in the forces, despite mining being a protected occupation. During the war years, production reached around 500,000 - 600,000 tons per year, all of which was now machine cut at the face and machine hauled to the pit bottom.

On 1 January 1947, the coal mining industry was nationalised and the National Coal Board took over the management of Cortonwood Colliery. During its first year in government ownership, 2,142 men produced 550,000 tons of coal. The Cortonwood Collieries Ltd was subsequently wound up with its shareholders receiving £538,100 for the company. One of the first improvements installed at the pit was the opening of Pithead Baths in 1950 with accommodation for 2,000 men. With the increasing use of mechanisation, coal output continued to rise whilst the number employed gradually decreased. In 1957, 732,000 tons of coal were produced, possibly the highest ever annual figure recorded at the pit.

In 1958 the NCB commenced a reconstruction scheme at Cortonwood Colliery. Skip winding was introduced in the shafts and electric winding engines were introduced at No 1 and No 2 shafts, replacing the old steam powered ones. Underground ventilation was now in the hands of an electrically powered fan and a new coal preparation plant was installed on the surface. By the end of the decade the pit employed 1,573 men who produced 541,000 tons.

In 1962, the coking and by-product plant closed due to a decline in the demand for coke within the UK steel industry. Cortonwood's output was now mostly dispatched to coking plants elsewhere. Despite the recent investment by the NCB, the pit's output continued to fall and by 1975 only 262,000 tons were produced by a workforce of 900. In that year, the Swallow Wood seam had become exhausted and operations were now focussed on the Silkstone seam. The pit still produced excellent quality coking coal for the steel industry but the fall in demand and in price were beginning to cause concern.

In the first four years of the 1980s the pit had lost £20,000,000 or approximately £20 for every ton of coal produced. On 1 March 1984, the NCB announced the immediate closure of Cortonwood Colliery, Polmaise Colliery in Scotland and Snowden Colliery in Kent due to the losses incurred. This was despite the men of Elsecar Colliery which had closed the previous year having been promised five years' work if they agreed to transfer to Cortonwood Colliery. These events triggered the yearlong national Miners' Strike of 1984/1985 and images from Cortonwood Colliery and Brampton became daily scenes in the media, which prominently featured the 'Alamo', the pickets hut erected at the junction of Pit Lane and Knoll Beck Lane. Cortonwood miners were amongst the first to go on strike during this acrimonious battle between Arthur Scargill and the National Union of Mineworkers and Margaret Thatcher over pit closures and the destruction of communities. The nearby bridge carrying Knoll Beck Lane over the railway line carried the famous graffiti slogan "We told Arthur No Surrender". Proceedings became increasingly bitter when a few men decided to return to work, coupled with a vast police force which frequently and aggressively clashed with the striking miners.

This culminated in dramatic scenes when the bowling green roller was launched down Knoll Beck Lane into the Police lines.

After the strike 800 men returned to work at the pit in March 1985 but on 28 October 1985 the NCB announced its immediate closure. Many of the men accepted enhanced redundancy payments but around 370 transferred to other South Yorkshire collieries. In 1986, the pit was demolished and the shafts filled in and capped; the spoil heap landscaped and grassed over. For several years, the site lay derelict but in 1998 the new Dearne Valley Parkway opened, complete with a junction for a new proposed retail park on the pit site. A new Morrison's supermarket opened on the site of the pithead baths and further retail units opened during the following years, with the pit shafts now buried beneath a DIY store.

A mining pit wheel in memory of those that had worked at the pit was positioned next to the war memorial on Knoll Beck Lane. It is believed that 87 men and boys died whilst working at Cortonwood Colliery, with the worst tragedies being an explosion of fire damp caused by shot firing on 9 December 1932 which killed 7 men; on 19 June 1961, 4 men died from gas emissions. However, even individual deaths are tragedies for the family concerned and one example is the death of G Logan on 5 March 1892, a lad of 17, who died when he was run over by coal tubs underground.

From 1996, part of the former South Yorkshire Railway Elsecar branch is now operated as a preserved steam railway, with passenger trains operating from the Earl Fitzwilliam's private railway station at Elsecar Heritage Centre as far as Tingle Bridge. Since 2006, the line has been operated by the Elsecar Heritage Railway Trust who intend to extend it from Tingle Bridge to a new Station adjacent to Cortonwood Colliery.

Above: A JV Postcard of Cortonwood Miners marching back to work along Knoll Beck Lane after the 1984/85 Miners Strike.

Hickleton Main Colliery (1892-1988)

Hickleton Hall, the home of Charles Lindley Wood, the second Viscount Halifax, is situated on the crest of a high limestone escarpment and, together with the adjoining cottages forming the picturesque estate village of Hickleton, enjoys a fine westerly prospect over the Dearne Valley towards Barnsley and a fine easterly prospect down the dip slope of the limestone escarpment towards Doncaster. This landscape feature forms the boundary between the exposed coalfield of the Dearne Valley and the concealed coalfield of Doncaster. At the bottom of the hill, the manor of Thurnscoe including Thurnscoe Hall was owned by the Reverend Thomas Thornely Taylor of Dodworth, whilst the farms and former turnpike tollhouse at Goldthorpe formed part of the Hickleton estate.

Around 1891, Robert Armitage and his business partners secured the options for the lease of 3,000 acres of coal beneath the estates of Viscount Halifax and Thomas Thornely Taylor. Robert Armitage lived at Farnley Hall near Leeds where his family owned the Farnley Iron Works Company, formed to exploit the mineral resources beneath his Leeds estate. He also served as Chairman of Brown Bayley's Steelworks Ltd of Sheffield. However, he was looking to spread his interests into coal (and politics – he later served as Mayor of Leeds and was Liberal MP for Leeds Central from 1906-1922). Therefore, he turned to some of his business contacts in the Sheffield steel industry to see if they wished to join him in developing the new Hickleton venture.

Consequently, on 31 December 1891 the Hickleton Main Colliery Company Ltd was registered with a capital of £150,000 in £100 shares with a registered office at 41 Norfolk Street, Sheffield. The new company was headed by Robert Armitage as Chairman and Ernest Hague as Managing Director. Other directors included David Davy of Sheffield, Charlie Markham of Chesterfield, Henry Tenant of York and Roland Philipson of Tynemouth. Other subscribers included Charles Edward Hunter of Selaby Park, Darlington, director of Manvers Main and Houghton Main Collieries; shipping magnate Arthur Wilson of Hull and Alexander Wilson of Sheffield, the Managing Director of Charles Cammell & Company Ltd. Arthur Badger served as the colliery company secretary.

David Davy was the Chairman of Davy Brothers Ltd and Charlie Markham owned Markham & Company Ltd, both engineering companies specialising in the manufacture of winding engines and colliery headgears. David Davy, Ernest Hague, Henry Tenant and Roland Philipson were all directors of the Manvers Main Colliery Company, which had successfully opened two pits at Wath-upon-Dearne.

With the capital in place the company decided to develop the new pit and commissioned the mining contractors Charles Walker & Eaton of Doncaster to undertake the work of sinking a pair of 18 feet diameter shafts to the Barnsley seam. The shafts were arranged in an east-west line and positioned 56 yards apart. A colliery site was purchased from Thomas Thornely Taylor to the south of Lidgett Lane, the road from Hickleton to Thurnscoe and easily accessible from the Swinton & Knottingley Joint Railway from which a short branch line was built to the colliery to bring in materials and sinking equipment. It was intended to lay out facilities for handling a production of 1,000,000 tons of coal per year with an output of 4,000 tons per day, and it was expected to take two years to sink to the Barnsley seam which was estimated to lie at a depth of 550 yards.

Above: Hickleton Main Colliery on a postcard by an anonymous photographer viewed from the colliery sidings to the west. A rake of the colliery company's private owner wagons has been loaded with coal from beneath the screens building and is awaiting collection for transport to market. The colliery company eventually owned over 3,000 of these wagons, all painted red with HICKLETON in white letters shaded with black. Note the term Thurnscoe East, used to designate the colliery village east of the railway line, with Thurnscoe West forming the older part of the village to the west of the railway lines. The terms Thurnscoe East and Thurnscoe West have now largely fallen out of use.

In the spring of 1892 preparations were made for developing the site. One of the first requirements was for the establishment of a brickworks for supplying bricks to line the shafts and for use in the construction of housing and surface buildings. The output from the small colliery brickworks was only 20,000 bricks per day and was supplemented with the purchase of 1,300,000 bricks from Houghton Main and Monckton Main Collieries, the Mexborough Brick Company, Micklethwait's Stairfoot Brickworks, Walker & Crawshaw of Conisbrough, James Gooddy of the Darfield Clay Works and the Sheffield Gas Company. To house some of the workers at the pit, a row of 30 houses known as Hickleton Terrace or Pit Row was erected on Lidgett Lane. The first of these 30 houses was occupied by Joe Taylor on 7 September 1892.

With materials and equipment in place, Reverend Thornely Taylor cut the first sods and sinking commenced in December 1892. The work was carried out by a team of 300 sinkers under the leadership of master sinker Sam Broadhead who lodged in a house in Great Houghton. The sinkers were housed in wooden huts on Lidgett Lane and had previously sunk the shafts at Cadeby Main Colliery. For example, the sinkers included John Taylor and his wife and together with his mother and two daughters they moved from Burcroft near Conisbrough where John Taylor had worked on sinking the shafts at Cadeby Main Colliery to live in the wooden huts on Lidgett Lane. Once the shaft sinking had been completed, the Taylor family settled in the area moving into one of the newly completed houses in Goldthorpe.

Temporary wooden headgears were used to sink the shafts serviced by temporary steam winding engines provided by Markham & Company of Chesterfield whilst the permanent equipment was erected above the operations. Two shafts were positioned 65 yards apart with the No 1 downcast shaft to the east and the No 2 upcast shaft to the west. Very little water was met during the shaft sinking although the shafts were lined with cast iron tubbing to a depth of 45 yards. The sinkers worked continuously day and night in six hour shifts with 16 men working in each shaft, sinking the shafts at a rate of 13 yards per week. On 28 June 1894, the Barnsley seam was reached at a depth of 542 yards. The seam was 8 feet in thickness and of excellent quality. During sinking operations, the Shafton seam had been intersected at a depth of 119 yards although it wasn't the intention to mine this seam.

On 6 July 1894, the sinkers and other workers were treated to a banquet held in one of the newly completed colliery buildings. David Davy, Ernest Hague and Dennis Hague represented the colliery company and the guests included Mr F Wardell, the Senior Inspector of Mines, and the Reverend Thornely Taylor. The shaft sinking had been completed without any loss of life or serious accident and Reverend Taylor promised to provide land in Thurnscoe and a donation towards the construction of new schools. With their work completed many of the sinkers moved on to sink the shafts at Grimethorpe Colliery, although some chose to stay and work at Hickleton Main.

The No 1 downcast shaft was equipped with an 85 feet high steel headgear and the No 2 upcast shaft was fitted with a 75 feet high wooden headgear. Both headgears and their steam powered winding engines were supplied by Davy Brothers Ltd of Sheffield. Both shafts were equipped to wind coal and fitted with double deck cages; 8 x 10cwt coal tubs could be wound up No 1 shaft and 4 x 10cwt coal tubs could be wound up No 2 shaft; therefore, 120cwt in coal could be wound to the surface with each draw of the cages. The upcast shaft was fitted with a steam powered Waddle type ventilation fan provided by Markham & Company of Chesterfield and steam raising was provided by the installation of 13 mechanically stoked Lancashire Boilers. Elsewhere on the surface, ancillary buildings, fitters and blacksmiths shops and coal screening and picking belts and a coal washing plant were constructed, together with a large brick chimney. A colliery owned locomotive was purchased for shunting duties and named Loco No 1, built by Markham & Company of Chesterfield in 1892 at a cost of £1,025. This was joined by a second engine, named, not surprisingly, Loco No 2 in 1899 and supplied by Chapman & Furneaux of Gateshead.

From July 1894, the pit bottom was opened out and headings were made through the 600-yard diameter shaft pillar, left intact to protect the surface buildings from subsidence. Beyond the shaft pillar longwall faces were opened out and men were recruited to work at the colliery, both locally and from further afield, particularly from Derbyshire and Staffordshire such that by the end of the year, 188 men and boys worked underground and 189 worked on the surface, a total of 387, 22 of which had joined the Yorkshire Miners Association. Mr J Eaton was appointed pit manager and J Meeklah the undermanager. Men worked underground in small groups in stalls positioned along the coal face, hewing the coal with picks and loading it into the coal tubs. These were then pony hauled to the main roadways from where the tubs were attached to an endless rope for haulage to the pit bottom.

In 1895, the capital of the colliery company was increased to £300,000 to pay for the development of the underground workings and the construction of housing. Around this time, Charles Markham left the partnership and was replaced on the board of directors by his younger brother, Arthur Markham, who later became Sir Arthur Markham, who became one of the leading developers of the concealed coalfield around Doncaster at the start of the 20th century.

The Barnsley seam was easily worked and coal production rapidly increased and by 1896 the workforce had increased to 851 employees. One week in July that year, 6,000 tons were raised and the undermanager Mr Meeklah, hosted a supper at the Horse & Groom in Goldthorpe for the officials and men. The royalty was increased by the purchasing of coal beneath smaller landowners - one example being the purchase of coal beneath 12 acres forming Chapel Fields at Thurnscoe for £1,802.

The colliery company had commissioned the Grange Iron Company of Durham to install a new steel headgear at No 2 shaft together with a new Wood & Burnett type coal screening plant with a capacity of 2,000 tons per day. The new headgear had already been delivered to the site when on 27 July 1898, the old wooden headgear at No 2 shaft caught fire - the flames were visible from several miles away. Normally any such disaster at a colliery would result in the workforce being thrown out of work whilst repairs were undertaken. Fortunately, the new replacement headgear was quickly installed without the need to dismiss the workforce of 1,727 men and boys and there was only a minor inconvenience to coal production. That year William Wilde was appointed pit manager and the company purchased Thurnscoe Hall from Reverend Thornely Taylor as a house for William Wilde and his family.

Relationships with the Swinton & Knottingley Joint Railway must have turned sour as in 1895 the colliery company approached the Hull & Barnsley Railway to build a branch line to the pit. The South Yorkshire Extension Railway was opened in 1902 in a partnership between Hickleton and Manvers Collieries and the Hull & Barnsley railway and a branch line and sidings were laid to the Hickleton pit yard. In 1897, another railway line was promoted in conjunction with Grimethorpe Colliery, Manvers Main and Houghton Main and the Lancashire & Yorkshire Railway, and, in 1906, the Dearne Valley Railway opened with another connection into the Hickleton pit yard. With three rail outlets from the pit, the colliery company could keep transport costs, down thus maximising their profits.

In April 1899, 2429 tons of coal were raised in a single 10-hour period which was claimed to be a world output record at the time. Flushed with success, the colliery company began to negotiate for additional landowners and the following year they successfully secured the lease for 6,807 acres of coal belonging to Herbert Thellusson of Brodsworth Hall at a rate of £35 per foot thickness per acre for the Barnsley coal and £27 per foot thickness per acre for all other seams. This new royalty was split into 1,605 acres beneath the Bilham estate and 5,202 acres beneath the Brodsworth estate. This enlarged the Hickleton Main royalty to over 10,000 acres and they intended to extract the Thellusson coal from the Hickleton shafts. The lease was effective from 1 January 1900 and included the lease of Hampole Priory for 89 years, the property possible intended as another company house for a colliery manager.

The company commissioned Vivian's Borehole & Exploration Company Ltd of Whitehaven to drill a borehole near the Great North Road at Red House to confirm the quality of the seam and plans were drawn up for the sinking of a ventilation shaft on Blacksmith Lane in Marr. The results of the borehole, completed by John Vivian in 1902, were unsatisfactory due to the presence of a geological fault. Nevertheless, the colliery company was convinced that coal was beneath the area but that it could only be accessed by the sinking of new shafts. Thus, the colliery company decided to form a subsidiary company and, after rejecting the name Thellusson Main in 1904, the Brodsworth Main Colliery Company Ltd was formed in 1905 with a capital of £300,000. Recognising the expense of developing the new company, the Hickleton director Sir Arthur Markham contacted his elder brother Charlie Markham (by now chairman of the Staveley Coal & Iron Company Ltd of Chesterfield) to see if they wanted to join them in the venture; Staveley subscribed for half the capital in the new company.

Above: A fine study by Edgar Scrivens issued as a postcard during the First World War, featuring No 1 headgear with No 2 headgear and the screens building nearest the camera. On the right, a wooden water cooling tower, brick built winding engine house and large chimney, the last bounded with steel hoops at regular intervals for structural strength.

In 1902, Ernest Hague died at his home at Castle Dyke in Sheffield. He had been Managing Director of Manvers Main and Hickleton Main Collieries and was the Chairman of Netherseal Colliery in Derbyshire. Recognising his influence in developing Brodsworth Colliery, a new mission church was constructed in his memory at Highfields in 1910. In 1903, David Davy passed away and he was succeeded on the board of directors by his son George Charles Hague Davy of Skellow Grange. At Hickleton Main, William Wilde was promoted to the role of Managing Director, with the role of pit manager awarded to John Minnikin, with Mr John Criddle appointed as undermanager. In 1911, John Criddle was promoted to Brodsworth Main colliery manager, an incredible achievement for a man who starred his mining career as a boy in 1892 helping to sink the shafts at Hickleton Main.

The first decade of the new century saw Hickleton Main break world coal production records, which enabled the company to enjoy a period of profitable prosperity. By 1906, 2,307 men and boys were employed at the pit, 1,962 of whom worked underground. On 4 December 1908, the colliery claimed the daily world production record from Mansfield Colliery when 4,214 tons were produced. On 13 January 1911, the *Colliery Guardian* claimed that the pit produced 1,100,000 tons of coal in 1910, believed to be a world record output at the time, an impressive achievement considering that all the coal was mined by hand and raised at the No 1 shaft; the colliery thus held world production records for daily (5,000 tons) and weekly

(26,000 tons) outputs. That year 3,049 men and boys were employed, 63% of which had joined the Yorkshire Miners Association Union.

Just after the 1912 national Miners' Strike, a gob fire broke out in the north-west district and rumours spread around the area that the pit had exploded entombing 400 men. Fortunately, the rumours were untrue and 60 colliery officials and fire fighters successfully extinguished the fire. Speaking in 1913, William Wilde stated that on the first day back after the strike the colliery produced 4,644 tons, a credit to the workforce, and during 1912 the pit produced an outstanding 1,250,000 tons of coal, despite the effects of the strike, a production record that they would eventually lose to their subsidiary Brodsworth Main. To celebrate that year the colliery company paid a 20% dividend to shareholders.

On August 1913, the Hickleton Main Colliery Company registered a new subsidiary company, the Llay Main Collieries Ltd with a capital of £250,000 of which the colliery company held 75% with the other 25% being owned by Rea Ltd, the Liverpool shipping company. The directors of the new company were Robert Armitage, George Davy, Charles Edward Rhodes, William Wilde and Alec Lionel Rea. The new company was formed to acquire a coal lease from Sir Arthur Markham in the Llay district of North Wales and in 1914 Llay Main Colliery commenced sinking. The Welsh pit was most unusual for receiving the suffix 'Main' betraying its Yorkshire owners.

Back in 1905, the colliery company introduced its own mining courses with an initial intake of 40 students to act as a primer for employees wishing to enrol at University Mining Departments. By 1913, 117 men were being taught on the courses and in the time since their inception they had produced 1 Mines Inspector, 2 colliery managers, 2 under managers, 1 Rescue Station Instructor and 1 Mining Surveyor.

Before the outbreak of the First Would War, Hickleton Main colliery employed over 3,000 men but in 1914, 1,607 men enlisted as soldiers. Nevertheless, the colliery could sustain an output of 1,000,000 tons of coal throughout the war years with the reduced workforce. To help the war effort, the pit decided not to sell coal above the price of 15 shillings per ton and in 1915 the workforce and their families were treated to a summer trip to Blackpool to help improve morale. Former employees on war service benefitted from a relief fund provided by several local collieries and by 1917 Hickleton Main had contributed £20,000 to the fund, which was used to purchase gifts for men who had distinguished themselves in action.

Despite the war, production had remained high at the colliery and the company had accumulated a considerable sum of war time profits which it decided to invest in other ventures. Following the cessation of hostilities, Hickleton, Brodsworth, Bullcroft, Markham Main and Yorkshire Main Collieries formed the Doncaster Collieries Association Ltd (DCA) with a capital of £500,000 equally subscribed by the five partners. The DCA acted as a selling agency for the coal produced from its member pits on a commission of 6d/ton and with its size could bulk buy at discount raw materials and equipment for its members. Later that year it was announced that Bullcroft Main Collieries & the Staveley Coal & Iron Company Ltd were looking for partners in the development of Markham Main Colliery at Armthorpe. Consequently, Hickleton Main Colliery and its subsidiary Brodsworth Main Colliery decided to subscribe £150,000 each in the share capital of the Markham Main Colliery Ltd, with each of the four partners taking a 25% stake in the new company who developed a pit at Armthorpe near Doncaster.

In 1920, William Wilde retired due to ill health and he was replaced with Robert Claytor as general manager; he had been agent to Yorkshire Main Colliery. However, two years later, Robert Claytor left the company to organise the purchase of the Shipley Collieries Ltd in Derbyshire which were up for sale. He would later return to South Yorkshire when he became Chairman of the Mitchell Main Colliery Company Ltd. At Hickleton Main, J T Greensmith of Markham Grange was appointed general manager. Incidentally, his son Tom Greensmith constructed a working model of the Hickleton Main shafts, it would be interesting to know if this model has survived.

Aware that the huge output at the pit was rapidly working its way through the reserves of Barnsley coal, the directors decided to develop the Parkgate Seam. In 1921 work commenced on the sinking of No 3 shaft and the deepening of No 2 shaft. The work was expected to take two years and increase the output of the pit by 1,000 tons per day which would sustain the pit for the following 100 years. Work on the new 21 ½ feet diameter No 3 shaft proceeded at a rate of 2 yards of excavations per shift and in 1923 the shaft had reached at depth of 909 yards, having intercepted the Parkgate seam at 789 yards and the Parkgate seam at a depth of 827 yards. Development of advancing longwall faces in the Parkgate seam commenced in 1925.

Two similar views of Hickleton Main Colliery taken from Lockwood Lane to the south.

Above Left: A 1920 postcard by Lamb of Barnsley featuring No 2 and No 1 headgears, and the construction of No 3 headgear and winding engine house centre right, together with the brickworks chimney far right. *(Andrew McGarrigle Collection)*

Above Right: A 1925 postcard by Edgar Scrivens showing the pit during its heyday, producing around 1,250,000 tons of coal per year and employing around 4,000 men. The new No 3 shaft, winding engine house, coal preparation plant and washery, together with its funnel shaped settling tank, have all been newly built on the right. No 1 headgear is now hidden behind a large wooden water cooling tower and No 2 Headgear is visible on the left.

On completion, the No 1 and No 2 shafts operated as downcast shafts and No 3 shaft operated as an upcast shaft. A new steam powered Waddle fan and standby electric fan were installed at the No 3 shaft to ventilate the underground workings. Markham & Company of Chesterfield supplied a steam powered winding engine and Lancashire Boilers, and the headgear was constructed from reinforced concrete with a brick collar to form an airlock. In 1922, the DCA purchased a new Baum washery and coal screening plant from Simon Carves Ltd with a capacity of 160 tons per hour to handle the increased output. To dispose of the increase in dirt from the new plant a large pylon supported aerial ropeway was installed stretching away over the fields to the east. The tipping covered the old brickworks as a new brickworks had been established to the north of Lidgett Lane to provide bricks for the construction of 1,500 new houses which were being provided by the colliery and the local authority in Thurnscoe.

The development of the Parkgate seam required the recruitment of an additional workforce and it was decided to provide colliery-owned housing. One of Robert Armitage's fellow Liberal MPs was Sir J Tudor Walters who owned his own architectural practice, the Housing & Town Planning Trust Ltd. In 1920, the colliery company together with Sir Tudor Walters established a subsidiary company named the Thurnscoe Housing Association who built 36 houses in George Street and 258 houses to the north of Lidgett Lane. In 1922, another partnership with the Industrial Housing Association under the directorship of Sir Tudor Walters saw 733 houses constructed at Thurnscoe East.

In 1923, the Hickleton Main Colliery Ltd decided to increase its capital by issuing £750,000 in 6% debenture stock. This was intended to pay for new shafts to the Parkgate seam at Hickleton and Brodsworth Main Collieries and for the full development of Llay Main Colliery (now employing 2,500 men) and Markham Main Colliery together with the erection of a proposed coke and by-product plant. The directors and their friends purchased £100,000 of the new shares and the remainder was issued to the public. To prevent the encroaching of coal workings into the royalties belonging to neighbouring collieries, in 1923 the colliery negotiated boundary agreements with the adjacent pits. The Barnburgh Cliff boundary line was established with Denaby Main and Barnburgh Collieries to the south east, and a boundary agreement was signed with Wath Main Colliery to the south, with Houghton Main Colliery to the west and with Frickley Colliery to the north. The area to the east was operated by the subsidiary colliery at Brodsworth, therefore there was no need to sign an agreement.

The 1920s continued to be profitable for the colliery company. Hickleton Main and Brodsworth Main were financially successful and production continued at around 1,250,000 tons per year from the Hickleton shafts. Profits recorded in 1923 were £147,562; in 1924 £140,388; in 1925 £119,202 although the 1926 General Strike caused the company in that year to record its first loss of £11,723. In 1926, a decision was made to sell their 75% stake in Llay Main Collieries to their Grimethorpe based neighbours, the Carlton Main Colliery Company Ltd. Thus, the company could use the sale proceeds to focus on developing Markham Main Colliery.

In 1926, the colliery was supplied by electricity from the 18-megawatt power station at Frickley Colliery 3 miles away, with the electricity delivered via overhead transmission pylons, some of the earliest pylons erected in the country. The electric supply was connected with the DCA electric ring main enabling electrical power to be distributed amongst the various collieries on the ring main. Electricity was also provided to the Dearne Electric Board to provide a domestic supply to customers in Thurnscoe, Goldthorpe, Bolton and Wath, as well as a direct supply to all the colliery owned houses in Thurnscoe. The development of the Parkgate seam enabled the workforce at the colliery to exceed 4,000 men for the first time in 1928 and by 1931, 4,145 employees were on the books. This was the second highest number of men employed at any British Colliery, only exceeded by the 5,224 men employed at Ashington Colliery in Northumberland in 1924. Incidentally, that same year the subsidiary colliery at Brodsworth Main employed 4,076 men, the third highest number at any British colliery.

However, the Great Depression during the 1930s caused by the Wall Street Crash the previous year saw the Government impose a standard tonnage on every British colliery to control production with effect from 1931. Hickleton Main negotiated a generous standard tonnage of 2,049,000 tons per year of which the Government permitted the colliery to produce 63% of this amount: 1,291,000 tons (720,000 from the Barnsley seam and 571,000 tons from the Parkgate seam). Any over production would be met with fines and a deduction from the following year's allowance. This caused widespread hardship throughout the country's coalfields as collieries decided to work 4 day weeks, impose pay cuts and dismiss staff. In 1932, around 1,000 men were dismissed at Hickleton Main Colliery leading to high levels of employment in the area. Despite this, the colliery company could sustain a high output and profit level and the following statistics provide for interesting reading, proving the levels of profit that could be sustained during periods of economic depression:

Year	Output (tons)	Profits	Dividend	Lease income	Bricks Produced
1931	1,092,000	£69,354	5%	£1,572	438,000
1932	1,041,000	£67,705	5%	£328	1,535,000
1933	1,087,000	£98,533	4%	£155	1,520,000
1934	1,155,000	£111,519	5%	£291	3,798,000
1935	1,231,000	£102,663	5%	£186	3,820,000
1936	1,280,000	£99,109	5%	No data	No data

The 43rd Annual Report of the Hickleton Main Colliery Company Ltd for 1933 revealed that the colliery company had a capital of £1,200,000 and held the following investments: £800,000 in Brodsworth Main, £250,000 in Markham Main, £100,000 in Doncaster Collieries Association, £40,906 in the Industrial Housing Association and £308 in the Thurnscoe Housing Association. Robert Armitage remained as Chairman and the other directors included Sir William Bird of Chichester; Major Cecil Fowler of Firth Manor in London; William Humble of Skellow Grange; Major Thirlwall Phillipson of Fordham Abbey in Cambridgeshire; John Armitage of Farnley Hall; and Captain George Davy of Beltrim Castle, Ireland.

The 43rd Annual Report also lists the shareholders in the colliery company. The largest shareholders were the executors of Sir Arthur Markham with 66,819 shares. The Armitage family held 65,390 shares and an additional 30,000 shares were held by their Farnley Investment Company. Charles Hague and family held 34,600 shares and William & Constance Humble owned 21,697 shares. The executors of William Wilde held 8.825 shares and John Greensmith held 9,895 shares. The Shaw family of Welbourne Manor near Kirkbymoorside in North Yorkshire owned 12,875 shares. The architect of Brodsworth Colliery's Highfields village, Benjamin Marson, held 500 shares, as did Clement Gatley, the company secretary. Leonard Hodges, the mining engineer of Barnburgh Hall, also owned 500 shares. Other colliery companies owned shareholdings: 19,740 shares were owned by Airedale Collieries Ltd and 10,000 by South Kirkby Featherstone and Hemsworth Collieries Ltd. Even British Electric Traction, the owner of local bus company Yorkshire Traction, owned 1,000 shares. There were also numerous other minor shareholders including furniture dealer Frederick Binnington of Kings Road Doncaster with 310 shares and newsagent Charles Cadman of 23 Laughton Road, Dinnington with 850 shares. All of them shared in the wealth generated from the huge output of coal produced at Hickleton Main.

Writing in *Mining Memories*, Ray Kennedy gives a vivid account of working at Hickleton Main Colliery during the 1930s when the skies were lit up at night by the burning muck stack and the pit buzzer governed life in the village. The whole community would be woken by the blowing of the pit buzzer at 4.30am which was repeated at 15 minutely intervals until 6am. The day shift would make their way to the pit for 6am and Ray would dress in his pit clothes ready for his shift: wearing clogs, an overcoat, knickers, a vest and his sister's beret on his head - long before the era of safety clothing and hard hats! His sandwiches were contained in his snap tin attached to his belt and a six pint Dudley (a metal vessel containing water) was slung from his shoulder. Ray was now ready for work and probably looking forward to 10am when the pit buzzer would sound for his 20-minute snap break, where he would enjoy his sandwiches, unless as Ray recalls, a resourceful pit pony had managed to steal them from his snap tin!

To enable the more efficient working of adjacent groups of collieries, the government had encouraged the creation of larger operational units and in 1937 the Doncaster Amalgamated Collieries Ltd was registered with a capital of £7,750,000. Doncaster Amalgamated Collieries (DAC) was formed by the merger of the Hickleton Main Colliery Company Ltd, Bullcroft Main Collieries Ltd and the Doncaster Collieries Association Ltd, together with the South Yorkshire operations of the Staveley Coal & Iron Company Ltd. Therefore, Hickleton Main joined Bullcroft Main, Brodsworth Main, Firbeck Main, Markham Main and Yorkshire Main as a department of DAC Ltd and its shareholders received DAC shares in exchange for their Hickleton shares. William Humble was the Chairman of the new company with Robert Armitage managing director. With its high output and directorial connections, Hickleton Main was more like the modern collieries of the Doncaster Coalfield rather than those of the Dearne Valley, therefore the merger was a natural progression.

Under the new ownership, an additional Simon Carves Ltd washery was installed in 1937 with a capacity of 200 tons per hour and production remained high, with 1,167,254 tons of coal recorded that year and 1,218,883 tons in 1940. Despite the outbreak of the Second World War, production remained high as did employment levels at around 3,600 men. To assist with the war effort the Meltonfield seam was developed at a depth of 385 yards via insets in the No 2 and No 3 shafts with drifts rising from this horizon to access the Newhill seam at a depth of 360 yards. The Meltonfield and Newhill seams were sometimes referred to as the Low Main and High Main seams respectively and leant themselves to mechanized mining using an American system of working known as "room and pillar" using coal cutting, mechanical loading and conveyor belt haulage to the pit bottom.

In 1944, Robert Armitage died. He had served as the Chairman of Hickleton Main Colliery Company from 1892 to 1937 and as managing director of DAC Ltd from 1937 to 1944. Unlike many of the other pits of the Dearne Valley, the owners of Hickleton Colliery had never shown any interest in the manufacture of coke and other by-products. However, in 1943, a new subsidiary company was registered as the Doncaster Coke & By-Product Company Ltd with the aim of establishing coking plants at Hickleton and Brodsworth Collieries at the end of the war. However, the nationalisation of the industry in 1947 saw these plans abandoned and, following nationalisation, DAC Ltd was paid £6,578,000 for its six collieries and the brickworks at Thurnscoe.

One of the first improvements initiated by the NCB was the introduction of pithead baths and on Saturday 20 August 1952, these were opened by General Sir Noel Holmes, the Chairman of the NCB North East Division. The baths had a capacity for 3,648 men. During the 1950s, the colliery muck stack caught fire and smouldered away for many years. One former miner recalled how he and the local boys would often unofficially ride in the buckets of the aerial ropeway, jumping into the soft spoil just before the bucket was upturned. The spoil heap was likened to a volcano with vents of steam and smoke and dangerous cracks in the surfaces revealed the glowing red embers of the fire below.

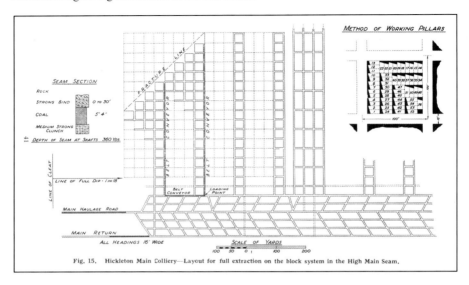

Fig. 15. Hickleton Main Colliery—Layout for full extraction on the block system in the High Main Seam.

Above: Plan depicting methods of working in the High Main (Newhill seam) at a depth of 360 yards using the American method of working pillars of coal between a grid pattern of roadways. *(Doncaster Amalgamated Collieries Brochure 1944)*

In 1956, reserves in the Barnsley seam were finally exhausted after 61 years of continuous working. The NCB had authorised a £4,000,000 reconstruction scheme with the introduction of a new pit bottom at a combined Meltonfield/Newhill level in No 1 and No 2 shafts and with the use of skip winding and coal haulage by high capacity mine cars, thus maintaining production above 1,000,000 tons per year. The skip in No 2 shaft had a capacity of 8 tons of coal and was fed by a 750-ton underground bunker, which itself was supplied by conveyor belts from mechanised mining in the Meltonfield and Newhill seams. A new electrically driven Waddle fan was installed to provide underground ventilation. The No 3 shaft was left unchanged apart from the replacement of its steam winder with an electric winding engine.

On the surface the old steel lattice No 1 and No 2 headgear and steam powered winding engines were replaced with new headgear and electric Koepe winders positioned at ground level rather than above the shafts. New screens and coal washing plant was installed which were connected to a new rapid loading bunker to supply coal fired power stations. The aerial ropeway was dismantled and a new tipping area to the south was developed, dirt being spread by a fleet of Euclid Trucks Company dumpers and spreaders.

In 1958, the 3,459 men at the colliery produced 1,064,000 tons but by 1964, these figures had dropped to 2,567 and 805,000 tons respectively and in 1973 to 1,400 and 585,00 tons respectively, despite the modernisation scheme. The reduction of manpower could be accounted for by the introduction of mechanised mining but the reduction in output was blamed partially on a high absenteeism rate at the pit, described sarcastically by the NCB Doncaster area director as "Fantastic! - the worst in Britain and probably the world." The colliery was now losing money and the workforce were disillusioned with managerial decisions and geological conditions and there was even talk of the pit closing.

However, a couple of recent developments saw the pit's future assured. In 1969, a new surface drift opened to intersect the Shafton seam workings from the adjacent Goldthorpe/Highgate combined mine. The new drift was positioned in the colliery pit yard and served as upcast ventilation for these workings. More importantly was the decision in 1975 to concentrate all workings on the Parkgate, Thorncliffe and Silkstone seams. It was hoped that this would sustain a profitable output of 750,000 tons of coal per year with a reduced workforce. A rapid loading bunker was constructed to load Merry-Go-Round trains with power station coal.

Production in the shallower seams finally ended in 1983 after which the deeper seams provided the pit's output. However, after the Miners' Strike of 1984/5 the pit was put on a 'development only' basis; full development of the deeper seams was intended to take place once work had finished at Goldthorpe Colliery. Workings in the Thorncliffe seam were abandoned due to poor geological conditions and on 1 January 1986 Hickleton merged with Goldthorpe Colliery to form the Hickleton/Goldthorpe combined mine. Many of the men at the Hickleton site were offered an enhanced redundancy package although a workforce of under 100 remained to run the operations from the Hickleton end. It was intended to redevelop the Hickleton reserves once Goldthorpe Colliery had exhausted its reserves in the Shafton seam.

Above: Following the Miners' Strike of 1984-85, the Hickleton Miners and their families and supporters assembled at the 'Big Lamp' at Houghton Road for the march back to work. The strike ended on 3 March 1985 nearly a year after it had begun and the Hickleton Miners returned to work on 5 March 1985. *(Peter Davies).*

In 1987, Cadeby Main Colliery was closed and its Shafton seam reserves allocated to Goldthorpe Colliery which meant an extended life for Goldthorpe at the expense of an increased delay to the redevelopment of Hickleton Main Colliery. Consequently, the British Coal Corporation decided that it was uneconomic to continue to develop the deeper seams and the pit was put on a 'care and maintenance basis', and, on 31 March 1988, the pit finally closed with the remaining men transferring to Goldthorpe Colliery. No 1 and No 2 shafts and most of the surface buildings were demolished shortly afterwards but No 3 shaft and the drift entrance remained in situ to serve as an emergency access to Goldthorpe Colliery, before being demolished in 1994. The shafts were capped and the No 2 shaft and drift were fitted with methane extractors; the methane was used to provide power to the local area. No 1 shaft was capped with a concrete plug although No 3 shaft was unmarked. Some of the ancillary buildings have found further uses, including the pithead baths which have been adapted as a business centre.

In 1992, the A635 Goldthorpe bypass was opened to the south of the spoil heap and a new access road was built to Thurnscoe and the pit site with the aim of stimulating the development of new industrial units. On 6 April 1993, a small pit wheel monument was constructed on Lidgett Lane as a memorial to the miners and their families who had suffered hardship and grief in the pursuit of coal from the mine. During its operational lifetime, 161 men and boys had died at the colliery. The first recorded fatality is possibly W Barlow, aged 45 who worked in the screens building on the surface and who died on 30 August 1896 when he was run over by railway wagons in the colliery sidings. In 1998, the spoil heap was landscaped and re-opened in 2001 as a country park named Phoenix Park which incorporated several works of art and sculptures created by the local community, together with an open-air climbing wall engraved with the face of a miner and the legend 'Hickleton Main Colliery 1892-1988'. On 20 June 2006, the Dearne Memorial Group unveiled a memorial in Thurnscoe Cemetery to the 161 men and boys who died at the pit.

Above: *"Leaving the Mine"*
– an atmospheric photograph of Hickleton Main pit bottom from the lens of Peter Davies.

Grimethorpe Colliery 1894-1992

The name Grimethorpe (or *Grimey* as it has always been informally referred to) is synonymous with coal, due to its colliery and world famous colliery brass band. Prior to 1894, Grimethorpe was a hamlet of farms and stone built cottages located on the 4,000 acre Grimethorpe and Brierley agricultural estate belonging to Francis John Savile Foljambe of Osberton Hall near Worksop. However, this rural backwater was about to change when on 16 December 1892, the *Colliery Guardian* reported that the Mitchell Main Colliery Company Ltd was undertaking negotiations for the coal beneath the Grimethorpe estate.

Located three miles to the south of Grimethorpe, Joseph Mitchell had established Mitchell's Main Colliery near Wombwell in 1871, sinking a pair of shafts to the Barnsley seam. After an unsuccessful attempt to sell the business in 1882 following an economic slump in the coal trade, his son Joseph Mitchell Junior restructured the family company as the Mitchell Main Colliery Company Ltd and decided to expand the firm's interests, securing additional leases beneath the untapped coalfield to the north, and, in 1892 he started negotiation with Francis Foljambe. On 21 January 1893, a lease was signed to extract the Barnsley seam for a period of 60 years, with the option to purchase land for the proposed colliery and brickworks and colliery village.

A site for the new pit was chosen to the south of the hamlet of Grimethorpe adjacent to the Midland Railway and it was hoped to commence sinking operations following the end of the 1893 National Coal Strike. In the meantime, a connection was made with the nearby Midland Railway and to the Great Central Railway's Stairfoot to Houghton Main branch line enabling materials to be brought to the site and a brickyard was opened nearby to supply the bricks required to line the shafts and construct the surface buildings. However, the shaft sinking work had to wait for the arrival of the sinking contractors Charles Walker & Eaton of Doncaster who were busy sinking the shafts at Hickleton Main Colliery; at the end of summer 1894, once their work had finished at Hickleton Main, they transferred to the site of the new Grimethorpe Colliery.

On Monday 8 October 1894, a rather grand 'turning of the first sods' ceremony was held in a field near Grimethorpe. Mr and Mrs Mitchell and the guests of the company met at Cudworth Railway Station and travelled in a special train laid on by the Midland Railway along the new branch line to the site of the pit where they were met by a crowd of shaft sinkers, workmen and local people. Mr Mitchell opened proceedings and invited the Reverend Husband of Cudworth Church to offer a prayer for God's blessing for the new colliery. Mr George Henry Turner, chairman of the Midland Railway then cut the first sod at the No 1 shaft before delivering a speech. At the No 2 shaft, in the absence of Mr Foljambe, the first sod was cut by Joseph Mitchell Junior who then delivered another speech. The party then adjourned to luncheon in the Sinkers Room following which further speeches and toasts were delivered amongst the eating of gourmet food and the drinking of wine and champagne. Delivering one of the additional speeches, Mr Tyas, whilst wishing the new venture every success, bemoaned the fact that the new colliery would take the best part of the Badsworth Hunting ground. Mr Tyas stated: "I can only hope that the Company will afford some means of easing poor fox hunters who have lost their nerve by providing gates, so that it may not be necessary for them to attempt the feat of jumping those high hedges." Whether Mr Tyas and his fellow poor fox hunters received their gates is unknown, however the ceremony continued with further speeches detailing the feat ahead. It was hoped to find the Barnsley seam at a depth of 500 yards and equip the pit for an output of 2,500 tons per day. The Mitchell Main Colliery

Company now controlled a coalfield of around 7,000 acres worked from pits at Wombwell and Darfield Main (purchased in 1894) and from the new venture at Grimethorpe, which would trade under a subsidiary as the Grimethorpe Colliery Company Ltd. It was estimated that it would cost £80,000 to sink the shafts and lay out railway sidings.

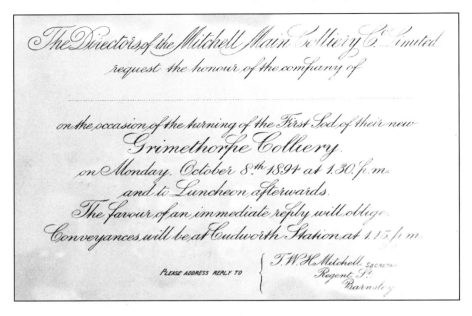

Above: An invitation from the Directors of the Mitchell Main Colliery Company to 'the turning of the First Sod of their new Grimethorpe Colliery'. *(Maurice Dobson Museum & Heritage Centre)*

Following the ceremony, work commenced on sinking two 19 feet diameter shafts under the leadership of Charles Walker. The shafts were positioned 80 yards apart with the No 1 downcast shaft to the south and the No 2 upcast shaft to the north. Almost immediately water began to flow into the shafts from the heavily fissured and porous sandstones. To overcome this, cast iron tubbing was inserted into the shafts as sinking work progressed. The Shafton coal seam was intersected at a depth of 72 yards but was sealed off by the iron tubbing which was carried down to a depth of 130 yards. This remedial work was time costly and expensive. Below the 130-yard level, shaft sinking was relatively straight forward and the shafts were lined with bricks. However, in 1895, the iron tubbing began to distort and fail, allowing water to flood the shafts. The costly corrective work required was beyond the means of the Mitchell Main Colliery Company Ltd and they decided to sell the colliery on 1 October 1896 to the Yorkshire & Derbyshire Coal & Iron Company. As part of the deal, Mitchell Main could nominate one of their directors to the board of the new company and, following this, they withdrew to concentrate their operations in developing the deeper seams at Mitchell Main and Darfield Main Collieries.

The Yorkshire & Derbyshire Coal & Iron Company Ltd was formed on 29 November 1872 with a capital of £73,000 by James Jenkins Addy and William Wake. James Addy was born in 1850 at Ecclesall Bierlow in Sheffield and William Wake lived in Bank Street in the same city. The two partners were proprietors of two small collieries near Dronfield on the

Yorkshire/Derbyshire border and they were looking to expand their interests. The new company was formed to develop a pit at Carlton near Barnsley and on 12 Nov 1873 they signed a lease for the Barnsley seam beneath 2,133 acres of land in the area belonging to the Earl of Wharncliffe (Edward Montagu Stuart Wortley Mackenzie) of Wortley Hall. The Earl of Wharncliffe cut the first sod of the Carlton Main Colliery shafts in 1873 and by 1876 the colliery was producing coal. Aware that they had limited reserves in the Barnsley seam, they were looking to expand their operations and the purchase of the adjoining Grimethorpe coalfield to the east was a natural progression.

Under the new ownership, the team of 127 shaft sinkers replaced the faulty iron tubbing and installed water pumps to drain the shafts. When this work was completed, shaft sinking recommenced and proceeded rapidly, striking the Barnsley seam at the end of 1897 at a depth of 581 yards. The seam was eight feet thick and of excellent quality and the shafts were continued to form a sump at the 600-yard level.

The previous owners had equipped the shafts with permanent steel lattice headgears and winding engines to carry out the shaft sinking operations. Both winding engines were supplied by Markham & Company of Chesterfield. The No 1 shaft was fitted with a triple deck cage carrying 4 x 10cwt tubs per deck and No 2 shaft was fitted with a double deck cage with 2 x 10cwt tubs per deck; therefore, 160cwt of coal could be raised with each draw of the winding engines. Steam raising was provided with a suite of 12 Lancashire boilers and the upcast shaft was equipped with a steam powered Schiele type ventilation fan installed by Crighton and Company. Two surface mounted engines provided underground haulage.

Above: This photograph by G A Fillingham was published as a postcard c1905 and shows Grimethorpe Colliery. The headgear above the No 1 downcast shaft and the screens building are on the left and the headgear above No 2 upcast shaft is on the right. Following typical practice, the headgear above No 2 shaft had been partially enclosed in a brick collar to form an airlock and increase the updraft for ventilation purposes. *(Chris Sharp / Old Barnsley).*

Men and boys were recruited to work the pit and move to the area and the colliery company provided housing in Grimethorpe although many men lived in nearby Cudworth. Once headways had been made through the shaft pillar, longwall faces were developed with men working in groups along the coal face. Coal was hand-loaded into tubs which were hauled by pony to the main roadways. From here, the tubs were conveyed by endless rope haulage to the pit bottom. After raising to the surface, each tub was weighed by the company and checked by the checkweighman with its weight and number recorded to generate the payment owed to the men in the group who had filled it. Coal was transported to the screens building for grading before dispatch via the railway sidings connected to the Midland Railway. However, James Addy was one of several local colliery directors who grouped together to establish the Dearne Valley Railway in 1897 and this line opened in 1902, providing an alternative outlet for Grimethorpe Colliery. This helped to lower railway transport costs with the competition generated by the two different railway companies helping to maximise the pit's profitability.

In February 1900, the Yorkshire & Derbyshire Coal & Iron Company Ltd formally merged with its subsidiary the Grimethorpe Colliery Company Ltd to form a new company under the chairmanship of William Wake, with James Jenkin Addy as Managing Director. The new company was named the Carlton Main Colliery Company Ltd and was registered with a capital of £410,000; a new head office and colliery offices were opened on Grimethorpe High Street. Most of the capital had been spent on developing Grimethorpe Colliery and securing the leases beneath the adjoining estate of William Warde-Aldham of Frickley Hall. This gave the company a royalty 9 miles long from Carlton in the west to Hooton Pagnell in the east, and in 1903 work commenced on sinking the shafts at the new Frickley Colliery, brought online to replace falling output at Carlton Main Colliery which was eventually closed in 1909. To pay for the new colliery the capital was increased to £700,000 and £290,000 in new shares were issued to the public.

At Grimethorpe, the colliery company laid out terraced houses to accommodate its growing workforce which by 1905 totalled 1,650 men. Around this time, a suite of Beehive coking ovens was opened to process the small coal into coke for sale to the steel industry, although this early coking plant had a short life as it was dismantled during the First World War. The colliery had been a tremendous success, with a high and increasing market fuelled by the coal boom during the Boer War. The colliery found a ready market for its coal and by 1911, the workforce had reached 2,608 when the company had completed the building of 238 houses forming the Grimethorpe 'seaside' estate.

On 26 April 1910, the colliery company signed a lease with Francis Foljambe for the Shafton seam beneath the Grimethorpe and Brierley estate for a period of 51 years from 1 January 1909. However, this coal was subleased to the Hodroyd Colliery Company Ltd. In 1910, this company commenced the sinking of Brierley Colliery, and, in 1915, they developed Ferrymoor Colliery to exploit this southern part of this lease. The latter pit was positioned on the site of the former Grimethorpe coke works and received the Brierley output via an overland tramway, which together with its own output was dispatched via the Grimethorpe Colliery sidings, although some of the output was loaded directly onto the Dearne Valley Railway at a loading plant half way along the tramway. This use of the Grimethorpe pit yard was explained by the fact that several of the Carlton Main directors sat on the board of the Hodroyd Colliery Company. In 1919, the Carlton Main Colliery Company took full control of the Hodroyd Colliery Company running it as a subsidiary operation.

During the First World War, plans were drawn up for the development of the deeper seams and, on 31 May 1917, a lease with Francis Foljambe was signed for all remaining seams of coal, ironstone and fire clay for a period of 99 years from 1 January 1917. A staple shaft was sunk from the No 1 pit bottom in the Barnsley horizon to the Parkgate seam and the No 2 shaft was deepened to the Parkgate seam at a depth of 851 yards. The seam was nearly 7 feet in thickness but separated into two layers by a band of mudstone. Insets were made in the shafts at the Haigh Moor seam horizon (661 yards) and Fenton seam horizon (789 seams) for future working, and longwall coalfaces were developed in the Parkgate seam first. Partially mechanised mining was introduced at these faces with conveyors and endless rope haulage replacing the use of pit ponies and the Parkgate coal was raised up the staple shaft to the Barnsley level from which it was wound to the surface.

The increasing output from the Barnsley and Parkgate seams saw the need to improve the surface plant. In 1912, a Simon Carves Ltd Baum type coal washing and screening plant had been opened and in 1918 this received an extension with an additional capacity of 180 tons of coal per hour. The washery was connected to a pylon supported aerial ropeway which extended to a new tipping site to the south-east. Waste material was conveyed in a series of buckets attached to the aerial flight and the contents were tipped to form a large spoil heap which ran parallel to the Midland Railway towards Houghton Main Colliery. The new coal preparation plant was installed to process the additional output expected from the development of the Parkgate seam.

The Carlton Main Colliery Company was increasingly becoming a very profitable concern with its two pits at Grimethorpe and Frickley capable of producing 2,000,000 tons of coal annually. During the 10-year period from 1912 to 1921, total profits of £1,821,640 were recorded and the company frequently paid dividends of 20 or 25%. This was an incredible sum for the time and demonstrated the immense profits that could be generated from the mining of coal. In 1919, the capital of the colliery company was increased to £780,000 with the issuing of £80,000 in additional shares. That year the company acquired the Hodroyd Colliery Company Ltd and a controlling interest in Rea Ltd of Liverpool, a shipping company with a fleet of stevedores and tugs and ideally positioned to handle coal exports. Rea Ltd also held a 25% stake in a new colliery being developed at Llay in North Wales. So much money had now accumulated in the colliery's reserve fund that it decided to issue a 150% share bonus. For every two shares held, shareholders received three complimentary bonus shares. This raised the capital of the company to £1,950,000 and the following year an additional £50,000 in new shares was issued to the public raising the capital to £2,000,000. The colliery company had also leased Cottage Farm, Foldhead Farm, Ringstone Hill Farm, Brierley Manor Farm and Brierley Lodge Farm from the Foljambe estate and on 21 October 1919, the Foljambe family sold the remaining 2,000 acre Grimethorpe and Brierley estate at an auction in the Royal Hotel in Barnsley, thus ending the Foljambe family's 300-year connection with the area. Many of the lots from the sale were purchased by the colliery company.

By 1922, 3,141 men were employed at the colliery producing around 1,000,000 tons of coal per year. To house the additional workforce, the colliery company constructed 228 houses on a separate site to the east. The brickwork of these houses was rendered with cement giving rise to the name 'White City'. Meanwhile, the local authority was providing its own housing schemes to the north along Brierley Road. A development of 68 brick built houses was given the name 'Red City' and the local authority also provided an additional 152 houses nearby in the mid-1920s; by 1926, 3,274 men and boys were employed at the colliery which became known as 'the pit with the golden pulley wheels' on account of its high production levels.

During the early 1920s the first generation of directors was succeeded by the next generation. James Jenkin Addy had moved to Hodroyd Hall near South Hiendley to oversee the development of the original Carlton Main Colliery. His son Roland Addy was born in 1893 and followed his father into the mining trade becoming managing director of the Hodroyd Coal Company and joining the board of the Carlton Main Colliery Company. The family later moved to Mount Osbourne House in Monk Bretton and in 1916, Roland Addy purchased Brierley Hall; after the end of the First World War he replaced his father as Managing Director. The colliery company's original chairman, William Wake, was succeeded by his son Phillip Kenyon Wake of Sheffield. Also on the board of directors were Sidney Gill of South Kirkby, Frederick Mawe of Malvern Wells, Harold Walker of Liverpool and Douglas Vickers of Sheffield steel and engineering conglomerate Vickers Ltd.

In 1924, the colliery company increased its capital to £2,500,000 to pay for several proposed projects. The first of these started in 1925 when work commenced on the sinking of No 3 shaft to the Parkgate seam at a depth of 850 yards. The new shaft was 21 feet in diameter and designated as an upcast shaft to assist with the ventilation of the expanded underground workings with the intention of raising Parkgate coal with skip winding facilities, one of the first such installations in the country. The shaft was equipped with a 7,500-horse power Metropolitan-Vickers electric winding engine, the largest in the country at the time and designed to raise 300 tons of coal per hour. However, a recession in the coal trade saw further development postponed and in the meantime, it was decided to work the Beamshaw seam from this shaft at a depth of 485 yards. Elsewhere in the colliery, drifts were sunk from the Barnsley horizon to exploit the Haigh Moor seam at a depth of 668 yards and drifts were taken from the Parkgate horizon to mine the Fenton seam at a depth of 821 yards.

In 1925, the Carlton Main Colliery Company opened a 18,000 KW Power Station at Frickley Colliery and electrical power was laid on to Grimethorpe Colliery as well as serving the villages of Grimethorpe, Brierley, Shafton and Cudworth; that year a profit of £218,579 was recorded. The following year the company expanded its operation with the purchase of the 75% stake held in Llay Main Collieries Ltd from the neighbouring Hickleton Main Colliery Ltd. The remaining 25% stake in Llay Main, which operated the largest pit in North Wales, was already controlled by Carlton Main through its Liverpool subsidiary Rea Ltd; therefore, Carlton Main now operated three collieries with the potential to produce 3,000,000 tons of coal per year and two smaller pits through the Hodroyd subsidiary.

Despite the 1926 General strike, the colliery company remained financially successful and in 1927 they purchased the Hatfield Main Colliery Company Ltd, who operated Hatfield Colliery near Doncaster. This brought another pit with a 1,000,000 ton per year capacity and the company intended to raise production to 5,000,000 tons per year from its collieries. To fund the purchase, £1,000,000 in additional shares were issued to the public. Around this time, Phillip Wake was replaced as Chairman by Douglas Vickers, bringing an end to the Wake family's connections with the colliery company. A selling agency, the Carlton Collieries Association, was established in 1927 to market the coal produced by the company's pits.

In 1929, 3,274 men were employed at Grimethorpe Colliery. However, the trade depression of the 1930s saw this drop by 40% to 2,033 by 1932 as the Government imposed a standard tonnage on the mining industry to avoid a collapse in price due to over-production. This caused considerable hardship in the region due to the rise in unemployment levels. On 12 December 1931, new pithead baths opened at the pit with facilities for £3,024 men at a cost of £26,000 provided by the Miners Welfare Scheme. Speaking at the opening, Douglas

Vickers, the colliery company chairman, addressed the economic situation of the time. He stated that there was very little prospect of employing more than 2,500 men due to the quota system imposed on the colliery. The consumption of coal at home and abroad had reduced due to the growth in the use of oil and a lot of the export trade had been lost as other countries developed their own coalfields

In 1934 sinking operations in the No 3 shaft were finally completed to the Parkgate seam. The No 3 shaft was installed with skip winding facilities using skips with 8-ton capacity. The pit was now producing coal from five seams. No 1 shaft was winding coal in tubs from the Barnsley, Haigh Moor Fenton and Parkgate seams and No 3 shaft was skip winding coal from the Beamshaw seam. The improving economic situation during the second half of the 1930s saw many of the unemployed men re-engaged and in 1938, the colliery produced 748,705 tons of coal. At the surface the spoil heap was enlarged by the tipping the dirt from side tipping wagons and using a second aerial ropeway. Meanwhile, the brickworks continued to expand and were now producing 200,000 bricks per week.

During the 1930s, the Carlton Main Colliery Company remained a profitable operation and in 1934 the Ruabon Coal & Coke Company Ltd was purchased. This company owned the Hafod No 1 and No 2 pits near Wrexham, employing 2,160 men. The company now owned Grimethorpe, Frickley, Hatfield, Brierley, Ferrymoor and South Elmsall collieries in Yorkshire and Llay and Hafod Collieries in North Wales, with a total production capacity of 6,000,000 tons. In 1937, Douglas Vickers died and was replaced by Harold Carleton Walker in the role of Chairman, with Roland Addy remaining as Managing Director.

In the 1940s, the Meltonfield seam was developed due to poor geological conditions in the Haigh Moor seam; this had suffered from extensive 'wash outs'. These were areas in which the original coal sediments had been eroded by the river sands above during deposition over 300 million years ago. The Meltonfield seam was now developed at a depth of 421 yards and was accessed from a pair of rising drifts from the Beamshaw horizon. All seams were now being mechanically mined with coal cutters and conveyors replacing the use of hand filled tubs. The Second World War had seen production at the pit increase and, in 1946, the workforce of 2,700 men produced 1,116,00 tons of coal.

On 1 January 1947, the colliery became part of the NCB North Eastern Division No 4 Carlton Area and the Government paid the Carlton Main Colliery Company Ltd £2,649,700 for its mining operations. In 1952, the Carlton Main Colliery Company went into voluntary liquidation and was officially wound up on 1 August 1962. Roland Addy and his father James Addy had run the company for 75 years, creating one of the largest colliery companies in the country. At nationalisation, Roland Addy sold Brierley Hall to Hemsworth Rural District Council and retired to live at Scarborough. Recognising the family's connection with the Barnsley area, in 1978 his wife Joan Addy left a bequest to the town's Cooper Art Gallery.

In its first year of public ownership, Grimethorpe Colliery produced 1,000,000 tons of coal, but this figure had dropped to 757,000 tons by 1955 when the NCB decided to implement an improvement programme. It was decided to combine the pit with Houghton Main, raising coal from the Meltonfield, Beamshaw and Winter seams at the Grimethorpe shafts and two locomotive haulage tunnels were driven underground to connect the two pits. The Barnsley seam was now exhausted and it was intended to raise all the output from the Parkgate and Silkstone seams at Grimethorpe within 15-20 years, leaving the shafts at Houghton Main for man-riding purposes.

The scheme also saw the reconstruction of the surface plant with skip winding introduced at No 1 shaft, and a third aerial ropeway was installed to tip dirt on a new site at Cudworth Common. In 1953, the underground haulage tunnel connecting the two pits opened in the Beamshaw level and coal from all the upper seams was now wound at the No 1 shaft which was equipped with a new Metropolitan-Vickers electric winding engine.

Electric power to the pit had been provided from Frickley Power Station, but this was now badly in need of refurbishment. Therefore, it was decided to build a new power station at the Grimethorpe site. This opened in 1958, complete with a chimney 300 feet high and a single distinctively shaped parabolic concrete cooling tower. The new power station was provided with coal from the Kent's Thick seam mined at a depth of 494 yards. Coal from this seam had a high ash content and was difficult to market, hence its internal consumption in the power station. The power station also supplied several other pits with electrical power, including Darfield Main and Houghton Main

In 1959 work commenced on deepening the No 2 and No 3 shafts to the Thorncliffe seam at a depth of 894 yards. No 2 shaft was equipped with a new headgear featuring a vertically mounted Koepe electric winding engine and the steel headgear at No 3 shaft was modified, giving it a somewhat distinctive appearance, described by some as ugly looking! A new coal preparation plant and washery opened in 1961 and a second underground connection with the Houghton Main workings was made at the Parkgate level, allowing all the output at the two pits to be raised at Grimethorpe Colliery. Despite the reconstruction scheme, output had fallen to 546,000 tons in 1964 when the pit employed 2,001 men.

In 1966, the large Coalite plant opened adjacent to the colliery producing smokeless fuel for the home market and further seams were developed in the early 1970s; the Fenton seam at a depth of 809 yards and the Newhill seam, the latter accessed via a surface drift. The colliery was now producing coal from six seams, Newhill, Meltonfield, Fenton, Beamshaw, Parkgate and Thorncliffe, but production remained relatively low and in 1975, only 441,000 tons of coal was produced, earning the pit the nickname of the 'sleeping giant', in spite there were still extensive reserves of coal remaining to be exploited. Most of the current output was now supplied to the Central Electricity Generating Board's power stations, although 20% was dispatched to coking works and 10% to the adjacent Coalite plant.

In 1979, work commenced on creating the Barnsley South Side Project, with the colliery becoming the centre of a £174,000,000 scheme designed to raise annually 3,000,000 tons of coal from Barnsley Main, Barrow Colliery, Darfield Main and Houghton Main Collieries. All these pits were linked and their output would be brought to the surface at Grimethorpe via a new drift mine completed in 1980; nearly nine miles of new underground roadways were constructed to connect the workings. Coal was brought up the new drift via conveyor belt to a huge new coal preparation plant, the largest in the country. The project was immediately successful and in the 1980-81 fiscal year, 1,255,486 tons were produced by the workforce of around 2,000 with 1,225,000 tons produced in the following year and the former sleeping giant of Grimethorpe was now living up to its earlier reputation as the pit with the golden pulley wheels.

At the surface, the coal was handled in the coal preparation plant via a series of covered conveyors and bunkers and dispatched into merry-go-round trains for transport to the power stations of the Aire and Trent valleys. Waste material was transported via covered conveyor onto the Cudworth Common tip where it was handled by 'the spreader', an unusual piece of machinery formed by a group of caterpillar-tracked mounted vehicles connected by conveyor belts that distributed the spoil around the tip like a scene from a surreal science fiction movie. However, the spreader seemed to frequently suffer from mechanical failure and was often out of action for extended periods of time.

Following the Miners' Strike, the colliery continued to achieve a high output of around 1,000,000 tons per year and in the 1991/1992 financial year, the 959 men employed at the pit produced 946,000 tons of coal and recorded a profit of £700,000. However, on 13 October 1992, the British Coal Corporation and the Government announced the closure of 31 out of the 50 remaining collieries to ready the industry for privatisation. The closure programme involved the loss of 30,000 jobs, with 10 pits earmarked for immediate closure including Grimethorpe Colliery.

Above: A splendid postcard of the famous Grimethorpe Colliery Band positioned in front of the Yorkshire Miners Association Grimethorpe branch outside the Cudworth Institute. The band was formed in 1917 by several members of a brass band at Cudworth which had disbanded, miners at Grimethorpe, the Colliery Institute and the Carlton Main Colliery Company Ltd and funded by voluntary subscriptions from officials and workmen. The band went on to achieve national and international success with a series of tours and television appearances. Following the closure of Grimethorpe Colliery in 1993 the band received sponsorship from RJB Mining, UK Coal and Powerfuel Ltd and is presently supported by Dransfield Properties Ltd, Carlton Brick Manufacturers and Besson of London. The band received prominent recognition from their appearance in the feature film Brassed Off and the soundtrack received a BAFTA. They also played at the 2012 Olympic Opening Ceremony at London and their current sponsorship deal takes them to 2019. *(Norman Ellis Collection)*

Despite the huge public outcry when thousands of people marched in demonstrations in London, with the Government - by now rapidly losing popularity - forced to introduce a partial reprieve, Grimethorpe Colliery was formally closed on 14 May 1993 with the loss of 950 jobs. The colliery was put up for sale to the private sector but no offers were received despite the huge amount of untapped coal reserves. When the Coalite plant closed the following year, the pit was subsequently demolished and the shafts filled in and capped. For several years, the site remained a derelict wasteland, with the drift entrance identifiable by its 1980 date stone clearly visible peeping above the rubble.

The area went into immediate decline and in 1994, a European Union study on deprivation listed Grimethorpe as the poorest village in the country. The scenes of deprivation attracted national interest as many people moved from the area leaving some of the streets abandoned and derelict. The callous pit closure programme was highlighted in the 1996 critically acclaimed film *Brassed Off*, starring Pete Postlethwaite, Ewan McGregor and Tara Fitzgerald and the Grimethorpe Colliery Brass Band. The movie was filmed in the streets of Grimethorpe with colliery scenes recorded at Hatfield Colliery because Grimethorpe pit had already been demolished. A particularly poignant scene was filmed on Pit Lane and saw Pete Postlethwaite's character suffer a heart attack; the film makers cleverly composited Hatfield Main Colliery's headgear into the background.

From 1996-2008, over £100,000,000 was spent on regenerating the area, with the money provided by the national government, Barnsley Council, the European Union, several development agencies and private enterprise. Businesses and warehouses opened on the colliery site with the new A6195 coalfields link road connecting the once isolated Grimethorpe with the rest of the Dearne Valley and the national motorway network. Many of the derelict houses were demolished and 500 new houses built which helped to improve the morale of the local community. The pit wheels were situated at the two entrances to the village and on 15 March 2003, the Grimethorpe Miners' Memorial Trust opened a memorial to the 154 men and boys who lost their lives working at Grimethorpe Colliery. Recorded on the memorial is the name of H Neatby, the first man to lose his life when on 14 March 1895 he fell from the headgear during the sinking of the shafts.

The spoil heap at Cudworth Common was landscaped and transformed into a nature reserve in 2005 as one of several South Yorkshire Community Woodlands created on former colliery spoil heaps; the Cudworth Common site incorporates Ferrymoor Flash and Edderthorpe Ings. In 2008, the original Grimethorpe spoil heap, spectacularly towering over the new A6195 road and which had remained derelict since its abandonment in the 1960s, was lowered and landscaped and transformed into the Park Springs Nature Reserve. However, still operating at the time of writing is the former colliery brickworks, trading as Carlton Main Brickworks Ltd, one of the last remaining operational brickworks in Yorkshire and fittingly still bearing the name Carlton Main, the original owners of Grimethorpe Colliery. However, 100 years after their formation in 1917, the Grimethorpe Colliery Band continue to perform to critical acclamation and have become the most famous brass band in the world, a fitting tribute to the colliery and community of *Grimey*.

Elsecar Main Colliery (1905-1983)

Although coal mining had been taking place in the Elsecar area since the mediaeval period, it was not until 1783, when William Fitzwilliam inherited the Wentworth estate and the house at Wentworth Woodhouse from the second Marquis of Rockingham, that mining operations were subsequently developed on a much larger scale. Prior to this date, some of the pits had been operated by private speculators under lease to the family, but Earl Fitzwilliam decided to take direct control of the Elsecar coalfield. Back in 1723, Low Wood Colliery was working the Barnsley seam and in 1742 Elsecar Old Colliery opened. In 1795, Elsecar New Colliery commenced production, stimulated by the forthcoming arrival of the Dearne & Dove Canal, of which William Fitzwilliam was one of the promotors.

One of the shafts at Elsecar New Colliery was equipped with a steam powered Newcomen beam engine, installed to pump water from the underground workings. This was a crucial step forward in the development of mining engineering, because, as the engine pumped out the water, it dewatered the surrounding strata enabling mining to take place at increasing depths. In 1816, Jump Pit commenced production, working the Barnsley coal at a depth of 60 yards, followed by Rainborough Park Pit near Tingle Bridge by the canal in the 1820s. Elsecar Low (Hemingfield) Colliery followed in 1840 with Simon Wood Colliery commencing production in 1853.

The Elsecar area was located on the northern edge of the Wentworth estate and Earl Fitzwilliam was also exploiting the coal on the southern edge of his estate in the Greasborough and Rawmarsh areas where he promoted the Parkgate Canal, a branch canal to serve these pits from the South Yorkshire Canal near Rotherham. Elsewhere on the Fitzwilliam estates in the Dearne Valley, the coal was subsequently leased to various colliery companies, for example, Cortonwood Colliery and Houghton Main Colliery. An outlying portion of the estate near Hemsworth in West Yorkshire was leased to the owners of Hemsworth Colliery who subsequently created the nearby settlement of Fitzwilliam, named after the family.

By the start of the twentieth century the Barnsley seam was mostly worked out in the Elsecar area and Earl Fitzwilliam was considering sinking a pit on his East Doncaster estate. However, on the advice of his mining agent, the East Doncaster estate was leased to Sir Arthur Markham so that Earl Fitzwilliam could concentrate on sinking to the deeper Parkgate seam beneath his core Wentworth estate. Consequently, New Stubbin Colliery near Rawmarsh was developed on the southern edge of the estate and Elsecar Main Colliery was sunk on the northern edge of the estate. Usually the suffix 'Main' after a colliery name was used to designate that the pit was working the Main or Barnsley seam, but at Elsecar the term was used to distinguish the colliery from the earlier pits.

A site was chosen for the new colliery to the south of the Great Central Railway's Elsecar branch and on 17 July 1905 the first sod above No 1 upcast shaft was cut by Thomas Newbold, general manager of Earl Fitzwilliam Collieries Ltd, who oversaw the sinking operations and that year 58 men commenced work on the site. The No 1 shaft was 16 feet in diameter and on 20 September 1906, the Parkgate seam was reached at a depth of 344 yards. The seam was 5 feet in thickness and of excellent quality. The first sod of the 18 feet diameter No 2 downcast shaft was cut on 28 September 1906 reaching the Parkgate seam on 18 February 1908. Sinking operations proceeded relatively smoothly despite the inflow of water and gas into the shafts. At the time, it was customary practice in the mining industry to designate the No 1 shaft as the downcast where air is drawn into the mine and No 2 shaft as the upcast where air is expelled from the mine, but at Elsecar Colliery the situation was reversed.

Above Left: Sinking operations at Elsecar Main Colliery. A postcard by F R Haigh taken from the south showing the temporary wooden headgear used to sink the No 1 shaft. The first sod had been cut on 17 July 1905 and the shaft had reached a depth of 36 yards by September that year. *(Norman Ellis Collection)*
Above Right: The pit site from the north looking across the canal and the railway line as featured on a postcard by Lamb of Barnsley c1907. Work on building the brick collar for No 2 shaft on the left is now underway. *(John Ryan Collection).*

The two shafts were situated 140 yards apart and arranged so that No 2 shaft was to the northeast and No 1 to the southwest. Sinking operations had been carried out using temporary wooden headgears and winding engines and in 1907 these were replaced with permanent headgears and winding engines. Above No 2 shaft a steel lattice headgear 80 feet high was constructed. The steel headgear at No 1 shaft was slightly smaller in height at 70 feet and was encased in a brick collar to form an airlock. The permanent winding engines by Bradley & Craven Ltd of Wakefield were housed in brick built engine houses to the south east of each shaft.

The No 1 shaft was equipped with a single deck cage for winding men and materials and was fitted with a ventilation fan provided by the Waddle Engineering & Fan Company of Llanelli in Wales. No 2 shaft was fitted with a double deck cage for winding coal with a capacity of 6 x10 cwt tubs per draw. Steam raising was facilitated by the provision of 10 Lancashire boilers, the exhaust from which was used to generate electricity via an exhaust turbo alternator. A screening plant was built to process the coal produced from No 2 shaft and this extended over 10 lines of railway sidings. The surface plant was equipped with a large brick built chimney nearly 200 feet high and the colliery was now ready to produce an output of 2,000 tons of coal per day. Working faces were opened in the Parkgate seam and mining operations commenced using the advancing longwall method with groups of men working in stalls along the face. Coal was hand cut and loaded into 10 cwt tubs. These were then hauled by one of the pit's 39 ponies to the main roadways and attached to an electrically powered endless rope for transport to the pit bottom.

Men were recruited to work at the pit, many having already been employed at Earl Fitzwilliam's other Elsecar collieries and they were housed in a series of high standard stone built terraced rows. These had been built during the previous century by Earl Fitzwilliam to provide accommodation for his workforce at the earlier pits in the district. The rows were built along Wath Road and named Old Row, Station Row, Meadow Row, Reform Row and

Cobcar Terrace. The cottages were architecturally superior to the standard of miners' accommodation at the time and some of the rows may have been designed by the noted architect John Carr of York. The 28 cottages forming Reform Row, complete with 1937 datestone, are particularly attractive as they follow the gentle curve of the road. The provision of high standard accommodation by Earl Fitzwilliam ensured a certain sense of loyalty from his workforce who would often doff their caps whenever "Earl Fitz Billy" passed by!

Above: By the time local photographer Frank Parkin produced this postcard of Elsecar Main Colliery in c1912, the pit had commenced full production. No 1 shaft is on the left together with the large screens building and No 2 shaft is on the right. The colliery was ideally situated for transport links and a train with a rake of Elsecar private owner wagons can be seen leaving along the former South Yorkshire Railway. The view is taken from Wath Road and obviously must have been photographed on a hot summers day as it features a group of lads playing on the banks of the Dearne & Dove Canal, and judging by the splash on the water it appears that one of them has just taken a plunge!

In 1922, compressed air was introduced to replace the use of ponies for coal tub haulage. In 1924, the workforce had reached 2,081 and it was decided to exploit the deeper seams. The No 1 shaft was extended to the Silkstone seam at a depth of 534 yards and workings in the Silkstone seam started in 1927; compressed air supply was used to power Siskol coal cutting equipment in this seam. A drift from the Parkgate workings was also tunnelled to the Silkstone seam to provide an emergency exit and complete the ventilation circuit. The increase in output saw the need for the installation of a modern coal preparation plant which was provided by Simon Carves Ltd in 1932. Colliery spoil was tipped across the meadows to the northeast near the old Hemingfield Colliery. The dirt was taken to a tippler which fed an extension dumping frame aerial ropeway which created the large muck stack at the pit.

Prior to 1933, mining operations on the Earl Fitzwilliam's Wentworth estate had been carried out directly under the control of the family. However, that year he formed the Earl Fitzwilliam Colliery Company Ltd with a registered capital of £1,500,000 and the royalties were transferred separately to the Earl Fitzwilliam Royalties Company. During the 1930s there was talk of nationalisation of coal royalties and Earl Fitzwilliam and several other landowners moved to protect their interests by creating various holding companies. Other nearby examples were the Wallsock Company, created by Sir Archibald White and the owners of Wallingwells Hall and Hodsock Priory to protect their royalties beneath Firbeck Main Colliery and the Elmsall Company, created by the trustees of Sir Charles Strickland to guard their coal royalties exploited by Upton Colliery. However, in 1938, mineral royalties were invested with the government and landowners received compensation.

In 1938, drifts were sunk from the Silkstone horizon to the Thorncliffe seam at a depth of 470 yards. Siskol coal cutters were used in this seam as well as the Silkstone but the Parkgate seam was still cut by hand. During the 1930s, the workforce averaged around 2,000 men, despite the implementation of the standard tonnage quota tempering the output. During the Second World War, work commenced on developing the Haigh Moor seam at a depth of 152 yards. A drift was tunnelled from the surface at a gradient of 1 in 5 to intersect the seam and the ventilation circuit was completed by opening an inset into the No 1 shaft. Production of mechanised faces in the Haigh Moor seam commenced in 1945 with the coal being brought to the surface along a conveyor belt up the drift.

The Barnsley seam around the picturesque estate village of Wentworth and beneath Wentworth Park had remained unworked and in 1942, controversial open cast operations commenced in the area to aid the war effort. In 1946, these were dramatically increased by Manny Shinwell, the Government's Minister of Fuel and Power, and were seen by many as an act of spite against Earl Fitzwilliam for having enjoyed the privileges brought by riches from coal royalties. The open cast operations were largely opposed by the local miners and the community, who had always enjoyed a good relationship with Earl Fitzwilliam and the National Union of Mineworkers even threatened strike action to save Wentworth Woodhouse from devastation.

However, open cast operations continued right up to the front door of Wentworth Woodhouse and involved the destruction of 2,000 acres of parkland, formal gardens, woodland, meadows and agricultural land; eventually open cast operations surrounded Wentworth village on four sides. In 1948, a small drift mine was opened on the estate but all operations finally ceased in 1955 following which the land was restored although it has since taken many years for the landscape to regain its traditional naturalised appearance.

In 1947, when Elsecar colliery was nationalised, the workforce totalled 1,760 who produced 700,000 tons of coal from the Haigh Moor, Parkgate, Silkstone and Thorncliffe seams. The NCB also took control of the nearby industrial workshops which became Elsecar Central Workshops. The NCB continued the mechanisation of the colliery with the introduction of underground haulage by diesel locomotive and mechanised methods of mining in the coal faces, including the use of power loading and the development of retreating coal faces in the Haigh Moor seam. The drift was an efficient method of transferring coal to the surface and output had increased to 782,000 tons in 1950, despite declining reserves in the Parkgate seam. By 1958, output had reached 883,000 tons.

In 1961, the steam powered winding engines were replaced with electric winding engines and a new coal washing and preparation plant was installed with a capacity of 250 tons per hour. By 1967, the retreating longwall coal faces in the Haigh Moor contributed 664,000 tons of coal. With 466,000 tons of coal being wound from the other seams, a total production of

1,130,000 tons of coal, the first time in the colliery's history that a figure over 1,000,000 tons had been achieved. The coal was sold for coke and gas production and was increasingly being used for electricity generation in the new Trent valley power stations.

In 1969, reserves in the Parkgate seam were exhausted followed by same happened in the Thorncliffe seam in 1972 and in the Silkstone seam in 1975, which caused a fall in production. This was partially replaced by extending the surface drift from the Haigh Moor horizon to intersect the Lidgett seam at a depth of 199 yards but geological conditions made the seam difficult to work and by 1975 production had dropped to 461,000 tons of coal. In 1979 workings were developed in the Kent's Thick seam from the surface drift at depth of only 30 yards beneath the surface. The shallow depth of the seam meant that frequent incursions from groundwater created difficult working conditions. Consequently, the decision was made to close the colliery with effect from 28 October 1983 and most of the workforce transferred to nearby Cortonwood Colliery with the guarantee of five years of further work.

Following the Miners' Strike the demolition of the surface buildings took place in 1985. The tall chimney was blown up, the bricks tipped down the shafts and the colliery spoil heap was landscaped and covered with agricultural fields. However, the colliery site remains derelict and in 2017 was still undeveloped and becoming overgrown. The NCB workshops at Elsecar and the Newcomen engine passed into the ownership of Barnsley Council in 1987 who subsequently developed Elsecar Heritage Centre as a major tourist destination in celebration of the industrial architectural importance of the area.

Above: This Scott's Series postcard probably dates from the late 1940s or 1950s and depicts some of the improvements made at the colliery, including the installation in 1932 of the large Simon Carves Ltd coal preparation plant and washery, complete with its distinctive funnel shaped concrete settling tank.

Barnburgh Main Colliery (1912-1989)

Above: A postcard depicting shaft sinking operations at one of the shafts. Shaft sinking was typically undertaken by using a large iron bucket, called a kibble, which was suspended from chains and lowered through the trap door into the shaft below. The kibble was used to lower men down the shafts and for raising the excavated material. Sadly, the identities of the men remain unknown: pure speculation maybe, but could that be master sinker Charles Walker standing in the bucket on the left with pit manager Arthur Thomson on the right? *(Norman Ellis Collection)*.

Barnburgh, sometimes spelt Barmborough, was famous throughout the area as the "Cat and Man Town", on account of its memorial to Sir Percival Cresacre, a 15th century knight who supposedly fought a long running battle with a wild cat or lynx whilst retruning to Barnburgh from Doncaster. The fight culminated in the church porch whereupon the knight fell dead from his injuries, his feet crushing the cat dead against the porch wall as he fell. One of the knight's descendents and owner of the Barnburgh estate married the son of Sir Thomas More, the chancellor to King Henry VIII and the medeival Barnburgh Hall was built for the family. In 1859, Thomas Peter More auctioned the hall and the Barnburgh estate was purchased by Andrew Montague of nearby High Melton Hall.

Andrew Montague had leased the Barnsley coal seam beneath his Conisbrough estate to Denaby Main Colliery Company in 1877 and the coal beneath his High Melton estate to the same company in 1894. However, at this time the coal beneath his Barnburgh estate remained unworked. Andrew Montague died in 1895 and the trustees of his will and his son Frederick James Osbaldeston Montague began negotiations with Manvers Main Collieires Ltd in 1906 for the coal beneath the 2,000 acre Barnburgh estate.

Manvers Main Collieries Ltd were already operating two pits near Wath-upon-Dearne and fuelled with profits driven by the coal boom created by the Boer War, they turned their attention to securing the neighbouring Barnburgh royalty. However, negotiations between Mr J F Thomson, the Manvers Main agent and general manager and the Montague trustees were long and protracted, but at the end of 1909 it was announced that the colliery company proposed to sink three shafts on a site near Harlington. One shaft was intended to mine the Barnsley seam at a depth of 550 yards, the second shaft would be sunk to the Parkgate seam at a depth of 800 yards and the third shaft would be a relief shaft and used for pumping water. It was intended to operate a colliery with an annual output of 1,000,000 tons per year and employing 3,000 men with Mr J F Thomson's son Arthur Thomas Thomson installed as the first colliery manager.

A contract was signed with John Eaton of the enginnering firm of Eaton, Son & Hinds. This firm had just started shaft sinking operations at Thorne Colliery near Doncaster and would undertake the work at Barnburgh once they had completed the Thorne shafts. The new colliery site would be adjacent to the new Dearne Valley Railway which had recently opened. The Dearne Valley Railway had been promoted by a number of colliery companies and one of its directors was Charles Edward Hunter, the son of one of the original promoters of Manvers Main Colliery. It was intended to deliver sinking apparatus and materials to the Barnburgh site via the newly completed railway.

In 1911, after five years of wrangling, negotitations were completed with the Montague estate for a coal lease of the Barnsley and Parkgate coal seams and a site for the proposed pit was purchased from the estate. One of the main reasons for the delay in signing the leases was the issue of colliery housing. The trustees wished to retain the rural nature of the Barnburgh estate and placed restrictions on the siting of houses. The lease stated that no housing was to be built to the north, east and south sides of Barnburgh Church or within one mile on the western side; the only exception would be for officials' houses adjacent to the proposed pit where such staff needed to be on site at short notice. Therefore all colliery housing had to be constructed over a mile away to the west, in the Bolton-on-Dearne and Goldthorpe areas. A proposed site for housing was purchased in Adwick-upon-Dearne from Earl Manvers but this was later used for the tipping of colliery spoil.

In June 1912, work commeced on sinking the shafts under the direction of Mr W Bunting, who had succesfully overseen the sinking of shafts at Brodsworth Main and Yorkshire Main Collieries. The No 5 downcast shaft was 18 feet in diameter and the No 6 upcast shaft was 16 feet in diameter and both were sunk to the Barnsley and Parkgate seams. In December 1912, work commenced on sinking the No 7 shaft to the shallow Shafton seam to provide water, although it wasn't the intention to work the Shafton seam at the time. The numbering of the Barnburgh shafts followed on sequentially from the four shafts at Manvers Main. The sinking had been carried out in record time and without the loss of any life.

 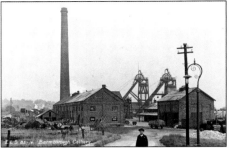

Above Left: This postcard view dates from 1911 and was produced by Regina Press Photographers of Doncaster. A connection was made with the nearby Dearne Valley Railway and a short branch line constructed to bring materials to the pit site. The steam powered crane was used to off load equipment from the railway. Barnburgh Church can be seen on the sky line.
Above Right: A fine study by Edgar Scrivens dating from c1920 depicting the surface buildings at Barnburgh Main Colliery. The two steel headgears above No 5 and No 6 shafts are prominent together with the much smaller No 7 shaft headgear visible beneath the legs of the No 5 shaft. *(Norman Ellis Collection).*

During 1913, water seeped into the shafts from the porous sandstones of the Oaks Rocks, a problem that had plagued the shaft sinkers at Manvers and Wath Collieries. A powerful water pump was brought to the site from Thorne Colliery to drain the shafts and work was concentrated on sinking the 12 feet diameter No 7 shaft to the Shafton seam at a depth of 86 yards. A pump was then installed in this shaft and the water used for colliery purposes; the water removed helped to drain the main shafts enabling shaft sinking to continue.

On 28 May 1914 the Barnsley seam was reached at a depth of 508 yards in No 6 shaft with No 5 shaft intersecting the seam on 13 June 1914. Pit bottoms were contructed at the Barnsley level before shaft sinking continued to the Parkgate seam. This seam was encountered in No 5 shaft on 28 February 1915 and in No 6 shaft on 3 March 1915 at a depth of 757 yards. The Barnsley seam was 8 ½ feet in thickness and the Parkgate seam was 5 feet in thickness. Following the succesful discovery of coal, Mr W Bunting left to oversee the sinking of the shafts at Markham Main Colliery at Armthorpe.

No 5 and No 6 shafts were equipped for coal winding and provided with steel lattice headgears 85 feet in height and coupled with steam powered winding engines, all provided by Markham & Company of Chesterfield. Steam generation was provided by a suite of Lancashire Boilers and both the shafts were equipped with double deck cages which could wind four tubs of coal with every draw of the cages. The remaining surface buildings were installed by Qualter Hall & Company and were all powered by elctricity delivered from the power houses and driven by steam turbines attached to the winding engines. An electrically powered fan was installed by the Waddle Engineering & Fan Company of Llanelli at No 6 shaft to ventilate the underground workings. Excess electricity generated on the site was used to provide power to the neighbouring villages of Barnburgh, Harlington and Adwick-upon-Dearne

Men were recruited to work at the new colliery and advancing longwall faces were first established in the Barnsley seam. Men worked in groups in various stalls along the face, hand-loading coal into tubs. This was then hauled by pony to the main roadways whereupon the wagons were coupled to an endless rope powered by an electric winding engine to the pit bottom. In April 1915 it was reported that 200 tons of coal per day were being raised from the Barnsley seam, although this probably represents coal released from the construction of the underground workings and from tunnelling through the shaft pillar. Access to the Parkgate seam was from a cage lowered by an elctrically driven winding engine from the Barnsley seam level; the development of the Parkgate seam followed shortly afterwards. However, extraction of this seam would be by retreating longwall faces and roadways were first tunnelled out to the extremities of the royalty where faces were formed along the royalty boundary. The faces were then worked backwards towards the shafts, with the roof being allowed to collapse in a controlled manner into the worked out regions.

By 1917, 1,215 men were employed at the pit and output was approaching 400,000 tons, all dispatched via the Dearne Valley Railway. The electric power supply generated at the pit was linked to the parent colliery at Manvers and the Doncaster Collieries Association electric ring main, which transferred surplus power between pits in the same group. To enhance the royalty, coal beneath land owned by several minor land owners in Barnburgh was purchased by the company and leases with larger land owners for coal in the area were signed with Earl Fitzwilliam, Henry Whitworth of Wath and the trustees of Sir Charles Watson Copley of Sprotbrough Hall.

In October 1921, pithead baths were opened at Barnburgh Main Colliery, the second such scheme to be provided at a Yorkshire colliery. The colliery manager, Mr T L Soar purchased the shower equipment from a former military camp at Ripon and devised the scheme to which 100 men signed up. The men paid 6d per week to use the baths but had to provide their own soap and towels. The pithead baths were replaced in 1926 with facilities provided by the Miners Welfare Fund with accomodation for 2,000 men.

In 1924, the colliery was connected by a private railway around two miles in length to Manvers Main Colliery and it was decided that all the output would now be transported along this line for washing and screening at Manvers. At this time 2,018 men were employed at the pit and output was around 700,000 tons, mostly from the Barnsley seam, as headings and retreat faces were still being established in the Parkgate seam. Many of the men walked or cycled to the pit from Goldthorpe and Bolton-on-Dearne.

In 1927 the Montague estates at Barnburgh and High Melton were sold to a consortium of Mexborough builders, although the Montague family retained the mineral rights. The new builders announced that they intended to build 1,000 houses in the area for miners, colliery officials and business men. However, the scheme seems to have foundered, and only 38 houses were built, including 19 semi-detached properties on Melton Mill Lane.

The introduction of the quota system in 1930 where each colliery was allocated a standard tonnage saw the development of the Parkgate seam suspended and operations were focussed on the Barnsley seam where 2,298 men produced around 800,000 tons of coal. To stop the encroaching of underground workings into the royalties of neighbouring pits a complex boundary agreement was drawn up with Hickleton Main Colliery, Brodsworth Main Colliery and Denaby Main Colliery which saw an exchange of outlaying areas of royalties between the four pits.

Improvements in the coal industry during the mid 1930s saw plans brought online for the development of the Parkgate seam and from other seams in the royalty. On 31 December 1935 the colliery company signed a 99 year lease for all other seams of coal with Frederick Montague who was now resident at Shortgrove Hall near Saffron Walden, Essex. The terms of the lease were £25/foot thickness/acre for the Silkstone seam, £22 10s/foot/acre thickness for the Shafton seam and £20/foot thickness/acre for all other seams. One of the clauses of the lease was that there was to be no subletting of coal to Denaby Main, Hickleton Main or Brodsworth Main Collieries. The Montague family probably saw very little in the way of royalties from these leases as the 1937 Mining Act transferred ownership of coal seams to the state, although landowners were compensated for their losses.

In 1936 a new screening plant was opened by Qualter Hall & Company of Barnsley ready to handle the enlarged output from the additional seams and a new powerful electrically driven Industructable ventilating fan was provided by Walker Brothers of Wigan. During 1937 skip winding was installed in the No 6 shaft ready to wind the Parkgate seam output with 8-ton capacity skips rather than the traditional coal tubs; it was believed to be the first installation of its kind in the country and a method which had provided efficient results on the continent. At the surface, the skips were tipped into a conveyor for transport to the new coal screens and the pit now employed 2,656 men. However, a series of lightning strikes, saw the temporary closure of the No 5 Barnsley seam pit for several months during 1938.

Once the disputes had been solved, machine coal cutting and mechanised mining and coal loading of the retreat faces in the Parkgate seam commenced in 1939, ready to replace dwindling reserves in the Barnsley seam. Unexpected geological difficulties with wash outs of the Parkgate seam (where the seam had been eroded by the deposition of the overlying river channel sandstones) saw rapid developments of other seams. Inroads into the Thorncliffe seam at a depth of 792 yards were made from drifts in the Parkgate horizon. From the Barnsley horizon, drifts were driven to access the Haigh Moor seam at a depth of 566 yards.

On Friday 24 April 1942, 17 miners working in the 109 area of the Parkgate seam in the North West district 400 yards from the bottom of the shafts, were trapped by an underground earth movement, described by some as an earthquake, as the vibrations rattled crockery and dislodged chimney pots in houses throughout Goldthorpe and Thurnscoe. The colliery agent described the event as a "weighting" or upheaval of the floor and that there had been no explosion and that a search was being made for the trapped men. A crowd gathered at the colliery gates to wait for news. One miner, Robert Fairhurst, who had crawled from the scene stated that "the floor seemed to come up and hit the roof".

The official report by the Divisional Inspector of Mines issued in December 1942 stated that the event had been caused by a "shock bump", an unusual phenomenon caused by the rising of the underlying strata following the collapse of overlying parts of the rock elsewhere in the colliery. The resulting shock wave had been transmitted throughout the area and was even recorded on the seismographs of the British Geological Survey at Kew in London.

There then followed what was described in the *Colliery Guardian* as "one of the greatest rescue attempts mounted by the coal mining fraternity, once again showing the tenacity, determination and dedication of the coal mining community when disaster strikes". The Wath Miners Rescue team were quick to the scene and were joined by Joseph Hall, the president of the Yorkshire Miners Association: the rescue attempt involved 451 men searching for the trapped miners. After being entombed for 44 hours, eight men were rescued and 5 more were later found trapped in rubble. Food and water was passed to the remaining trapped men who were all resuced after 66 hours. However, despite the best efforts of the rescue team, four men were unaccounted for. Their bodies were later found some 100 hours after the event; they apparently died instantly from the effects of the upheaval. The four fatalities were W Cope, A Lackenby, W Rodgers and G Southwell; 30 others were injured in the event.

Following the event, miners returned to work at the pit under a subdued atmosphere although it was still necessary to produce coal to help the war effort. In 1945 entries into the Newhill seam were made at a depth of 340 yards and in 1947, the 2,299 men employed at the pit produced 775,000 tons of coal when the colliery was nationalised and transferred into the ownership of the National Coal Board.

As part of the Manvers Main reconstruction scheme, the NCB proposed to modify the operations at Barnburgh Colliery with the introduction of underground transport of coal in 6-ton capacity mine cars hauled by diesel locomotives for skip winding at the shafts. The Winter seam was opened out and accessed by sinking two staple shafts from the Newhill seam level and the main shafts were extended to the Thorncliffe seam at a depth of 788 yards. At No 5 shaft a new 3,500 horsepower electrical winding engine was installed, capable of winding coal from all the levels of the mine. This engine had been manufactured in 1944 in the USA for a Russian coal mine but the Second World War had seen it repatriated to the UK - it was possibly the largest winding engine in the country at the time. No 6 shaft was adapted for winding men and materials and the air flow was reversed, with No 5 shaft becoming the upcast and No 6 the downcast, following the installation of a new ventilation circuit in 1955. All the output would now be sent along the private railway to the new coal preparation plant at Manvers Main Colliery and the sidings with the Dearne Valley Railway were removed.

Following this, the colliery produced 1,036,000 tons of coal in 1957 and production remained around the 1,000,000 ton level for several years. In 1962 the Meltonfield seam was entered at a depth of 328 yards. By 1965 all of the other seams had been abandoned and production was focused on the Newhill and Meltonfield seams. That year output had fallen to 779,000 tons produced by a workforce of 2,090 men. By 1978 all the coal was mechanically produced by retreat mining methods leading to a decline in workforce levels. By 1984, only operations in the Newhill seam remained and the pit was producing 450,000 tons of coal. After the Miners' Strike, production continued in the Newhill seam but adverse geological conditions caused the colliery to record a loss of £2,800,000 in 1988. The British Coal Corporation decided to close the colliery on loss making grounds from 16 June 1989. The remaining workforce of 750 men were offered enhanced redudancy packages and some transferred to other pits in the area.

Demolition occurred in 1990 when the No 6 headgear was blown up on 8 June, followed by the blowing up of the No 5 headgear on 10 August. For several years the site lay abandoned with the three concrete shaft pillars standing proud amongst the rubble but eventually the area was landscaped and now forms part of a country park. Part of the private railway line was adapted for use as a section of the new national Trans Pennine Trail and one of the winding wheels was mounted as a memorial to the colliery and situated near the junction of Westfield Lane and Hollowgate near Barnburgh. On 4 June 2006 Barnburgh Colliery was one of four local collieries commemorated in the unveiling of a new stained glass window at Goldthorpe Church.

Mining the Shafton Seam

Introduction

The Shafton seam is a shallow coal seam which outcrops along the northern side of the Dearne Valley and derives its name from the village of Shafton. From here, the outcrop can be traced eastwards through Grimethorpe, Little Houghton, Darfield and Billingley to Bolton-on-Dearne. The seam is around five feet in thickness and provides an excellent steam-raising coal; it was much in demand for railway locomotives. The coal had been sporadically mined along the outcrop and in the area to the immediate north for many years prior to the industrialisation of the Dearne Valley via a series of adits (horizontal or gently inclining tunnels into the hillside) or by shallow shafts. In 1838, the Wakefield firm of J & J Charlesworths were working Old Billingley Colliery at a depth of 60 yards, although the venture was short lived. Lying at a relatively shallow depth beneath the surface, mining operations usually employed the use of the pillar and stall method, with large blocks of coal were left intact to protect the surface from subsidence. The Shafton seam was also notoriously wet, its shallow depth enabling groundwater to percolate into the workings.

In the 20th century, an organised and large scale initiative commenced to exploit the seam and several collieries were developed to the north of the outcrop. These were, from east to west: Brierley Colliery, Ferrymoor Colliery, Dearne Valley Colliery, Billingley Drift Mine, Highgate Colliery and Goldthorpe Colliery. Several of these pits accessed the shallow Shafton seam via drifts as opposed to shafts, a more economical way of transport coal to the surface.

Above: The surface appearance of a drift mine is notably different to a shaft mine, as evidenced by this Haigh Brothers postcard of Dearne Valley Colliery. The entrance to the drift tunnel is on the left from which coal tubs are hauled to the small screens building on the right. *(Andrew McGarrigle Collection)*

Brierley Colliery

Above: Brierley Colliery depicted on a postcard by Walter Roelich of Doncaster c1915. The pit was one of the last in the country to be equipped with wooden headgears. No 1 shaft is on the left with No 2 shaft on the right.

The Hodroyd Colliery Company Ltd was registered on 29 July 1910 with a share capital of £30,000, subscribed jointly by the New Monckton Collieries Ltd of Royston and the Carlton Main Colliery Company Ltd of Grimethorpe. The new company was formed to purchase Hodroyd Colliery and to develop additional pits exploiting the Shafton seam. Hodroyd Colliery was already working the seam beneath the Hodroyd Hall estate belonging to Viscount Galway in the South Hiendley area further to the west.

On 26 April 1910, the Carlton Main Colliery Company signed a lease with Francis Foljambe for the Shafton seam beneath the 4,000 acre Grimethorpe and Brierley estate for a period of 51 years effective from 1 January 1909. However, this coal was subleased to the Hodroyd Colliery Company Ltd with the intention of sinking two pits at Brierley and Ferrymoor near Grimethorpe. In 1910 work commenced on sinking a pair of shafts to the south of Brierley village and two permanent wooden headgear were erected to sink the shafts. These were possibly the last wooden headgears constructed at any British colliery as the 1911 Mines Act prohibited the use of such structures made from wood.

Both shafts were 14 feet in diameter and were named the No 1 downcast and No 2 upcast. On 23 April 1912, both shafts reached the Shafton seam at a depth of 220 yards; the seam was over five feet in thickness. The No 1 shaft was designated for coal winding purposes and equipped with a steam powered winding engine and a double deck cage carrying 4 x 10cwt tubs of coal. Men and materials were wound at the No 2 shaft which was equipped with a steam powered 'indestructible ventilating fan' installed by Walker Brothers of Wigan. Steam raising was generated from four Lancashire boilers and the surface plant was completed with a coal screening building and brick built chimney.

Men were recruited to work at the pit and the colliery company constructed 28 houses adjacent to the pit yard in 1916 and called Hodroyd Cottages in 1916. Another 14 houses were provided in the centre of Brierley village. Underground workings were initially operated by the pillar and stall method but were later converted to the more efficient advancing longwall faces employed at other pits in the area. Coal was hand cut and loaded into tubs for transport to the pit bottom for raising to the surface screens. The colliery was not connected directly to the railway network and the output was conveyed along a tramway 800 yards in length to the Dearne Valley Railway at Peter Wood near Engine Lane (the road connecting Shafton to Grimethorpe). Tubs of spoil were also conveyed along the tramway for tipping at Peter Wood and the tramway was nicknamed the 'ginny run'.

The outbreak of the First World War hampered the development of the colliery and in 1919 the Hodroyd Colliery Company Ltd was integrated as a fully owned subsidiary of the Carlton Main Colliery Company Ltd. The surface plant at Brierley Colliery was completely modernised with the replacement of all the steam powered plant by electrically powered and compressed air driven machinery. Electric power was supplied direct from Grimethorpe Colliery and a new electric winding engine installed at No 1 shaft. At No 2 shaft a smaller winding engine was powered by compressed air and used for emergency purposes only. The surface screens and chimney were dismantled and the tramway was extended 1,000 yards from Peter Wood to connect with the screening and coal washing plant at Ferrymoor Colliery. The new tramway opened in 1923 and featured a raised concrete gantry across Engine Lane and the fields to the south. The original Hodroyd Colliery was closed in 1922 and efforts were concentrated on developing Brierley and Ferrymoor Collieries.

The improvements were immediately successful and by 1923, Brierley Colliery employed 1,175 men. However, the shallower workings to the south were suffering from water inundation so operations were concentrated in the other districts of the pit. In 1927, the year after the General Strike, the colliery recorded its highest ever manpower levels at 1,561, with 1,329 men employed underground and 232 on the surface. The quota system and standard tonnage imposed during the 1930s saw employment levels drop to only 595 by 1933. However, during that decade, mechanised coal cutting was introduced at the pit and by 1936 output that year totalled 281,906 tons, all dispatched along the tramway to Ferrymoor Colliery.

By 1940, the workforce had increased to 940 and the government had lifted the national quota system and ordered all collieries to increase production to aid the war effort; in 1941, Brierley Colliery produced 335,242 tons of coal. However, the Shafton seam was suffering from poor geological conditions caused by the development of a 12-inch band of dirt in the middle of the seam. This was exacerbated by the effects of flooding in the southern districts of the pit and the decision was made to concentrate production at Ferrymoor Colliery and run down Brierley Colliery and in 1946 most of the workforce transferred to Ferrymoor and Grimethorpe Collieries.

At the Brierley site, a small workforce was retained and the colliery was used as a pumping station. Following nationalisation, the pit was used as a training ground until 1963 when it was subsequently demolished. In 1960, the Peter Wood spoil heap was partially removed for use in road building projects and the remainder of the tip was landscaped and planted with coniferous trees. The former railway loading point adjacent to the Dearne Valley Railway became the NCB Shafton Central Workshops & Stores before closing in 1985. The colliery site was developed as a housing estate with new houses surrounding the original Hodroyd Cottages, although the former "ginny run" tramway remains as a footpath.

Ferrymoor Colliery

Following the development of Brierley Colliery, the Hodroyd Colliery Company sunk its second new colliery on Ferrymoor Common adjacent to Grimethorpe Colliery and the venture was initially known as the New Hodroyd Colliery. Two shafts measuring 14 feet in diameter were sunk in 1915, the No 1 downcast and No 2 upcast. In 1916, the shafts intercepted the Shafton seam at a depth of 70 yards and the seam was found to be nearly six feet in thickness. Both shafts were equipped with steel headgears and the No 1 shaft was used for winding coal and the No 2 shaft was designated to wind men and materials. The downcast shaft was equipped with a double deck cage with a capacity of 4 x 10cwt tubs of coal and the upcast shaft was fitted with a Walker Brothers of Wigan steam powered 'indestructible ventilating fan'. Steam raising was provided by four Lancashire Boilers.

Because of the shallow nature of the seams, the underground workings used the pillar and stall method, with large blocks of coal left in place to protect the surface from subsidence. At the surface, coal was handled in a screening building and dispatched into railway wagons in the colliery sidings. The railway sidings connected with those in Grimethorpe Colliery and the output was conveyed to markets along the Midland and Dearne Valley Railways. Spoil from the washery was transported to the adjacent Grimethorpe Colliery for tipping. Men were recruited to work at the pit and in 1917, the workforce totalled 136, mostly engaged on development work.

In May 1919, the Hodroyd Colliery Company was taken over by the Carlton Main Colliery Company and the pit at New Hodroyd was renamed Ferrymoor Colliery. The new owners restructured the surface buildings at Ferrymoor and its sister pit at Brierley. The steam raising plant was replaced with machinery powered by electricity and compressed air supplied by Grimethorpe Colliery. The winding engine at No 1 shaft was replaced with an electric winder and a compressed air powered winding engine was installed at No 2 shaft, although this was only designated for emergency purposes.

In 1923, the screens and coal washery were enlarged and it was decided to handle all the output from Brierley at Ferrymoor so the Brierley Colliery tramway was extended to Ferrymoor Colliery to convey the output to the screens. By 1924 the workforce had increased to 696 and this had reached 840 in 1926. Workings in the shallow Shafton seam were effected by frequent water incursions which led to the flooding of the eastern districts of the pit and in 1938 the colliery was closed for several years whilst water was pumped out of the pit, although the screens building remained open to process the output from Brierley Colliery.

During the Second World War the government encouraged the nation's collieries to increase production and Ferrymoor Colliery re-opened in 1944. Around this time, a surface drift was sunk from the pit yard reaching the Shafton seam on 21 September 1945 and the pit was reconfigured into a drift mine, although the No 1 shaft was retained to complete the underground ventilation circuit. New mechanised faces were developed in the Shafton seam with the intention of developing production following the forthcoming closure of Brierley Colliery.

In 1947, 253 men at the pit produced 162,000 tons of coal and following nationalisation and the closure of Brierley Colliery, the manpower levels increased as men were transferred to the pit. In 1965, the uneconomic pillar and stall method of working (which left around 50% of the coal in situ as pillars), was abandoned in favour of developing fully mechanised retreat mining faces in the Shafton seam. Annual production remained around the 175,000-ton level produced by a workforce of around 450 men.

In 1970, a new drift to the Shafton seam was sunk at South Kirkby Colliery some three miles away, known as Riddings Drift, connections were made to the Ferrymoor workings. On 1 April 1973, Ferrymoor Colliery and Riddings Drift were combined to form Ferrymoor Riddings Colliery with all coal being raised at the South Kirkby site so production at the Ferrymoor site ceased. The new development produced 670,000 tons of coal in 1975 from a workforce of only 200 men and the colliery broke several production records. Until the opening of the new Barnsley East Side Coal Preparation Plant at South Kirkby in 1980, the entire output from the Riddings Drift was transported by a fleet of lorries for processing in the washery at Ferrymoor Colliery.

In 1980, the Ferrymoor Colliery shafts were capped and filled in and the surface buildings demolished and all output was processed at the South Kirby site where production continued at high levels with 621,000 tons recorded in the 1981/1982 financial year. However, the site of Ferrymoor Colliery was subsequently covered by the expansion of Grimethorpe Colliery's Barnsley South Side development.

Dearne Valley Colliery

On 18 January 1901, the Dearne Valley Colliery Company Ltd was registered with a capital of £30,000 to acquire the Shafton seam in the Little Houghton and Great Houghton areas. The directors of the new venture included Richard Borrough Hopkins of Moor Allerton Hall in Leeds as Chairman; J T Collins of Harrogate; H Ellison of Cleckheaton; J A Jopling of Newcastle; R Watkin of Darfield and W Wood of Bradford. Messrs Hopkins and Collins were directors of the Micklefield Coal & Lime Company which operated Peckfield and Ledston Luck Collieries near Castleford; however, the other directors appear to have had no previous connection with the mining industry. Most of the capital was subscribed by Walton Cliffe and Joseph Wood, shareholders in the Micklefield Coal and Lime Company.

The Dearne Valley Colliery Company had secured the option to lease the coal beneath the estates of Major Marmaduke Nesfield Wright at Little Houghton; Robert Crewe-Milnes, (Earl of Crewe) at Great Houghton and William de Meuron, (Earl Fitzwilliam) at Great Houghton and Billingley. A total royalty of 2,000 acres had been secured although the leases were not actually formally signed until several years later. The lease with Earl Fitzwilliam was signed on 29 August 1906 granting the colliery company the right to extract the Shafton seam for a period of 40 years at a royalty of £97 per acre.

A site for the new venture at Little Houghton adjacent to the Midland Railway was purchased from Marmaduke Wright and in 1900 work commenced on sinking two drifts and a ventilation shaft. The drifts were sunk in a northwards direction at a gradient of 1 in 10 passing underneath Middlecliffe Lane. The Shafton seam was reached the following year at a depth of 200 yards and pillar and stall faces were opened with production commencing in 1903. The coal was hand-loaded into 10cwt tubs and hauled by pony to the main drift roadways. From here the tubs were attached to an endless rope that hauled them up the drift tunnels to the surface. The coal was tipped from the tubs into the screens buildings for sorting and grading and onward dispatch in the company's fleet of sky blue coloured private owner wagons with the name DEARNE VALLEY emblazoned on the side. Two sets of sidings were constructed to the north of the Midland Railway. Steam raising was provided by four Lancashire boilers and electricity was generated in the power houses to drive the endless rope haulage and supply underground lighting. The pit had a large brick built chimney, built in a square shape rather than the traditional round shape. Spoil from the screens was tipped on a site between the eastern sidings and the Midland Railway.

Dearne Valley Colliery was located near Houghton Main Colliery but separated from the latter by the hamlet of Little Houghton. Men were recruited to work at the pit and by 1905, 232 men and boys were employed at the colliery. Many of the miners lived at Darfield and walked to the colliery or travelled on one of the many pit buses that plied the route from Wombwell to Dearne Valley and Houghton Main Collieries. However, a few men lived locally in a small development of terraced houses constructed by the company in Little Houghton and Middlecliffe. Beech Farm and the appropriately named Colliery Farm were purchased from Marmaduke Wright to provide feed and hay for the ponies used underground. However, the farms were later sold to Houghton Main Colliery.

By 1917, 399 men were employed at the colliery. The pit enjoyed a very good reputation as a 'family pit', and several men and their sons worked at the mine, many ultimately spending their whole lives working at the colliery; relationships between the men and the management were often good. By 1924 the colliery employed 605 men. As a drift mine, output per man was relatively high, because a drift mine with continuous transport of coal from the faces to the surface was often a more efficient form of working, rather than the stop-start method required by waiting to wind coal in cages up a shaft. Despite this, underground working conditions were difficult as the Shafton seam was very wet and a pumping station was established to drain the underground workings.

In 1927, the colliery company was reconstituted as Dearne Valley Colliery (1927) Ltd with a capital of £90,000 following the deaths of the three major shareholders. The executors for Joseph Wood, Walton Cliffe and F T Hunt represented £65,160 of the company's capital and they decided to continue operating the colliery as a going concern under the name Dearne Valley Trust. The colliery was subsequently restructured a third time, reverting to its original name of Dearne Valley Colliery Company Ltd. The workforce remained stable at around 600 employees throughout the 1930s and 1940s. In the 1940s, 'Siskol' type mechanical coal cutters were introduced to cut coal and bore new roadways, but the colliery was still using pit ponies to transport coal tubs to the main headways long after their use had ceased at surrounding pits.

In 1947, when the pit transferred to NCB ownership, 534 men produced 160,000 tons of coal. On 17 November 1951, a new canteen and medical centre together with pithead baths with accommodation for 540 men were opened at the colliery. In 1957, the workforce of 632 men produced 202,000 tons of coal. During the 1960s, British Rail introduced a programme of replacing steam locomotives with diesel locomotives. Subsequently, demand for the excellent steam raising properties of the Shafton coal fell and 100 men were transferred to the neighbouring Houghton Main Colliery; in 1964, the remaining workforce of 474 produced 155,000 tons of coal. In 1965, hand filling of coal tubs finally ceased with the introduction of fully mechanised longwall faces.

Reserves in the Shafton seam were due to run out in 1972 when it was planned to close the colliery. However, a reprieve came with a new plan to sink drifts to access coal in the Sharlston Top seam and Sharlston Yard seam, below the Shafton seam horizon with the development of retreating longwall faces, a very economical method of mining where two roadways and a coal face are developed at the very extremity of the royalty before the coal is worked back to the base of the drifts or shafts. During the fiscal year 1976-77 the pit produced 212,000 tons of coal with a workforce of 408.

In 1980, the colliery output was transported by an overland covered conveyor to a new coal preparation plant at Houghton Main Colliery for grading and washing and then onwards by Merry-Go-Round trains to the Central Electricity Generating Board's power stations. In 1982, a new ventilation shaft was sunk near Great Houghton and intersected the Sharlston Yard seam at a depth of 330 yards below the village. Coal was subsequently transported via an underground shaft to the deeper workings of Houghton Main Colliery for transport via locomotive haulage road for treatment at the new coal preparation plant at Grimethorpe Colliery as part of the Barnsley South Side Complex.

Following the Miners' Strike, the colliery passed into the control of the British Coal Corporation on 5 March 1987 and produced 350,000 tons the following year. However, geological problems in the Sharlston Yard seam caused a loss of £2,000,000 in 1990 which was expected to be repeated the following year. Consequently, British Coal decided to close the colliery with effect from 5 April 1991 with the loss of 266 jobs. The site was cleared and a stone bearing the legend DEARNE VALLEY COLLIERY 1901 was positioned on Middlecliffe Lane at the former entrance to the pit.

Above: A 1956 photograph of Dearne Valley Colliery by K W Buckley taken from Ings Lane bridge over the former Midland Railway. Empty NCB wagons are waiting in the sidings prior to loading under the screens building. The small-scale nature of the drift mine is apparent *(Maurice Dobson Museum & Heritage Centre)*

Billingley Drift Mine

J & J Charlesworth, the Wakefield coal masters, had opened Old Billingley Colliery in the 1830s beneath 40 acres of land that they owned in the area. Old Billingley Colliery was sunk to a depth of 60 yards to exploit the Shafton seam but by 1848 the pit had closed. The pit site was to the north of the A635 road, in an area subsequently reworked by open cast mining in the 1990s. The coal beneath Earl Fitzwilliam's 360 acre Billingley estate had been leased to the Dearne Valley Colliery Company in 1906 but in 1948 the NCB announced proposals to develop a new drift mine at Billingley to help contribute towards an increase in the region's coal production. The new venture was located to the south of Billingley Green on the A635 and the drift tunnels were driven in a northwards direction beneath the village to access the Shafton seam at a depth of 33 yards.

In 1951, the colliery commenced production and underground workings used the pillar and stall method due to the shallow nature of the seam, with the coal being hand cut and loaded into traditional 10 cwt tubs. These were then attached to an electrically driven endless haulage rope for transport up the drift to the surface. The colliery had very little in the way of surface buildings and no railway connection and the coal was simply loaded into lorries for transport to other collieries for treatment. In 1952, 76 men were employed at the pit, including 6 working on the surface, the highest workforce recorded at the pit.

The colliery was connected underground in the Shafton seam to Highgate Colliery where the coal was worked by mechanised methods of mining, and, after only five years of operation, the decision was made to close Billingley Drift mine as the output could now be worked from Highgate Colliery. On 7 September 1956, the pit formally closed and the remaining 31 employees transferred to adjacent pits. The drifts were sealed and the mine has now passed into memory.

Above: A 1956 photograph of Billingley Drift Mine by K W Buckley showing this relatively small-scale operation to the south of Doncaster Road. The drift mine only existed for five years from 1951-1956. In the 1990s, the open cast working of the Highgate and Shafton seam around the A635 road destroyed all traces of Billingley Drift Mine and the colliery, the smallest of all the Dearne Valley pits, has now largely been forgotten *(Maurice Dobson Museum & Heritage Centre)*

Highgate Colliery

Described by the *Colliery Guardian* on 1 September 1916 as a "new colliery in miniature...somewhat of a novelty in this district of deep shafts", Highgate Colliery was located at the western end of Goldthorpe to the northeast of the cross roads at Highgate on a site bounded by the Dearne Valley Railway's Hickleton Colliery branch to the west and the Hull & Barnsley Railway to the east. The colliery was accessed by road from Goldthorpe and had a railway connection to the Dearne Valley Railway and a land sale yard on Barnsley Road. A private syndicate had acquired the leases of the Highgate and Shafton coals from beneath 600 acres belonging to the Reverend Thornely Taylor beneath his Thurnscoe estate. On 28 October 1916, the Highgate Colliery Company Ltd was registered with a capital of £5,000 in £1 shares, with the first directors of the new venture being W Baxter, J Hawksworth, E Downing and H B Denton.

Work on sinking a pair of shafts commenced in May 1916. The No 1 downcast shaft was 10 feet in diameter and the No 2 upcast shaft to the south was 8 feet in diameter. Both shafts were equipped with electric winding engines and steel headgears and both could wind coal. The small cage in each shaft could raise a single 10 cwt capacity tub of coal. On 23 August 1916, the workable Highgate seam was reached at a depth of 14 yards and the Shafton seam was reached the following year. At the surface, steam raising was provided by two Lancashire boilers and electrical generation was via a 250 KW turbo alternator. A small screens building was erected over two sidings on the Dearne Valley Railway but the colliery lacked a coal washing plant. Spoil from the screens was tipped to the south of the colliery.

Due to the shallow nature of the Shafton seam, the pillar and stall method of working was adopted with pillars of coal left intact to protect the surface from subsidence. Coal was hand cut and loaded into tubs which were then hauled to the pit bottom by an electrically powered endless rope. From the pit yard, a 195-yard-long drift was driven to intersect the workings in the western district. It was intended to produce 100 tons of coal per day, and, in 1917, 42 men worked at the pit, mostly on development work. By 1923, 200 men were employed at the colliery and production had increased to 1,000 ton per week when operations were suddenly suspended. The colliery subsequently changed hands and was sold to the Flockton Colliery Company Ltd. This company owned the Hartley Bank Pit near Netherton in West Yorkshire and was controlled by the Elliott family of Lepton; Benjamin, George, Stanley & Ralph Elliott became the new directors of the Highgate Colliery Company Ltd.

The new management started re-equipping the pit with a new screening plant to process an increased output and the colliery re-opened in 1924, and by 1927, 192 men were employed, including 34 on the surface. Electric pumps were installed in the shafts to drain the wet Shafton workings and the surplus water was sold to Hickleton Main Colliery, and the royalty was enlarged by the leasing of coal beneath the freehold land owned by Hickleton Main.

During the 1930s, mechanized mining was introduced into the underground workings with the use of Siskol coal cutting machines and, in 1936, 75,413 tons of coal were produced. Output remained small but consistent and in 1943 the colliery company was reconstituted as the Highgate Colliery Company (1943) Ltd with a capital of £100,000. In 1946, work commenced on a new surface drift to access an additional 385 acres subleased from Hickleton Main Colliery. In 1947 when the pit was nationalised, 242 men produced 97,000 tons of coal. The NCB finished the construction of the drift mine and developed a second return drift to ventilate the underground workings; in 1953 pithead baths with facilities for 800 men were opened.

The royalty was enlarged with the addition of 1,000 acres of Shafton seam belonging to Wath Main Colliery and 850 acres formerly owned by Frickley Colliery. The new royalty was intended to prolong the life of the pit for 40-50 years at an extraction rate of 1,000 tons of coal per day. By 1955 the first longwall faces were opened in the Shafton seam and 416 men produced 166,000 tons of coal that year. An underground connection was made with the Billingley Drift Mine to raise the combined output at Highgate Colliery. Following the installation of 12 longwall mechanised faces complete with conveyor belts transport up the drifts, the original shafts were capped and filled in during 1960. The old colliery spoil heap was removed, carried away by lorry, used for the construction of motorway embankments along the new A1(M) Doncaster bypass.

By 1964, 569 men at the pit had produced 343,000 tons of coal and the output per man shift was exceptionally high. In 1966, an underground link was made with Goldthorpe Colliery and the two pits were combined to form Goldthorpe/Highgate Colliery. All output was now transported to the surface via the new Bella Drift at Goldthorpe Colliery for dispatch to power stations. However, the drifts at the Highgate site remained in use for the transport of men and materials. Production in the Highgate Colliery workings was now from two fully mechanised faces in the Shafton seam, extending north-eastwards beneath the Brodsworth area. The new combined mine was an immediate success and broke several production records' frequently producing over 1,000,000 tons of coal per year.

Following the 1984-85 Miners Strike, deteriorating geological conditions forced the closure of the Highgate coalfaces although those in the Goldthorpe Colliery districts remained open for a further eight years. The Highgate site was demolished and in 1992 the new A635 Goldthorpe bypass was driven across the site. New warehouses were subsequently opened on the site of Highgate Colliery. On 4 June 2006, a ceremony was held in St John & St Mary Magdalene Church in Goldthorpe where a new stained glass memorial window designed by Martha Maguire was unveiled commemorating Barnburgh, Goldthorpe, Hickleton & Highgate Collieries. The ceremony was attended by local poet Ian McMillan and locally born Hollywood actor Brian Blessed. A wrought iron memorial to the colliery also features in the Goldthorpe Miners Welfare Hall portico, now used as the Dearne Play House.

Goldthorpe Colliery

Shallow mining operations had been carried out in the Goldthorpe area on a small scale since 1678. However, in 1909, the Shafton seam beneath Lord Halifax's 1,500 acre Goldthorpe and Hickleton estate was leased to Henry Lodge & Sons Ltd. Henry Albert Lodge was born in 1844 in Skelmanthorpe in West Yorkshire and owned Bloomhouse Green Colliery near Darton. When this pit closed in 1868, Henry Lodge moved into the role of colliery proprietor, sinking Ryhill Main Colliery to the Shafton seam in 1874. Following his death in 1889, the colliery was taken over by his son Henry Lodge Junior. In 1896, the company was registered as Henry Lodge & Sons Ltd with a capital of £35,000. With expertise gained working the Shafton seam at Ryhill Main, Henry Lodge was looking to develop a second venture extracting this seam.

On 21 May 1909, it was announced that a new colliery was to be sunk adjacent to the Dearne Valley Railway at Goldthorpe and it was hoped to find work for 500 men and equip the pit to produce 1,000 tons of coal per day. A colliery site was purchased from Lord Halifax and on Tuesday 27 June 1909, a ceremony to mark the cutting of the first sods was held. The sod above the No 1 downcast shaft was cut by Mr R C Irwen, chairman of the Lancashire & Yorkshire Railway who operated the adjacent Dearne Valley Railway. The sod above No 2 upcast shaft was cut by Barron Kilner, owner of the Calder Vale Glass Works in Wakefield. Barron Kilner was related to the famous glass bottlers Kilner Brothers of Dewsbury and Conisbrough, and, when not managing his glass works, he played rugby for Wakefield Trinity. Mr J Whitfield was appointed manager of the new pit; he had formerly been manager of Glasshoughton and Rotherham Main Collieries.

The 14 feet diameter No 1 shaft reached the Shafton seam in January 1910 at a depth of 63 yards. The seam was five feet in thickness and by July of that year 140 men were raising 200 tons of coal per week from the roadway excavations through the shaft pillar whilst the No 2 upcast shaft was being sunk. This measured 12 feet in diameter and reached the Shafton seam at the end of August 1910. To celebrate, the management entertained the pit sinkers to a congratulatory dinner. During sinking operations, water flowed into the shafts from the surrounding strata but this was removed with electric pumps whilst the water proof brick lining was installed. Permanent headgear was used to sink the shafts; that above the No 1 shaft was of steel construction and equipped with a cage to wind 2 x 10cwt tubs of coal. The headgear at No 2 shaft was much smaller by comparison, made of wood and used to wind men and materials.

In 1911, a steam powered ventilating fan was installed at No 2 shaft by the Waddle Engineering & Fan Company of Llanelli and production commenced from pillar and stall workings. Coal was hand cut and loaded into tubs which were then hauled by pony to the main roadways. From here endless rope haulage conveyed the tubs to the pit bottom. At the surface, the tubs were tipped into the screens building and once sorted and graded, the coal was dispatched into sidings alongside the Dearne Valley Railway. The company purchased several private owner wagons with HENRY LODGE painted on the sides. The coal was much in demand for railway locomotives and as a general house coal. The steam powered engine at No 1 shaft was contained within a brick built engine house and steam raising was provided by two Lancashire boilers. Steam and smoke was exhausted by a tall square sectioned chimney, similar to that provided at Dearne Valley Colliery. Spoil from the screens was tipped on a field to the west, parallel with the railway line.

Above Left: This scene of the pit bottom at No 1 shaft is one of a set of commemorative postcards issued by *The Miner*, the journal of the National Union of Mineworkers. The double deck winding cage was built to accommodate several men or wind four of the coal tubs (lower right) at a time. The relatively shallow workings were vulnerable to the influx of groundwater earning the pit the nickname of 'the sludge pit'.

Above Right: Coal was wound up the shafts in coal tubs to a level about 10 feet above the surface into a covered structure called the heapstead. From here the tubs were transported along the gantry to the screens building where the coal was sorted and graded and loaded into the Henry Lodge private owner wagons which passed beneath the screens building. Once loaded the wagons were ready for onward transport via the national railway network. A c1920 postcard by Edgar Scrivens.

Above: A postcard by Edgar Scrivens c1920, illustrating the difference in the two shafts at Goldthorpe Colliery. No 1 shaft (left) was equipped with a large steel headgear to bear the weight when raising coal and alleviating the stresses exerted by the winding engine, which could pull over a lesser headgear. The No 2 headgear on the right was much smaller and made of wood and consequently only used for winding materials, including the stack of pit props in the foreground.

By 1917, 462 men were employed at the colliery but a trade depression in the summer of 1923 saw the dismissal of 200 men. Fortunately, most of these found work at Hickleton Main and Barnburgh Main Collieries which were still recruiting. At this time, Henry Lodge Junior decided to close Ryhill Main Colliery due to the spiralling costs of sinking to the deeper seams and the increase in competition from other pits in the area so on 3 September 1923 he sold Goldthorpe Colliery to Old Silkstone Collieries Ltd of Barnsley. This company was chaired by Sir Archibald Mitchelson and owned Dodworth Colliery, Barugh Green Coking Plant, Garforth Collieries Ltd near Castleford and the Allerdale Coal Company near Whitehaven. Goldthorpe Collieries Ltd was registered with a capital of £50,000 and the new management intended to fully develop the pit; by 1929, 408 men were back on the books and output was averaging around 250,000 tons per year.

On 16 September 1930, the royalty was enlarged when 1,800 acres of Shafton coal were leased from beneath the Barnburgh estate of Frederick Montague of High Melton Hall. With the Shafton seam dipping ever deeper under the limestone beneath the concealed coalfield around Hickleton, a move was made towards changing to more efficient advancing longwall methods of mining, although these would take several years to implement. In 1937, a new electrically powered ventilation fan replaced the old steam powered fan to improve the ventilation to the expanding underground workings. During a phase of increased production to assist the war effort, a record output of 3,241 tons was recorded for one week in December 1942.

In 1947, when the colliery was nationalised, production had dropped to 97,000 tons produced by a workforce of 336 men. The NCB introduced advancing longwall faces to raise production but was faced by the fact that the surface plant and small diameter shafts were insufficient to handle any increase in output. Consequently, in 1954 a reconstruction scheme was commenced with the principal work being the construction of a new drift beneath Bella Wood to access the Shafton seam beneath the concealed coalfield. The first sods of the new Bella drift were cut in February 1955 and the work was carried out by Cementation Mining Ltd of Bentley. The contractors drove a 2,250-yard-long tunnel in an easterly direction down a gradient of 1 in 9 to intersect the Shafton seam workings. The drift was fitted with an endless rope for the haulage of men and materials and a continuous conveyor for the transport of coal mined from the mechanised longwall faces. At the surface, new plant was constructed to handle the output and, by 1960, 238,000 tons of coal were raised with a workforce of 516 men.

In 1966 Goldthorpe Colliery was linked underground with the adjacent Highgate Colliery and from that date all output from the combined mine was brought up the Bella drift. In November 1967 work started on a return drift to complete the ventilation circuit which would allow the closure of the original Goldthorpe Colliery shafts. The return drift was sunk from the Hickleton Colliery pit yard in an easterly direction down a gradient of 1 in 6.7 for a length of 1,550 yards. Two electric ventilation fans were installed at the top of the Hickleton drift. In the meantime, work commenced on a new coal preparation plant at Goldthorpe linked directly to a new 3,000-ton capacity rapid-loading bunker built alongside the former Dearne Valley Railway. This bunker could load 950 tons of coal into continuously moving Merry-Go-Round trains within one hour. New pithead baths were provided at the Goldthorpe site with facilities for 800 men and a new tipping site for colliery spoil was opened to the east of the colliery. The original Goldthorpe shafts were capped and filled in during 1973.

Above Left: Edgar Scrivens photographed this detailed study of the No 1 headgear with several miners visible on the gantry in c1920. The headgear was removed in the 1960s following the conversion to a drift mine.
Above Right: This large bunker was completed in the late 1960s to supply merry-go-round trains. The bunker was fed by continuous conveyor from the drift mouth and was demolished in 1995.

The new Goldthorpe Drift Mine was a tremendous success and output increased rapidly; in 1975, 807,000 tons of coal were produced from four highly mechanised faces, two in the former Highgate Colliery workings from beneath the Brodsworth area and two from Goldthorpe workings in the Hickleton and Barnburgh areas. In the 1976-77 fiscal year production had increased to 1,003,921 tons of coal and Goldthorpe Colliery joined the ranks of the 17 British Collieries which produced over 1,000,000 tons that year.

In the 1980s the Goldthorpe drift mine was believed to be producing the cheapest coal in the country. After the 1984-85 Miner's Strike, production from the Highgate faces ceased, due to deteriorating geological conditions, but output remained high at Goldthorpe. On 1 January 1986, Goldthorpe Colliery was merged with Hickleton Main Colliery, with the Hickleton site put on a developmental basis with the aim of working the deeper seams once the Shafton seams were exhausted. However, the closure of Cadeby Main Colliery caused additional areas of the Shafton seam beneath High Melton and Sprotbrough to be allocated to Goldthorpe Colliery. Whilst this had the effect of prolonging the life of Goldthorpe Colliery, it sounded the death knell for the Hickleton Colliery site which subsequently closed.

During the 1988-89 financial year, 1,000,000 tons of coal were produced for the second time in the history of the colliery. Work commenced on accessing the Shafton seam in the Cadeby Main royalty by extending the drifts through the Southerly Don Fault and new retreating longwall faces were opened. In the first three years of the 1990s, the pit produced 1,442,00 tons, 1,379,000 tons and 1,124,000 tons respectively, the last figure in the 45-week period up to 4 February 1994. However, on that date the colliery was put on a care and maintenance basis despite having made a profit of £70,000,000 in the last 5 years whilst producing the cheapest coal in the country and 410 men were made redundant. It was claimed by some that the pit had become a victim of its own success and the high production rate had eaten through its remaining reserves.

The subsequent privatisation of British Coal saw the colliery being offered for sale to the private sector, but despite the existence of 5,000,000 tons of coal reserves and the profitable operations, there were no bidders. The pit closed in 1994 and the following the year the surface buildings were demolished. The Bella drift was capped with a methane extracting device and the colliery spoil heap was landscaped. For many years, the site lay abandoned until it was subsequently covered with new housing estates. On 4 June 2006, a stained-glass memorial window was unveiled in Goldthorpe Church commemorating the pit and a wrought iron art work featuring Goldthorpe Colliery installed at the entrance to the Welfare Hall, now the Dearne Play House. The two colliery banners were once on display in Goldthorpe Library.

The last train of coal left the rapid loading bunker in April 1994 thus ending the history of deep coal mining in the Dearne Valley of South Yorkshire, which had contributed millions of tons of coal to the furnaces of industry. There followed a limited period of coal reworking from some of the colliery spoil heaps, together with the open cast working of Highgate and Shafton seams in the area between Highgate and Darfield and between Little Houghton and Grimethorpe. However, these operations ceased in 1999, bringing coal production in the area to an end. Now, a generation later, the pits are just a memory but the people of the Dearne Valley can be proud of their contribution to the success of the nation, a nation that owes them a debt for the many lives lost and hardship suffered in the pursuit of coal.

Above: Following the cessation of deep mining operations with the closure of Goldthorpe Colliery in 1994, several smaller coal extracting processes continued for a few more years. Many of the coal tips were reworked to remove older coal and there were extensive open cast operations between Darfield and Goldthorpe and Grimethorpe and Middlecliffe. This photogaph shows open cast operations to the west of Houghton Main Colliery in 1998, illustrating the depths that these open pits could reach. The layered nature of the Coal Measures strata shows up well in the cliff face, as does the exposure of the Shafton seam to the right of the bulldozer. Dump trucks are tipping overburden (material removed from above the coal seam) into an area where the coal has already been excavated. During operations, several remains of early mining equipment were found including a medieval rag and chain pump – now on display at the Maurice Dobson Museum & Heritage Centre in Darfield.

Above: The yearlong Miners' Strike was called to prevent the widespread closure of collieries and the destruction of mining communities, following the announcement by the NCB of a series of pit closures including Cortonwood Colliery. The strike commenced on 6 March 1984 and at its height involved 142,000 employees; this was the largest scene of industrial action since the General Strike of 1926. Pits were picketed and the bitter conflict pitched the miners against a determined Government led by Prime Minister Margaret Thatcher. This photograph depicts the pickets' hut on Golden Smithies Lane at Manvers Main Colliery. Many of these huts were known as 'Alamos' after the Battle of the Alamo in 1836, a pivotal event in the Texas Revolution, as memorably depicted in the film *'The Alamo'*. *(Peter Davies)*

The annual Miners Demonstration and Gala organised by the Yorkshire National Union of Mineworkers was held throughout Yorkshire towns during the 20th century. These spectacular events provided a proud occasion when miners and their families could march behind the pit banner before assembling to hear speeches and enjoy the afternoon's festivities. **Above:** The 1993 demonstration was held in Wakefield and this scene features the Grimethorpe Colliery banner passing along Wood Street. **Below:** The 1994 demonstration was held in Doncaster and shows the Sheffield Women Against Pit Closures banner on High Street. This group established the Houghton Main Pit Camp in 1992/3 to protest against the closure of the colliery. *(Norman Ellis)*

Part 2 Dearne Valley Communities

Above: Many of the Dearne Valley colliery communities developed into thriving commercial centres, as illustrated on this 1920s postcard of Goldthorpe by Edgar Scrivens, depicting a busy Doncaster Road. The shopping parade on the left was named Stone Row and was constructed in 1895 as part of the first development of housing for Hickleton Main Colliery. The Globe Tea Company was a national chain of shops that opened premises throughout the country, the supermarkets of the day. The view is little changed today although the building on the left now trades as a public house, the Rusty Dudley, the name reflecting the mining heritage of the area.

Above Ladycroft in Bolton-upon-Dearne consisted of 50 cottages built in the 1870s to house the first workers in the area and is typical of the inferior quality of the cottages provided at the time. The houses of Ladycroft were cleared in 1955 and new housing was built on the site.

Below: This charming scene of Bridge Walk at Little Houghton was issued as a postcard by Barnsley Photo Company c1910. Bridge Walk was on the popular walking route from Darfield to Houghton Main and Dearne Valley Collieries – the chimney of the latter can be seen on the skyline. Three of the young men have coal dust covered faces – having obviously just come off shift.

Introduction

Many of the settlements of the Dearne Valley were recorded in the Domesday survey of 1086 and generally evolved into medieval villages of stone built cottages situated above the flood plain of the River Dearne. The region remained a quiet rural backwater with most of the villagers working in agriculture, although there were several watermills on the Rivers Dearne and Dove. The first signs of the impending onslaught of industry occurred in the 1790s when teams of navvies descended on the area to excavate the Dearne & Dove Canal. However, this was developed to tap the coal in the western extremity of the region at Elsecar and Worsbrough, and the remainder of the Dearne Valley was left largely untouched by industry. Nevertheless, the arrival of deep mining spurred on by the opening of the South Yorkshire Railway in 1850 saw a rapid development of the coalfield, together with the urgent need to provide houses for the workforce, often in isolated locations away from the existing settlements.

Above: The original rural nature of the Dearne Valley is reflected in the cottages and farms built from local sandstone, as depicted on this postcard of West Melton High Street c1910. The rural aspect continued into the 20th century and horse drawn vehicles were a common sight. The postcard is from an anonymous photographer and date from c1900.

There was only a limited supply of accommodation in the older villages. Therefore, rows of terraced cottages (cottage being the term used for housing at the time) were constructed. Unlike the older buildings, the new rows had walls of brick, typically supplied by the colliery brickworks, and roofs of Welsh slate imported via the railway network. Some of the better-quality rows would often be brick built to the rear and sides, but have a stone frontage facing the road. Apart from the construction of larger houses for management and officials, the building of new houses was generally left to private enterprise as the return on the investment was not considered high enough for the colliery company. Local builders typically undertook the task of building colliery housing, and many of their rows would bear their names.

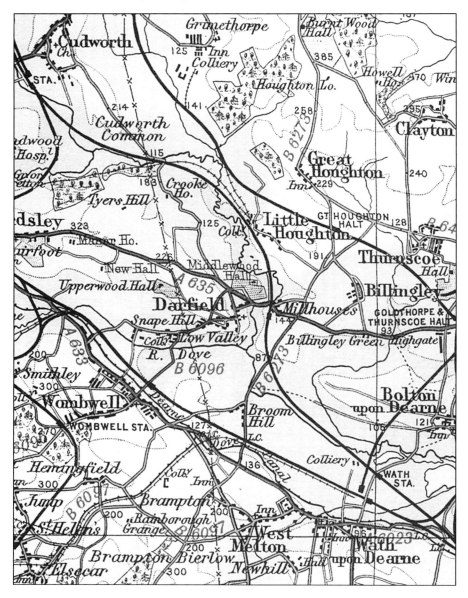

Above: An extract from 1928 Bartholomew's Half Inch to the Mile Map of the Dearne Valley, showing some of the communities mentioned in the text.

The new houses varied in quality, but many were 'jerry' built - constructed to very basic standards with little in the way of facilities. They were often in the form of a four-room tenement, with a front room and coal fire, a kitchen with a Yorkshire range, and two bedrooms upstairs. Outside earth closets and privies were provided in the back yards although there was very little in the way of proper sewage facilities and water supplies. When the houses were completed and let to the new workforce, the local builders would then collect the weekly rent themselves or lease or sell the new cottages to the colliery company who guaranteed the rent in exchange for their building services. With numerous people migrating to the area, it was a widespread practice for the householders to take in one or more lodgers; thus, many of the new colliery communities became overcrowded, with an average of five or six people living in a typical house, with some cottages housing ten or more people.

However, some colliery promotors saw the benefits of building their own company houses. These would then be solely available for their own employees and, as rent could be deducted at source from the miners' pay, there would be no possibility of any arrears. Company owned housing could be used as a controlling tool over the workforce as once a man left the pit's employment (or if he was dismissed) he and his family would have to vacate the colliery owned cottage. Colliery owned housing could also be used as a tool of leverage over a workforce in times of industrial dispute with the threat of eviction often used to subjugate the strikers, a threat carried out in 1876 at Manvers Main Colliery, in 1877 at Cortonwood Colliery, in 1902 at Denaby Main Colliery and famously in 1905 at Hemsworth Colliery to the north of the study area. Examples of other colliery owned housing include the concrete cottages of Brampton owned by Cortonwood Colliery Company and the 'Seaside Estate' at Grimethorpe, owned by the Carlton Main Colliery Company Ltd.

New settlements required shops and services. Initially a small shop might have been opened in a front room by an enterprising miner's wife, but soon established shopkeepers moved in, opening stores for the sale of provisions. The Barnsley British Co-operative Society was also keen to serve the new settlements and opened many handsomely built new branches. These were well supported, due to the promise of the dividend paid on purchases for their members. Other enterprising individuals opened small wooden lock-up shops, especially for the selling of sweets and cigarettes or for use as fish and chip shops. However, shopping facilities were often limited in the new colliery communities whilst some of the nearby older settlements developed into shopping centres and small towns, for example Wombwell, Wath, Hoyland and Mexborough.

Nearly as important as shopping facilities (if not more so in some cases!) was the establishment of licensed premises, either in the form of 'beer-offs', private social clubs or purpose built public houses. Substantial profits were to be made from these as mining was thirsty work and the local breweries competed to open large public houses. More formal colliery institutes were provided by some colliery companies but these were typically alcohol-free until the establishment of the Miners Welfare Fund in the 1920s which opened many Miners Welfare Halls & Institutes, with adjoining sports and recreational facilities. Other communal buildings for leisure purposes included billiard halls, public swimming baths, skating rinks and cinemas, whilst the colliery communities were surrounded by numerous allotments, popular amongst the men for the growing of flowers and vegetables and for the housing of racing pigeons.

The establishment of the 1870 Education Act required the compulsory schooling of all children from the ages of 5-12. Prior to this, children from the new mining settlement attended

Church of England Schools in the older villages but these quickly became overcrowded due to the expanding population. Some of the colliery companies also provided their own schooling, employing their own teaching staff. From 1870 onwards, the West Riding County Council took over the responsibility for the provision of schools and large brick built schools were provided throughout the Dearne Valley on behalf of the various Parish Councils, Local Boards and Urban District Councils.

The spiritual needs of the new population were attended to with the construction of churches and chapels – the latter largely provided by the Wesleyans, Wesleyan Reform, Primitive Methodists, Congregationalists, Baptists and Roman Catholics, the last being popular with many of the Irish immigrants. The churches encouraged the involvement of the local community with the affairs of the region and eventually miners were elected on to local parish councils, often replacing local landowners, and colliery owners. Several of the new parish councils sought an increasing influence in the governance of the area and many became Urban District Councils.

Above Left: The Barnsley British Co-operative Society was established in 1864 and branches quickly spread throughout the area. This is the 28th branch which opened at Hemingfield in 1884 and which was captured on this postcard c1910, possibly with manager George Hemsworth in the doorway.
Above Right: Wombwell John Street Infant and Junior Schools were built by the West Riding County Council and opened in 1910 with accommodation for 420 children. The schools were demolished in 1995, as - like many of these handsome old school buildings - they are no longer deemed fit for purpose. This postcard was published by Edgar Scrivens in 1920.

During the 20th century as the pits expanded their output and deeper seams were exploited, additional housing was required. During the First World War, very little house building had been undertaken throughout the country which caused concern within the government. The establishment of the 1919 Housing Act which implemented the findings of the 1917 Tudor Walters Report, enabled local authorities to take advantage of government loans and subsidies to provide council houses - built to much better standards than the earlier pre-war housing. This subsidy was also available to the colliery companies through the establishment of colliery owned public utility societies and many of the pits provided their own housing during the 1920s.

Following the Second World War, council house building continued and the NCB established the Coal Industry Housing Association in 1952. This organisation provided 19,842 houses for miners in the manpower deficiency regions of the Yorkshire and East Midlands Coalfield and many of these came to be occupied by miners from Northumberland, County Durham and Scotland where their own pits had closed. From the 1960s, private housing developments began to appear throughout the Dearne Valley and many of the original cottages and terraces of some of the older colliery communities were no longer deemed fit for purpose and were demolished. In 1947, the NCB inherited 140,000 houses and it was a reluctant landlord and keen to dispose of their housing stock, by a combination of demolition, sale to individuals or sale to local authorities. In 1974, the West Riding County Council and the various Dearne Valley urban district councils were abolished and administrative duties were split between the new Metropolitan Boroughs of Barnsley, Doncaster and Rotherham. Local governance is now provided from these towns and the former urban district councils, once proudly independent and well-respected organisations, were missed by many. The Right to Buy policy introduced by the Government in the 1980s saw tenants entitled to buy their council properties and many of these passed to their owners or to absentee landlords. Increased provision of private housing estates and the selling of many of the former council houses has continued into the 21st century and the remaining council stock is now managed by a variety of housing associations on behalf of the three Metropolitan Borough Councils.

Over the following pages, a potted chronological history of the growth of most of the Dearne Valley colliery communities during the 19th and 20th centuries is presented. The villages are discussed in alphabetical order, although the larger towns of Barnsley and Mexborough situated at either end of the study area have been omitted in favour of concentrating on the smaller settlements. Please note that this account is not intended to be a comprehensive history of any location and readers wishing to explore the historical aspects in further depth are requested to consult the texts listed in the bibliography and the excellent work conducted by the many local history societies and heritage groups in the area.

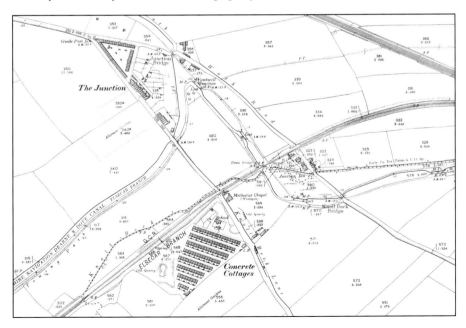

Above: Extract from the 1903 Ordnance Survey 1:2500 Map showing the colliery communities of Wombwell Junction and Concrete Cottages built to house miners at Cortonwood Colliery (See the Brampton Bierlow section for more information)

Bolton-upon-Dearne

Bolton-upon-Dearne (sometimes referred to as Bolton-on-Dearne or simply Bolton) was an ancient agricultural settlement of stone built cottages and a church dating back to Anglo-Saxon times, situated to the north of the River Dearne on a sandstone outcrop above the flood plain. Bolton was recorded in the Domesday Survey of 1086 as *Bodeton* and following the Norman Conquest, the area passed into the ownership of Roger de Busli of Tickhill Castle. In 1700, the manor of Bolton and Goldthorpe and the surrounding 2,000 acres came under the control of William Henry Marsden of Burntwood Hall near Great Houghton. The Marsden family developed small scale 'day hole' collieries to mine shallow coal seams in the Goldthorpe area but these operations had ceased by 1778. The area subsequently passed into several other hands with Viscount Halifax of Hickleton Hall assuming the role of Lord of the Manor and extending his Hickleton estate with the purchase of land in the Goldthorpe area, whilst the land around Bolton-upon-Dearne passed into the ownership of several other families, particularly John Bingley, Philip Smelter Cadman, Charles Otter, Sir Theodore Brinckman, Earl Fitzwilliam and Joseph Mitchell of Bolton Hall.

Prior to the arrival of coal mining, the district was rural in nature; its inhabitants were employed in agriculture and, in 1851, the population of Bolton and Goldthorpe was recorded as 604. As well as Bolton St Andrew's Church and the village cottages, other buildings included Bolton Hall, Manor Farm, a Post Office, Primitive and Wesleyan Methodist Chapels, two public houses (the Angel Inn and the Cross Daggers Inn) and a sandstone quarry that provided building stone. A village Board School had opened in 1880 and on the River Dearne were two corn watermills, named Lower Mill and Upper Mill. However, in the early 1870s, the landowners of the Bolton area leased the coal beneath their lands to a partnership of industrialists who developed Wath Main Colliery in 1873.

Wath Main Colliery was positioned some distance away from Bolton at the southern extremity of the royalty, adjacent to existing railway connections. However, a brickyard was opened on Furlong Road and speculative builders provided areas of brick built terraced housing around Station Road and Mexborough Road. The largest development was at Ladycroft where 50 houses, arranged in two long rows, were built shortly after the arrival of the Swinton & Knottingley Joint Railway (Bolton Railway Station was opened on 1 July 1879). Adjoining Ladycroft, a new brick built public house was constructed. This was the Collingwood Hotel and named after Baron Collingwood who served under Horatio Nelson during the Battle of Trafalgar. During the 1870s and 1880s people migrated to the area, both from Yorkshire and from further afield and the new houses were occupied by a combination of miners, railway workers, quarry workers and agricultural labourers. In 1881, the population of Bolton was recorded as 927 but this had increased to 1,205 by 1891.

With the development of Hickleton Main Colliery to the north and the laying out of 242 terraced houses in the hamlet of Goldthorpe in 1895, together with the pits at Wath and Manvers to the south, all attracting additional families to move to the area, the local parish council decided to seek urban powers to provide a greater influence on the new settlement. In 1899, Bolton-upon-Dearne Urban District Council was formed and the new council provided improved services to the local inhabitants which that year numbered 3,233 (1,454 in Bolton and 1,779 in Goldthorpe). In 1897, the 41st branch of the Barnsley British Co-operative Society opened.

The new urban district council continued to improve conditions for the local area. The former board school built in 1880 was vastly overcrowded and in 1896, new council schools were opened and these were subsequently enlarged ten years later. In 1912, a new infants school was opened by the West Riding County Council in Priory Road. In 1890, the Bolton-upon-Dearne Gas Company supplied gas for street lighting from their gas works near the railway station, but from 1901, a gas supply was laid on from the Wath & Bolton Gas Board's new works at Wath Station Road. Many of the new houses were provided with a water supply and the council constructed their own sewage works, although many of the older cottages were still reliant upon wells for their water supply, with privies and outside lavatories in the back yards. In 1902, a new railway was opened skirting the area to the west and operated by the Hull & Barnsley Railway (Wath Branch). However, this was built primarily to carry coal and no stations were provided in either Bolton or Goldthorpe on the new line.

Above: Viewed from the eastern end of Station Road, the first property in Ladycroft was used as Bolton-on-Dearne Post Office and William Trickett, probably the man in the white coat, was post master. The postcard by Edgar Scrivens dates from around 1918.

In the early 20th century, building operations continued and around 70 stone-fronted, brick-built, terraced houses and two shops were laid out by speculative builders along the eastern side of Mill Lane (now Dearne Road) and these were occupied by miners at Wath Colliery. Additional houses were built in Furlong Road, Chapel Street and Edna Street, the last possibly constructed by Goldthorpe entrepreneur and builder Sidney Hamilton, and named after his daughter Edna. People continued to migrate to the area to work at the surrounding collieries, and by 1911 the population of Bolton and Goldthorpe had increased to 8,675, nearly ten times what it was 30 years earlier. The rapidly increasing population meant an increasing death rate and the graveyard at St Andrew's Church became full and was closed for burials. A cemetery had been provided in the fields to the south, but this had closed due to flooding. Therefore, in 1905 the council provided a new cemetery in Furlong Road.

Above Left: The Collingwood Hotel was located at the junction of Station Road and Furlong Road. There often appeared to be a gaggle of children ready to appear in the photograph. This was because at the time portrait photography was expensive and any photographer setting up his equipment in the street would attract attention. By appearing in the resulting postcard which would be sold for a penny at the Post Office, this was a cheap way of sending photographs to friends and family.
Above Right: In 1905, new council offices and a free library were opened at a cost of £3,500, contributed by the Scottish-American philanthropist Andrew Carnegie on behalf of Bolton-on-Dearne Urban District Council. The postcards are from the lens of Edgar Scrivens and date from around 1908 and 1918 respectively.

Bolton Hall had been occupied by Joseph Mitchell and Thomas Wilfred Howe Mitchell, the sons of Joseph Mitchell Senior who had developed Mitchell's Main Colliery at Wombwell. Following Joseph Mitchell's death in 1895, Bolton Hall and its surrounding gardens and fields were purchased by Wath Main Colliery and the hall became the Dearne Valley Social Club. Most of the new housing in Bolton had been constructed with bricks supplied by the brickyard in Furlong Road, but, around 1910, Wath Main Colliery decided to open Wath Main Brick Works on a site on Ingsfield Lane. This was adjacent to the Hull & Barnsley Railway and provided bricks for the colliery company's own proposed housing development on part of the Bolton Hall estate. This development consisted of 108 houses laid out along the north side of Ingsfield Lane and Wath Road, of which 28 larger houses on Wath Road were allocated for colliery officials. The houses were built from a distinctive red brick and constructed in blocks of four and six and built to a very high standard with spacious accommodation. The end properties of each block featured large gables with a patterned brick effect and strips of wooden cladding. Altogether, this new development provided a very impressive frontage to Ingsfield Lane and Wath Road which is still striking today.

After the First World War, and empowered by the 1919 Housing Act, Bolton Urban District Council constructed numerous council houses at Goldthorpe and Bolton with loans and subsidies provided by the Public Works Board. These houses were built in pairs or blocks of four and included front and rear gardens. Unlike their pre-war cousins, they were much larger in size and featured flushing indoor toilets, bathrooms, built in kitchens, and water, gas and electricity supplies. Around 1923, the council constructed 108 houses on Furlong Road and The Crescent and an additional 70 houses were built in 1924 along Prospect Road, The Green, Highgate Lane and Thurnscoe Road. This latter development incorporated tennis courts and bowling greens, together with recreation grounds and allotments. In addition to the council housing, a private builder constructed 22 semi-detached houses was built on Furlong Road.

The economic boom of the early 1920s attracted more people to move to the area to work in the surrounding pits and this influx of population also stimulated other developments. The Cross Daggers public house was replaced with much larger premises around 1923 and at the same time, the Barnsley British Co-operative Society opened their second Bolton store in Furlong Road. In 1924, the street tramway operated by the Dearne District Light Railway opened, connecting Bolton with Thurnscoe, Goldthorpe, Wath and Barnsley. A major recreational scheme was opened at Goldthorpe Green by the Miners Welfare Fund, which included sporting facilities and a finely appointed Miners Welfare Hall.

Above Left: This Edgar Scrivens postcard must date from between 1924-1933 as there are tram lines and overhead wiring along Wath Road, although it must have been captured on a quiet morning as very little is happening in the street. The smartly appointed buildings on the right were built by Wath Main Colliery Company in 1912.

Above Right: A 1930s postcard by James Simonton featuring The Green, one of several housing developments constructed by Bolton Urban District Council in the 1920s. Most of the local authority housing constructed following the 1919 Housing Act was built to very high standards. *(Chris Sharp – Old Barnsley)*

Additional council houses were provided by the local authority along a stretch of Furling Road to the north of the Swinton & Knottingley Railway bridge, and in several locations in Goldthorpe. By 1926, Bolton Urban District Council had built 904 houses in Bolton in only four years, an incredible achievement for such a small local authority; most of these houses were occupied by miners and their families moving to the area to work at the local pits. The local council even provided public urinals in Furlong Road and Wath Road, a feature now long gone.

During the 1930s, the Great Depression caused a dramatic cessation to most developments in the area. The local collieries were working to an imposed quota system, many were on short time and about a third of the mining workforce had been dismissed. This led to severe hardship and levels of poverty in the area with extremely high unemployment levels, a situation that only gradually improved throughout the rest of the decade. However, the outbreak of the Second World War saw the local pits reverting to maximum production to aid the war effort, although war time restrictions continued to hinder local developments. During World War II, Bolton Hall was requisitioned by the army and a heavy anti-aircraft (HAA ATAC) military gun site was constructed on Lowfield Lane and was known as Station H17. The remains of this structure have now been scheduled as an Ancient Monument by English Heritage.

After the end of the Second World War, the local council (now named Dearne Urban District Council following the merger in 1937 between Bolton and Thurnscoe Urban District Councils) restarted its house building programme. A development of 138 houses was provided to the north of Carr Field Lane, including Crofton Drive and Hall Broome Gardens. Some of these houses were steel framed structures provided at the end of the 1940s. They are known as 'BISF' Houses and were manufactured by the British Iron Steel Federation as part of a national government scheme to provided post-war housing under the Ministry of Works 'Emergency Factory Made Housing Programme'. They featured walls of precast reinforced concrete panels and steel sheet cladding. Around 1950, Dearne Urban District Council purchased a block of land bounded by Carr Field Lane and Carr Head Lane for the site of its largest individual housing programme. This was used for the construction of the Ringway estate, a development of 414 semi-detached houses, which also included two shopping parades, a post office, a church hall, a community centre and a new public house called the Dearne Hotel.

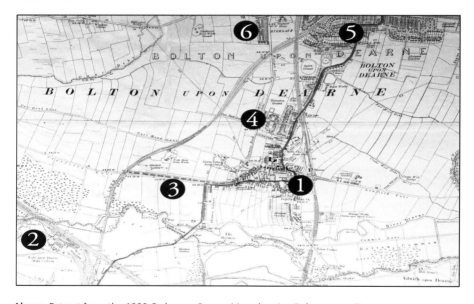

Above: Extract from the 1932 Ordnance Survey Map showing Bolton-upon-Dearne.
1: Bolton Village. **2:** Wath Main Colliery. **3:** Ingsfield Lane Pit Houses. **4:** Prospect Road BUDC Council Housing (1924). **5:** BUDC Housing at Goldthorpe Green (1924). **6:** George Street – early BUDC Council Housing (1912) – see Goldthorpe section. *(Taken from the Dearne District Traction Act Map – Paul Fox Collection)*

The massive house building programme of the 1950s was due to the National Coal Board's policy of encouraging miners and their families to move from the older coalfields to the highly productive South Yorkshire Coalfield, where massive investment was being undertaken in the local pits. In 1953, the NCB's Coal Industry Housing Association, constructed two large housing estates to the north and south of Ingsfield Lane on land inherited from Wath Main Colliery. These developments were used to house miners recruited from the older coalfields who transferred to work at Manvers Main and Wath Main Collieries. A total of 694 houses were provided by the Coal Industry Housing Association, all built in blocks of two or four and constructed from grey PRC panels (Prefabricated Reinforced Concrete). The northern development featured 300 houses in Maori Avenue, Vancouver Drive, Edinburgh Avenue, Canberra Rise, Melbourne Avenue, Commonwealth View, Princess Close and Coronation Drive. These street names were all derived from connections with the British Commonwealth although Coronation Drive reflects the 1953 coronation of Queen Elizabeth II. To the south of Ingsfield Lane, 394 similar houses were laid out along Broadwater, Mill View, South Drive, Heath Grove, Broomhill View and Dearne Road. The Ings Lane Sports and Social Club, with adjoining recreation ground, was provided by the Coal Industry Welfare Social Organisation for the inhabitants of the new pit estate. Two working men's clubs were now open elsewhere in Bolton; the British Legion Club on Station Road and the Bolton-upon-Dearne Club on Abraham Hill and Angel Street.

In a period of five years, a total of 1,246 additional houses had been provided by the local authority and the NCB, resulting in a massive increase in the local population. However, one aspect often overlooked in a male dominated industry like coal mining is the potential for high levels of female unemployment. To address this, in the 1960s, the Barnsley British Co-operative Society opened a large clothing factory on Lowfield Road and many miners' wives and daughters found employment here. This factory was later converted to manufacture kitchen units but has since closed and been demolished. In the early 1970s, the local authority provided another housing estate. This was adjacent to Billingley View, a new road constructed to connect Carr Head Lane with Carrfield Lane. On this new site, approximately 180 houses were constructed forming the 'Radburn Estate'. These houses were built under the 'Radburn Principle' with the rear of the properties facing the streets and the fronts of the houses facing communal yards or grassed areas. The concept is named after Radburn in New Jersey, USA, a new town established in 1929 which pioneered this type of housing under a 'ready for the motor age' policy. Elsewhere in the area during the 1960s and 1970s, the former Hull & Barnsley railway cutting (where trains had ceased operating in 1929) and the Wath Main brick pits were filled in and the land reclaimed. The Bolton brick pits were also reclaimed and transformed into a new country park and fishing ponds. The 1970s was also notable in that the first major developments of private housing were constructed on Highgate Lane, together with new schools - Carrfield, Heather Garth and Lacewood Primary Schools.

The Miners' Strike and the subsequent closure of the surrounding collieries hit the Bolton area hard although it may be fair to say that it didn't suffer as much as some of the other Dearne Valley communities. There has been very little demolition of older housing stock in Bolton, except for slum clearance schemes initiated by the local council in 1938 which compulsorily purchased and demolished some of the stone built cottages and yards in the old village -and again in 1955 when the terraces of Ladycroft were cleared, together with some houses in Mexborough Road which were affected by mining subsidence. Reflecting recent national trends, many of the local working men's clubs have closed and the Cross Daggers and Dearne Hotel have both been demolished. To attract new industry to the area, the Goldthorpe Industrial Estate was built at Highgate and many Bolton people now work in the new employment opportunities created there and on the site of Manvers Main Colliery. The recent opening of a national retail distribution warehouse for ALDI UK has created further employment prospects. Although Bolton never traditionally had a colliery of its own, there is therefore no mining memorial as such, although one recent pleasing development was the dedication on 3 August 2014 of a new Dearne Towns War Memorial in Bolton Cemetery. This is a particularly splendid structure commemorating the 100th anniversary of the First World War and listing the names of the men from Bolton, Highgate and Goldthorpe who lost their lives during the two world wars - a credit to the people of Bolton.

Brampton Bierlow

The parish of Brampton Bierlow was originally agricultural in nature and comprised the hamlets of Brampton, Melton Green and West Melton. The first consisted of a small group of cottages, farms, a school and the Bulls Head Inn - clustered around Brampton Hall owned by Sir George Ellis. Melton Green and West Melton were larger settlements to the south, each comprising several cottages and farms. The name Brampton is derived from the Old English word *Brantone* – an enclosure with bramble bushes. Bierlow is derived from an old Norse word *Byar Log* an area where some form of self-government or law is imposed and Bierlow is a relatively common place name throughout the country. Melton is derived from the Old English *Midleton* – the middle farmstead. Melton later received the prefix of West to distinguish it from High Melton near Mexborough.

Brampton Bierlow was recorded in the Domesday Survey of 1086 when the area was owned by Ilbert de Laci of Pontefract Castle; the village subsequently passed into the ownership of the monks of Monk Bretton Priory and Bolton Priory. Following the Dissolution of the Monasteries, the area passed into the hands of several landowners, prominent amongst which were Sir George Ellis of Brampton Hall and Earl Fitzwilliam of Wentworth Woodhouse. In 1819, the Brampton & Hooton Roberts turnpike road opened and the foundation stone for a new church at West Melton was laid on 8 November 1853 by the 5th Earl Fitzwilliam.

Coal mining had taken place on a very small scale in the area for several hundred years, as the shallow Meltonfield, Abdy and Newhill coal seams outcrop towards the west and were easily worked - a small day hole pit was recorded at Cortworth in 1486. Early mining operations were centralised around Melton Green and along the valley of the Knoll Beck where in the 1800s, New Brampton Colliery, Cortwood Colliery (later renamed Willow Main) and Greenland's Colliery were working the shallow seams. However, it was the opening of Cortonwood Colliery in 1875 that saw the development of a large colliery community to the north of Brampton.

The colliery company had purchased land in 1876 from Sir George Ellis and, on an isolated site near the Dearne & Dove Canal, it built 106 cottages forming the colliery community named Concrete. These houses were unusual in that they were constructed out of concrete - hence the name - and had flat roofs; therefore, they were known as 'Concrete Cottages'. However, the development quickly gained the unofficial name of 'Little Palestine' or 'Jerusalem', due to the resemblance with the flat roofed externally plastered houses of the Holy Land. There were eight streets of terraces, varying in length from four to nineteen houses. Cottages were built along one side of each street, so that the front of each property faced the back yard of the house on the next row.

Internally, the cottages were relatively spacious compared to other colliery housing of the time. On the ground floor was a living room with a fireplace and a kitchen. The latter contained a Yorkshire Range for cooking, a stoneware sink with a single cold-water tap, and a 'copper' - a basin used for boiling water and washing clothes. A gas supply laid on from the colliery was used to illuminate the downstairs rooms. Upstairs were three bedrooms; a large bedroom with a fireplace and two smaller rooms. A cellar under each property was used for the storage of coal and potatoes. Each cottage contained a private yard to the rear at the end of which was an earth closet. The colliery company also constructed a school containing two classrooms and paid the salaries of the teachers until the West Riding County Council took over the responsibility for education. On the eastern side of Knoll Beck Lane, a tin chapel was opened by the Wesleyan Methodists. Three of the concrete cottages contained small shops trading from the front rooms whilst No 1 became a Post Office. A wooden lock up shop was opened as a fish and chip shop and the colliery company provided a large site to the south for allotments.

Above: This Edgar Scrivens postcard from 1925 is captioned 'New Bridge, Concrete, Wombwell', and shows the newly constructed bridge and embankment provided to carry Knoll Beck Lane over the Knoll Beck stream, the railway and the canal to Elsecar. Dearne District Light Railway tram number 12 can be seen operating to Barnsley. Off camera to the left the railway was carried over the canal by a unique lifting bridge that operated rather like a draw bridge. The bridge featured two iron bastions to hold the winding apparatus embossed with the legend 'South Yorkshire' referencing the original South Yorkshire Railway of 1850. It was a shame that this unusual railway bridge was not preserved. The flat-topped houses of Concrete Cottages can be seen to the right together with the early village school; Nabot House stands prominently on the left. In the distance, some of the houses built by the Industrial Housing Association have been constructed along Knoll Beck Lane. To the right of the tram is Pit Lane, where the pickets' 'Alamo' hut was situated during the 1984/84 Miner's Strike. New Bridge was the scene of violent clashes between the police and pickets during the dispute. During the conflict, the bridge wall to the left of the tram was graffitied with the famous slogan 'We told Arthur No Surrender'. New Bridge was replaced with a modern structure to allow the Dearne Valley Parkway to pass underneath, but the scene is still recognisable today. *(Chris Sharp – Old Barnsley)*

The provision of the colliery owned housing of Concrete Cottages succeeded in attracting a workforce to the area, as Cortonwood Colliery was a relatively late arrival compared to some of the other Dearne Valley collieries and therefore the competition for labour would have been more intense. The provision of colliery owned housing had the advantage that rental payments were deducted from the miners' pay packet preventing rental arrears. This was a problem that many private landlords experienced, for when the rent collector called every week, the inhabitants were often 'not in'! The provision of company owned housing was also beneficial in times of industrial unrest. In 1877, during a dispute at Cortonwood Colliery, the striking men were instructed to leave Concrete Cottages and after the end of the strike, part of an agreement was that all the workers re-engaged must reside in the colliery owned settlement, presumably because the threat of eviction was a major control on the discipline of the workforce by the colliery owners.

The 1881 census indicates that families came from all over the country to live at Concrete Cottages, particularly from Yorkshire, the West Midlands, Derbyshire and London, although several of the cottages were uninhabited at the time. However, by the time of the 1901 census, 580 people were living in the 106 cottages and many families had taken in lodgers. None of the streets were named, the entire community was simply numbered 1- 106 Concrete. In the 1880s another isolated colliery community was constructed to the north of the canal at Wombwell Junction, named after the junction of the Dearne & Dove Canal and the canal branch to Elsecar and not far from The Junction public houses. At this location, 55 houses were provided in three terraces arranged around a triangular plot of land. At the northern apex of the triangle at the junction of Wath and Knoll Beck Lane, a new public house opened called the Guide Post Inn. Migrants moved into the houses of Wombwell Junction and the area gained a certain notoriety and received the local nickname of 'three cornered hell'! It was sometime referred to as New Wombwell although this also applied to the houses at Concrete as well.

By 1903, the area around Melton Green was being targeted by speculative builders and terraces were built along Packman Road, Content Terrace and Mount Terrace. Whitworth's Wath Breweries opened a new public house named the Cottage of Content. These new developments were supplied with bricks from two new brickworks named West Melton Brickworks and Melton Field Fire Clay Works. Shortly afterwards, Joseph Carnley sold a 21-acre site for building at West Melton and speculative builders laid out Carnley Street, West End Road, Hoober Street, Linden Road, Woodfield Road and Brampton Road. This development was served by the opening of a branch of the Barnsley British Co-operative Society in 1914.

In the 1920s the colliery company were opening out the deeper seams and consequently seeking to recruit a larger workforce. This led to a major phase of house building, complete with new shops, schools, a Wesleyan chapel and a Miners Welfare Institute. Two sites for development were purchased to the west and east of Knoll Beck Lane from Earl Fitzwilliam, Charles Wright and the Trustees of the George Ellis Charity. The western site was smaller, but the larger eastern site bounded by Knoll Beck Lane, Pontefract Road, Wath Road and the canal totalled 59 acres and included the old Cliffe Fields and the Bulls Head Inn. In 1922, the colliery company commissioned the Housing & Town Planning Trust to construct a development of 60 houses forming Knoll Beck Avenue on part of the western site. These were much larger properties than those provided before the war and were arranged in blocks of two and four with front and rear gardens. The scheme also included twelve large properties for colliery officials facing Knoll Beck Lane.

In 1924, the colliery company sold the remaining portion of the western site and the eastern site to the Industrial Housing Association. This was an organisation established by a group of colliery companies to provide company owned housing throughout the country and they were active within the Dearne Valley at Brampton and Thurnscoe. The Industrial Housing Association was chaired by Lord Aberconway who was also the Chairman of Cortonwood Collieries Ltd; it could obtain loans and subsidies from the government to assist with its house building projects. The Industrial Housing Association drew up plans for a development of

358 houses named Cortonwood Village, with 67 houses on the western site and 291 on the eastern site. In 1924, the first batch of 67 houses were built forming Knoll Beck Crescent. The following year, 147 of the remaining 291 houses were built along Knoll Beck Lane, Dearne Road, Chapel Avenue, Wath Road and Cliffe Road. All the houses were built to a high standard in blocks of two, three and four. The corner blocks constructed at road junctions were angled and thus expensive to build. This led to the scheme being praised by Sir Patrick Aberconway, the leading town planner in the country. Each house was provided with small gardens to the front and large gardens to the year.

However, certain areas of the site were sold, including plots for a new Barnsley British Co-operative Store and for a block of four shops incorporating a new Post Office named Concrete Post Office. The Miners Welfare Fund provided a Miners Welfare Institute, with football and cricket pitches, recreation grounds, tennis courts and bowling greens in 1925. On 13 November 1926, a 1,980-square yard site was conveyed to the trustees of the Brampton Bierlow Wesleyan Methodist Church who built a handsome new chapel to replace the original tin chapel opposite Concrete Cottages. The new housing developments were connected to Barnsley and the rest of the Dearne Valley in 1924 by the opening of the Dearne District Light Railway along Knoll Beck Lane and the trams were housed in a depot opposite the houses at Wombwell Junction. The Bulls Head Inn remained the property of the colliery company but this was leased to the Wath Brewers, Whitworth, Son & Nephew.

Above: This road junction on Wath Road was originally known as Tunstall Cross and is depicted on this 1920 postcard published by Doncaster Rotophoto. Everill Gate Lane to the left leads to Broomhill and the road to the right leads to Hemingfield. In the distance can be seen the Guide Post Inn and houses at Wombwell Junction. The fact that cows are being driven down the road amongst the rows of cottages provided by speculative builders is typical of the curious juxtaposition of rural and industrial that existed in the Dearne Valley prior to the Second World War. The smartly dressed ladies on the right appear to be amused by the situation!

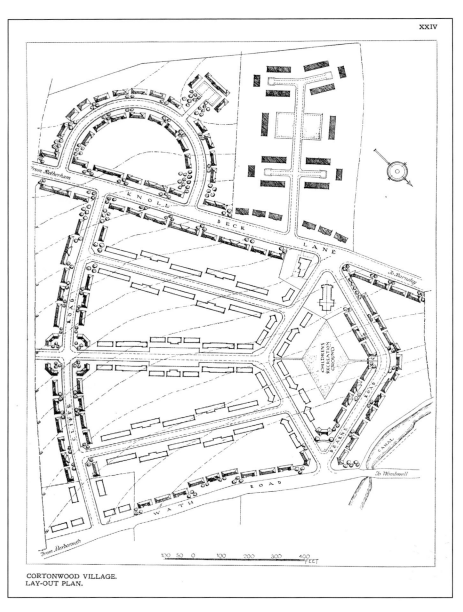

Above: This layout plan showing Cortonwood Village appeared in the book *The Building of 12,000 Houses*, by Sir Tudor Walters. The book depicts the estates constructed on behalf of various colliery companies by the Industrial Housing Association. Cortonwood village originally consisted of 358 houses together with a children recreation ground and a site for a new church and shop. However, the houses shown in white were never built and the central area was sold to Rotherham Rural District Council.

358 houses named Cortonwood Village, with 67 houses on the western site and 291 on the eastern site. In 1924, the first batch of 67 houses were built forming Knoll Beck Crescent. The following year, 147 of the remaining 291 houses were built along Knoll Beck Lane, Dearne Road, Chapel Avenue, Wath Road and Cliffe Road. All the houses were built to a high standard in blocks of two, three and four. The corner blocks constructed at road junctions were angled and thus expensive to build. This led to the scheme being praised by Sir Patrick Aberconway, the leading town planner in the country. Each house was provided with small gardens to the front and large gardens to the year.

However, certain areas of the site were sold, including plots for a new Barnsley British Co-operative Store and for a block of four shops incorporating a new Post Office named Concrete Post Office. The Miners Welfare Fund provided a Miners Welfare Institute, with football and cricket pitches, recreation grounds, tennis courts and bowling greens in 1925. On 13 November 1926, a 1,980-square yard site was conveyed to the trustees of the Brampton Bierlow Wesleyan Methodist Church who built a handsome new chapel to replace the original tin chapel opposite Concrete Cottages. The new housing developments were connected to Barnsley and the rest of the Dearne Valley in 1924 by the opening of the Dearne District Light Railway along Knoll Beck Lane and the trams were housed in a depot opposite the houses at Wombwell Junction. The Bulls Head Inn remained the property of the colliery company but this was leased to the Wath Brewers, Whitworth, Son & Nephew.

Above: This road junction on Wath Road was originally known as Tunstall Cross and is depicted on this 1920 postcard published by Doncaster Rotophoto. Everill Gate Lane to the left leads to Broomhill and the road to the right leads to Hemingfield. In the distance can be seen the Guide Post Inn and houses at Wombwell Junction. The fact that cows are being driven down the road amongst the rows of cottages provided by speculative builders is typical of the curious juxtaposition of rural and industrial that existed in the Dearne Valley prior to the Second World War. The smartly dressed ladies on the right appear to be amused by the situation!

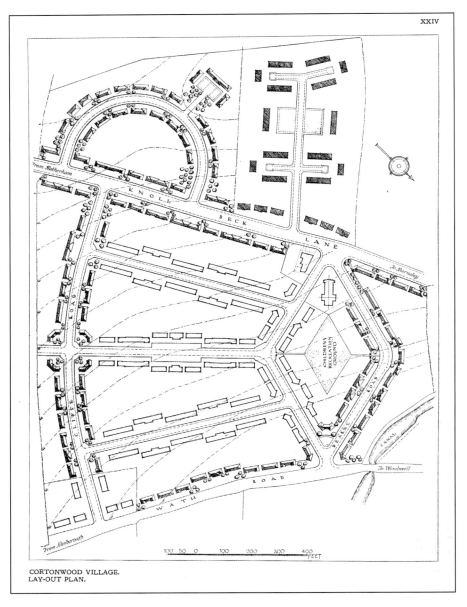

Above: This layout plan showing Cortonwood Village appeared in the book *The Building of 12,000 Houses*, by Sir Tudor Walters. The book depicts the estates constructed on behalf of various colliery companies by the Industrial Housing Association. Cortonwood village originally consisted of 358 houses together with a children recreation ground and a site for a new church and shop. However, the houses shown in white were never built and the central area was sold to Rotherham Rural District Council.

On the 21 April 1927, the remaining 14 acres in the middle of the site were sold to Rotherham Rural District Council. On part of this a new West Riding County Council School opened around 1930, allowing the original school at Concrete Cottages to close. The Rural District Council also provided its own houses with 105 properties being built along Chapel Avenue, Rother Street and Becknoll Road in 1928. The Rotherham Rural District Council purchased another area for the building of 74 houses in 1929 on Pontefract Road, Melton Street, Melton Avenue with a southern extension to Becknoll Road. An additional area of 40 council houses was provided along the northern side of Wath Road in 1929. All the Rotherham Rural District Council Houses were built in groups of two, three and four and provided with gardens to front and rear.

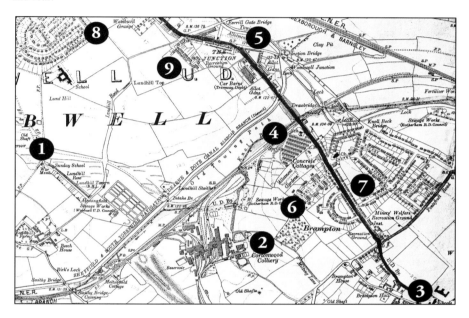

Above: Extract from the 1932 Ordnance Survey Map showing the Brampton Bierlow area.
1: Site of Lundhill Colliery and Lundhill Row. **2:** Cortonwood Colliery. **3:** Brampton Village. **4:** Concrete Cottages. **5:** Wombwell Junction. **6:** Housing & Town Planning Trust Estate (1922). **7:** Industrial Housing Association Estate (1925). **8:** Wombwell Urban District Council Housing (mid-1920s). **9:** Housing Estate provided for Dearne District Light Railway employees. *(Taken from the Dearne District Traction Act Map – Paul Fox Collection)*

In 1930, a development of 25 houses and two shops was constructed on the remaining portion of land at the junction of Pontefract Road and Wath Road. This completed the major phase of house building at Brampton and the colliery community now totalled 679 houses: 106 at Concrete; 55 at Wombwell Junction; 60 provided by the Housing & Town Planning Trust; 214 by the Industrial Housing Association; 219 built by Rotherham Rural District Council and 25 provided by a private builder.

The depression of the 1930s and the Second World War suppressed any further development (apart from 40 private houses in Westfield Road, Brampton Road and Highfield Road in the 1930s and the opening of St Albans Mission Church in Cliffe Road). However, in the mid-

1950s, Rotherham Rural District Council commenced another large house building programme. This included the construction of 92 houses in Moorebridge Crescent and 172 houses along an extension to Knoll Beck Avenue which linked up with Westfield Road and incorporated Wyn Grove, Wynmoor Crescent and Ellis Crescent. These houses were built in pairs and provided with large gardens. In 1958, the Concrete Cottages and the houses at Wombwell Junction were no longer judged fit for purpose and were demolished; many of the residents moved into the new council estates. The council also provided a development of pensioners' bungalows and flats on the site of the concrete cottages. However, the Concrete name survived into the 1970s as the name of the Post Office.

Following the closure of the Cortonwood Colliery in 1985, a large development of private housing was constructed on colliery land accessed from Westfield Lane. The colliery spoil heap was landscaped and the pit site redeveloped as the Cortonwood Retail Park. The new A6195 now passes beneath Knoll Beck Lane and runs parallel to the canal and former railway. A war memorial and winding wheel to commemorate those that worked at Cortonwood Colliery has been erected opposite the Miners Welfare building.

Broomhill

Very little has been written about Broom Hill (now referred to as Broomhill), a hamlet located on the flood plain of the River Dearne by a road junction formed by the meeting of Everill Gate Lane, (the lane from Wombwell Tunstall Cross) and the B6273 from Brampton to Darfield Millhouses. The settlement, originally referred to as Broom Hill, is not recorded in the Domesday Survey although it subsequently guarded an ancient crossing over the River Dearne known as Marle's Bridge. In 1855, there were a handful of cottages and a new public house, the Railway Inn which opened following the arrival of the Midland Railway in 1840 and it is possible that the hamlet originally developed as a small railway community. The land in Broomhill was in the hands of several small owners, although Earl Fitzwilliam owned Wombwell Ings, Billingley Ings and Bolton Ings and a large farm house at Old Moor, all forming part of the flood plain of the River Dearne.

With the arrival of the Dearne & Dove Canal, the railways, the local brickmaking industry, and Cortonwood Colliery, Broomhill developed as a community of around 100 houses during the 1870s and 1880s. In 1873, the hamlet was provided with a Local Board School with accommodation for 258 children; there were a couple of shops, an Institute and a Primitive Methodist Church and several allotments. In 1880, a borehole was sunk to provide water to the surrounding Dearne Valley villages and the Dearne Valley Water Works opened on Everill Gate Lane. By 1910, an additional 40 houses had been built together with a new Methodist Church and a Mission Room. Many of the small landholders in the area, including William Casson and Emily Cash, sold their land for housing and the coal beneath to Cortonwood Colliery.

In the 1920s, a recreation ground was opened, including a football pitch, bowling green and tennis courts, possibly provided by the Miners Welfare Fund and a bus service was provided from Broomhill to Wombwell Market Place. However, in the following decades, the hamlet was affected by a series of floods partially attributed to mining subsidence which had lowered the level of the surrounding flood plain. It was estimated that around 12 feet of coal had been removed from beneath the area, causing extensive mining subsidence. By 1962, most of the older houses had been demolished and areas of derelict land remained between the other buildings. With a substantially reduced population, the School, Mission Room and Institute were subsequently closed and demolished. Meanwhile the surrounding meadows and the flood plain had become permanently inundated with areas of water known as 'flashes'.

One night, in 1984, the driver of a Yorkshire Traction double decker bus who was transferring the vehicle from Doncaster depot to Wombwell depot, took a wrong turn through Broomhill and decapitated the top deck on the low bridge that carried the Midland Railway over the B6273. Returning with a recovery truck from the depot to retrieve the roof from the side of the road, the engineering staff were somewhat surprised to find the bus roof had disappeared, possibly taken to a local scrap yard by an enterprising individual or cut up for use on allotments! Whatever, Yorkshire Traction subsequently converted the vehicle to an open top bus and it spent the remainder of its days carrying holidaymakers from Skegness to Butlin's Holiday Camp.

In 1985, the opening of the Wombwell Bypass truncated Everill Gate Lane, and in 1988, the B6273 to the north of Broomhill was closed and replaced with a new link road built on a high embankment above the flood plain bypassing the hamlet. This road now forms the A6195 Dearne Valley Parkway. Consequently, Broomhill has become a forgotten backwater and receives little through traffic. However, new housing has since been built on the vacant plots of land and the Railway Inn has been renamed the Old Moor Tavern. The surrounding area has now become a haven for wildlife following the opening of Broomhill Flash and the RSPB Old Moor Visitor Centre & Nature Reserve at Old Moor Farm. Broomhill has become a peaceful and pleasant residential area adjacent to the Trans Pennine Trail, a new coast to coast cycling and walking route that opened in 2001.

Above: An interwar postcard of Broomhill depicting the Railway Inn located at the junction of the B6273 and Everill Gate Lane, the road leading to Wombwell. Most of the houses and the Methodist Church in the distance have been demolished, although the pub remains open. *(Chris Sharp – Old Barnsley).*

Darfield, Snape Hill & Low Valley

Darfield is situated on a prominent hill top position, overlooking an ancient bridging point over the River Dearne and the valley of the River Dove. Roman coins have been found in the area and All Saint's Church features Saxon foundations. Darfield was recorded as *Derewelle* in the Domesday Survey of 1086 when the Lords of the Manor were *Alsi* and *Chetelber*. The place name later evolved to Darfield derived from the Saxon terms *Dere* – where deer roamed - and *Field* – an area of pastureland. The land in the area subsequently passed to the monks of Monk Bretton Priory and, following the Dissolution of the Monasteries, into the hands of a variety of landowners, who constructed several large houses in the area: Tyers Hall, New Hall, Wood Hall, Netherwood Hall, Upperwood Hall and Middlewood Hall.

Above: Church Street in the old village centre as depicted on a postcard by Edgar Scrivens dating to around 1920. The rural nature of the old stone built cottages is shown in this view, which included the Cross Keys pub on the right and Darfield Church. Apart from the church, most of the buildings shown here have been demolished and the Cross Keys has been rebuilt and set back from the road. The church tower was badly damaged by mining subsidence but has been repaired and the graveyard contains the 1857 Lundhill Colliery Disaster Memorial, the 1886 Houghton Main Cage Disaster Memorial and the grave of Darfield's most notable resident: Ebenezer Elliott, the 'Corn Law Rhymer.'

Prior to the arrival of mining, the parish of Darfield was extensive and included Billingley, Great and Little Houghton, Wombwell and Worsbrough - and a population of 648 was recorded in 1841. The village was agricultural in nature, with the population engaged in working on the local farms although sandstone quarrying was a small but significant industry. To the north east, the River Dearne crossing was guarded by the Old Bridge Inn, a public house originally established in 1450 to serve travellers on the road between Barnsley and Doncaster. This road was turnpiked in 1740 when a tollhouse was built to collect tolls from passing traffic. The main centre of the village consisted of the Norman Darfield Church and its Rectory, the Cross Keys public house, a Post Office, a National School and several houses, cottages and farms. At Darfield Bridge was a watermill, whilst a second watermill was located on the River Dove adjacent to Netherwood Hall. The area around Darfield Bridge is often known as Millhouses – named from the old houses by the watermill. From Darfield village centre, a road extended south westwards from Darfield, passing down Snape Hill and twisting and turning across the flat flood plain of the River Dove at Low Valley, before rising to end in the town of Wombwell.

In 1840, Darfield Railway Station was opened by the Midland Railway and a handful of cottages for railway workers was built at Darfield Bridge. In 1850, the Low Valley Clay Works were established by James Gooddy who lived in Poplar House in Darfield. The clay works manufactured sanitary pipes, tiles and bricks from clay excavated from a series of open pits. However, the local landowners, including Francis Taylor of Middlewood Hall and Charles Harvey of Park House, leased the coal beneath their land to a consortium of Pontefract industrialists who developed Darfield Main Colliery in the low-lying valley of the River Dove in 1860. This area was known as 'Low Valley' or simply as 'Valley', and a new colliery community developed at Low Valley during the 1860s and 1870s.

Within the pit yard, a row of eight substantial houses was erected for officials and deputies. This row was known as Tiger Row and adjoined two large houses for colliery management called Netherwood Cottages. Another row of five cottages nearby was named Rabbit Row, built in the shadow of the coke ovens. The road from the colliery to Low Valley, originally named Netherwood Lane, was subsequently renamed Pit Lane at its western end and Pitt Street (spelt with two letter *t*'s) at its eastern end where it joined the road from Darfield to Wombwell. Housing for the rest of the colliery workforce was provided at Low Valley but this was left mostly to speculative builders, although some of the rows were owned by the colliery company – one such row on George Street was known as Company Row and was built in 1875. At Low Valley, a settlement of around 300 terraced houses was laid out forming a grid pattern along Pitt Street, Hope Street, Providence Street, James Street, Henry Street and George Street. It is possible that James, Henry and George were the names of some of the colliery proprietor's children, although George Street may be derived from George Pearson, the leading promotor of the pit. The population of the new colliery community was 139 in 1861 but ten years later this had increased to 661 as the colliery grew and employed more workers.

Men were encouraged to move to Low Valley to work at Darfield Main Colliery and most of the new migrants were from the Yorkshire area. However, others moved from the coal mining areas of the Black Country counites of the West Midlands - Staffordshire, Shropshire, Warwickshire and Worcestershire. The collieries of the Black Country were facing the exhaustion of their coal reserves and suffering from drainage problems; the miners were relatively low paid, as the unpopular 'Butty System' of payment was used – this being a method where a single man was paid for all the coal mined by his team; he subsequently and often unfairly subdivided the payment amongst his team members. The colliery company employed the services of recruitment agents, for example Paul Roper of Bilston in Staffordshire, who encouraged men to move from Staffordshire to Low Valley. Other important migrants were Daniel and Joseph Hammerton from Wolverhampton. The Hammerton's were building contractors and they built most of the houses at Low Valley and Snape Hill. Migrants from the West Midlands totalled around 10% of the local population in

1861 which had increased to 21% by 1871. Other significant influxes of migrants to the area were from Nottinghamshire & Derbyshire (9%) and Ireland (6.5%).

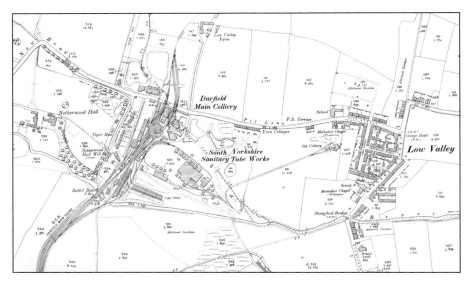

Above: Extract from the 1906 Ordnance Survey 1:2500 Map of Darfield Main Colliery, showing the close relationship with the adjoining Brickworks (now trading as South Yorkshire Sanitary Tube Works following the death of James Gooddy in 1893) and the colliery community of Low Valley. The Old Colliery marked just to the west of Low Valley was a pumping shaft and this area was later covered with the Darfield Muck Stack. *(Maurice Dobson Museum & Heritage Centre)*

The houses of Low Valley were built with bricks supplied from James Gooddy's brickworks and were arranged in long rows of four roomed tenements, with shared backyards and outside privies. There was no electricity or gas lighting, although the kitchen was fitted with a Yorkshire Range and copper for boiling water and there was a coal fire in the front room. Some of the houses incorporated little shops and a sub post office and in 1863 a Primitive Methodist Chapel opened in Pitt Street. The children of the new settlement attended the National School in Darfield until the opening of St Matthew's Mission Church which included school rooms for girls, boys and infants. On the corner of George Street and Pitt Street, a public house opened called the George Hotel but known locally as the 'corner pub'. Many of the early houses were 'jerry built' with no proper sewage disposal system and no water supply - in the 1870s there were 23 wells in Low Valley and another 18 at Snape Hill which provided the water. Infant mortality was substantially higher than the national average and the health situation reached critical levels during the scorching summer of 1874. The River Dearne had become polluted with sewage and effluent and with little water in the river due to the drought conditions, pollution levels were running high and the local wells were contaminated. The unhealthy conditions caused outbreaks of contagious diseases like small pox and scarlet fever to sweep through the area with disastrous results. Consequently, during the following year a sewage scheme was implemented by the local authorities and a water supply was laid on to the houses following the opening of the Dearne Valley Waterworks at Broomhill.

Sporadic building operations continued throughout the 1880s and by 1891, additional houses had been provided to the south of the River Dove off Ings Road (96 houses at Queen Street and Elliott's Terrace) with 22 houses built on Station Road near Wombwell, complete with a new public house, the New Station Inn. Isolated rows of houses were also built elsewhere, including 14 houses named Kent Row, 16 houses forming Littlefield Terrace, 14 houses called York Cottages and four houses named PB Terrace on Pitt Street. In 1872, a Wesleyan Methodist Church opened on George Street followed by a second village school, Low Valley Infants School, which opened on 9 January 1888.

In 1878, Houghton Main Colliery commenced production but most of the miners were housed some distance away at a new settlement known as Snape Hill, located on Snape Hill Road between Darfield and Low Valley. A small brickyard was opened here and between 1877 and 1894, Daniel Hammerton submitted plans for the erection of 73 houses forming New Street, and a row of 16 houses called College Terrace, together with a large detached property named Cambridge House which was built as a new home for himself. These houses were built on land purchased from Cambridge University's Trinity College, and this is reflected in the naming of the properties. Another 70 houses were constructed in a loop around the brickworks forming Havelock Street and additional properties were built along both sides of Snape Hill Road. These included several shops and branch number 18 of the Barnsley British Co-operative Society opening in 1880.

Above: Snape Hill developed as an important commercial thoroughfare following the building of cottages to house miners at Houghton Main Colliery. This photograph is by Darfield photographer W Stables and was issued as a postcard by Haigh Brothers of Barnsley in 1910. The street was lit by the solitary gas lamp and the carrier's cart adds interest to the scene. Most of the buildings shown here have since been demolished, apart from the five shops on the left – and many of these no longer function as commercial premises. *(Andrew McGarrigle Collection)*

By 1881, the population of Snape Hill was 596 as men and their families moved to the area to work at Houghton Main Colliery. Although most of these were from Yorkshire, there was another significant influx of migrants from the Black Country, Nottinghamshire and Derbyshire, reflecting the pattern of migration that had occurred at Low Valley a few years earlier. Many men would walk to the pit from Snape Hill, via Darfield Village, School Street, Little Houghton Lane and across the River Dearne on a footbridge and up Ings Lane to Houghton Main Colliery. This was probably a pleasant walk before a shift on a sunny day in Summer but a very tiring walk back after completing a shift. In later years, enterprising transport operators including Greenhow & Sons and George White provided pit buses at shift times, departing Wombwell Market Place and picking up miners in Low Valley, Snape Hill, Darfield and Middlecliffe before running to Houghton Main Colliery.

The increase in population saw the opening of the Victoria Inn and Darfield Workings Men Club at Snape Hill plus the Low Valley Workings Men Club and the Brick Layers Arms at Low Valley. By 1891, the population of Darfield, Snape Hill and Low Valley had reached 3,414 and in 1896 Darfield Urban District Council was established. In 1897, 92 houses were laid out in Darfield Village itself, on Victoria Street, Queen Street, Coronation Street and School Street and shortly afterwards another block of housing was constructed on Garden Street, Barnsley Road and Snape Hill Road including the 63rd branch of the Barnsley British Co-operative Society. These terraced houses were fronted in stone, possibly reflecting their location near the sandstone cottages of Darfield village, perhaps an early attempt at blending in new architecture with older buildings. Darfield had been developing at the same time as Snape Hill, with a Reading Room opening in 1879 and Barnsley Road Methodist Church in 1887 (replacing an earlier chapel which became the Conservative Club) together with a new Police Station. Additional houses were provided by speculative builders in the village as well as at Darfield Bridge and Millhouses near the Railway Station, where a sub post office opened together with another public house, the Station Hotel.

In the 1890s and 1900s, further brick built housing was constructed on Snape Hill Road, Stonyford Road and Station Road, the new houses forming a ribbon development linking Darfield, Snape Hill, Low Valley and Wombwell. The opening of Dearne Valley Colliery in 1903 brought more workers to the area. A Roman Catholic School was built on Stonyford Road and another school was provided in Darfield Village. The Urban District Council introduced many improvements, noticeably the provision of water supplied from the Dearne Valley Waterworks at Broomhill and the proper disposal of sewage following the opening of the sewage works. In 1870, the Wombwell and Darfield Gas Company had opened a gas works for the supply of gas for street lighting; this later also provided a domestic supply. In 1898, the first electrical supply was laid to the village, but this was mostly used for street lighting.

By 1911, the population of Darfield, Snape Hill and Low Valley had nearly doubled in ten years to 6,284 following the rapid expansion of the Darfield Main, Mitchell's Main, Houghton Main and Dearne Valley Collieries and another major influx of workers and their families moved to the area. In anticipation, the West Riding County Council opened new schools on Snape Hill Road on 27 January 1910: a mixed school for 480 children and an Infants School for 240 children. Opposite the schools a fine new Wesleyan Methodist Church opened on 9 June of that year. Snape Hill and Low Valley were surrounded by allotments but the provision of leisure facilities now included a cinema which opened in 1914 on the corner of Snape Hill Road and George Street. This was initially known variously as the Briton Picture Palace, the Cinema Palace or the Astoria Cinema, but the building functioned as Low Valley Hall after the war, a venue for public meetings and performances. Another cinema opened near Darfield Church, the Darfield Empire which became a church hall in 1956. In 1929, two stadiums opened, Ings Road Stadium and South Yorkshire Sports Stadium and both were used for speedway with greyhound racing also being held at the later.

In 1915, Daniel Hammerton and his son Ernest Hammerton were now living at The Poplars in Darfield and were both working for Darfield Urban District Council where Daniel was Collector and Assistant Overseer and Ernest was a Surveyor and Sanitary Inspector. Another branch of the family, Holin Hammerton, ran a Joiner's shop on Snape Hill, where another member of an influential local family, Thomas Septimius Camplejohn, owned a grocery shop. Other members of the Camplejohn family lived in Alderney Cottage and operated the area's first bus service to Barnsley. The Poplars was later used as offices by Darfield Urban District Council.

Above Left: George Street and Stonyford Road were originally named Low Valley Lane and formed the main thoroughfare between Darfield and Wombwell. This view looking north shows some of the earliest housing constructed in the 1860s and 1870s – most of which has since been demolished. Both postcards were published by Edgar Scrivens c1920.
Above Right: Stonyford Road runs between Stonyford Bridge over the River Dove to Cockstool Bridge over the Bulling Dike in the distance which marks the junction with Ings Road and Station Road. These houses were provided in the 1890s as part of a new phase of building for Darfield Main Colliery following its purchase by Mitchell Main Colliery.

Following the end of the First World War, Darfield Urban District Council exerted an increasing influence upon the provision of housing and services in the area, establishing a new cemetery on Saltersbrook Road and provided the first council houses. These consisted of a development of 24 houses at Millhouses near Darfield Bridge in 1922, followed by 114 semi-detached houses on Nanny Marr Road, Barnsley Road, West Street, South Street and South View. In the mid-1920s, the local authority and the Miners' Welfare Fund opened Darfield Park, which included flower gardens, recreation grounds, bowling greens and tennis courts. Meanwhile, in Low Valley another branch of the Barnsley British Co-operative Society was opened in 1929 on Stonyford Road. Towards the end of the 1930s, the local council constructed another 164 houses on North street, East Street and Illesley Road and, together with eight cottages owned by the local authority, this brought the total number of Darfield Urban District Council houses to 310. The 1930s also saw the provision of private housing on Nanny Marr Road and Barnsley Road in Darfield. In 1934, Ernest Hamilton, by now a private architect and surveyor, drew up plans for 58 houses on a plot of land owned by his son, Daniel Hammerton, who was named after his grandfather, Daniel Hammerton, who had built some of the first houses in Low Valley and Snape Hill. This new development of 58 houses formed Tempest Avenue. Finally, in 1938, a small single storey branch of the Barnsley British Co-operative Society opened on Nanny Marr Road.

Above: This postcard of George Street published by Edgar Scrivens, c1914, shows some of the developments at the northern end of Low Valley. The schools and Wesleyan Methodist Chapel opened in 1910, the latter replacing the earlier Methodist Chapel in Pitt Street. In 1914, the Low Valley Picture Palace opened as a venue for meetings, theatre and cinema performances. The schools were demolished in 2007 and replaced but the cinema building is now used as a fishing supplies warehouse.

The building of council housing, private housing and speculatively built terraced housing saw an increase in the population, particularly in the Darfield area, which put a strain upon the existing schools. To address this in 1940, the West Riding County Council opened Foulstone Secondary Modern School although the school was not officially opened until 17 May 1943. Following the end of the Second World War, the local authority stepped up the provision of council housing following the 1946 Housing Act. An additional 490 houses were provided in the late 1940s and early 1950s. Some of these developments were instigated due to a government scheme to provide post war housing under the Ministry of Works 'Emergency Factory Made Housing Programme', when housing was quickly required; as bricks were in short supply, alternative methods of construction were needed. A development of 108 'Cornish' houses was built on Rose Avenue and Bellbrooke Avenue constructed by the Central Cornwall Concrete & Artificial Stone Company. These houses were manufactured from concrete panels and featured mansard roofs. Another 48 'BISF' houses were provided by the British Iron Steel Federation, manufactured from concrete panels and steel sheet cladding. These houses were built on Bly Road, Clarney Avenue and Clarney Place. The remaining 334 houses were provided later in the 1950s when brick supplies became more readily available and included houses and bungalows on Barnsley Road, Bly Road, Morrison Road, Schofield Road and Ridgeway Avenue.

Darfield Urban District Council continued its building programme throughout the 1960s providing additional houses, flats and bungalows, and another 386 properties were built in the block of land between Barnsley Road and Saltersbrook Road. During its lifetime from 1896 to 1974, Darfield Urban District Council constructed 1,186 houses. A new public house, the Darfield Hotel, known as the 'new un' was built, with the Longbow Pub opening on Barnsley Road. Meanwhile 150 houses and flats were constructed at Upperwood Road in Snape Hill in the 1960s and many of these houses were occupied by miners moving to the area from the Scottish coalfields. This development also included new premises for the Darfield Working Men's Club.

Some of the new houses on Upperwood Road and in another development at Cover Drive and Norville Crescent were occupied by families displaced from Low Valley as, during the early 1960s, most of the original colliery houses in Hope Street, Providence Street and George Street were demolished after a life of 100 years. In 1971, when the population of Darfield had reached 7,739, further demolition occurred in the Snape Hill area and many of the houses provided for Houghton Main Colliery miners in Havelock Road and New Street were cleared. Additional demolition of colliery housing in Low Valley saw Elliott's Terrace demolished and become the site of a council depot and houses have also been cleared in Station Road. At the same time, extensive private house building activities were taking place in Darfield, particularly along Upperwood Road.

At the time of writing, the former colliery community of Snape Hill consists of a handful of properties on Snape Hill Road that escaped the demolition programme of the 1970s, although some of these are presently derelict. Although most of the older houses of Low Valley and the George Hotel have been demolished and replaced with modern housing, several of the later colliery houses remain on Stonyford Road and Station Road. Some of the chapels, schools and clubs in Low Valley have been demolished or rebuilt, both sports stadiums have disappeared and a new industrial estate has been built at Low Valley following the closure of the local pits. The water filled clay pits which once provided an impromptu swimming pool during the 1926 General Strike, have been infilled and the Darfield Colliery muck stack, once smouldering away and towering above the houses of Low Valley, has been totally removed from the landscape.

However, the history and heritage of the area is promoted by the Darfield Amenity Society and one of the society's greatest achievements has been the opening in 2001 of the Maurice Dobson Museum & Heritage Centre. Here visitors can view the unusual antiques and curios collected by local shopkeeper Maurice Dobson, visit the art gallery and café, whilst upstairs rooms feature a whole plethora of local history items, including bricks from James Gooddy's brickyard, coal from local pits, cigarette dispensing devices issued by Camplejohn Brothers, toys produced in Arthur Greenwood's Darfield Toy Factory and working models of colliery headgears created by modelmaker Alan Mellor.

Elsecar, Hemingfield & Jump

Elsecar is pleasantly situated in the valley of the Knoll Beck, a small tributary of the River Dearne. Although it wasn't mentioned in the Domesday Book in 1086 when the country was documented following the Norman Conquest, Hoyland to the north was recorded as *Holand* and Wentworth to the south was recorded as *Winteworde*, both these settlements being located on higher ground and overlooking the Elsecar valley. The name of Elsecar is probably derived from *Aelfsige*, an Old English personal name, and *kjarr*, an old Norse name meaning brushwood. The land in the area had been awarded to Roger de Busli of Tickhill Castle and Earl de Warenne of Conisbrough Castle. However, the estate subsequently passed into the hands of Thomas Watson-Wentworth (1693-1750). Thomas Watson-Wentworth was the Earl of Malton and the first Marquis of Rockingham and he constructed Wentworth Woodhouse in 1725 as a family home.

Coal mining in the area had been undertaken on a small scale since medieval times and in 1161, the monks of Kirkstead Abbey were working the Parkgate seam near Thorpe Hesley to the west. However, the Barnsley coal seam, at a shallow depth beneath the Knoll Beck valley, became the main prize and in 1750 Richard Bingley was working Elsecar Old Colliery on a lease from the Marquis of Rockingham with coal being transported to overland markets. In 1752, Thomas Watson-Wentworth took control of the pit from Richard Bingley, subsequently sinking additional shafts, but these operations were very small affairs and, by 1771, Elsecar only consisted of six cottages near Elsecar Green. The surrounding area was rural in nature featuring many scattered farms and cottages owned by the estate. However, in 1783, William Fitzwilliam, the fourth Earl Fitzwilliam, inherited the Watson-Wentworth estates, making him one of the largest landowners in the country. Earl Fitzwilliam was keen to exploit the coal reserves on his estate and, together with several other landowners, he promoted the Dearne & Dove Canal Company which received royal assent in 1793, with the canal opening a terminal basin at Elsecar in 1798.

On 25 September 1795, Earl Fitzwilliam opened Elsecar New Colliery as a fresh venture intended to export coal via the forthcoming canal network to markets throughout the country. The new colliery was in an area which became known as Distillery Side following the opening of a short-lived distillery. The pit was equipped with a Newcomen beam engine - an atmospheric steam engine which pumped water from the underground workings. This crucial step forward in mining technology had the effect of lowering the water table and draining the water from the rocks beneath the surface, enabling the safe working of the coal. In 1795, Earl Fitzwilliam constructed a row of 15 substantial stone built cottages facing Elsecar Green. These cottages were known as Old Row and were built to accommodate the first workers and six more were built at Skiers Hall.

Following the opening of the canal, in 1800, another ten cottages, now known as Station Row, were constructed on Wath Road. At the time the famous architect, John Carr of York, was working for Earl Fitzwilliam and these cottages may represent some of his work. They are very elegantly designed with the two end and two central cottages being three storeys in height and projecting forward of the building line. With more workers now engaged at the pit, production increased and in 1810, 26,462 tons of coal were dispatched by barge from Elsecar Basin on the Dearne & Dove Canal.

In 1837, a row of 28 stone cottages was erected along Wath Road and named Reform Row after the 1832 Reform Act. These cottages gently follow the curve of the road and were again built to a very high standard. Later that year Earl Fitzwilliam opened another colliery at Jump. This was located some distance from the canal; therefore, a wagonway was constructed along the valley of a little stream to convey the coal to wharfs on the canal. Another inclined wagonway was built from the Elsecar Canal Basin across Elsecar Green in front of the cottages of Old Row to the Milton Iron foundry and blast furnaces at Stubbin operated by ironmaster George Dawes. This wagonway continued further westwards to ironstone pits in Tankersley Park and coal and pig iron was now exported from Elsecar with limestone imported for use in the ironworks. Cottages were constructed at Stubbin Bottom, New Houses and Milton Road for foundry workers and in 1840, the fifth Earl Fitzwilliam built the Church of the Holy Trinity on Church Street at a cost of £2,500, together with a Reading Room and Sunday School. Elsecar was subsequently established as an independent parish in 1844 formed from part of the parish of Wath-upon-Dearne.

Above Left: The cottages of Low Row were constructed in 1795 to house miners at Elsecar New Colliery and were built to a very high standard. Just visible beneath the caption on this postcard by an anonymous photographer are the rails of the incline railway that was installed in the late 1830s to Milton Ironworks. Today Low Row forms part of the Elsecar Conservation area fronting Elsecar Green. The first families may have come from elsewhere on the Fitzwilliam estate, having previously worked at the many farms, but diverted to work in the Earl's more profitable mining venture, returning to assist on the farms during harvest time or when demand for coal was low.

Above Right: An important development in 1853 was the opening of the Miners Lodging House on Fitzwilliam Street. This was a handsome three storey structure which provided 22 rooms for single miners and featured the first indoor bath in the village, together with a hot water geyser. The building later became Elsecar Working Men's Club as shown in this postcard by Frank Parkin. However, for a long time the hostel stood derelict, but, on 23 April 1974, its architectural significance was recognised when it became a Grade II listed building. In 1982, the building was tastefully restored and converted into 14 apartments by the architectural practice of Nuttall Yarwood & Partners.

In 1840, Earl Fitzwilliam opened another pit further down the canal at Tingle Bridge. This was called Elsecar Low Colliery and was provided with a canal basin and eight new cottages. A further ten cottages were built at Tingle Bridge together with a public house named the Elephant & Castle. Shortly afterwards, Earl Fitzwilliam renamed some of his pits: Elsecar Old Colliery of 1750 was renamed Elsecar High Colliery; Elsecar New Colliery of 1795 was renamed Elsecar Mid Colliery; and Elsecar Low Colliery of 1840 was renamed Hemingfield Colliery. The high quality of housing provided by Earl Fitzwilliam for his workforce was recognised by the government's Mines Inspector Seymour Tremenheere, when in 1845 he published a Report on the 'Mining Population in parts of Scotland and Yorkshire'. He described the Elsecar accommodation as 'of a class superior in size and arrangement, and in the conveniences attached, to those belonging to the working classes'. Tremenheere described the Elsecar cottages as consisting of 'four rooms and a pantry, a small back court, ash pit, pig sty and a garden which is kept neat with flowers and paving stones and walled in with a low gate to prevent children from straying into the road'. He stated that 'proper conveniences were attached to every six of seven houses and kept perfectly clean. The rent for the cottage and garden is two shillings per week and each man can also hire an additional 300 square yards for potato ground'.

In 1851, the population of Elsecar and Stubbin was recorded as 977 and the settlement was home to numerous colliery and iron workers. That year the South Yorkshire Railway opened a terminus adjacent to Elsecar Canal Basin, thus securing additional markets for Elsecar coal. Around this time, Earl Fitzwilliam opened a series of industrial workshops to service the manufacturing needs of his estate and a private railway station was built named Rockingham Station, used to convey the Earl and his guests to race meetings at Doncaster. In 1836, a small village school had opened on Distillery Side but this was now hemmed in between the canal and railway. Therefore, in 1852, a new National School was provided on Church Street. Meanwhile, the road to Hoyland was named Fitzwilliam Street and additional cottages were built together with a public house, the Milton Arms, and the Miners Hostel on Fitzwilliam Street opened in 1853. That year Elsecar Mid Colliery closed and was subsequently used as a pumping station and a new pit named Simon Wood Colliery was opened nearby.

In the meantime, Earl Fitzwilliam continued to improve the facilities on his booming industrial empire at Elsecar. In 1856, a new market opened and, in 1857, the newly established Elsecar, Wentworth & Hoyland Gas Light & Coke Company erected coke ovens to generate gas for street lighting. Several shops opened in the village including a Post Office and another public house named the Market Hotel. In 1860, another 15 cottages were constructed at Cobcar Row and over the following years further housing and facilities were built on St Helen's Street, Cherry Tree Avenue and at Stubbin which was developing as a commercial centre along the road from Elsecar to Hoyland. St Helen's Roman Catholic Church & School opened in 1864, Elsecar Congregational Church in 1881, and a Primitive Methodist Chapel and Wesleyan Reform Methodist Chapel were also constructed. Additional public houses now included the Butchers Arms, the Forge Inn and the Fitzwilliam Arms. In 1870, a market hall opened, later named Milton Hall, with the Barnsley British Co-operative Society erecting a branch on Church Street in 1893.

By 1881, the population of Elsecar had reached 2,500 and further housing was provided at Meadow Row on Wath Road, together with another public house named the Ship Inn, with St John's Wesleyan Methodist Chapel opening behind. The school was enlarged to accommodate 430 children and by the canal was a large flour mill named EFW Mill (Earl Fitzwilliam's Wentworth Mill). By now the growing of vegetables and flowers was catered for in numerous allotments and, in 1892, a cricket ground and pavilion opened on Armroyd Lane. In 1891, a Local Board had been elected to run the affairs of the community and they adapted the Hoyland Mechanics Institute for use as a Town Hall; in 1894 the Local Board became Hoyland Nether Urban District Council. The village of Hoyland located on the hill a mile north of Elsecar, subsequently developed into a small town of 10,000 people with churches, chapels, schools, shops and a popular market all serving the local colliery communities; such pits included Hoyland Silkstone Colliery and Rockingham Colliery on the Barnsley side of Hoyland.

Above: Earl Fitzwilliam was a keen supporter of community events in the village and, on 29 April 1911, a rifle range was opened at Milton Ironworks and a series of commemorative postcards were published by Edgar Scrivens; this one features Countess Fitzwilliam firing a rifle in front of a crowd of onlookers. Usually the relationship between the men and their master was a particularly sour one in the history of coal mining in this country. However, there was a lot of affection for 'Earl Fitzbillie' from the Elsecar miners and at the christening of Earl and Countess Fitzwilliam's son in 1911, a large silver cup was presented at the festivities. When open cast mining in the 1940s threatened to damage Wentworth Woodhouse, the Elsecar miners threatened to go on strike to protect the huge house belonging to their landlord. *(Brian Brownsword Collection)*

In 1903, Elsecar High and Elsecar Mid Collieries had ceased working and the Barnsley coal seam was now worked out in the valley. Earl Fitzwilliam decided to sink a large new colliery to exploit the deeper reserves across the whole area. This pit was sunk to the south of the canal and named Elsecar Main Colliery; it commenced production in 1908. By this time Earl Fitzwilliam owned around 150 cottages in Elsecar and many more had been provided by speculative builders. However, Earl Fitzwilliam created a new settlement on Cobcar Lane to house some of the new workforce at Elsecar Main Colliery. The new development was built following the popular Garden City Principles of the time and was named Elsecar Model Village and 78 houses were constructed in 1911 on Lifford Place and Strafford Avenue. These commodious houses were built in pairs, and groups of three, four and five and were provided with front and rear gardens and three or four bedrooms. The building line and housing types varied with large gables and various amounts of exposed brick and cement render.

In 1910, the area adjoining Elsecar Reservoir opened as Elsecar Park which incorporated flower gardens, tennis courts, bandstand, paddling pool and a tea pavilion. However, Frank Parkin, a keen amateur photographer who owned a barber's shop on Fitzwilliam Street, decided on an unusual scheme to promote the Elsecar Park as a tourist destination and inland resort. He submitted some photographs of the park and reservoir to the *Sheffield Star* with the caption 'Elsecar-by-the-Sea' and touted the idea that the steel workers of the industrial City might like to visit Elsecar-by-the-Sea for a day of leisure and pleasure. The idea was tremendously successful, and train loads of visitors arrived at Elsecar Railway Station having travelled from Sheffield. The shores of the reservoir were lined with sand and named 'the beach' and 'the north shore' and boat landing stages were constructed. During the summer months, thousands of visitors came to Elsecar-by-the-Sea from Sheffield, Rotherham, Barnsley and the Dearne Valley. The day trippers could paddle and bathe in the reservoir and take boating trips. The enterprising Frank Parkin produced souvenir postcards of Elsecar-by-the-Sea to sell to visitors and their sales funded his developing photographic business. Over the following years, he produced a substantial photographic archive depicting Elsecar, Hoyland and Wentworth.

Above: Two of Frank Parkin's postcards of Elsecar-by-the-Sea depicting 'The Children's Corner' and 'The Beach'. The captions to most of Frank Parkin's photographic work feature his initials FP and represent a fine record of photographs focused on Elsecar and district. It would be a worthy tribute to the man to perhaps one day see an exhibition of his work.

During 1912, King George V and Queen Mary undertook a series of tours of the industrial and mining regions of the country with the aim of 'acquainting themselves with the lives, work and homes of their industrial subjects'. The first tour was to South Wales and the second trip was a four-day tour of the West Riding of Yorkshire and the royal party were accommodated at Wentworth Woodhouse. On 9 July 1912, the royal party visited Rotherham Clifton Park, Silverwood Colliery and Woodlands Model Village before breaking for lunch at Hickleton Hall. In the afternoon, the cavalcade passed through the Dearne Valley villages of Goldthorpe, Bolton, Wath and West Melton to Elsecar where the King descended Elsecar Main Colliery. The tour was extremely popular and many thousands of people lined the route and bunting and flags decorated the villages.

In 1914, the Elsecar Midland Working Men's Club opened together with the Electra Picture Palace near the Railway Station. However, the First World War arrested any future developments. During the post-war period, Elsecar Main Colliery recruited additional men and participated in the economic boom of the early 1920s. Hoyland Nether Urban District Council erected 152 council houses on Cobcar Avenue, Strafford Avenue and Howse Street in Elsecar and similar estates in Hoyland. These were all built in semi-detached pairs and provided with front and rear gardens. After the Second World War, to alleviate the housing shortage, the local authority provided 142 prefab bungalows on Bevan Avenue and Tomlinson Avenue.

Above: The Royal tour of 1912 was accompanied by Regina Press of Doncaster who issued numerous picture postcards of the event, including this example showing the arrival of the King at Elsecar Colliery. The King descended the pit and toured the underground workings, despite having just received news of the terrible explosion at Cadeby Main Colliery. Later that evening the King and Queen made an unscheduled visit to the offices of the Denaby & Cadeby Main Collieries Ltd at Conisbrough where crowds had gathered at the pit gates waiting for the news about the men trapped underground and the fate of the rescue parties who were affected by a second explosion. The explosion killed 91 men, including William Henry Pickering, the Chief Inspector of Mines for Yorkshire & the North Midlands. A memorial was unveiled to the victims of the disaster in Denaby Main Cemetery in 2012, and in 2017, the Friends of Hyde Park Cemetery in Doncaster commenced an appeal to restore William Pickering's grave.

In the early 1950s, the NCB established the Coal Industry Housing Association to construct new estates intended to house miners and their families displaced from the older coalfields of the country in favour of the highly productive Yorkshire and East Midlands Coalfield. At Elsecar, 132 houses were built on Welland Crescent. These were all identical in style to other CIHA estates and constructed from precast reinforced concrete panels. At the same time, Hoyland Nether Urban District Council constructed 184 houses and bungalows in Gray Street, Zetland Road and Cobcar Lane and many Scottish miners moved into these new developments. During the 1960s and 1970s private housing estates have been built in the area and Elsecar has grown with Hoyland and Jump to form one continuous area of urban development. In 1983, Elsecar Main Colliery was closed bringing the era of coal mining in the area to an end; there was also demolition of some of the cottages on Fitzwilliam Street due to mining subsidence.

Above: The streets of Elsecar were decorated with bunting to celebrate the visit of King George and Queen Mary and were captured in a series of photographs published by Frank Parkin. This example shows Reform Row festooned with bunting and the Yorkshire Mining Association's Hemingfield Colliery banner was hung across Wath Road. The Ship Inn was one of numerous public houses in the Elsecar area. Unlike some landowners who were keen to imposed temperance ideas on their communities, Earl Fitzwilliam obviously had no problems with the 'evils of alcohol'! The pub was one of many owned by the Wath brewery, Whitworth Son & Nephew, and at the time of the photograph, Enoch Baxter was the landlord. The Ship Inn was demolished in the 1920s and rebuilt as new premises set further back from the road.

Above: Two views captured by Elsecar photographer Frank Parkin featuring the Model Village: the development of 78 houses constructed by Earl Fitzwilliam for miners at Elsecar Main Colliery on Cobcar Lane, Strafforth Avenue and Clifford Place. The two last street names represent Fitzwilliam family connections; Lifford Place is derived from William Fitzwilliam, Baron of Lifford in County Donegal, Ireland, and Strafford Avenue is named after Thomas Wentworth, first Earl of Strafford.

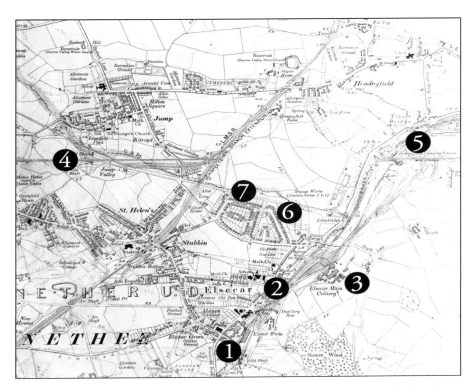

Above: Extract from the 1932 Ordnance Survey Map showing the Elsecar, Hemingfield and Jump area. **1:** Elsecar Workshops (now Elsecar Heritage Centre). **2:** Elsecar Canal Basin. **3:** Elsecar Main Colliery. **4:** Jump Pit. **5:** Hemingfield Pit. **6:** Elsecar Model Village. **7:** Hoyland Nether U D Council Housing (mid-1920s). *(Taken from the Dearne District Traction Act Map – Paul Fox Collection)*

However, recognising the unique architecture of the Elsecar Workshops, the Newcomen engine and the industrial settlement of Elsecar, the West Riding County Council designated the area as a conservation area in 1974 and Barnsley Council subsequently created the Elsecar Heritage Centre as a tourist attraction, complete with small industrial units, shops, galleries, a museum, an antiques centre and an exhibition hall. Following the awarding of National Lottery Heritage Grants, the unique Newcomen engine was restored to working order in 2010 and the site now hosts open days for visitors. The Elsecar Heritage Railway operates a passenger service using preserved locomotives along the former South Yorkshire Railway from Earl Fitzwilliam's Rockingham Station, passing the sites of Elsecar Colliery and Hemingfield Colliery to a proposed terminus near Cortonwood Colliery. Restoration work on the canal basin has seen the holding of waterway festivals and boating trips and in 2014 the Friends of Hemingfield Colliery took over the former Hemingfield pumping station with the aim of restoring the buildings together with the Hemingfield canal basin. The Dearne and Dove canal reservoir has been incorporated into Elsecar Park where the annual Elsecar-by-the-Sea festival is held and the whole area, together with the attractions in Wentworth village, makes for a charming visit, a fitting celebration of the industrial heritage of the area through the pursuit of coal.

Hemingfield & Jump

The two small hamlets of Hemingfield and Jump overlook Elsecar and the valley containing the Knoll Beck and the branch of the Dearne & Dove Canal.

Prior to the opening of Earl Fitzwilliam's Elsecar Low Colliery at Tingle Bridge in 1837, the hamlet of Hemingfield consisted of a handful of cottages including Skiers House and Beech House and several farms: Hill Top Farm, Hemingfield Farm, Low Farm and Lundhill Farm. The hamlet was situated a short distance to the east of Jump along the lane to Wombwell and, like Jump, it enjoyed a pleasant southerly aspect. In 1826, the Ellis Church of England School was built by the Trustees of the George Ellis Charity. The school was later extended in 1877 to accommodate 300 children and was partially funded by shares invested by the charity in the Dearne & Dove Canal. Following the opening of Elsecar Low Colliery, cottages were built by speculative builders along the main street and at Hemingfield Green, whilst at Tingle Bridge, a small colliery community developed adjacent to the canal which included a public house, the Elephant & Castle. In Hemingfield shops and a Post Office were provided together with a public house named the Milton Arms; the Hemingfield Working Men's Club and a branch of the Barnsley British Co-operative Society were also opened. Miners from Lundhill Colliery also lived in the local community and Elsecar Low Colliery was renamed Hemingfield Colliery. In 1886, a Wesleyan Methodist Chapel opened and the Dearne Valley Water Board provided two reservoirs to supply the area with water. Shortly afterwards in 1893, Wombwell Urban District Council opened Hemingfield & Jump Cemetery between the two settlements and the main road through the settlement was named Cemetery Road. In the 1920s, the Miners Welfare Fund provided a recreation ground. Hemingfield Colliery closed in 1920, but the pit passed into the ownership of the South Yorkshire Pumping Association who maintained it as a pumping shaft to drain the underground workings. In 1940, they erected the small but distinctive concrete headgear, together with a similar headgear at their other site at Elsecar Mid Colliery. Today the site belongs to the Friends of Hemingfield Colliery who have embarked on the commendable task of restoring the location.

Before Jump Pit was opened by Earl Fitzwilliam in 1840, the surrounding area consisted of a couple of cottages at Kit Royd and Halfway House at the junction of the roads to Hoyland, Elsecar and Wombwell. However, following the opening of the colliery, an area of housing was laid out for the new workforce at Milton Square and houses were built on Milton Road, Fitzwilliam Road, Wentworth Road, Arundel View and along the lane that subsequently became Church Street. The new housing was built by speculative builders and it is said that the settlement received its unusual name because miners had to jump across a stream to get to the pit. The stream flowed down a small valley, known as the Jump Valley or Cobcar Valley, to join the Knoll Beck near the canal; this valley was used to build an incline railway or wagonway to convey coal from the pit. In 1865, a Church of England school opened with accommodation for 220 children on Church Street and in 1880 a Board School was provided with places for 330 children on Roebuck Hill. In 1882, St George's Church and Sunday School was opened as a Chapel of Ease for the parish church in Wombwell. Jump also included a Wesleyan Reform Methodist Church, several shops, a Post Office, a branch of the Barnsley British Co-operative Society and a public house named the Flying Dutchmen. The area was surrounded by allotments and in the early 20th century, a recreation ground with gardens, bowling greens, pavilion and tennis courts was opened. In the 1920s, Wombwell Urban District Council constructed 60 council houses in two small estates either side of the cemetery at Preston Avenue and Hallsworth Avenue. Jump pit closed in the 1890s but its incline railway remained in operation for several years as it now served Hoyland Silkstone

Colliery; today it forms a pleasant walking trail. For a long time the settlement was served by the famous 'Jump Circular' buses of Yorkshire Traction. When intending passengers asked the driver "is this bus was going to Jump?" and were told yes, they always replied "well hold it down while I get on!"

Above Left: Looking east along Cemetery Road into Hemingfield from the railway bridge showing a charming rural scene at the turn of the 20th century, depicted on postcard published by Lamb of Barnsley. Horses and carts were the normal method of transport and on the skyline in the distance is the smoking chimney of Cortonwood Colliery. The building in the centre has now disappeared and some of the housing on the right has been demolished but the five cottages on the left remain.

Above Right: This photograph was taken by Frank Parkin in 1910 and shows a view in the colliery community of Jump showing Church Street from Wentworth Road. Jump Post Office is on the right with the Wesleyan Reform Methodist Church on the left. Most of the buildings depicted in this view have since been demolished although the ones in the centre remain – one housing a shop currently selling the best Pork Pies in the country!

Below: Once known as the bicycle pit due to the arrangement of its winding wheels, the modern concrete headgear at Hemingfield Colliery was installed in 1940 when the pit served as a pumping station. The site is currently managed by The Friends of Hemingfield Colliery. *(Chris Allen, 2015. Licenced for reuse under Creative Commons Licence http://www.geograph.org.uk/photo/4358423)*

Goldthorpe & Highgate

At the time of the 1891 census, Goldthorpe consisted of Hall Farm and six cottages on Goldthorpe Lane with another cottage at Goldthorpe Green, together with a public house, the Horse and Groom Inn, at Goldthorpe Lane Ends. This was the name given to the junction of Goldthorpe Lane and the Barnsley to Doncaster turnpike and a tollhouse was situated at Highgate to the west. The area was governed by Bolton-upon-Dearne Parish Council and the Lord of the Manor was Viscount Halifax of Hickleton Hall, located in the estate village of Hickleton one mile to the east.

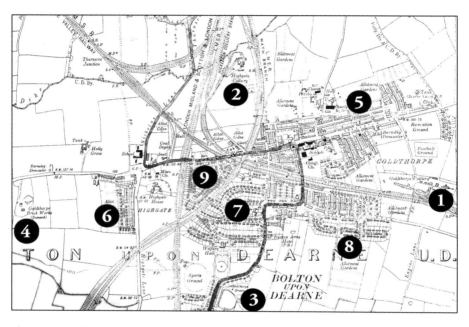

Above: Extract from the 1932 Ordnance Survey Map showing Goldthorpe and Highgate.
1: Goldthorpe Colliery. **2:** Highgate Colliery. **3:** Bolton Brickyard. **4:** Highgate Brickyard. **5:** Hickleton Main Colliery 242 Houses (1895) – Hickleton pit to the north. **6:** George Street BUDC Council Housing (1912). **7:** BUDC Council Housing (1923). **8:** BUDC Council Housing (1924). **9:** Probert Avenue BUDC Council Housing (1925). *(Taken from the Dearne District Traction Act Map – Paul Fox Collection)*

Although mining operations had been recorded in the area when William Marsden was working the Shafton seam, these operations had ceased by 1778 and Goldthorpe remained a rural backwater until 1892 when shaft sinking at Hickleton Main Colliery commenced. Even then, the shaft sinkers lived at Thurnscoe East, where a row of 30 houses had been built and it was expected that most of the colliery houses would be provided at Thurnscoe. However, in 1894, the colliery company purchased a block of land to the north of Doncaster Road from Viscount Halifax and then worked with local builders to lay out a development of 242 terraced houses. This new development was initially referred to as New Goldthorpe to distinguish it from the older cottages on Goldthorpe Lane. The houses were all built by 1895 and occupied by incoming miners and their families, many migrating to the area from elsewhere in

Yorkshire and the old mining districts of the Black Country in the West Midlands. However, the new settlement lacked any educational facilities and for the first few years, New Goldthorpe was quite a raw community, with the children having to walk to the Board Schools in Bolton-upon-Dearne. It wasn't until 1897 when the houses were numbered and the streets given names - West Street, Main Street, East Street and Central Avenue. Many of the new houses were overcrowded, with large families the norm, and in addition, many families took in one or more lodgers who worked at the pit. The back yards were unclean and sewage facilities were primitive, so diseases were rife and infant mortality rates high.

Anticipating the drinking requirements of New Goldthorpe, the Horse & Groom Inn had been purchased by Whitworth's Wath Brewery in 1894, and a handful of properties facing Doncaster Road were used as shops, together with a few wooden lock-up buildings. However, in 1896, to serve the shopping needs of this new community of around 1,000 people, the Doncaster Mutual & Industrial Co-operative Society purchased a site on the south side of Doncaster Road and their new branch opened to the public on 27 January 1897.

In December 1895, Goldthorpe's first church opened on Lockwood Lane. This was a tin structure known as St Alban's Mission Church. In 1897, a small Primitive Methodist Chapel and Goldthorpe Working Men's Club & Institute were both built on Lockwood Lane. However, there was some concern about the overcrowding of the schools in Bolton-upon-Dearne; therefore, in 1897, the West Riding County Council provided new schools at Goldthorpe Lane Ends.

Hickleton Main Colliery Company had opened its own brickworks in 1892, but another site was opened at Goldthorpe Green known as Bolton-on-Dearne Brickyard. Many of the men who worked here were housed in a row of 24 cottages provided by a speculative builder – this later became known as 'Packies Puzzle.' At the time, most house furnishings were purchased on 'easy terms' and when the debt collector or 'packet man' came to collect the weekly payments, a knocking on the internal walls travelled the length of the terrace, giving the inhabitants time to hide from the debt collector, who would be left somewhat puzzled by the fact that nobody in the 24 houses was at home every time he came calling!

In 1899, the population of New Goldthorpe had reached 1,562 with an additional 68 living in the old hamlet and 149 in Packies Puzzle. Therefore Bolton-upon-Dearne Parish Council decided to seek urban status and became Bolton Urban District Council. This enabled the new local authority to exert increased power and influence over the affairs of the area and their first initiatives were the completion of proper sewage facilities, the laying on of fresh water, and a gas supply from the Wath & Bolton Gas Board. This last was initially used for street lighting, for shops and public buildings, but was soon supplied to all the houses. However, Goldthorpe remained a 'rough and ready' settlement at the edge of the mining frontier in the Dearne Valley, likened by some to a town from the Wild West of America. Drinking and public disorder were frequent occurrences, and alcohol fuelled fights were especially common, especially between the women! Therefore, in 1900 the West Riding Constabulary opened a new police station to keep an eye on the inhabitants and many a drunken miner slept the night in the cells!

At the turn of the century, Hickleton Main Colliery continued to expand and further housing was required. This was provided mostly by two builders: Mr Leadley, working at the west end, and Mr Hamilton, working at the east end. Work started around 1902 to the north of Barnsley Road when Mr Leadley over the following years laid out around 200 houses along

King Street, Queen Street, Elizabeth Street, Whitworth Street and Charles Street. Meanwhile, Sidney Hamilton purchased land from Viscount Halifax at the eastern end of Goldthorpe. On this plot, he built the Goldthorpe Family & Commercial Hotel of which he was the proprietor and landlord, the Goldthorpe Hippodrome and Goldthorpe Market. Behind this he also built around 100 houses on Hamilton Road, Doncaster Road, St Mary's Road, Kathleen Street and Nora Street - the last two streets possibly named after his daughters. The Hippodrome burnt down in 1914 but was re-built as the Astoria Dance Hall.

With the increasing building developments, the whole area was now referred to as Goldthorpe from 1904 onwards and Goldthorpe Lane was renamed High Street. At the same time, a large railway cutting was under construction for the Dearne Valley Railway. Mr Leadley purchased the triangular piece of land bounded by the new railway, High Street, and Barnsley Road and constructed an additional 156 houses - including Jackson Street, Railway View and Leadley Street. Many of the houses constructed by Mr Leadley feature a distinctive brick band between the downstairs and upstairs windows and the upper storey was often rendered with cement. This became his 'signature style' and was repeated when Mr Leadley was awarded the contract to construct 1,000 houses forming a Model Village for Askern Main Colliery in 1911.

Above: Goldthorpe Empire Cinema is shown on this postcard of Doncaster Road published by Edgar Scrivens in the late 1920s. Doncaster Road was the main commercial centre – note that most of the shops have their sun blinds lowered. Two small buses are awaiting passengers for Doncaster, the nearest vehicle belonging to G S T Deverew of Thurnscoe. Meanwhile, the group on the right includes a man in a wheelchair - possibly an unfortunate victim of an accident in one of the local pits?

Above: Goldthorpe owes a lot of its development to Sidney Hamilton, who was instrumental in developing Goldthorpe Market. One of Goldthorpe's entrepreneurs, Mr Hamilton also owned the Goldthorpe Hotel, the Hippodrome / Astoria Dance Hall, a motor garage with petrol station and houses in several streets in the area, all built with bricks supplied by his own brickworks named Highgate Brick Company. This view of Goldthorpe Market on Nora Street was published by James Simonton in 1910.

Building operations continued to the south of Doncaster Road at Goldthorpe. Approximately 220 houses were built on Co-operative Street, Victoria Street, Beever Street, Doncaster Road, Cross Street and Claycliffe Terrace. Some of these houses were occupied by miners working at Goldthorpe Colliery which opened in 1910. These housing developments caused the population of Goldthorpe to increase rapidly as people migrated to the area to work in the pits. In 1902, the Primitive Methodist Church moved to larger premises on Doncaster Road, and, in 1904 the schools were enlarged; in addition, the Goldthorpe Working Men's Club moved to larger premises in Co-operative Street. In 1910, Goldthorpe Empire Cinema opened. Two years later a second cinema, Goldthorpe Picture House, joined it. In addition to Goldthorpe Market on Nora Street, another Market Place was provided by the local authority on Market Street.

Above: At Highgate, prior to 1905, the only buildings were the old tollhouse and Highgate House Farm. However, speculative builders turned their attention to this area and around 180 houses were laid out along Barnsley Road, Highgate Lane, William Street and George Street, together with extensive allotments. This postcard view c1910 of Barnsley Road shows two different building styles – a stone fronted brick built terrace (left) and a traditional brick built row (right). In the 1920s, the Halfway Hotel, the Highgate Working Men's Club and a new branch of the Barnsley British Co-operative Society were opened. In 1923, Viscount Halifax donated land for St Michael's Mission Church.

In 1910, Bolton Urban District Council expressed its concern at the standard of the new housing erected and what they thought was profiteering by the private builders in the area. The council therefore proposed to build their own high-quality housing by obtaining loans for their construction and letting the new properties to residents at competitive rates. Following a delay in raising the finances, in 1912, 40 semi-detached council houses were built on George Street and Edward Street in Highgate, complete with large front and rear gardens. This development was one of the earliest council building schemes by a local authority in the country and represents the pride by which the urban district wished to represent its people. It is shame that they were not refurbished as they were demolished in the 1980s. In 1911, the West Riding County Council provided a new school at Highgate.

Following the opening of Barnburgh Main Colliery, Mr Leadley commenced further building operations at Goldthorpe to the south of the Dearne Valley Railway. 178 houses were laid out along Frederick Street, Albert Road, Poplar Avenue, Wellington Street, Princess Road and Barnburgh Lane. Sixty additional properties were constructed as semi-detached houses and many of these were occupied by colliery officials. To the west other speculative builders were active at the same time near the old hamlet of Goldthorpe. The old cottages were demolished and housing was constructed along High Street, Straight Lane, Lesley Road, Orchard Street, Hall Street, with another 120 houses constructed, plus 40 additional semi-detached houses known as 'The Avenues'. By the outbreak of the Second World War, around 1,500 houses had been built at Goldthorpe for miners at Hickleton, Goldthorpe and Barnburgh Collieries. With another pit at Highgate was due to open.

Above: Although St Alban's Mission Church had opened in 1895, the provision of a larger church was considered desirable, and, in 1913, Lord Halifax came to the assistance of the South Yorkshire Coalfields Churches Extension Committee, (an organisation created to raise funds to provide for the spiritual needs of the new colliery communities), with an offer to build and furnish a new church. In 1914, the architect, Alfred Nutt of Slough, drew up plans for a distinctive and most unusual church and vicarage, both constructed from ferro-concrete. This Regina Press postcard shows the arrival of Lord and Lady Halifax for the dedication and opening of the Church of St John the Evangelist and St Mary Magdalene on 18 May 1916. This saw the designation of Goldthorpe as an independent parish of approximately 4,500 people, created from part of the parish of Bolton-upon-Dearne. The unusual ferro-concrete church is well worth a visit.

When the new Goldthorpe church opened, it was reputed that Goldthorpe was still a wild place, vastly overcrowded, and noted for its hard drinking, brawls and fist fighting - Sergeant William Rouston and his team of seven police constables at Goldthorpe Police Station were probably kept very busy. Indeed, whilst raising money for the church, Reverend Saxton stated that there was more need for conversion to Christianity in Goldthorpe than in Africa! Whether the new church had a calming influence on the locals is unknown; however, Goldthorpe Church - described by Sir Nikolaus Pevsner as 'an early example of the use of reinforced concrete in a curious out-of-the-way style'- has certainly gained architectural recognition in the intervening years and is now a Grade II listed building.

Following the end of the First World War, returning service men established the Comrades Club on High Street in 1919, subsequently renamed the Union Jack Club. The local collieries began to increase production and during the early 1920s, recruitment drives led to more families moving to the area. The 1919 Housing Act had empowered local authorities to construct council housing and this largely replaced the provision of housing by speculative builders. Consequently, Bolton Urban District Council constructed a series of estates, with the houses provided with front and rear gardens. Houses were built in pairs or blocks of four and were now of an improved standard compared to their pre-war cousins. To provide bricks for future housing developments, the council purchased the Bolton Brickyard on Furlong Road, stamping their bricks with the legend BUDC. Work commenced in 1922 with the construction of 70 houses in Furlong Road and Park End Road followed by 14 larger properties at Goldthorpe Green and 46 houses in Market Square. In 1923, 276 houses were laid out along Homecroft Road, Hope Avenue, Welfare View and Washington Road. This large development was also served by a new public house, the Buxton Arms, and adjoined the new Miners Welfare Hall & Recreation Ground.

Above Left: The Mining Industry Act (1920) established the British Miners' Welfare Fund which received a penny for every ton of coal produced in the country. The funds raised were used for 'purposes connected with the social well-being, recreation and conditions of living of workers in and about coal mines'. In 1923, the Welfare Hall and Recreation Ground at Goldthorpe Green, one of the finest such developments in the country was opened. The scheme included a cycling and running track, a cricket ground, tennis courts, bowling greens and a park with a bandstand. A football ground was added after the war. In many former mining communities, these Welfare Halls have since been demolished, although the handsome building at Goldthorpe now survives as the venue for the Dearne Valley Play House. Between the pillared portico are a series of artworks commemorating local collieries. The illustration is from a postcard published by Edgar Scrivens in 1923.
Above Right: The Miners Welfare Fund also provided a second recreation ground on Doncaster Road, as shown on this postcard by Arjay Productions of Doncaster dating from the 1960s. The Recreation Ground incorporated playing equipment and sports fields and was positioned between Doncaster Road and Goldthorpe Colliery. The circular water tower, partly visible behind the house on the left, was erected in 1951 and replaced an earlier water tank provided by the Dearne Valley Water Board. The mast behind the house (directly in line with the girl on the roundabout) was the terminal pylon for the Hickleton Colliery aerial ropeway

In 1924, 126 council houses were constructed on Barnburgh Lane, Windermere Avenue, Derwent Gardens and Lindale Gardens. Many miners from Barnburgh moved into these houses, located only a short walk or cycle ride from the pit. Finally, around 1925, to the south of Barnsley Road near Highgate, 168 council houses were built along Probert Avenue, Sankey Square and Lincoln Gardens. Sankey Square was named after the Sankey Commission - led by Sir John Sankey - which led to the passing of the 1919 Coal Industry Commission Act; Probert Avenue was named after Jack Probert, a local councillor.

The economic depression throughout the 1930s put paid to any further housing developments, but three other events are of note: the first was when, following an accident at Hickleton Colliery, photographer and amateur filmmaker, Charles Hanmer, made a film named *Black Diamonds – the true story of coal*. The film depicted daily life in the local collieries and received its premier at London's Marble Arch Cinema, receiving critical acclaim for its realism and gritty depiction of mining life. The second event was the opening of the new Bolton Secondary Modern School in 1936, which later became Dearneside Comprehensive School. The third occurred in 1937 when Bolton-upon-Dearne Urban District Council and Thurnscoe Urban District Council merged to form Dearne Urban District Council. In 1960, a new town hall and council offices were built in the Miners Welfare Park, unfortunately necessitating the removal of the bandstand.

Above: Probert Avenue is named after Jack Probert, a prominent member of Bolton Urban District Council - the local authority which did much to enhance the welfare of the local community. In 1925, a development of 168 houses was provided on Barnsley Road forming the Probert Avenue estate. These two postcards were published by Edgar Scrivens in 1925 and illustrate the new housing.

Following the end of the Second World War, very little further house building occurred in the Goldthorpe area, as the National Coal Board, Dearne Urban District Council and private builders concentrated their efforts in the Thurnscoe and Bolton areas. In 1959, the Arndale Shopping Parade opened in Doncaster Road, replacing some of the first houses dating from 1895, and the new Goldthorpe Library opened in the 1968 designed by architect Neville McMahon – the author's uncle! For a long time the main A635 through Goldthorpe and Highgate was covered with red tarmac, lending the name of 'Red City' to the town - at the time of writing, patches of red tarmac are still visible at Highgate. During the 1950s, 1960s and 1970s, Goldthorpe formed a busy shopping area with a well-supported market and a thriving community. However, the Miner's Strike during 1984-85 caused major hardship in the district, and in November 1984, two teenage brothers, Paul and Darren Holmes, died whilst digging for coal in a railway cutting at Goldthorpe.

Following the Miner's Strike, the closure of the local pits at Highgate (1985), Hickleton (1988), Barnburgh (1989), and Goldthorpe (1994), saw the heart ripped from the local community. Many of the shops, clubs and pubs have closed and many people have left the area. The Buxton Arms, Halfway Hotel and Recreation Club have been demolished, a fate that also surely awaits the Goldthorpe Hotel. However, recent events have seen some renewal in the area. The Miner's Welfare Hall now hosts the Dearne Valley Playhouse and the entrance to the building features artworks depicting the local pits and a new Health Centre has been built on the site of the Dearne Urban District Council Offices. In 2011, the new Dearne Advanced Learning Centre opened and Dearneside Comprehensive School was subsequently demolished. In 2012, derelict housing in Main Street and Central Street was demolished to make way for a new primary school which replaced the original school near the Police Station.

Above Left: Although Doncaster Mutual & Industrial Co-operative Society had opened a store in Doncaster Road in 1897, the Barnsley British Co-operative Society provided a shop on Barnsley Road to serve the new housing developments at Highgate in the 1920s. The Highgate branch, housed in this rather splendid building, was the supermarket of its day. As well as selling general food provisions and supplies it also housed a drapery and furnishing department and sold clothing and shoes. During the 1920s there was no need for the villagers of Goldthorpe to visit other towns as all their shopping requirements could be supplied by the local shops - whether it was a new pair of pit boots from the Co-op or a set of false teeth from Christine Creser's artificial teeth shop! This postcard was published by Thomas Rogers of Goldthorpe around 1925 and the Co-operative building has since been converted into residential flats.

Above Right: Working Men's Clubs were a type of social club that was very popular in industrial areas of the country. The clubs were run on a not-for-profit basis by a committee of local men on behalf of their members and included educational facilities, pool and snooker tables and a licensed bar. They were particularly popular on Friday and Saturday nights when an act or 'turn' would be provided for the entertainment of the members. Another highlight was the annual trip to a coastal resort, which typically involved the chartering of a train or the hiring of a fleet of Yorkshire Traction buses, with some of the larger clubs requiring up to 30 buses or coaches for the trip. The clubs also served as bases for numerous sports teams and Goldthorpe had several such establishments, including the Recreation Club which opened in 1910 and is pictured above in 1925 on this postcard by Thomas Rogers. The building was recently demolished with new housing built on the site.

In 2011, a memorial to the two teenage brothers, Paul and Darren Holmes, was erected in the town centre. However, the scars of the destruction of the coal mining industry remain deep in the area, particularly concerning the way in that the life of the local community was destroyed by the policies of Prime Minister Margaret Thatcher, and, on her death in 2013, many people in Goldthorpe celebrated with a parade culminating with the burning of an effigy of the former Prime Minister.

Great Houghton, Little Houghton and Middlecliffe

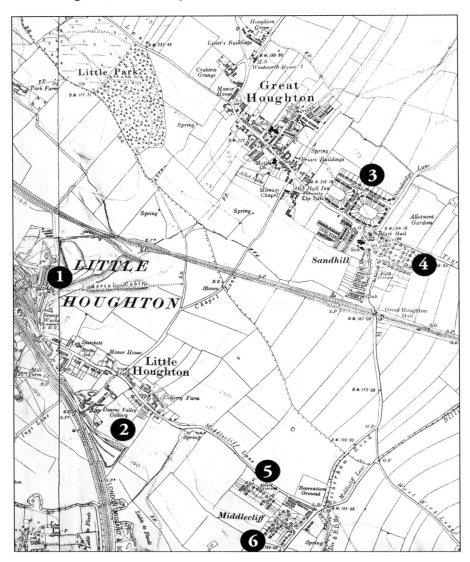

Above: Extract from the 1932 Ordnance Survey Map showing Great & Little Houghton and Sandhill. **1:** Houghton Main Colliery. **2:** Dearne Valley Colliery. **3:** Houghton No 1 Housing Scheme (1921). **4:** Houghton No 2 Housing Scheme (1924). **5:** Little Houghton No 1 Housing Scheme (1924). **6:** Little Houghton No 2 Housing Scheme (1925). *(Taken from the Dearne District Traction Act Map – Paul Fox Collection)*

The hamlets of Great Houghton and Little Houghton were both recorded in the Domesday survey as *Haltone*, when the Lord of the Manor was named *Richard de Sourdeval*, who had been awarded the area following the Norman Conquest. The two settlements became known as Houghton Magna and Houghton Parva respectively and formed part of the Parish of Darfield. Great Houghton was the larger settlement, a typical medieval planned village with cottages lining the main street with long strips of land behind each property. The area passed into the ownership of Sir Edward Rodes who constructed an Elizabethan mansion - Old Hall - as his home and a Chapel of Ease in 1650 for the use of his tenants, saving them the walk to Darfield Church. By 1801, the population of Great Houghton had reached 257 and most people were employed on the local farms.

Prior to the arrival of coal mining in the 1870s, the Lordship of the Manor of Great Houghton had passed into the hands of the Marquis of Crewe, although Earl Fitzwilliam of Wentworth Woodhouse owned 1,000 acres of land in Great Houghton and Billingley. Old Hall had now become an inn and the village featured a Post Office, a Wesleyan Methodist Church and a Public Elementary School which had opened in 1873 with accommodation for 150 boys and girls and 70 infants. At the western end of the village, near Houghton Green, was a Manor House and Crabtree Grange, whilst sandstone quarries were being worked adjacent to Park Lane, the bridleway leading to Grimethorpe.

In 1871, Little Houghton was a small hamlet with a population of 96. The settlement consisted of stone built cottages adjoining an ancient cross, a watermill on the River Dearne, a Manor House and several farms: Mill Farm, Beech House Farm, Park Farm, Edderthorpe Farm and Colliery Farm - the last possibly named from early shallow coal mining operations in the area. A footpath led across the fields to the north to Great Houghton and another one crossed the River Dearne to the south leading to Darfield. Little Houghton and its 800 surrounding acres were now owned by Charles Wright of Bolton Hall in Bolton-le-Bowland in North Yorkshire. However, on 1 January 1873, Charles Wright signed a lease with a consortium of colliery promotors for the Barnsley seam of coal beneath his estate and Houghton Main Colliery was sunk adjacent to the Midland Railway line, with coal production commencing in 1878.

However, rather surprisingly, the main colliery workforce was initially housed some distance away at Snape Hill in Darfield, which entailed a rather long walk to the pit across the fields and over the footbridge on the River Dearne. The reason for this is unclear: perhaps a clause in the lease prohibited the provision of colliery housing on Charles Wright's estate. Speculative builders also built isolated terraces elsewhere, including several small rows in Great Houghton village, a row of 15 houses named Lister's Buildings at Houghton Green and 20 houses near Billingley Cross Roads at a location that subsequently became known as Middlecliffe. Another small isolated colliery community was constructed at Sandhill near Great Houghton.

In 1903, Dearne Valley Colliery opened. Additional families migrated to the area and most of these were accommodated at Snape Hill, Darfield Bridge and Middlecliffe. By 1911, the population of Little Houghton and Middlecliffe numbered 498, Great Houghton totalled 1,735, with the rural village of Billingley numbering 193. In 1908, a new Wesleyan Methodist Chapel and School was erected in Great Houghton at a cost of £1,400. The following year saw the opening of the 45th branch of the Barnsley British Co-operative Society. Additional speculatively built terraces were constructed on Milton Street and School Street and Great Houghton Working Men's Club opened in the High Street. The expanding population had caused the village school to become overcrowded; therefore, the West Riding County Council constructed a new school at Sandhill in 1910 with accommodation for 160 junior children and 110 infants. Adjoining the school another area of housing was provided in the same year with 85 houses built in Rotherham Road, Cross Street and Dearne Street. Fifty of these houses feature gables above the bedroom windows and may be the work of Messrs Green Brothers of Rotherham, as they appear identical to houses provided by that firm at Dinnington Colliery and at Langwith Colliery in Derbyshire.

Above Left: At Little Houghton, the colliery company provided housing for colliery officials and management. The first colliery houses formed this row of twelve cottages known as Deputy Row, on Ings Lane. As the name implies, these were provided for colliery deputies, although Number 4 was used as a sub Post Office. By 1891, the population of Little Houghton was 288 with 620 in Great Houghton. This postcard was published c1905 by W Stables of Darfield and the houses were demolished in the 1970s

Above Right: Sandhill developed as a colliery community in the 1890s and 1900s and is pictured here on this postcard by an anonymous photographer. It is taken from the railway bridge over the Dearne Valley Railway. Around 120 cottages were built on Sand Hill Terrace, Victoria Terrace, Field Terrace, Rotherham Road, Turner Road, New street and Edward Street. The settlement included Sand Hill Working Men's Club – known as the bottom club - William Clarkson's grocers and off-licence, a newsagent and a fish and chip shop. *(Chris Sharp – Old Barnsley)*

Following the end of the First World War, housing developments were provided by Hemsworth Rural District Council, taking advantage of government loans and subsidies made available to local authorities to encourage house building to a higher standard. The early 1920s were a period of economic growth for the collieries of the area and, by 1925, Houghton Main Colliery employed a workforce of 2,523. In 1921, Hemsworth Rural District Council prepared plans for the Houghton Number 1 Housing Scheme, a development of 96 properties on Rotherham Road, Mount Avenue, Pleasant Avenue and Stone Bridge Lane, designed by architect's H G Wagstaff of Doncaster and R Higginbottom of Thurnscoe. The houses were built in blocks of two and four and included a gas, water and electrical supplies and inside were flushing toilets, facilities lacked by most of the pre-war houses. Three bedrooms and a bathroom were provided upstairs and the new estate incorporated front and rear gardens and two large communal areas intended for recreational grounds. The houses were built from a distinctive red brick and are identical to the Red City houses at Grimethorpe constructed at the same time.

In 1923, the Miners Welfare Fund constructed the Welfare Hall and Miners Welfare Club at the junction of Rotherham Road and Thurnscoe Lane and in 1924 Houghton Number 2 Housing Scheme was constructed by Hemsworth Rural District Council. This was a development of 50 houses (extended to 60 houses in 1925) forming Byron Street, Ebenezer

Street, John Street and Thurnscoe Lane. These were all semi-detached properties with their upper storeys covered in concrete render and again built to a high standard, with gardens and three bedrooms and a bathroom upstairs.

At the same time, Hemsworth Rural District Council were undertaking building operations at Middlecliffe. The Little Houghton Number 1 Housing Scheme of 1924 consisted of 30 houses on George Street, John Street and Albert Crescent. Some of these houses were built in blocks of four and featured a downstairs bathroom, so that as miners came off shift in their dirty clothing, they could go straight to the bathroom without soiling the rest of the house, as this was a time before the widespread use pithead baths. In 1925, the local authority constructed Little Houghton Number 2 Housing Scheme, a development of 50 semi-detached houses on Rotherham Road, Charles Street and Mary Street. Hemsworth Rural District Council also constructed a sewage works to serve Sandhill and Great Houghton and Barnsley Rural District Council constructed another sewage plant to serve Middlecliffe and Billingley. With these developments, Hemsworth Rural Council provided 146 houses at Sandhill and 80 houses at Middlecliffe, but another proposed council development of 12 houses and a park on Albert Crescent was never built. At Little Houghton, four semi-detached houses were built opposite the Manor House for Houghton Main colliery officials and six semi-detached houses were built opposite Beech House for Dearne Valley Colliery officials; however, it is unclear whether these houses were provided by the local authority or the colliery companies themselves. Around 1925 the Miners Welfare Fund opened a recreation ground and sports pavilion at Middlecliffe and another smaller recreation ground at Little Houghton together with a Miners Institute building.

In 1907, the Dearne Valley Railway had opened a new railway passing beneath Rotherham Road at Sandhill. They provided a railway station named Great Houghton Halt, and provided an infrequent passenger service to Grimethorpe and Wakefield in one direction and Goldthorpe and Edlington in the other. However, bus operators stepped forward to provided quicker and more direct services to local towns and, by 1930, Sydney McAdoo, Camplejohn Brothers, George White and Larratt Pepper were operating from Great Houghton to Barnsley; George White, Greenhow Brothers and Camplejohn Brothers were providing links to Wombwell including several pit buses from Houghton Main and Dearne Valley collieries, and George White, F Stewardson and Yorkshire Traction were operating to Doncaster.

By 1930, the housing developments at Sandhill and Great Houghton were only separated by single fields on both sides of Rotherham Road. However, the economic depression during the 1930s and the Second World War put a stop to any future developments apart from the building of some bungalows in Great Houghton for retired miners in 1936. However, in the 1950s, the Coal Industry Housing Association constructed 88 prefabricated reinforced concrete houses at Middlecliffe on Queens Avenue and Windsor Crescent. These were provided for incoming miners mostly from Scottish coalfields where some of the pits were facing closure and where the NCB was encouraging men to move to South Yorkshire. Hemsworth Rural District Council also provided another 26 houses on Potts Crescent, although some of these may have been temporary prefabs as they have since been demolished. However, at Sandhill, a larger development of houses and bungalows was proposed for Wescoe Avenue, Norfolk Road and John Street, although only 86 properties were eventually built.

In the 1960s and 1970s, several of the old farms at Little Houghton were demolished, together with Deputy Row on Ings Lane and the Miners Institute. The area was now situated in the shadow of the Houghton Main spoil heap, which was over 300 feet in height. In 1982, this was grassed over and landscaped under a scheme promoted by South Yorkshire County Council. However, one of the saddest losses to the area was the demolition of the Elizabethan Old Hall Inn at Great Houghton following a fire, although a modern replacement public house was constructed on the site. Modern houses have filled the gap between Great Houghton and Sandhill and the combined settlement is now commonly referred to as Great Houghton.

In 1991 Dearne Valley Colliery closed, followed by Houghton Main Colliery in 1994, and the colliery buildings were cleared. Some open cast mining took place on the site and in 1998 a new road was constructed from Middlecliffe to Grimethorpe to improve transport links with the surrounding area. The original village school in Great Houghton has been demolished, together with the earlier Wesleyan Methodist Chapel and the replacement Old Hall Inn. In 2007, the school built back in 1910 was demolished and replaced with a new school constructed under a Public Private Finance Initiative. Great Houghton Welfare features a memorial garden to all those who worked in the coal mining industry and one of the pit wheels has been erected as a memorial at Little Houghton. However, what is striking about Little Houghton is how quiet it is now; most of the houses have been demolished and replaced by woodland and the colliery site is grassed over and silent, although a large warehouse has been built on the site of the coal preparation plant to the west. The lane to Little Houghton is a dead end with no through traffic and the peace is only disturbed by the bus service that still turns around in the former colliery car park, a far cry from when thousands of miners would be bussed into the pit or walk across the fields from Darfield and Great Houghton.

Above: Rotherham Road pictured in the 1930s by James Simonton. The bus belongs to George White and is shown parked outside the family home, one of the new properties provided by Hemsworth Rural District Council in 1921. The vehicle is a Reo Sprinter with seating for 20 passengers and was registered WX 3855 in 1930. George White operated service buses from Great Houghton to Wombwell and Barnsley but these were sold to Yorkshire Traction on 28 November 1936. However, he continued to operate pit buses until 1952.

Grimethorpe

Grimethorpe was first recorded in the 13th century as *Grim's torp* deriving its name from '*Grim*' - a Viking invader who had settled in the area and '*torp*', a Scandinavian name for an outlying farm or hamlet. In contrast, the nearby village of Brierley was a much older settlement located on the hilltop to the north and was first recorded in the Domesday Survey of 1086. Brierley consisted of cottages, farms and Brierley Hall plus the medieval deer park and manor house at Hall Steads. This overlooked Grimethorpe which prior to 1891 was a simple hamlet consisting of Ferry Moor Farm, Foldhead Farm, Manor Farm, Oak House, Mill Cottages and Grimethorpe Cottages, together with a small school erected in 1868 and a Primitive Methodist Chapel which opened the following year. To the north, Grimethorpe Hall had been built in 1669 for the Seaton family; the Lindley Family occupied Brierley Hall. However, in 1617, the Lord of the Manor of Brierley and Grimethorpe and its agricultural estate of 4,000 acres passed to Sir George Saville of Rufford Abbey in Nottinghamshire. During the 1700s, the Saville family were mining the Shafton seam, possibly along the outcrop at Brierley, but these operations were short lived and the area soon returned to agriculture.

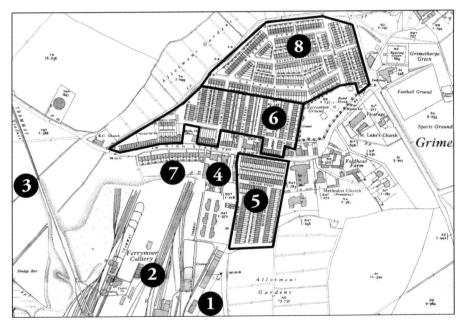

Above: Extract from the Ordnance Survey 1930 1:2500 Map showing the centre of Grimethorpe: **1:** Grimethorpe Colliery to the south. **2:** Ferrymoor Colliery. **3:** Tramway from Brierley Colliery. **4:** Carlton House – the Colliery Offices. **5:** First area of housing pre-1900. **6:** Second Area of housing 1900-1905. **7:** Deputy Row c1907. **8:** Seaside Estate 1910-1912.

In 1869, St Pauls Church was built in Brierley as a Chapel of Ease to St Peter's Church in Felkirk some distance away. By this time, the estate had been inherited by George Savile Foljambe of Aldwarke Hall near Rotherham and subsequently passed to Francis John Savile

Foljambe of Osberton Hall near Worksop - who signed a lease for the coal beneath the estate with the Mitchell Main Colliery Company in 1893. The latter subsequently commenced work on sinking the shafts at Grimethorpe Colliery. Coal was reached in 1897 when the colliery was taken over by the neighbouring Carlton Main Colliery Company Ltd which also opened a brickyard. From 1894, recognising the forthcoming industrial developments, the Grimethorpe area was placed under the jurisdiction of the newly established Hemsworth Rural District Council.

To work the new pit, the colliery company recruited men from the local area as well as from the older coalfields of Nottinghamshire, Derbyshire and the West Midlands. Several men transferred from Carlton Main Colliery near Barnsley which was facing the exhaustion of its coal reserves. To house the new workforce the colliery company laid out 133 terraced houses in six rows to the south of High Street around 1898, together with a detached building named Carlton House which served as the colliery offices. The northern side of High Street was designated as the main shopping area and it included a Post Office, the Grimethorpe Hotel, the 52nd branch of the Barnsley Co-operative Society a new Wesleyan Methodist Chapel and a parade of shops provided by a speculative builder. Building operations continued to the north of High Street with a series of terraced rows built perpendicularly to High Street totalling 103 houses.

Above Left: The rural nature of Grimethorpe is evident from this postcard of Church Street published by G A Fillingham of Cudworth which features Grimethorpe Club and the Mill Cottages. The postcard dates from around 1910 when Grimethorpe Green became Church Street; St Luke's Church is behind the railings on the right.
Above Right: A direct contrast to the rural view above is provided by this James Simonton postcard depicting a grim looking western end of High Street totally devoid of any vegetation. These houses were built around 1905 and include 20 houses forming Deputy Row on the right constructed by Herbert Mollekin. *(Andrew McGarrigle Collection)*

By the time of the 1901 census, the population of the new colliery community and the old Grimethorpe hamlet had increased to 1,684 and many of the new houses were vastly overcrowded – and many families took in lodgers, usually single men who worked at the pit. Several of the streets were not named, being simply referred to as One Street, Two Street, Three Street etc. The original village school was overcrowded, despite having been enlarged in 1898 by the colliery company, and the new settlement lacked a permanent church, although worshippers had been using a wooden hut as a temporary building. However, on 11 June 1902, the Ecclesiastical Parish of Grimethorpe was established from within the parish of Felkirk and plans were brought forward for a new church and school. The colliery company owned Fold Head Farm and donated sites for the new school and church; the latter was constructed at a cost of £6,500 subscribed by Francis Foljambe. Designed by Charles Hodgson Fowler, the prolific ecclesiastical architect, the new St Luke's Church and Vicarage opened in March 1904 next to a new village school provided by the West Riding County Council.

In the early 1900s, the streets of the new colliery community were properly named. To the south of High Street, the roads were termed Carlton Street, Cudworth View, and Queen Street. The streets to the north of High Street were named King Street, Chapel Street and Joseph Street. Further house building continued with the laying out of 104 houses along New Street, Rockingham Street, North View and along the northern side of High Street, with a row of 20 larger properties erected along the southern side of High Street intended for colliery officials. These houses were provided with front gardens and were known as Deputy Row. To relieve the monotony of the long rows of terraced houses, Deputy Row featured individual gables above the bedroom windows and a continuous brick band running between the windows - they were probably designed by the building contractor Herbert Mollekin of Maltby.

Above: Margate Street was one of the roads forming the Seaside Estate constructed around 1910-12. The end houses of each block featured large gables above the bedroom windows, and two brick bands were carried along the fronts of each terrace between the lower and upper storey windows, the lower brick band arching over the doors and windows. This architectural feature was a 'signature style' of builder Herbert Mollekin, and is visible in his other colliery housing constructed elsewhere in South Yorkshire. The Seaside Estate suffered from deprivation following the closure of Grimethorpe Colliery and remained in a semi-derelict state for several years with some tenants having to live next door to burnt out and vandalised properties and most of the housing was demolished in the early 2000s. This postcard was published by an anonymous photographer shortly after completion of the houses – note the solitary gas street light.

By 1911, the population of Grimethorpe had increased to 3,262. The colliery company provided an Institute on Brierley Road and Grimethorpe Working Men's Club had recently opened. To accommodate the increasing population, the schools had been extended and a new Roman Catholic Church and Primitive Methodist Chapel opened on High Street. The colliery company was now working with Herbert Mollekin to provide additional colliery housing, both at Grimethorpe and at Moorthorpe - the latter for Frickley Colliery. At Grimethorpe, a development of 238 houses was laid out forming Cromer Street, Margate Street, Brighton Street and Hastings Street. With their streets named after seaside towns, this development subsequently gained the colloquial name of 'the Seaside Estate'.

Allotments were provided to the north of the Seaside Estate and to the south of the initial area of housing constructed in 1898. The Grimethorpe Picture Palace opened around 1912 and in 1913 motor buses provided by Barnsley & District Traction Company were operating from the Grimethorpe Hotel to Barnsley. The outbreak of the First World War put a stop to any further developments, but in 1915 Hemsworth Rural District Council prepared plans for the laying out of 96 'workmen's dwellings' along a new street proposed to be named Manor Avenue and situated opposite Manor Farm. This development would have featured 16 larger semi-detached houses fronting Brierley Road with 80 houses arranged in a series of parallel terraces behind. However, the plans were shelved, possibly due to wartime restrictions.

In 1919 Colonel Foljambe sold the remaining 2,000 acres that he owned in Grimethorpe and Brierley; many of the lots were purchased by the local authority and the colliery company for housing developments. The colliery company also purchased most of the farms in the area and the older cottages in the original Grimethorpe hamlet, as well as Brierley Hall which was used as a home for Roland Addy, the Managing Director of the Carlton Main Colliery Company. In 1921, when the population had reached 4,692, Hemsworth Rural District Council prepared plans for another housing development, this time on an entirely new site on Brierley Road opposite Grimethorpe Hall. Taking advantage of the loans and subsidies paid to local authorities under the 1919 Housing Act, this new estate, known as the Grimethorpe Number 1 Housing Scheme of 1922, featured 68 houses constructed in blocks of two and four together with front and rear gardens, all arranged around Manor Crescent. The scheme was designed by architects, H G Wagstaff of Doncaster and R Higginbottom of Thurnscoe, and built from a distinctive red brick - it soon gained the name 'Red City'.

In 1924, Hemsworth Rural District Council constructed Grimethorpe Number 2 Housing Scheme, consisting of 50 semi-detached houses in Brierley Road and Dell Avenue. To relieve the design, the upper storeys were rendered with concrete roughcast over the brickwork. In 1925, Grimethorpe No 3 Housing Scheme was constructed. This featured 102 semi-detached houses arranged along Park Road, Park Avenue, Central Avenue, Clifton Road and Willow Dene Road. This latest development brought the number of Hemsworth Rural District Council houses to 220, all built to a higher standard than their pre-war cousins, with ample accommodation, gardens, an electrical supply from the colliery, and a water and gas supply. Around the same time the colliery company provided similar housing at White City. On Cemetery Road, four larger properties named Woodhall Villas were constructed together with a Doctor's house - since converted to a public house called the Red Rum

The early 1920s were a boom time for the local coal industry. Grimethorpe Colliery was now capable of producing around a million tons of coal per year and the Shafton seam was being exploited at two new subsidiary pits: Brierley Colliery and Ferrymoor Colliery; the entire operation now employed around 4,000 men. The original village school had been demolished in 1917 and a new park, recreation ground and bandstand were laid out on the site by the Miner's Welfare Fund in 1925. The fund continued to improve recreational facilities providing a cricket ground, football ground, tennis court, bowling greens and a Miner's Welfare Recreation Ground. The growing population meant an increasing need for burial space and a new cemetery was opened by the local authority on Common Lane which was renamed Cemetery Road.

By 1925, the local authority had provided 220 houses and the colliery company owned around 830 houses. However, the General Strike and the deteriorating economic situation following the Wall Street Crash of 1929 put paid to any further developments. Nevertheless, the population had increased to 4,692 by 1931. However, the local pits were working on short time, Ferrymoor Colliery had temporarily closed and around a third of the workforce had been dismissed at Grimethorpe Colliery, leading to hardship and poverty in the area. This was only alleviated towards the end of the 1930s when coal production increased in anticipation of the Second World War. The only building activity during this time was the provision of 16 houses plus four bungalows for retired miners on Mount Road, although plans were underway for the development of Michael's Estate.

Above: During the early 1920s, the colliery company provided 230 houses on a site adjacent to Lady Wood, an area somewhat detached from the rest of Grimethorpe and accessed via Cemetery Road. The new streets were named Nancy Road, Burntwood Road, Lady Wood Road, Cross Street and The Square. The earliest phase of 40 houses on Burntwood Road and Nancy Road took place c1920. The white reinforced ferro-concrete panels gave it the name 'White City'. Due to structural problems caused by deterioration of the steel and concrete, these houses were later demolished, although the other 190 houses of White City - being constructed from traditional brick with render applied to the upper storeys - remain standing today. *(Chris Sharp – Old Barnsley)*

Following the end of the Second World War, the Government encouraged the newly nationalised coal industry to increase production and assisted local authorities with the provision of additional housing. Hemsworth Rural District Council laid out Michael's Estate on the plot of land that they had originally earmarked for their first council house building programme back in 1915. Michael's Estate consisted of 106 brick built bungalows arranged in blocks of four, five and six, specifically for retired miners and men demobbed from the military. However, during the late 1940s and 1950s building materials were in short supply and alternative methods were adopted. The Mile End Estate was built adjacent to Michael's estate and consisted of 50 prefabricated bungalows constructed from concrete panels. Another 50 similar prefabricated bungalows were erected at Mount Pleasant near Mount Road.

Two 1930s postcard views from the lens of James Simonton of Balby.

Above Left: The Empire Palace Cinema was built by the Grimethorpe Picture Syndicate and it probably dates from 1910-12. The Grimethorpe & District British Legion Club opened next door in 1919 – this is now called the 'Bullet' ex Servicemen's Club. In the distance are Grimethorpe Working Men's Club and Grimethorpe Colliery Institute; the stone buildings on the left form part of Manor Farm.

Above Right: On Brierley Road, Hemsworth Rural District Council provided several housing developments during the 1920s and properties from the Grimethorpe Housing Number 2 Scheme are shown on this James Simonton postcard of Brierley Road c1930. The Manor Inn was owned by Barnsley Brewery and dates from the mid-1920s but has been recently demolished. Several shops and a Post Office were built along Brierley Road. *(Chris Sharp – Old Barnsley)*

At the same time the Coal Industry Housing Association had been established by the NCB to encourage men from the older coalfields, particularly in Scotland, to move the highly productive Yorkshire & East Midlands coalfield. Starting in 1953, a development of three separate estates of pit housing was built by the Coal Industry Housing Association, all in blocks of two, three or four and of concrete panel construction. The first development was an extension to the original White City, and 117 houses were built on Chestnut Street, Oak Street, Poplar Street, Sycamore Avenue and Woodland Terrace, the street names reflecting the nearby Lady Wood. The second development comprised 232 houses on Cemetery Road, Raymond Avenue, Oldroyd Avenue, Charles Street, Duke Road, Taylor Road and Coronation Avenue - the last named after the 1953 coronation of Queen Elizabeth II. The third development was built by Foldhead Farm where 20 houses on Elizabeth Street and Cemetery Road were constructed. This brought a grand total of 369 houses provided by the Coal Industry Housing Association during the 1950s.

With the increasing availability of bricks towards the end of the 1950s, Hemsworth Rural District Council provided an extension to Red City and 110 semi-detached properties were laid out on Windmill Avenue and Manor Grove. The council also built 62 bungalows on Clear View. The rapid post-war building programme by the local authority and the NCB saw a large migration of people into the Grimethorpe area and, by 1961, the population of Brierley and Grimethorpe had increased to 8,259. The educational facilities of the area were supplemented with the opening of Brierley Grimethorpe County Secondary School (later Willowgarth High School) together with two additional junior schools: Ladywood Primary School at White City and Milefield Middle School at the western end of the village.

Around 1970, some of the original colliery housing was demolished on John Street and Chapel Street and the prefab bungalows of the Mile End Estate were replaced with 58 new bungalows on Meadow Crescent, Milefield View and Springfield Road although it wasn't until the mid-2000s when the prefab bungalows at Mount Pleasant were demolished and replaced by private housing. However, the closure of Grimethorpe Colliery in 1993 saw the heart torn from the local community; the area went into decline and suffered from terrible social problems, with extreme levels of unemployment, petty crime and drug use - indeed many people left the area. In the 1980s, the NCB, by now reluctant landlords, were keen to dispose of their housing stock to local authorities and, coupled with the Government's Right to Buy Policy, many of the houses were purchased by their owners. Several remained with the council but a sizable proportion were bought by private landlords who struggled to maintain their properties and find tenants. Derelict houses with boarded up windows and burnt out roofs were a common sight and it took several years of investment and regeneration to improve the local environment, with varying degrees of success. The declining population meant that the village schools were demolished and replaced with a supermarket.

In the 1990s, further streets in the original colliery village were demolished, as well as most of the houses forming the Seaside Estate, although some of these were refurbished. New roads were built through the derelict colliery site and in 1998 the newly constructed A6195 connected Grimethorpe with the rest of the Dearne Valley and the Motorway network, helping to improve transport links to the once isolated colliery community; this brought new industries to the area. Further demolition of colliery housing continued in the early 2000s together with the construction of new houses built near the colliery and on the site of the Seaside Estate. Reflecting national trends in the falling use of public houses and clubs, the Manor Inn and Grimethorpe Hotel have been demolished but the Miners Welfare Institute has been rebuilt. Willowgarth High School was demolished and replaced with a new Advanced Learning Centre at Shafton and the Old Folks Centre has been pulled down - this building featured prominently in the film *Brassed Off* as the band's practice hall.

In December 2000, *Brassed Off* actor Pete Postlethwaite returned to the area to open the Millennium Green, a recreational area near St Luke's Church and in 2003 a memorial was positioned in High Street in memory of all those who had lost their lives at the pit. Today, mining is now a memory in 'Grimey' but it remains a proud feature of the heritage of the area. Ironically, the name Grimethorpe is now recognised throughout the world, thanks to the tours of the famous Grimethorpe Colliery Band, whether they are performing in the local region, the national stage of London's Royal Albert Hall, or the international stage of Sydney Opera House.

Swinton

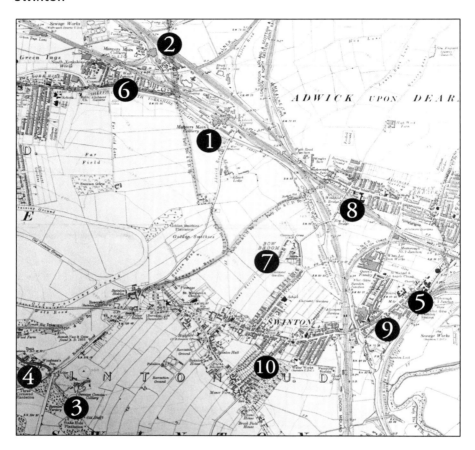

Above: Extract from the 1932 Ordnance Survey Map showing Swinton and Manvers Main Colliery. **1:** Manvers Main No 1 Pit. **2:** Manvers Main No 2 pit. **3:** Swinton Common Colliery. **4:** Site of Rockingham Pottery (1745-1842). **5:** Site of Don Pottery (1801-1893). **6:** Colliery Community of Nash Row (See Wath Section) **7:** Bow Broom. **8:** Roman Terrace. **9:** Swinton Bridge. **10:** Swinton Urban District Council Housing 1920s. *(Taken from the Dearne District Traction Act Map – Paul Fox Collection)*

Swinton was mentioned in the Domesday Survey of 1086 as *Swintone* - the name derived from the Old English for 'Swine Farm' - and the area was awarded to Roger de Busli of Tickhill Castle following the Norman Conquest. A small 12th century Norman Chapel was built in the village, possibly by the Knights of St John and Jerusalem, who held one of the manors of Swinton. Over the following years, the land passed on to other landowners including the Canons of Nostell Priory near Wakefield and the Marquis of Rockingham, before being inherited by Earl Fitzwilliam in 1783. The settlement occupied an elevated position between the valleys of the River Don and River Dearne, and its cottages and farms were spread out along Mexborough Road from Swinton Common in the west towards

Swinton Bridge in the east, all forming part of the parish of Wath-upon-Dearne. In 1817, with the building of St Margaret's Church, Swinton was designated its own parish of around 1,700 acres.

Although small scale coal pits and day holes had been operational on Swinton Common during the 1600s, the first major industrial activity of note occurred in 1745 with the establishment of a pottery at Swinton Common by Edward Butler on land owned by the Marquis of Rockingham. The pottery later passed into the hands of William and John Brameld who renamed it Rockingham Pottery. Under the ownership of the Brameld Brothers, the pottery achieved considerable fame and, during the 1820s and 1830s, around 300 people were employed, producing high quality porcelain and earthenware. A notable commission was for a 200-piece dinner service for King William IV and for the creation of two large 'Rhinoceros' vases. In 1801, another pottery was established at Swinton Bridge named the Don Pottery and this too became well known for its pottery output. Today, Rockingham and Don Pottery is highly sought by collectors; the two Rhinoceros vases are on public display – one in the Clifton Park Museum in Rotherham and the other in the Victoria & Albert Museum in London.

In 1794, work commenced on constructing the Dearne & Dove Canal from Swinton to Barnsley and in 1819, the Rotherham to Swinton turnpike opened followed nine years later by the Swinton to Conisbrough branch. The Midland Railway arrived in 1840 and opened a Railway Station at Swinton Bridge on 30 June that year. Following this, the main road through Swinton was renamed from Mexborough Road to Station Street. However, coal mining was becoming an increasingly important industry in the surrounding area. In the late 1840s, Warren Vale Colliery was in operation, followed by Swinton Common Colliery, and, in 1858, Kilnhurst Colliery was sunk to the Barnsley seam. These three pits were all owned by the Wakefield coalmasters J & J Charlesworth, but apart from Kilnhurst Colliery, they were relatively small-scale operations - Warren Vale Colliery was connected to the canal at Kilnhurst by a wagonway whilst Swinton Common Colliery had no rail or canal outlet.

The forthcoming opening of Kilnhurst Colliery led to the establishment of a separate parish to serve this area which became effective from 26 October 1860. A Wesleyan Methodist Chapel had opened in 1850 and Kilnhurst Church opened in 1859. In 1870 a United Methodist & Primitive Methodist Chapel was provided followed by a Board School in 1879. On 1 January 1861, Kilnhurst Co-operative Society was established operating from premises on Victoria Road. Two additional branches were later opened opposite Meadow View and on Clay Pit Lane in Rawmarsh. This led to the formation of Swinton Co-operative Society in 1864, but the venture was unsuccessful and the village was later provided with the 21st branch of the Barnsley British Co-operative Society.

However, the development of Manvers Main Colliery in 1867, designed to extract the Barnsley seam from beneath Earl Manvers Mexborough estate and from beneath Earl Fitzwilliam's Swinton estate, brought widespread industrialisation to the Swinton area. The opening of Manvers Main Colliery saw the need for additional housing. Some of this was provided by the colliery company themselves at Nash Row in Wath-upon-Dearne, but speculative builders constructed houses and created three colliery settlements within Swinton Parish: – Bowbroom, Roman Terrace and Swinton Bridge. These colliery communities with their rows of brick built terraces were situated in relatively isolated locations at some distance from the village of Swinton with its church, stone cottages, old hall, public houses, old Toll Bar and Swinton Stables which featured Earl Fitzwilliam's Private Race Course.

Above: Six Postcard views of Swinton Bridge, the heart of the industrial end of Swinton.

Top Left: Bridge Street looking east, one of a series of postcards issued by C F Hurst to commemorate the opening of the Mexborough & Swinton Tramway in 1907.
Top Right: Swinton Bridge looking west with the original stone built Canal Tavern on the right.
Middle Left: This busy scene on Bridge Street was captured on a postcard by Edgar Scrivens in 1908, prior to the installation of overhead wiring for the trams.
Middle Right: The Canal Tavern on the right was rebuilt around 1912 and despite its recent demolition, the scene is instantly recognisable today. Swinton Railway Station closed in 1968 as part of the Beeching cuts but in 1990 a new station opened a site to the south of the bridge. The postcard was published in 1920 by Edgar Scrivens. *(Paul Fox Collection)*
Lower Left: William Street was constructed in the 1870s to house workers at Manvers Main Colliery, South Yorkshire Glass Works and Swinton Foundry. It is shown here in this 1905 photograph by C F Hurst issued as a postcard by Crowther-Cox.
Lower Right: Bridge Street developed as a busy commercial centre, as can be seen on this postcard by C F Hurst / Crowther-Cox c1905 with the Don Hotel on the right. The area in the distance near Market Street was occasionally used as an open-air market. However, the photographer has captured the annual arrival of Swinton Feast, a travelling fair.

In the 1870s, around 100 houses were built at Bowbroom, an isolated settlement near the Dearne & Dove Canal and not far from Manvers Main Colliery. The houses at Bowbroom were laid out on Queen Street, Albert Street and Thomas Street, and the community also included a small Wesleyan Reform Methodist Chapel and a public house – the Cresswell Arms.

The colliery company also worked with speculative builders to provide terraced housing at Roman Terrace, and around 100 houses were built on Wath Road, together with shops and a branch of the Barnsley British Co-operative Society and two pubs, the Plant Hotel and the Roman Hotel. In the 1890s, Roman Terrace was enlarged with the provision of several hundred additional houses on Cambridge Street, Oxford Street, Victoria Street, Chapel Street, Spencer Street, Barker Street, Frederick Street, White Lea Terrace and Wragby Row.

At Swinton Bridge, around 400 houses were constructed by speculative builders on Bridge Street, William Street, White Lee Road, New Station Road and Walker Street. Additional houses were provided to the west of the Railway Station on Charles Street, Crossland Street and Wortley Avenue. Swinton Bridge was surrounded by various industries and it developed as a mixed industrial settlement. As well as miners working at Manvers Main Colliery, there was also a boatyard on the canal, the Don Pottery (which closed in 1893), the Don Chemical Works, the Swinton Iron Works, the South Yorkshire Glass Bottle Company (later Dale Brown & Company's glassworks), Hattersley Brothers Ltd producing kitchen stoves and grates, and the railway sheds at Mexborough.

In 1860, Swinton Church School became Swinton Fitzwilliam Junior & Infants School under the patronage of Earl Fitzwilliam. However, the school was becoming overcrowded as families moved to work at the new industries in the area. Therefore, in 1876, the Swinton Local Board was established to oversee the governance of the area and to provide services to the growing population. The Swinton Local Board organised the construction of Swinton Bridge Board School at a cost of £6,000. This opened in 1878 and was enlarged in 1895; it could accommodate 900 children. The following year Kilnhurst Board School opened with places for 320 children. In 1884, Roman Terrace Board School was built with a capacity for 500 children and this was later extended to cater for 855 children.

In 1876, the population of the area was recorded as 6,983 and Swinton Local Board was concerned at the poor water supply and sewage facilities (or lack of) both in the old village, where there was a reliance upon wells, and in the new colliery communities, where a lot of the new building had been to poor standards, with outside privies and earth closets being the norm. The lack of proper sanitation was having a detrimental effect on the health of the inhabitants, contributing to a relatively high death rate of 19/1000. Therefore in 1882, a scheme at a cost of £25,000 was implemented, which included the sinking of a borehole and the construction of a waterworks on Wortley Avenue. This supplied a reservoir built at the top of the village on Race Course Road from which the houses could draw a water supply. Sewers were laid along the main streets to a new sewage works near the River Don.

St Margaret's Church had opened in 1817, but was destroyed by fire in 1897; it was subsequently rebuilt, incorporating some of the arches from the Norman Chapel in the churchyard. As early as 1875, there was concern over the lack of church facilities at Swinton Bridge, but after some delay, a Chapel of Ease was provided on a site donated by Earl Fitzwilliam. This was named St Michaels and All Angels Church and was consecrated in 1901. Other religions sought to provided facilities for their worshippers. In 1865, St John's

Wesleyan Methodist Church opened on Station Street whilst nearby, in Milton Street, the Ebenezer Wesleyan Reform Chapel was built in 1873. In 1869, a Primitive Methodist Chapel opened at Swinton Bridge and another was provided in 1880 at Roman Terrace. In 1882 the Congregationalists opened a school room followed by the Congregational Church on Station Street in 1902. Finally, in 1911, a large Wesleyan Methodist Chapel was built on Wath Road in Roman Terrace.

By 1891, the population of Swinton had increased to 9,697 as people flocked to the area; ten years later the population numbered 12,217. Consequently, under the 1894 Local Government Act, Swinton Local Board sought urban powers and became Swinton Urban District Council, purchasing Highfield House for use as their offices. Highfield House and Swinton Hall had previously been occupied by members of the Brameld family. By now Bow Broom was linked to Swinton Village by ribbon development along Queen Street, and Swinton Village was linked to Swinton Bridge which in turn was now linked to Roman Terrace and the larger settlement of Mexborough.

Above: Station Street developed as the main commercial thoroughfare in the centre of Swinton, as shown on these c1915 postcards by C F Hurst.
Left: Looking east towards Swinton Bridge.
Right: Looking west towards Swinton Common and featuring the Midland Railway Express Parcels Traffic delivery horse and cart.

In the meantime, Swinton was becoming a centre of transport networks. The Canal had opened in 1798 and the original Midland Railway Swinton Station of 1840 was replaced with a new station to the north of the road which opened on 2 July 1899. This was renamed Swinton Town Station to distinguish it from Swinton Station, which had opened on 18 March 1871 on the South Yorkshire Railway. In 1907, the Mexborough & Swinton Traction Company provided a street tramway to Mexborough and Rotherham and, in 1915, it opened a trolleybus serving Roman Terrace on a route between Mexborough and Manvers Main Colliery. A gas works had been built in 1856 and this was taken over by the Swinton & Gas Light Company in 1872. Gas was supplied to Swinton, Mexborough and Kilnhurst and in 1911, the works were purchased jointly by the Urban District Councils of Swinton and Mexborough and gas was supplied directly from Manvers Main Colliery from 1920.

In the meantime, Swinton was developing as a commercial centre and numerous shops opened along Station Street and at Swinton Bridge. In 1906, the Carnegie Library opened, and, in 1908, the West Riding County Council provided Queen Street School. In 1910, St John's Methodist Church was rebuilt with a new church hall opening next door in 1913 on the site of the old Norman Chapel. However, Swinton was becoming famous for its number of pubs:

The Woodman Inn, the Kings Head, the Gate Inn, the Ring of Bells, the Travellers Rest, the Sportsman Inn, the Robin Hood, the Butchers Arms, the Station Hotel, the Canal Tavern, the Ship Inn, the Red House and the Don Hotel. These were complemented by the opening of the Swinton Workings Men's Club, the Victoria Club and the United Services Club.

Around 1925 the Miners' Welfare Fund provided a recreation ground on the land behind Highfield House. This development was known as Swinton Miners Welfare and was opened by Countess Fitzwilliam It included tennis courts, bowling greens and a cricket ground with a wooden pavilion. Another Miners Welfare Ground opened at Kilnhurst, again with facilities for cricket, tennis and bowling. An additional recreation ground was provided at Roman Terrace and was opened by Earl Manvers. Film shows had been held in the United Services Club on Station Street. However, in 1929 the Swinton Picture House opened across the road – this building was later known as the Roxy Cinema and 'going to the pictures' became a popular pastime.

Above: On 1 April 1938, the Roman Terrace area, consisting of 32 acres, 616 houses and a population of 2,440 was transferred to the jurisdiction of Mexborough Urban District Council. This was a natural progression as Roman Terrace was much nearer to Mexborough than to Swinton. The housing at Roman Terrace had been built within the boundaries of Swinton Parish, with the streets to the north of Wath Road suddenly ending where they met the fields of Highwoods Farm; the latter were already within Mexborough Parish and on the estate of Earl Manvers. The two postcard views were published by Crowther-Cox in 1907 and show Wath Road (left) and Frederick Street (right)

Following the First World War, Swinton Urban District Council provided their first council houses. A development of 42 houses was constructed at Piccadilly on Elmfield Avenue and Beechfield Avenue around 1922. In the late 1920s, around 200 houses were built on Slade Road, Manor Road and Brookfield Avenue. These houses were provided in pairs or blocks of four and featured front and rear gardens - they were an improvement on the pre-war housing.

In 1937, Swinton Urban District Council provided another council estate. At Swinton Bridge, 52 houses and bungalows were built on Walker Street and Coronation Road. At the western end of the village, land to the south of Rockingham Road was designated for a larger development and around 200 semi-detached houses and bungalows were constructed on Rockingham Road, Brameld Road, Griffin Road, Highfield Road, Toll Bar Road and along the northern side of Rookery Road. The naming of the streets reflects the area, Rockingham, Brameld and Griffin from the Brameld family who once owned Rockingham Pottery – whose trade mark was a griffin - whilst Highfield Road, Rookery Road and Toll Bar Road are named after older houses in the village. The local authority also provided similar houses and bungalows at Meadow View and at Kilnhurst, where several of the streets were named after former leaders of the council. During the interwar period, Swinton Urban District Council built a total of 783 houses and 68 bungalows. During the 1920s and 1930s, private housing was constructed along Church Street, Rockingham Road, Race Course Road and Romwood Avenue.

Following the end of the Second World War, the dire shortage of housing was addressed with further developments on the fields of Highfield Farm and plans were drawn up for a new 'Garden City' – the Highfield Farm Estate. Around 1946, the council purchased 128 prefab bungalows and these were erected on Woodlands Crescent and Broadway and on Piccadilly where they formed the Wood End Estate. Meanwhile, plans were drawn up for 548 permanent semi-detached houses and bungalows. Building commenced in the early 1950s with the laying out of Rookery Road, Central Avenue, Park Road, Valley Road, East Avenue, South Avenue, The Rise, The Crescent, The Croft, The Lea, Grange Road and Brookside. The Highfield Farm Estate incorporated wide streets with grass verges and avenues of Lime trees and areas of open space – each provided with a little concrete plinth displaying a 'No Ball Games'. On Broadway, a shopping parade of eight shops with flats above was provided. In 1953, Swinton Fitzwilliam Infants School was built on Rookery Road and a Teacher Training College opened nearby. This was quickly adapted and extended to become Swinton Secondary School to serve the new population.

Above: The Toll Bar was demolished and replaced with this shopping parade in the early 1950s, which included Swinton Common Post Office, suitably festooned for the Coronation of Queen Elizabeth II in 1953. This postcard was published by James Simonton. *(Andrew McGarrigle Collection)*

In 1948, the local council purchased 22 acres of woodland stretching from Swinton Common to Piccadilly from Earl Fitzwilliam. These woods were named Creighton Woods, after Alderman Creighton and were provided for the benefit of the new residents of the Highfield Farm Estate. On Warren Vale, a Lych Gate was constructed to form an entrance feature to

Creighton Woods. The structure was a gift to the people of Swinton from Enid Harrop and was in memory of the men who had served in the two world wars. Enid Harrop (who in 1913 wrote a booklet on The Four Churches of Swinton) wished the lych gate to be a joint gift with her sister Beatrice and today the structure is known as the 'Sisters Lych Gate'.

Meanwhile, on another site near the hamlet of Bowbroom, the Coal Industry Housing Association were developing a scheme to provide housing for miners displaced from the Scottish Coalfields who had been encouraged to move to work at Manvers Main Colliery. On Broome Avenue, in 1954, 50 houses were built in blocks of 2, 4, 5 & 6, all from precast grey reinforced concrete panels. The development was incorporated into a new Swinton Urban District Council estate known as the Bowbroom Estate or Cresswell Estate. These houses were built to a different design to those provided on the Highfield Farm Estate and the development included 96 bungalows and 330 houses – the latter built in blocks of 2, 3 ,4 & 6. These were laid out on St John's Road, Thomas Street, St Marys Crescent, Storey Street, Goodwin Crescent. As part of this scheme, the Cresswell Arms was rebuilt and the Bowbroom Working Men's Club was opened. Meanwhile, Swinton House on Fitzwilliam Street was adapted for use as a club for the colliery management and deputies. In the centre of the village, Swinton Civic Centre was constructed – a new shopping parade, library, and premises for the Butchers Arms, all replacing many of the older cottages of the area.

During the 1960s and 1970s, the local authority continued to provide additional housing, notably in the form of several low-rise housing developments and blocks of flats and, in the 1970s, the Swinton Fitzwilliam Estate opened. These modern houses featured central heating and had flat roofs – leading to the nickname 'Jerusalem' but they are now known as the 'Swinton Patios'. Further areas of private housing were constructed during the 1970s, but around the same time, some of the original terraces in Swinton Bridge and Roman Terrace were demolished.

In 1801 the population of the Swinton area was only 653 but by 2011 this had increased to 15,599. Swinton now features a mixture of older cottages, terraced housing, former council estates and private housing and has become a popular residential area, with frequent train services to neighbouring towns and the new industries on the site of Manvers Main Colliery to the north.

Thurnscoe

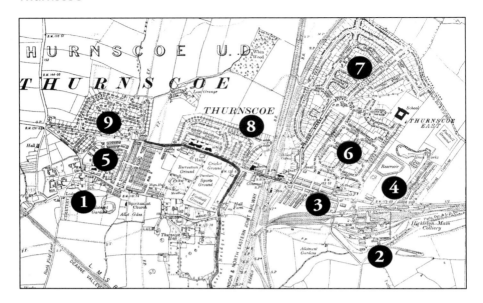

Above: Extract from the 1932 Ordnance Survey Map showing Thurnscoe.
1: Thurnscoe Village. **2:** Hickleton Main Colliery. **3:** Lidgett Lane Housing pre-1900. **4:** Spike (George Street). **5:** Housing 1900-1914 including the Dole Backs. **6:** Thurnscoe Housing Association Lidgett Lane Scheme (1920) **7:** Industrial Housing Association (1923-1925). **8:** TUDC Housing No 1 Scheme (1921). **9:** TUDC No 2 Scheme (1925). *(Taken from the Dearne District Traction Act Map – Paul Fox Collection)*

Thurnscoe was recorded in the Domesday survey of 1086 as *Ternusc* when the Lordship of the Manor belonged to *Richard de Sourdeval*, who was awarded it following the Norman Conquest. During the mediaeval period, most of the land in the area was under the ownership of the monks of Roche Abbey, who owned High Grange Farm and Low Grange Farm, the term Grange indicating that the area formed an outlying portion of a monastic estate devoted to farming. Following the Dissolution of the Monasteries, the village passed into other hands, including Thomas Shirecliffe who constructed Thurnscoe Hall from 1670-1701 and thence to Reverend Simpson. In 1868, Reverend Simpson sold the 1,500-acre manor of Thurnscoe to Thomas Edward Taylor, a Barnsley linen manufacturer who lived at Dodworth Grange. On his death, he was succeeded by his son, Reverend Thornely Taylor, and, in 1891, when the population of the village was 217, the colliery company signed a lease for the Barnsley coal seam.

Prior to the opening of Hickleton Main Colliery, Thurnscoe consisted of a few cottages, a school and schoolhouse, almshouses and the Butchers Arms, together with St Helens Church. However, the pit was situated some distance away in Lidgett Lane, the lane that led up the hill to Hickleton Hall, the home of Viscount Halifax, who had also leased the coal beneath his Hickleton and Goldthorpe estates to the colliery company. Temporary accommodation in the form of wooden huts for the shaft sinkers was provided on Lidgett Lane and, in 1892, the colliery company opened a brickyard and constructed a row of 30 houses named Hickleton

Terrace. When coal was discovered in 1894, the colliery company worked with speculative builders to provide the accommodation, and the following year, building work commenced in the hamlet of Goldthorpe; 242 houses were built for the new workforce.

However, speculative builders were also active in Lidgett Lane and, by the turn of the century, 194 additional houses had been built and the new colliery community was termed Thurnscoe East, to distinguish it from the old village. Opposite the pit, a row of 12 larger houses was constructed for colliery officials, plus two houses for colliery management, together with offices for the colliery company. To the east, George Street was laid out consisting of a development of 38 houses plus an isolated terrace of 24 houses at the northern end, together with allotments. George Street was always referred to as 'Spike' - the reason why having now passed into time - and Thurnscoe East was often referred to as 'Top End'. By 1901, the population of Thurnscoe had increased from 217 to 2,366, indicating the huge migrating into. Consequently, Thurnscoe Church yard was closed for burials and a new cemetery opened in 1902.

The rapid increase in population caused the school in the old village to becoming vastly overcrowded; therefore, Reverend Thornely Taylor gifted a plot of land on Back Lane to the West Riding County Council which opened Houghton Road Junior & Infants School on 3 May 1897. These schools were extended in 1910. During his lifetime, Reverend Taylor made several gifts of land for the benefit of the district and, in 1898, Thurnscoe Institute opened in the old village. Meanwhile, following the opening of Hickleton & Thurnscoe Railway Station on the Hull & Barnsley Railway's branch line to Wath in 1897, the Station Hotel, known as 'the Drum' opened to serve the new population at Thurnscoe East. In 1898, the colliery company opened a reservoir to the north of Lidgett Lane to provide the houses of the village with a water supply and in 1900, Thurnscoe Market Place opened near the railway station.

At the beginning of the 20th century, speculative builders turned their attention to providing housing adjacent to the old village of Thurnscoe, and streets of terraced housing were laid out along Butcher Street, Orchard Street, Edward Street, Albert Street. A block of 160 houses were built on Church Street and Chapel Street, and some of the terraced rows on this development were 22 houses long. At the top of Chapel Street, a Wesleyan Methodist Church opened to serve the new population. Shops were laid out on High Street and Back Lane (now Houghton Road). In 1914, builders including Messrs Turner Brothers of Barnsley provided a development of 80 terraced houses built in barrack like rows in Kingsway. These streets were named as the Avenues and together with Chapel Street and Market Street became known unofficially as 'the Dole Backs', although the area was known as 'Thurnscoe West' or the 'Bottom End'.

The rapidly developing community had been served by Thurnscoe Parish Council since its formation in 1893, although Doncaster Rural District Council remained responsible for the provision of most of the facilities. However, on 8 September 1908, the parish council was granted urban status and Thurnscoe Urban District Council was established, with meetings held in the parish hall in Lidgett Lane. Mark Lane Nokes was the Chairman of the new authority and William Wilde, the colliery manager, was Vice-Chairman. In 1909, the Church of England provided a large tin church, St Hilda's Mission Church, to serve the religious needs of the people of Thurnscoe East, thus relieving the pressure on St Helen's Church in Thurnscoe village. In 1911, when the population had increased to over 4,000, Reverend Taylor donated six acres of land to form a recreation ground and park which opened next to the Hickleton Main cricket ground. The following year, the colliery company constructed

Hickleton Main Institute which opened at a cost of £460. Further shops and a few private houses were built in Shepherd Lane.

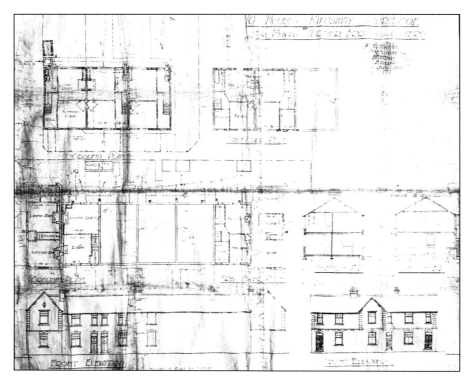

Above: Although in poor condition, this architectural plan of the Kingsway Dole Backs is included for its historical nature. The houses were arranged in blocks of ten in eight parallel rows named Marlborough Avenue, Foljambe Avenue, Lansdowne Avenue etc. They probably gained their nickname during the depression of the 1930s when many men were unemployed. The simple four room tenements of the Dole Backs were built to poor standards and resembled the earlier rows of the 1860s and 1870s rather than the more progressive building initiatives of the time. The dole backs were demolished in the 1960s. *(Thurnscoe Local History Group)*

However, the outbreak of First World War brought an end to any further developments and it wasn't until the establishment of the 1919 Housing Act that house building operations recommenced. The Act empowered local authorities and utility societies to take advantage of government subsidies and loans to build houses to an improved standard. An 18-acre site was purchased from Reverend Thornely Taylor in 1919 to the north of the Thurnscoe Garden Village for the provision of council housing under a scheme named the Thurnscoe Housing Scheme Number 1. The following year, Thurnscoe Urban District Council constructed 256 houses in blocks of two, four and six to the designs of the council surveyor, Thomas Bull. These houses formed Thornely Crescent, Taylor Street and extensions to School Street, Garden Street and John Street. Two of the new streets were named in honour of the Reverend Thornely Taylor whilst John Street takes its name from his son. This new estate was sometimes referred to as the Thurnscoe Hall Estate due to its road name connections with Thurnscoe Hall.

At the same time, the colliery company was also looking to provide their own housing to accommodate an additional workforce required to work the deeper seams at the pit. On 29 July 1920 at a meeting convened by the colliery company at the Midland Grand Hotel in London St Pancras, the Thurnscoe Housing Association was established. This was a public utility society, formed to take advantage of government loans and subsidies under the 1919 Housing Act. The Thurnscoe Housing Association was formed under the guidance of Sir Tudor Walters, an influential town planner and author of the 1917 Tudor Walters Report. He also owned the architectural practice known as The Housing & Town Planning Trust Ltd and was a fellow Liberal MP with Robert Armitage, the chairman of Hickleton Main Colliery Company.

Above: An illustration from the *Colliery Guardian* depicting housing developments at Thurnscoe East in 1925. In the centre is the newly completed Thurnscoe Housing Association Lidgett Lane Scheme with its geometric street plan. Meanwhile building is underway forming the streets of the Industrial Housing Association development. Note Windsor Street under construction on the left

The first scheme announced by the Thurnscoe Housing Association was the George Street Scheme and details of the development have survived in the archives. The Association purchased land in George Street for £1,826 from the colliery company on which to construct houses designed by Sir Tudor Walters. On the western side of George Street, 28 houses were built by builders Messrs R Hann Smith of Rotherham at a cost of £19,040. On the eastern side of George Street, a contract was signed with Thurnscoe builders Messrs A Bull & Company for eight houses at a cost of £6,280. The entire scheme of 36 houses and the purchase of the land had cost £27,146 – an average of £754 per house. A third of this cost was paid through government subsidies and the remainder through Public Works Board Loans. A larger site to the north of Lidgett Lane was purchased from the colliery company for a development of 258 houses forming the Lidgett Lane Scheme. On this development, Tudor Street, Saxon Street, Stuart Street, Dane Street and Norman Street were laid out, with the street names derived from invading tribes and royal dynasties, apart from Tudor Street, which was named after Sir Tudor Walters, despite its name coincidentally being the name of the Tudor royal dynasty. The Thurnscoe Housing Association records provide details of a third housing plan named the Thurnscoe Hall Scheme, although this project was completed by Thurnscoe Urban District Council.

In 1922, Hickleton Main Colliery Company was one of several colliery companies that established the Industrial Housing Association. This essentially operated along the principles of the Thurnscoe Housing Association but on a national scale, constructing colliery estates throughout England and Wales for its member companies, again under the guidance of Sir Tudor Walters and to designs drawn up by his architectural practice. The Industrial Housing Association purchased High Grange Farm and its surrounding fields from Reverend Thornely Taylor for the development of an estate of 733 houses, with High Grange Farm used as accommodation for colliery management. This huge development incorporated numerous different house designs, constructed in blocks of two, three, four and six. The scheme included three and four bedroomed properties with the bathrooms provided downstairs, ideally positioned for miners to bathe in straight from the pit. The development also included 24 larger houses for deputies, six 'cottage shops', a public house provided by John Smiths Brewery named the Fairway Hotel, recreation grounds, allotments and a site for a new school, Thurnscoe Hill School, was opened by the West Riding County Council on 10 January 1927 and was subsequently extended in 1934.

In 1923, the fields around Low Grange Farm were purchased from Reverend Thornely Taylor by the Thurnscoe Urban District Council for the development of another local authority housing estate named Thurnscoe Housing Scheme Number 2. On this site, the council built 266 smartly appointed semi-detached houses. The new estate was laid out along Houghton Road, Lorne Road, Horse Moor Road, Common Road, Westfield Crescent, Wensley Street, Manor Road, Merrill Road, Monsal Street, Richmond Street and Pear Tree Avenue, the last named after the nearby Pear Tree Cottages. The scheme also incorporated public lavatories and waiting shelters at the 'Big Lamp', a large gas light on Houghton Road, a short distance from the terminus of the tram network provided by the Dearne District Light Railways.

In 1926, all the new houses received an electrical supply from the pit, a gas supply from the Wath & Bolton Gas Board and water from the colliery reservoir. The combined development of 1,549 houses (522 by Thurnscoe Urban District Council, 294 by Thurnscoe Housing Association and 733 by the Industrial Housing Association) during the 1920s was probably one of the largest building schemes at any mining village in the country, all resulting from Hickleton Main's 1920s heyday when the pit was an absolute powerhouse employing over 4,000 men and producing 1,250,000 tons of coal per year. However, following the General Strike of 1926 and the economic depression that followed the pit was now working short time and by 1929 there were 340 unoccupied houses in Thurnscoe. Nevertheless, by 1931, the population of the village had increased to 10,500.

Above: Lidgett Lane became the main thoroughfare of Thurnscoe East and houses were built on Hickleton Terrace, King Street, Queen Street, Grange Terrace, York Terrace, Clarence Terrace. Whitworth's Buildings, together with a Post Office, shops and a Primitive Methodist Chapel were also constructed. The Parish Hall on the right was built in 1905 on a site provided by the colliery company and at the expense of Reverend Taylor. The Hall was built in memory of Ernest Hague, the manging director of the Hickleton Main Colliery Company Ltd. This postcard was published by Lamb of Barnsley c1908

Above Left: In connection with the Thurnscoe Housing Number 2 Scheme, Back Lane was renamed Houghton Road and extended along a new concrete road shown in the above postcard published by Edgar Scrivens in 1931. The smart appearance of the scheme is evident – these were some of the finest council houses constructed in the country.

Above Right: The Barnsley British Co-operative Society's Thurnscoe branch opened in 1901 and shortly afterwards 40 houses were provided in School Street, Garden Street and John Street - the development was known as Thurnscoe Garden Village. This postcard illustration was published by an anonymous photographer c1910.

The 1920s also saw a further development of shops and community buildings in the western part of Thurnscoe. A parade of shops with mock-Tudor upper story frontages opened on Houghton Road to serve the new housing developments and, in 1924, this shopping parade formed the terminus of the new tramway belonging to the Dearne District Light Railway which operated through the Dearne Valley to Barnsley. Opposite Houghton Road Schools, a new Wesleyan Methodist chapel opened in 1929, next to the three-storey high Broadway Buildings. This contained shops on the ground floor and a dance hall and billiard hall on the upper floors; later it incorporated a garage and petrol station. To the west of Broadway Buildings, a new public house opened named the Thurnscoe Hotel - referred to as the 'new un' by the locals. Further shops were constructed along Shepherd Lane together with a new library provided by the West Riding County Council. A new direct road was laid from the Big Lamp as Houghton Road. This new road removed the need for through traffic to pass along Lorne Road and Common Road near the old village of Thurnscoe.

Above: Norman Street was one of the streets laid out in 1920 by the Thurnscoe Housing Association as part of 258 houses forming their Lidgett Lane Housing Scheme. The project was divided into three contracts: 130 houses at the cost of £115,708 with Messrs R Hann Smith; 128 houses at a cost of £114,932 with Messrs A Bull & Company; and a joint contract with the two building firms of £18,571 for the construction of roads and sewers. Trees were planted along the pavements to relieve the monotony of the building line as shown in this postcard by James Simonton which dates to 1930. *(Chris Sharp – Old Barnsley)*

Above: Thurnscoe Cinema House was built by the Thurnscoe Cinema Company and opened on 12 May 1922 with accommodation for 728 patrons. The Hickleton Main Silver Brass Band held an opening concert and one of the first films shown was *A Dogs Life* starring Charlie Chaplin. Next to the cinema was Thurnscoe Market Place and the Roman Catholic Church of the Holy Family. Bingo was introduced in 1962 and the cinema showed its last film in 1967, becoming a permanent bingo hall thereafter - the premises were later used as a snooker club. The cinema, church and market place have since been cleared and recently replaced with a new supermarket.

Overleaf: This plan of Thurnscoe Village was published in the book *The Building of Twelve Thousand Houses* by Sir Tudor Walters and features the 733 houses laid out by the Industrial Housing Association and the 258 houses built by the Thurnscoe Housing Association. The naming of the streets on the estate continued the connection with British history, being Windsor Street, Roman Street, Briton Street, Briton Square, Hanover Street, Hanover Square, Cromwell Street, Brunswick Street and York Street. Additionally, Grange Crescent took its name from High Grange Farm and Deightonby Street was named after the lost settlement of Deightonby, the name of a deserted medieval village between Thurnscoe and Frickley. To provide for the construction of the large council and colliery housing developments, the colliery company opened a new brickyard to the north of Lidgett Lane in 1920.

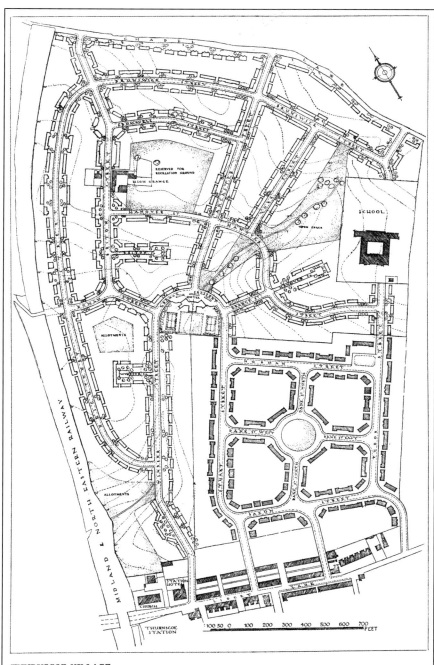

THURNSCOE VILLAGE.
LAY-OUT PLAN.

In 1923, the colliery company decided to improve the welfare facilities and plans for an open-air swimming pool were made. However, the Miner's Welfare Fund took over the implementation of this scheme and shortly afterwards the Hickleton Main Miner's Welfare & Institute opened which incorporated the earlier Institute and cricket pitch. The scheme also included a football ground, running track, pavilion, tennis courts, bowling green and putting green. The Institute was well used by several clubs and societies, including the renowned Thurnscoe Harmonic Male Voice Choir which had been established in 1924. The Miner's Welfare Fund also provided swimming baths on Station Road in 1928, although these became the responsibility of Thurnscoe Urban District Council. Thurnscoe owed much of its development to the generosity of Reverend Thomas Thornely Taylor, who sold and donated land to the colliery company and local authority. He was notable for owning the first vehicle registered in the Barnsley Borough, a motor car with the registration HE 1. After his death, his son John disposed of the remaining 640 acre Thurnscoe Estate; Thurnscoe Hall was purchased by the colliery company as a residence for William Wilde. The colliery company also bought 22 assorted properties: two cottages on Shepherds Lane; Hall Farm, Home Farm Cottage, Rose Cottage, The Lodge, Pear Tree Cottages, Rosslyn House, Hall Cottage, High Grange Cottages, High Grange Farm and Low Grange, (the last lived in by the colliery agent, John Minnikin). Together with the 30 houses forming Hickleton Terrace, the 294 houses constructed by the Thurnscoe Housing Association and the 733 houses provided by the Industrial Housing Association, the colliery company ultimately owned 1,080 properties in Thurnscoe. High Grange Farm was later used as the colliery's estate office.

Despite the economic depression of the 1930s, developments continued through this decade and the West Riding County Council provided a library in Shepherd Lane. In 1931, the colliery company donated a seven-acre site in Chapel Lane to serve the Hill School, and playing fields and a football ground were opened. In 1934, the education system was reorganised and Houghton Road School became a Junior and Infants School and the Hill School was adapted as a secondary modern school. An extension to the Hill School was also built to house the Juniors and Infants. On 2 March 1935, the new St Hilda's Church opened on Hanover Street and was consecrated by the Bishop of Sheffield, allowing the old mission church to close. The handsome new stone built church with accommodation for 450 worshippers opened on Hanover Street. Grants for the building of St Hilda's Church were received from Lord Halifax of Hickleton Hall, Ralph Warde-Aldham of Frickley Hall and Saint John Warde-Aldham of Hooton Pagnell Hall.

In 1935, the council provided 50 bungalows on Low Grange Road, constructed in a field donated by John Minnikin. In 1937, the council merged with Bolton-upon-Dearne Urban District Council to form Dearne Urban District Council. The new authority completed the housing on Low Grange Road with the provision of 70 semi-detached council houses in 1938. Following the end of the Second World War, further housing for miners was provided by the Coal Industry Housing Association (CIHA), an organisation established by the NCB to provide accommodation in the Yorkshire and East Midland coalfields. The NCB encouraged miners and their families to move to the area from the older coalfields of Scotland and North-East England. At Thurnscoe, building operations were centred on Thurnscoe Bridge Lane from 1952, and 168 houses were provided on a western site (Derry Grove) and 104 houses on the eastern site (Lindley Crescent). Dearne Urban District Council also provided further housing in the 1950s. The first phase of this was a short extension to Merrill Road which accommodated six small blocks of flats, 24 apartments in total. Building operations continued throughout the decade and the local authority provided 234 houses forming the Whin Wood Estate - Merrill Road, Burnside, St Peter's Gate, Challenger Crescent and Whinside Crescent.

This development also included a small supermarket, playing fields and a new public house named the Whin Wood. In the 1960s School Street was extended to link up with Lingamoor Leys and Merrill Road and 166 'Reema' houses were constructed. Reema houses were made from a series of prefabricated reinforced concrete panels, and were supplied by Reed & Mallik of Salisbury, (Reema being a contraction of their manufacturers names). The new estate also included 24 flats. On Clayton Lane, Thurnscoe High School and Gooseacre Infants and Junior School were built. During the 1960s and 1970s, some demolition of older housing occurred, including some of the speculatively built terraced housing at Thurnscoe West and George Street. In 1974, the housing stock owned by Dearne Urban District Council passed to Barnsley Metropolitan Borough Council and in the 1980s they undertook a major refurbishment of the Thurnscoe Hall Estate, demolishing many of the properties. The NCB was looking to dispose of its housing stock and most of its 1,300 Thurnscoe houses passed to Barnsley Council, private landlords or were purchased by the tenants.

Above Left: During the First World War, 1,607 Hickleton Colliery miners had joined the forces and on Saturday 20 September 1920, Thurnscoe Park, with a new War Memorial was opened by the colliery company. The park passed into the ownership of Thurnscoe Urban District Council which continued to improve the facilities, building a bandstand and sunken garden with two pagodas, one of which is shown in this Edgar Scrivens postcard published in 1931. Note the smoking chimneys of Hickleton Main Colliery in the distance.

Above Right: A postcard issued by the South Yorkshire Times depicting NCB houses in Derry Grove, constructed by the CIHA. These were built in pairs and blocks of four from precast reinforced concrete panels, lending a grey finish to the appearance of the properties, and were amongst 24,070 houses completed by the Coal Industry Housing Association. They were often given nicknames like 'Concrete', 'Canyon' and 'White City'. In 1977, all CIHA and Thurnscoe Housing Association estates transferred to the NCB which disposed of them to local authorities. *(Andrew McGarrigle Collection)*

With the closure of the colliery in 1988, the heart of the local community was removed and many of the public buildings have since been demolished, including the Houghton Road Schools, Broadway Buildings, the Wesleyan Methodist Chapel, Thurnscoe Cinema and Thurnscoe Baths; the population has since declined as people have moved away from the area. Thurnscoe has suffered from extreme levels of deprivation which have only recently been addressed by the local authorities. In the 21st century, the Reema estate was demolished due to structural problems, together with many of the speculatively built terraced houses at Thurnscoe East; some of the derelict properties on Brunswick Street and Dane Street have also been removed and replaced with new social housing. However, the community spirit endures and there has been a renewed interest in the area fostered by groups including the Friends of Thurnscoe Park and the Thurnscoe Local History Group.

Wath-upon-Dearne

Above: During the 18th century, Wath was known as the 'Queen of Villages' due to its Georgian properties and the village remained picturesque well into the 20th century, as can be seen on this 1930 postcard of High Street, published by Edgar Scrivens. The premises of beer retailer Alfred Smith front the former Market Square and tram number 17, belonging to the Dearne District Light Railway, can be seen heading away from the camera towards Manvers Main. However, the attractive buildings on the left have been demolished and replaced with a brutalist modern shopping parade and library, but Alfred Smith's property remains, a reminder of the times when Wath was the Queen of Villages.

Wath-upon-Dearne (commonly referred to as Wath) was recorded as *Wade* in the Domesday Survey of 1086, and the name is derived from the Norse word Wath, meaning a ford. The area was given to Roger de Busli, a Norman baron who accompanied William the Conqueror in 1066. However, the village may have an older ancestry as it is believed that a branch of the Roman Road named Ryknield Street passed through the area crossing the River Dearne en route from Templeborough to York and Castleford. The village, like neighbouring Wombwell, is located on the spring line marking the change of rock types from porous sandstone to impermeable clay, and situated above the floodplain. With extensive fertile agricultural lands in the area and access to sandstone for building, the village grew during the medieval period, clustered around the Norman All Saints Church. An early market was established and a National School was opened in 1663. Wath served as a small market town for the neighbouring area, with Wath Hall constructed as a residence for a branch of the Savile family in 1770 on the site of a mediaeval Manor House.

The land in this area subsequently passed on to other landowners which included Henry Payne of Newhill Hall, William Smelter Cadman of Handsworth Grange in Sheffield, Robert Charles Otter of Royston Manor in Clayworth, Earl Manvers of Thoresby Hall and local brewer Spedding Whitworth of Dunford House. Earl Fitzwilliam was the Lord of the Manor and owned land to the south of Wath, including a private race course at Swinton Common. The Dearne & Dove Canal reached Wath in 1798; the Midland Railway opened a station in 1841 and the South Yorkshire Railway opened one in 1851. Wath was becoming the centre of a transport network developed to exploit the coal reserves of the Dearne Valley and industrialists were beginning to focus their attention on the area. However, Wath retained its rural and pleasant aspect, even though in 1841, the population was recorded as 1,453.

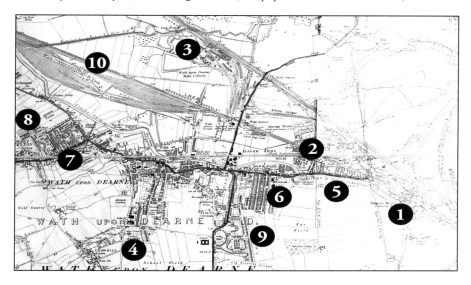

Above: Extract from the 1932 Ordnance Survey Map showing Wath-upon-Dearne.
1: Manvers No 1 Pit. **2:** Manvers No 2 Pit. **3:** Wath Main Colliery. **4:** Site of Newhill Colliery. **5:** Nash Row. **6:** Gore Hill. **7:** Winterwell. **8:** WUDC Housing Scheme (1923). **9:** WUDC Housing Scheme (1924). **10:** Wath Concentration Yard. *(Taken from the Dearne District Traction Act Map – Paul Fox Collection)*

The first colliery sunk in the area was Newhill Colliery on Cemetery Road to the south of Wath which opened in 1866. The pit was not very successful financially, and so was reconstituted as a company with a capital of £30,000 and another shaft was sunk in 1877 to the Meltonfield seam at a shallow depth. However, output was very small and was sold in the local vicinity; by 1900 the pit had ceased working. Nevertheless, a small community had developed at Newhill, which included Newhill Hall, Newhill Grange, Newhill Farm and the Crown Inn. This formed a hamlet of stone cottages which housed agricultural labourers, quarry workers and miners. A few brick-built rows were added together with a Wesleyan Reform Methodist Church and All Soul's Mission Room.

However, three much deeper and larger collieries were sunk adjacent to the new railway network. The first was Manvers Main Number 1 Pit, sunk in 1867, followed by Wath Main Colliery in 1873, with Manvers Main Number 2 Pit following in 1875. Wath, once the Queen of Villages, suddenly found itself on the cusp of being transformed into an industrial town. Three principal areas of housing were built: on Doncaster Road including Nash Row, on Barnsley Road including Winterwell, and in an area within Swinton Parish named Roman Terrace – now largely considered part of Mexborough.

In the 1870s, the Manvers Main Colliery Company opened a brickyard to assist the development of a new colliery settlement at Wath Staithes on Doncaster Road to the east of Wath. This new community was known as Nash Row and included two public houses, the Lord Nelson Inn and the Manvers Main Inn. Around 90 houses were built along Doncaster Road, Park Lane and Little Moor Road and around two communal yards known as Court No 1 and Court No 2. The 1881 census recorded a population of 246 people living at Nash Row and, of these, nearly 100 were born outside Yorkshire, mostly in Lancashire and the counties of the Black Country. The new houses were simple 'two-up two-down' cottages, with a fire place in the front room and a kitchen with a Yorkshire Range and a copper to boil water and wash clothes. Privies were built in the backyards and allotments provided. The new settlement was owned by Manvers Main Colliery and, during a strike in 1876, the management evicted many of their workers from the houses. Another row of 12 houses was built to the north of the railway line near Manvers No 2 Pit yard, mainly for deputies. In the 1890s, another block of housing was built to the west of Nash Row, consisting of 96 similar houses forming Winnifred Road, Edna Street and Common Lane. The colliery company built a footbridge across the railway line from the northern end of Park Lane to provide access to Number 2 Pit. To the west at Gore Hill, another 75 houses were built by speculative builders on Cadman Street and Doncaster Road. Several of the men living here worked at the adjacent malt house and the South Yorkshire Works - an oil, soap and chemical manure factory.

Above: The colliery community of Nash Row was situated on Doncaster Road to the north of the Dearne & Dove Canal, with the chimneys of Manvers Number 1 Pit visible in the background. The building nearest the camera is Manchester House, a drapery store owned by George Garrett which was later converted into a Billiard Hall. Other shops in Nash Row included Joseph & Michael Whitfield's general store and John Pyatt's grocery shop. The Dearne District Light Railway was built along Doncaster Road in 1924, the tram poles being built into the wall on the left. In the 1960s the whole area was demolished and Doncaster Road was rerouted to run along the bed of the canal. However, the wall on the left remains, complete with three truncated tram poles. This postcard was published in 1920 by Edgar Scrivens.

As well as shops, the new community at Nash Row and along Doncaster Road was provided with various churches and chapels. St Joseph's Roman Catholic Church opened in 1879 on Doncaster Road, mostly paid for by the Cadman family. Around 1890, a Primitive Methodist Chapel opened near Common Bridge which carried Doncaster Road over canal. In 1900, St James's Mission Church and Sunday School opened, which saved worshippers a walk to the mother church in Wath.

Above Left: The National School at Wath Town End had become overcrowded, so the Wath Local Board provided new schools at Gore Hill. These were named the Victoria Schools after the golden jubilee of Queen Victoria on 21 June 1887. The schools were extended in 1911 to accommodate 732 infants and junior children, some of which are shown on this postcard by Hawley of Hillsborough. The schools were recently demolished and replaced with a new building.

Above Right: Around 1905 and 1906, a large development of approximately 450 houses was built to the south of Doncaster Road, including Dearne View, Beech Road, Avenue Road and Sandymount Road. These were provided by local builders and used to accommodate miners moving to the area to work the deeper seams at Manvers Main Colliery. King George V celebrated his Silver Jubilee in 1935 when the inhabitants of Avenue Road festooned the street with flags and bunting, as shown on this postcard by an anonymous photographer.

At Wath Town End to the west, building operations were taking place on the Winterwell Fields in the 1880s and 1890s. Initially, Winterwell House stood in isolation at the junction of Melton Road and Barnsley Road. However, a grid of terraced housing was constructed by speculative builders and around 600 houses were built in Winterwell Road, Victoria Road, Albert Road, York Street, Princess Street, Co-operative Street, Barnsley Road and Melton Road. The development also included a Primitive Methodist Chapel and a Wesleyan Methodist Chapel; a house called Westville which became West Melton Working Men's Club; a public house on Barnsley Road named the George & Dragon Inn; a new branch of the Barnsley British Co-operative Society; a Gospel Hall on Barnsley Road and a Police Station - ideally situated to keep an eye on the new residents. People migrated to Winterwell to work at Cortonwood, Wath and Manvers Collieries and the settlement was surrounded on four sides by allotments. Nearby several isolated rows were built, including ten houses at Oakland Terrace, erected by the canal and with no road access and 50 houses on Hollowgate Avenue. Further houses were built on Vicar Road and Norton Road and, on 24 March 1913, the Wath & West Melton Cinema Company opened the Grand Cinema on Norton Road, with accommodation for 600 patrons. On Barnsley Road, Wath National School dated back to 1663 and a Church of England Infants School was built in 1895. However, most of the children at Winterwell attended new West Riding County Council Schools. These were opened in 1906 on Park Road and extended in 1911, although they were built some distance away across the valley of the Brook Dyke on Cemetery Road in Wath. The new schools had places for 800 children.

Above Left: Around 600 houses were built in the area known as Winterwell / Wath Town End / West Melton in the 1880s and 1890s, but this picture shows some of the better-quality properties constructed around 1905 on Melton Road (now Melton High Street), in front of a small school (St Joseph's Roman Catholic School which had opened in 1881?) The scene remains relatively unchanged today, although the wooden lock-up shops on the right have gone. Both postcard views date from around 1910 and were published by Edgar Scrivens.

Above Right: The Cross Keys Inn once stood in isolation on Doncaster Road and was one of many public houses in the town: others including the Lord Nelson Inn, Manvers Main Inn, the Red Lion Hotel, the White Bear, the George & Dragon and the New Inn. On the right is St Joseph's Roman Catholic Church, erected in 1879 at the expense of the Cadman and Nicholson families. The church in the distance is St James Mission Church, built at a cost of £2,000 in 1900, and recently demolished. Burman Road was built to the right in 1924.

The local governance of Wath had been the responsibility of the Wath Local Board and, in 1868, it opened a new cemetery with two mortuary chapels near Newhill Hall. In 1853, it promoted the Mechanics Institute which was rebuilt in 1883 by public subscription and subsequently grew to have 400 members. In 1885, a new Market Place was opened in the town, and in 1894, the Wath Local Board was reconstituted as Wath Urban District Council, operating from premises at Wath Hall which became the Town Hall. With increased 'urban' powers, the new authority could improve facilities in the area. It constructed a water works near Wath Wood and laid on a water supply, together with sewerage to the new corporation sewage works. A gas supply was introduced from the gas works on Station Road and a hospital was built by the Wath, Swinton & District Joint Hospital Board. The town was provided with a Methodist Church & Sunday School and a Primitive Methodist Church and became a thriving commercial centre. Several large properties were built in Fitzwilliam Street, Chapel Street and Cross Road which housed the better-off people of the town.

By 1901, the population of Wath township had increased to 8,515 and by 1911 it totalled 11,830 (7,736 in Wath and 4,494 in West Melton), all looking to Wath for their shopping and leisure needs. In 1899, local brewer Spedding Whitworth had provided a recreation and athletics ground on Moor Road as a gift to the people of the area. This incorporated a running track, football ground, cricket pitch and a fine pavilion building. In 1904, a parade of fine houses was built in Wharncliffe Crescent, including a new Post Office.

In 1910, the Olympia Skating Rink opened to serve the roller-skating craze that was sweeping Edwardian Britain at the time. The craze was short lived, and in 1912, it was converted into the Empire Cinema by the West Riding Electric Theatre Company with accommodation for 950 patrons. However, on 26 March 1920 the cinema burnt down and the building was rebuilt as the Empire Hall. In 1911, a Drill Hall opened in Moor Road as well as new public swimming baths next door, the latter at a cost of £2,500.

Following the First World War, Wath Urban District Council continued to improve services and facilities in the area. The local authority provided its own council houses, taking advantage of loans and subsidies from the Public Works Board. At Winterwell, 122 houses were built on Oak Lea Avenue and Stokewell Road in 1923. These houses were provided in blocks of two and four and included front and rear gardens in direct contrast to the earlier cramped housing of the area. In 1924, a large plot of land was purchased to the east of Sandygate. On this site 440 houses were built forming Burman Road, William Street, Henry Road, Charles Road, Riley Road, Winfield Road, Oak Road, Ash Road, Hawthorne Road and Sycamore Crescent.

Above Left: A postcard of Riley Road published by James Simonton in 1930 showing some of the 440 houses constructed by Wath Urban District Council on this site which included 60 large semi-detached properties at the northern end of Burman Road. The houses were built in blocks of two and four and featured spacious accommodation, with small front gardens and larger rear gardens. The development also included a new branch of the Barnsley British Co-operative Society. Burman Road is named after Frederick James Burman, the Medical Officer of Health to Bolton and Wath Urban District Councils.
Above Right: Although not in the parish of Wath, Roman Terrace near Mexborough was built to house many of the miners at Manvers Main Colliery. Many of the houses were built to poor standards, as evidenced by this photograph from the 1950s showing dishevelled properties on Wath Road. Roman Terrace featured a Methodist Chapel, the Roman Hotel, the Plant Hotel a park and schools with accommodation for 855 children. The block of housing on the left has since been pulled down and replaced with bungalows. The trolleybus belongs to Mexborough & Swinton and is operating to Manvers. *(Peter Mitchell / S J Butler)*

In 1913, the Barnsley & District Traction Company provided a bus service from Barnsley to West Melton and this was extended to Wath in 1914. However, the Urban District Council joined forces with three neighbouring local authorities to provide their own street tramway. This opened in 1924 as the Dearne District Light Railway and provided connections to Barnsley, Bolton, Goldthorpe and Thurnscoe. A short branch operated along Doncaster Road to the Manvers Main Inn at Nash Row whilst another branch was proposed to operate along Sandygate to Swinton. However, this was diverted to run along Burman Road to serve the new council housing estate.
In 1924, a new road, Montgomery Road, had been created to provide a more direct access for the trams and, as part of this scheme, the Town Hall Gardens were turned into a new public

park. In High Street, Wath Theatres Ltd built Wath Majestic Cinema Theatre with a seating capacity for 950 patrons. This new building was opened on 2 August 1926 by Arthur Thomson of Manvers Main Colliery. Because of the increasing population during the 1920s, new schools were needed. On 17 February 1923, Wath Secondary School was opened by the West Riding County Council in temporary buildings adjacent to Park Street School. However, in 1930 the school moved to a new building on Sandygate which became Wath Grammar School the following year.

During the 1920s and 1930s, private builders constructed several more streets: Woodland Terrace, Sandygate Crescent, Quarry Hill Road, Campsall Field Road and a southern extension to Fitzwilliam Street. However, the economic depression and the outbreak of war put a halt to any major developments by the local authority. Nevertheless, the post-war demand for housing saw Wath Urban District Council provide additional housing and, in the late 1940s, 72 prefabricated bungalows were built on Campsall Field Road.

In 1953, Wath Urban District Council compulsorily purchased Newhill Hall and its estate for the site of new council housing. The last family resident had left Newhill Hall in 1944; the property was demolished and 442 houses and bungalows were built on Campsall Field Road, Varney Road, Buckleigh Road, Crowley Drive, Cemetery Road, Quaker Close, Grange Road, Wombwell Avenue and Ellis Avenue. Some of the Newhill Hall grounds were incorporated into a new park, Newhill Park, which also included the now Grade II listed Payne Mausoleum built in 1834. Another 172 houses were built to the north of Newhill Park in Newfield Crescent, Cutts Avenue, Hall Drive and Nicholson Avenue. The new housing developments saw the building of a new road named Festival Road, after the 1951 Festival of Britain. On Festival Road, the Central Primary School and extensions to Wath Grammar School were opened.

During the mid-1950s, Wath Urban District Council was undertaking another large house building programme when it purchased the Winterwell Fields near West Melton. A development of around 760 houses, bungalows and flats was laid out and the streets were given literary names: for example, Masefield Road, Burns Way, Dryden Road, Byron Crescent, Ruskin Close, Wordsworth Road, Tennyson Rise, Browning Road, Blake Avenue & Coleridge Road. The development also included an Old People's Home and the Albert Working Men's Club.

The new housing estates were available to anybody and many miners moved into these new houses. However, most of the miners who came down from Scotland to work at Wath and Manvers Collieries in the 1950s were accommodated at a new pit estate in Bolton-on-Dearne. Wath Urban District Council continued to provided housing throughout the 1960s and early 1970s and a large 'Radburn' estate of houses, bungalows and three storey flats was built to the west of the town centre; it included shops and a rebuilt White Bear public house. Many of these houses were laid out on the 'Radburn Principle', with open plan communal spaces and access to the rear of the properties. The streets were named Valley Drive, Pinfold, Denman Road, Keble Martin Way, Saville Road, Gawtress Row, Fleming Square - many of the street names derived from family connections with the town.

To make way for the development of the Radburn Estate, several of the older stone cottages at the west end of the town were cleared. Demolition continued throughout the 1970s when the entire settlement of Nash Row was pulled down, together with areas of housing to the north of the village and at Town End, where many of the speculative built terraces of

Winterwell were cleared. A new town community centre named Montgomery Hall was built and a new road was constructed diverting Sandygate away from the town centre, together with additional housing provided at Strathmore Grove by South Yorkshire County Council. In 1985, a new relief road was built along the line of the derelict Dearne & Dove Canal. However, the closure of the surrounding pits at the end of the 1980s caused major hardship in the area and the town went into decline; some of the flats on the Radburn estate were demolished.

There has however been a recent revival in the town's fortunes. Wath Marshalling Yard and Manvers Main Colliery have provided a huge site for new industry: warehouses, call centres for example. These have attracted investment and provided employment opportunities in the area. Nevertheless, this has generated traffic problems at peak times and traffic is now constant along Biscay Way following the opening of a new supermarket on the site of Wath Brewery. Still, the town has remembered its mining heritage with memorials to both Wath and Manvers Collieries. Meanwhile, at the site of Nash Row, the Lord Nelson Inn, once the scene of numerous union meetings, now survives as a printing workshop; the Manvers Main Inn has been rebuilt as the Staithes Public House.

Above: The Wath Gas Works were established in 1844 at premises on Station Road from which gas was supplied for street lighting and public buildings, and later, to domestic properties, following the formation of the Wath & Bolton Gas Board in 1901. Two gasometers were built to hold coal gas generated at local coking works and by-product plants. The older 'two lift braced column supported' telescopic gasholder in the may date from the 1850s and is typical of such structures provided during the Victorian era. The second spirally guided gasholder was constructed in the 1890s and two additional gasometers were later provided. Most towns and cities had their own gasworks, but the 1948 Gas Act saw gas generation pass to twelve Local Gas Boards which formed British Gas in 1973. Gas generating was centralised and many of the smaller plants like the one at Wath were closed and dismantled during the 1970s, when coal gas was replaced with methane gas extracted from the North Sea oilfield. This postcard was published in 1905 by John Crowther-Cox of Rotherham.

Wombwell

Wombwell is located above the flood plain of the River Dove at the base of the dip slope of the Woolley Edge Rock, a band of sandstone within the Coal Measures which is overlain by clays and mudstones; the change in rock type leads to natural springs and forms an ideal location for a settlement. The village may date back to Saxon times as Womba's Well - the village with the well in the hollow - but it was recorded as *Wambella* in the Domesday Book of 1086, when the area was awarded to several Lords following the Norman Conquest: Roger de Busli of Tickhill Castle, Ilbert de Laci of Pontefract Castle and Walter of Aincort. Wombwell was one of several villages that formed the parish of Darfield, and in the 13th century, a Chapel of Ease was built.

Over the succeeding years, the district passed into a variety of landowners, including Sir George Wombwell, Member of Parliament for Huntingdon and Chairman of the East India Company. The family took its name from the area and originally lived at Wombwell Hall, but later moved to Newburgh Priory in North Yorkshire, and Wombwell Hall was pulled down in 1865. Other landowners included the Vernon-Wentworth family of Wentworth Castle; Earl Fitzwilliam of Wentworth Woodhouse; the Rimington-Wilson family of Broomhead Hall near Stocksbridge; Sir Theodore Brinckman of Clewer, Berkshire; Charles Taylor of Middlewood Hall, Darfield; and the Garland family of Netherwood Hall.

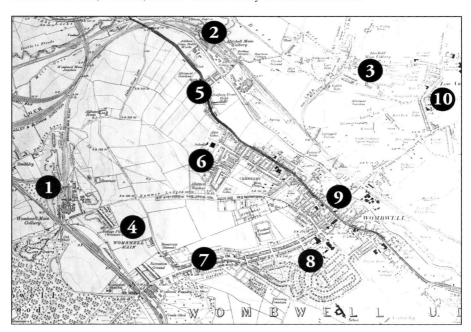

Above: Extract from the 1932 Ordnance Survey Map showing the Wombwell area.
1: Wombwell Main Colliery. **2:** Mitchells Main Colliery. **3:** Darfield Main Colliery. **4:** Wombwell Main. **5:** Mitchell's Terrace. **6:** Bartholomew & Main Streets. **7:** Hough Lane Ribbon Development. **8:** WUDC Housing Scheme (1923). **9:** Wombwell Town Centre **10:** Low Valley.
(Taken from the Dearne District Traction Act Map – Paul Fox Collection)

There had been small scale mining operations in Wombwell Woods for many years but these worked inferior seams. In 1804, the Dearne & Dove Canal opened, although its main aim was to transport coal from the Worsbrough district, higher up the Dove valley. However, the opening of the South Yorkshire Railway in 1851 enabled colliery development to take place on a far greater scale. Henry Herbert Wombwell signed a Deed of Assignment for his 1,007 acre Wombwell estate with Charles Bartholomew, a railway and transport industrialist from Doncaster who represented a consortium of promotors wishing to develop a new colliery. The promotors successfully sank Wombwell Main Colliery near Wombwell Woods, one mile to the east of the village. Adjoining landowners leased their land to other colliery speculators, and Lundhill Colliery was sunk in 1853, Darfield Main Colliery in 1856, Swaithe Main Colliery in 1860, Mitchell's Main Colliery in 1871, and Cortonwood Colliery in 1872. Therefore, Wombwell quickly found itself surrounded by new pits and colliery communities and developed as a thriving commercial centre.

Above Left: Wombwell High Street developed as a busy shopping thoroughfare as can be seen on this postcard by an anonymous photographer which dates to 1910. On the left can be seen the three golden balls denoting the pawnbroker's shop belonging to John Guest & Sons. Many people would pawn their belongings on Mondays, retrieving them on Saturdays for the weekend. The building on the right is Wombwell Town Hall which opened in 1897. Apart from the growth of motor traffic, the scene is little changed today.
Above Right: A 'Greetings from Wombwell' Multiview published by Edgar Scrivens in 1920, depicting five views of the town: Wombwell Church, Wombwell Main Colliery, Great Central Railway Station, High Street and Park Street. The last features the Wombwell Empire Cinema which opened in 1910 and was rebuilt in 1913 with its fine frontage featuring stone from the quarries at Wombwell Main and bricks provided by Earl Fitzwilliam's brickworks at Skiers Spring near Hoyland.

In 1851, the population of Wombwell township was 1,627, but the village remained relatively small as the local pits had not yet been developed. St Mary's Church had been enlarged in 1835 and cottages were situated along the High Street, together with two farms, Town End Farm at the end of High Street, and Polar Farm opposite Wombwell Hall in Park Street. Aldham House Farm was situated to the north-west and there was a watermill at Aldham Bridge, where Barnsley Road crossed the River Dove, and there was another watermill near Netherwood Hall. The village contained shops and a Post Office but lacked its own school, children having to walk to The Ellis Church of England School at Hemingfield.

However, with the opening of the new collieries, people migrated to the area, both from elsewhere in Yorkshire and from the older coalfields of the country. Adjacent to Wombwell Main Colliery, the colliery company constructed a new settlement for their workforce named Wombwell Main, taking its name from the pit; the provision of accommodation in the cottages of the new company settlement would have been a persuasive factor in recruiting a workforce. The opening of brickworks and the importing of roof slates saw a different building style for the new houses at Wombwell Main, in direct contrast to the older stone built cottages of the area. Six houses were built along Pit Lane adjoining the colliery and these may have been reserved for deputies, although one was used as a smithy. On the opposite side of the road, 32 houses were arranged in four rows and numbered 7-15; 16-25; 26-35 and 36-42 respectively. The new houses, or 'cottages' as they were referred to at the time, were rather simple affairs, consisting of two bedrooms upstairs, a front room downstairs with a fireplace, and a kitchen with a Yorkshire Range and copper for boiling water and washing clothes. Several blocks of communal earth closets or privies were provided in the back yards. However, the colliery company provided a gas supply and water supply and the accommodation was probably far superior to the standards provided in many of the older cottages in the area, which relied on wells and candle light.

Wombwell Main had been built in the 1850s, prior to the 1870 Elementary Education Act which introduced compulsory schooling for children aged 5-12. However, the colliery company built their own school in the pit yard and employed their own teaching staff. Another building, number 42A, was used as Thomas Hinchcliffe's butcher's shop as the colliery company wanted a fresh supply of meat available to keep their men fit and healthy. In the 1880s, the colliery company built a chapel in the pit yard and opened a covered swimming pool. The new settlement of Wombwell Main was built within the shadow of the smoking colliery chimneys and adjacent to the brick kilns that provided its bricks. However, despite the immediate industrial nature and grim setting, the community was built in a rural and isolated position and the surrounding fields and nearby Wombwell Woods formed an ideal playground for the children - and probably an ideal poaching ground for the local miners!

In the 1860s, the colliery company provided another area of housing near Hough Lane. This settlement was also called Wombwell Main, although it was separated from the first Wombwell Main by two fields. This second new colliery community consisted of two long rows of terraces. The first row was numbered 43-70, whilst the second row was split into three blocks numbered 71-78, 79-89 and 90-101. No 43 was occupied by Arthur Hinchcliffe and used as a grocers and drapers. Nearby on Hough Lane, a public house opened; it was known as the Sir George's Arms, after Sir George Wombwell. The colliery company also provided a football and cricket ground, although this was later when the Midland Railway opened in 1895. The new colony of Wombwell Main was a close-knit community and the pit was known as 'the family pit' due to its close relationship between the men and their masters – one of the latter being Samuel Roberts of Sheffield who would be conveyed from Dovecliffe Station in a pony and trap on his frequent visits to inspect Wombwell Main.

A mile to the south of Wombwell Main, another isolated settlement was constructed at the same time for the miners of Lundhill Colliery. This consisted of a single row of 53 cottages named Lundhill Row, again built with bricks from the colliery brickworks. An adjacent stone barn was converted for use as a Wesleyan Methodist Chapel and Sunday School and a new public house opened, named the Lundhill Tavern. However, there was no school and children had to walk to the school in Hemingfield. When Lundhill Colliery closed in 1895, its assets were acquired by Wombwell Main Company Ltd, including the 53 cottages of Lundhill Row. Another colliery community was developed at Low Valley for Darfield Main Colliery in 1860 to the north of Wombwell (this has already been covered in the Darfield, Snape Hill & Low Valley section of this book). Other settlements at Broomhill and Hemingfield all looked to Wombwell for their services.

Above Left: The colliery community of Wombwell Main is shown on this postcard by an anonymous photographer c1905. This view looks towards Hough Lane from Wood Walk and features the second development of cottages, dating from the 1860s. Note the washing hung out in the yard between the two rows. The station master's house on the left opened in 1895 with the arrival of the Midland Railway. The 42 cottages forming the first development at Wombwell Main and the 59 cottages forming the second development were both cleared in the 1970s. *(Chris Sharp – Old Barnsley)*

Above Right: In 1871, Charles Bartholomew of Wombwell Main Company Ltd purchased 56 acres of land on Barnsley Road; this was subsequently split into lots and sold to private builders and the colliery company for housing. The northern end of Main Street (shown here in a postcard by John Crowther Cox of Rotherham) was built in the 1880s with the southern end following in the 1890s. Charles Bartholomew gave his name to an adjacent street of similar houses. On 22 May 1944, the Wombwell Main Company auctioned off their housing stock in Main Street, Bartholomew Street and Blythe Street.

With the opening of Mitchell's Main Colliery, a new colliery community was developed in the late 1870s about one mile to the northwest of Wombwell. This new settlement was initially known as Mitchell's Main, which, like Wombwell Main, took its name from the colliery. This feature - in naming a new settlement with the term 'Main' after the colliery - was also repeated at Denaby Main near Mexborough - discussed in an earlier book by the author on Denaby & Cadeby Main Collieries. The new brick built housing of Mitchell Main was provided in the block of land between Barnsley Road and the Dearne & Dove Canal. A settlement of around 90 terraced houses were laid out on Barnsley Road, Bradbury Balk Lane, Myers Street & Hammerton Street - the last possibly named after Daniel Hammerton, a building contractor from Darfield or after Messrs Dickinson & Hammerton, the owners of the nearby Aldham Glass Bottle Works. The houses fronting Barnsley Road were named Mitchell's Terrace, and this name was later applied to the whole settlement. To the north of the canal within the pit yard, a terrace of six larger properties known as Pit Cottages provided accommodation for colliery officials. The settlement contained two shops, and allotments were provided on Barnsley Road, but there was no school; children had to walk to the newly opened school in Wombwell. In 1893, the Mount Tabor Wesleyan Reform Church opened on the opposite side of Barnsley Road and around the same time a large public house was built, initially known as the Halfway Hotel and later as the White Rose.

The opening of Cortonwood Colliery saw houses provided at Concrete Cottages and Wombwell Junction, as has been discussed in the Brampton Bierlow section of this book. However, by the mid-1880s, Wombwell was surrounded by colliery communities at Lundhill, Wombwell Main, Mitchell Main, Low Valley, Concrete and Wombwell Junction, all separated from the larger village by fields but looking to it for their services and shopping requirements. Reflecting its growth, Wombwell had been established as an Ecclesiastical Parish in 1864 and the following year a Local Board was formed to assist with the governance of the area. The village was beginning to thrive and grow into a small town, with a market established in 1875 in an old quarry, and numerous shops opening. These included rather grand premises forming the 3rd branch of the Barnsley British Co-operative Society which opened in 1869. There were several public houses, including the Royal Oak, the Railway Hotel, the Horse Shoe Hotel and the Prince of Wales Arms.

Above: Bradbury Balk Road contained 22 of the 90 cottages forming the colliery community of Mitchell's Main or Mitchell's Terrace, constructed in the late 1870s. In 1901, the population of the settlement was 434. The housing of Mitchells Main was cleared in the 1970s although Aldham Cottages – a row of 23 houses provided for the Aldham Glass Bottle Works in 1895, remains today. The postcard was published by Edgar Scrivens in 1920 and incorrectly captioned Bradbury Road. This bridge over the Dearne & Dove Canal can be seen in the distance. *(Norman Ellis Collection)*

The Local Board supplied the area with water from the Dearne Valley Waterworks at Broomhill and installed sewers and sewage works. In 1870, the Wombwell & Darfield Gas Company opened in Station Road and the gas was supplied by the Local Board in 1879. The rapidly increasing population also meant that the number of deaths correspondingly increased and a new cemetery was provided on Cemetery Road in 1868. As well as mining, other industries were opening in the area, including the Mineral Water Manufactory and the Dearne & Dove Glass Bottle Works, both located adjacent to the canal.

By 1881, the population of Wombwell was recorded as 8,451 and the development of the Parkgate coal seam at Wombwell Main Colliery saw more workers to move to the area. Houses were provided in the 1880s in the block of land between Barnsley Road and Blythe Street, including the lower part of Main Street, Victoria Road, Bond Street, York Street and School Street. Some of these houses were built by speculative builders and some by the colliery company. Additional housing was constructed for Wombwell Main Miners in the

1890s and 1900s, on Main Street, William Street, Princess Street, Frederick Street, William Street, West Street, the southern side of Blythe Street and Bartholomew Street. Blythe Street takes its name from John Blythe, the agent to the Wombwell Main Company.

Elsewhere, speculative builders provided additional housing along the roads radiating from Wombwell to the various colliery communities: along Summer Lane to Wombwell Main; along Hough Lane to the second development at Wombwell Main - linking up the once isolated Sir George's Arms; along Barnsley Road to Mitchell Main; along Station Road to Low Valley; and along Park Road and Wath Road to Wombwell Junction. The population of the area increased rapidly, to 10,952 by 1891 and to 17,536 by 1911.

In 1894, the Wombwell Local Board was reconstituted as Wombwell Urban District Council and on 22 June 1897, a foundation stone was laid for the new Wombwell Town Hall by Mrs Mitchell of Bolton Hall, the wife of Joseph Mitchell Junior, a partner in Mitchell Main Colliery. The stone also commemorated the diamond jubilee of Queen Victoria. Another member of the Mitchell family, Major Thomas Mitchell was the chairman of the new local authority.

The rapid increase in population saw the desperate need for the provision of new schools in the district. In 1876, Barnsley Road Junior and Infants School opened with accommodation for 800 children. This was followed in 1894 with the opening of Park Street Junior and Infants School on a site opposite Wombwell Hall with places for 850 children. The West Riding County Council opened a third school in 1910, John Street School, with room for 420 children. St Mary's Church, by now inadequate for the district's needs was pulled down on 21 December 1896, and Viscount Halifax laid the foundation stone for the new replacement church which was consecrated on 21 April 1898 with the tower subsequently being added in 1914. The religious needs of other faiths were catered for with new buildings. In 1867 Wombwell Congregational Chapel opened, followed by a Wesleyan Methodist Chapel, a Zion Chapel, a United Reform Church on Hough Lane and the splendid Primitive Methodist Connexion Henry Adams Memorial Church on Barnsley Road. Park street became home to St Michael's and All Angels Roman Catholic Church and School. Following mining subsidence effecting their old barracks on Station Road, the Salvation Army moved into their new citadel on Park Road.

The Barnsley British Co-operative Society opened an additional branch in 1902 on Barnsley Road and had branches at Park Street, Station Lane and Wombwell Main. Meanwhile the leisure needs of the new community were beginning to be addressed. The Wombwell Working Men's Club & Institute opened in 1899 and was extended ten years later, the new premises proudly featuring four prominent foundation stones. In 1905, a new public library opened in Station Road, provided by the philanthropist Andrew Carnegie at a cost of £3,270. In 1910, three entertainment venues opened in the town. The first was the Pavilion Roller Skating Rink in Marsh Street which became the Pavilion Cinema the following year. On 12 May 1910, the Wombwell Empire opened in Park Street with a skating rink on the first floor and a cinema underneath. Finally, on 20 August 1910, the Wombwell Hippodrome opened on the junction of Hough Lane and Jardine Street. Roller skating was an immensely popular activity at the time, but the fashion was short lived and replaced by a new craze for 'going to the pictures', and the black and white silent movies of the era played to huge audiences. The Empire Cinema removed its skating rink and was rebuilt in 1913. In 1914, Wombwell Urban District Council provided public swimming baths on Hough Lane, as 'going to the baths' was another popular activity during that time.

Following the end of the First World War, Wombwell Urban District Council decided to embark on a council house building programme. A large plot of land was purchased and starting in 1922, 464 houses were laid out on Jardine Street, Mellor Road, Hadfield Street, Roebuck Street, Pickup Crescent, Goodyear Crescent, Wright Crescent, Hall Road and Elliot Avenue. This development differed greatly from the older areas of colliery housing. The houses were mostly built in pairs with large front and rear gardens and arranged around a series of geometric patterns and curving crescents. As part of this development, the West Riding County Council provided two new schools - Kings Road Primary School and Wombwell County Secondary School - the latter built around a series of quadrangles. The council also opened Wombwell Park, featuring tennis courts, bowling greens, flower beds and an attractive rock garden known as the Dingle. At Wombwell Main, the Miners Welfare Fund provided a recreational ground including football and cricket pitches.

In 1924, the local authority formed the Dearne District Light Railway and opened a street tramway linking Wombwell with Barnsley and the other Dearne Valley villages. More people moved to the area and the local pits were now exploiting deeper seams; Wombwell was becoming a thriving commercial centre. The 1920s perhaps represent the town's heyday and it is hard to believe how busy it was, especially on market days and on Friday and Saturday evenings. In 1929, the South Yorkshire Stadium opened on Station Road, home to the Wombwell Colliers Speedway team, and the stadium also hosted greyhound racing, both activities being popular with miners.

Above Left: The first houses were built on Hough Lane in the 1890s near the Sir George's Arms and ten years later housing had spread along Hough Lane from Wombwell Main to the town centre. The Sir George's Arms was a rather grand public house, possibly built in the 1880s to serve Wombwell Main, which can be seen in the far distance. This postcard was published by Edgar Scrivens in 1920.
Above Right: As well as miners, several of the new houses were occupied by workers at Wombwell Iron Foundry, and shops and services opened along Hough Lane, including this tin chapel which served as the United Methodist Church. The tin chapel was replaced with a brick structure in 1928. This postcard was published by John Crowther-Cox in 1905.

Despite the economic depression of the 1930s, the council's house building programme continued on a new site to the north of Hough Lane and 96 houses were built on Copeland Road, Stubbs Avenue and Loxley Avenue, with 70 bungalows being built on Copeland Road, Burrows Grove and Tune Street. After the Second World War, bricks and materials were in short supply; therefore, the local authority purchased 224 BISF houses from the British Iron & Steel Federation. These houses were constructed from concrete panels and steel sheeting and were quick to build. They were laid out on Wooley Avenue, Bondfield Crescent, Foley

Avenue, Washington Avenue, Sokell Avenue and Windmill Road. Again, the scheme featured curving crescents and was completed in the early 1950s with an additional 118 brick built houses on Washington Avenue, Rutland Place, Bird Avenue and Burrows Grove. Wombwell Urban District Council embarked on another house building programme in the 1950s and 458 houses and bungalows were built on Wilson Street, Rose Place, Rose Grove, Wainwright Avenue, Wainwright Place, Yvonne Road, Kitchin Road, Jones Avenue, and Turner Avenue.

In 1947, the colliery-owned settlements of Wombwell Main and Lundhill Row passed into the ownership of the NCB, together with other houses in Windmill Avenue and Park Street, as well as Smithley Farm and a large house near the colliery named Woodleigh. The NCB were looking to dispose of their housing stock by a combination of sale and demolition and after the closure of Wombwell Main Colliery in 1969, the entire settlements of Wombwell Main and Lundhill were demolished during the 1970s.

House building continued into the early 1960s with 370 houses and flats constructed on the Aldham House Estate around Pearson Crescent, followed by the provision of the Aldham House Radburn Estate at the end of the decade: 270 houses and flats built on the open plan Radburn Principle. This brought the total number of houses constructed by Wombwell Urban District Council to well over 2,000; new schools were built, for example Highfields Primary School, and new public houses were provided, for example the Periwinkle at Aldham House. As well as the council housing and the housing built for miners before the war, private builders contributed to Wombwell's housing stock in the 1930s and especially since the 1960s. Today, Wombwell is still a relatively busy shopping centre but, following the closure of the surrounding collieries, most of the people work elsewhere, many finding employment in the warehouses, industrial units, retail parks and distribution centres built on the former colliery sites.

Part 3 Dearne Valley Transport

Above: A scene in Montgomery Road, Wath, captured on a 1920s postcard by Edgar Scrivens. The conductor of Dearne District tram number 30 has just changed the pole for the return journey to Manvers or Swinton whilst a competing Barnsley & District motor bus has stopped to allow a passenger to alight. The vehicle is fleet number 98 (registration HE 1827), a 1924 Leyland SG11 motor bus with Brush bodywork for 32 passengers. Today, Montgomery Road is occupied by Wath Bus Station and the ivy clad property on the right has been demolished to make way for Wath Library.

The Road Network

Although our prehistoric ancestors used ancient trackways to move around and trade with other regions, it was the expansion of the Roman Empire and the introduction of its military road network that introduced the concept of highways as we think of them today. The Roman invasion of Britain in AD43 by Emperor Claudius sought to subjugate the Iron Age tribes of the country, initially by conquest and perhaps more successfully, by implementing the appeal of the Roman lifestyle. The Romans began to expand their road network from their principal fort at London, their new military roads being ideally suited to moving legions to various areas in the new Roman province. From their fort at Lincoln, they pushed northwards to Doncaster, where a fort guarded the crossing of the River Don, before continuing to York where they established a provincial capital in AD71. From Doncaster, another road led southwards to the Roman fort at Templeborough near Rotherham, approximately following the line of the modern day A630. From Templeborough it was thought that a roman road headed northwards through the Dearne Valley to link up with the Roman settlement at Castleford. The exact route of this road heading through Wath-upon-Dearne (Wath being an old name for a ford across a river) is now lost and can only be partially traced on modern maps. Another conjectured Roman road is believed to have headed north from Conisbrough, crossing the River Don at Strafforth Sands near Mexborough, before passing between Barnburgh and High Melton and possibly linking up with the road through the Dearne Valley from Templeborough.

The withdrawal of the Roman occupation in AD410 saw Britain enter the Dark Ages. Saxon, Viking and Norman invasions followed which increased the population and stimulated trade. Following the Norman invasion of 1066, the Dearne Valley was divided up into a series of manorial estates which fell under the jurisdiction of Roger de Busli of Tickhill Castle and William de Warenne of Conisbrough Castle. In 1147, the granting of land to religious orders saw the founding of Roche Abbey by the Cistercians and, in 1154, Monk Bretton Priory near Barnsley was established by monks of the Cluniac monastic order. The latter built a large watermill on the River Dearne near Stairfoot. The development of trade continued through the medieval period, enhanced locally by the granting of market charters at Doncaster in 1248, Barnsley in 1249, Rotherham in 1250, Sheffield in 1296 and Wath-upon-Dearne in 1312. Local villagers looked to trade at these new markets and new roads and tracks were formed to link these together.

The Dissolution of the Monasteries and the collapse of the feudal state saw land tenure pass to a multitude of owners. However, trade continued to grow throughout late medieval times, with goods being transported long distances along a growing network of pack horse roads, the most famous locally being known as the 'Salter's Gate', established to bring salt from Cheshire to Barnsley and Doncaster and now forming the modern day A635. Much later, a growing need for passenger transport was serviced by a network of horse drawn stage carriages between the major towns and cities, although most local people still relied upon a horse drawn cart or pony and trap for transport.

Increasing concern at the perilous state of the road network led to the formation of Turnpike Trusts. These were organisations established by an Act of Parliament, with powers to collect tolls on goods and people using the roads, the revenue raised used for continuing improvements and highway maintenance. In the Dearne Valley area the following turnpike roads were established:

1740 Doncaster-Barnsley-Saltersbrook (Yorkshire/Cheshire Border).
1741 Doncaster-Wakefield
1742 Doncaster-Boroughbridge (Great North Road)
1764 Rotherham-Wentworth
1764 Sheffield Tinsley-Rotherham-Conisbrough-Doncaster
1809 Rotherham-Swinton
1818 Brampton Bierlow-Hooton Roberts (with the Swinton branch to Conisbrough)
1825 Barnsley-Hemsworth-Pontefract

By the mid-19th century, turnpike roads were increasingly seen as inefficient, with the frequent stops to pay tolls seen as a barrier to the free movement of trade. Most freight traffic had now transferred to the new canal and railway network, creating a dramatic collapse in turnpike revenues; and a movement to de-turnpike roads was gaining traction. The Local Government Act of 1888 transferred responsibility for road maintenance to newly formed county councils and the roads of the Dearne Valley passed into the control of the West Riding of Yorkshire County Council from 1889.

Above: Three forms of transport meet at Wath-upon-Dearne. In the foreground is Doctor Fred Easter's De Dion Bouton motor car registered C1552. Meanwhile on Station Road bridge, tram car number 30 belonging to the Dearne District Light Railway crosses the Dearne & Dove Canal whilst en route to Thurnscoe. In 1985, this area was redeveloped as part of the A633 Wath bypass and a new roundabout now occupies this site.

The increase in the use of motorised transport in the early 20th century saw the introduction of the Road Fund through the 1920 Road Act. This was designed to raise revenue for road maintenance and improvements from the rapidly rising number of petrol-powered public and private vehicles using the roads. Revenue was raised from vehicle excise duty and from a tax on fuel. The 1920 Road Act also established a classification scheme for the roads of the country, and, from 1923, the familiar A-road and B-road numbering system was introduced.

Former turnpikes and other roads were linked up to create new A roads, those passing through or near to the Dearne Valley including:

A1 London-Doncaster-Edinburgh
A61 Sheffield-Worsbrough Bridge Barnsley-Leeds
A628 Barnsley-Hemsworth-Pontefract
A630 Sheffield-Rotherham-Doncaster
A633 Rotherham-Wath-Wombwell-Barnsley
A635 Doncaster-Goldthorpe-Darfield-Barnsley-Manchester
A6022 Mexborough-Swinton Woodman Inn
A6023 Wath-Manvers-Mexborough-Conisbrough

Roads of lesser status were designated B roads and these were often of relatively short length and linked up with the A road network. Those in the Dearne Valley were numbered:

B6089 Wombwell-Brampton-Rotherham
B6090 Wentworth-Hooton Roberts
B6092 Swinton Blackamoor Road (one of the shortest B-roads in the country)
B6096 Hoyland-Wombwell-Darfield
B6097 Hoyland-Elsecar-West Melton-Wath
B6098 Manvers-Bolton-Goldthorpe
B6100 Stairfoot-Worsbrough
B6273 Hemsworth-Great Houghton-Broomhill-Brampton
B6411 Great Houghton-Thurnscoe-Hickleton

Above: One of the attractive West Riding finger posts that were installed following the 1920 Road Act featuring the new A and B road designations. This example was at Swinton Woodman Inn at the junction of the A633, A6022 and B6092, captured by Stan Smith in 1932, whose bicycle bell and handle bar is pictured in the foreground. The tram belongs to the Dearne District Light Railway and is about to depart for the short run to Wath and West Melton. Off camera to the right was Swinton Common Colliery which closed in 1936. A roundabout was installed at this junction in the late 1950s and the sign post has long since disappeared. *(Stan Smith / Paul Fox Collection)*

Apart from new suburban roads serving housing developments, very little road building took place until the construction of the national motorway network, but the new motorways skirted the Dearne Valley. The A1(M) Doncaster Bypass opened in 1961 and the M1 London-Wadworth Motorway opened in 1967. During construction, it was decided to extend the M1 to Leeds, passing to the west of Barnsley; this opened in 1968 and the short spur to the A1(M) at Wadworth was renumbered M18.

Apart from the opening of the Mexborough bypass on the A6023 in 1968, the only other major phase of road building occurred in more recent times following the collapse of the mining industry. This was proceeded by the opening on 24 October 1985 by the South Yorkshire County Council of the Wath Bypass (Biscay Way) and the much longer Wombwell Bypass (Mitchells Way & Valley Way) along which the A633 was now routed. In 1988, a new road opened replacing part of the B6273 between Broomhill and the A635 at Darfield Cat Hill, and this new road was designated as the Dearne Valley Parkway.

Following the closure of many of the pits in the late 1980s and early 1990s, the shafts were capped, the surface buildings demolished and railway sidings removed. However, the derelict pit sites, spoil heaps and abandoned railways remained undeveloped for several years. This created what was believed to be the largest area of dereliction in Europe, a huge tract of land stretching for nearly 10 miles from Elsecar to Barnburgh. The land remained the property of the British Coal Corporation, the successor to the National Coal Board, but, following the privatisation of British Coal's remaining mining operations in 1994, the land passed into the ownership of English Partnerships, a government developmental agency. The Dearne Valley was designated as an Enterprise Zone in 1995 and benefited from national and European grants to create new roads and areas of employment.

The Goldthorpe bypass on the A635 was opened in 1992, passing to the south of the Hickleton Main Colliery spoil heap, and the Dearne Valley Parkway was extended westwards to the M1 near Hoyland in 1998 and designated as the A6195; it linked with the new retail park at Cortonwood Colliery and enabled new industrial units to be constructed on colliery sites near Hoyland. In the same year, the A633 was rerouted along a new road through the former Wath Marshalling Yard from Wath to link up with the A6195. At Wath the A633 met another road, an extension of the A6023 from Mexborough, passing through the site of the former Manvers Coal Preparation Plant and serving new offices, call centres and the newly opened Dearne Valley College. From Cat Hill roundabout, the A6195 was extended in 2003 to Grimethorpe, connecting Grimethorpe to the rest of the Dearne Valley for the first time and new warehouses and manufacturing centres have recently been opened on the site of Houghton Main and Grimethorpe Collieries. The A6195 was extended to Shafton in 2004, finally linking up with the new Cudworth bypass on the A628, which opened in 2010.

Today the road network has been greatly enhanced and the Dearne Valley Enterprise Zone has created thousands of new jobs. However, pressures on the road network remain, especially at peak times due to the increased use of private transport. Major traffic jams are now prevalent during rush hour, many along the single carriageway sections of the newly constructed A633, A6023 and A6195, roads which, with the benefit of hindsight, perhaps should have been built to dual carriageway standards when ample space was available through the former colliery sites. These pressures at peak times are bound to continue.

The Dearne & Dove Canal.

In 1726, a group of Sheffield Cutlers and Doncaster Corporation established the River Dun (sic) Navigation Company to improve the waterway for commercial barge traffic, by constructing a series of canal cuts and longer sections of canal to bypass the many weirs along the course of the River Don. By 1751 the waterway was navigable as far as Tinsley, five miles short of Sheffield. However, the new navigation was mostly of benefit to the metal working regions of Sheffield, and the Dearne Valley remained a rural backwater. The River Dearne was too shallow for the use of commercial barge traffic, therefore, in 1772, the Marquis of Rockingham proposed the construction of an 18-mile long canal to help develop the new coalfields. The canal was intended to leave the River Don at Conisbrough and to proceed up the Dearne Valley via Barnsley to terminate at Haigh near West Bretton. However, these plans never came to fruition, possibly due to issues involved in raising finance, and it would be a further 20 years before the development of the first canals in the Dearne Valley, with the establishment of The Dearne & Dove Canal.

On 20 October 1792, a meeting was held at Barnsley between the River Dun Navigation Company and The Aire & Calder Navigation Company to co-ordinate rival schemes to bring navigable canals to the Barnsley region. The Aire & Calder Navigation Company proposed to construct the Barnsley Canal between their existing waterway at Wakefield to a point near Hoyle Mill in Barnsley where it would meet a scheme proposed by the River Dun Navigation Company. This was initiated by the Dearne & Dove Canal Act which was approved by an Act of Parliament on 3 June 1793. This authorised the construction of the new canal and the raising of £60,000 in shares and £30,000 in mortgages.

Shareholders in the new Dearne & Dove Canal Company included several prominent landowners and coal royalty owners in the area: Earl Fitzwilliam of Wentworth Woodhouse; Thomas Osbourne the Duke of Leeds; Sir Lionel Copley of Sprotbrough Hall; Sir George Wombwell of Wombwell Hall; and Sir Francis Wood of Monk Bretton. The development of proposed collieries on the estates of the landed gentry would generate extensive royalty payments to landowners, hence their interest in the opening of new coalfields. The canal company proposed to build a 10-mile-long waterway from the River Don at Swinton to Hoyle Mill near Barnsley. Along its length, the canal would rise a total of 127 feet via 19 locks, with most of the locks being grouped into short flights to increase efficiency. Two short branches were authorised: one along the tributary valley of the Knoll Beck to Elsecar Basin, the centre of Earl Fitzwilliam's industrial empire; the other branch along the tributary valley of the River Dove to Worsbrough Basin, the focus of the Mitchell family's coal and iron businesses.

Construction of the canal commenced at Swinton in 1794 and by 1798 the canal had reached Elsecar. By 1800 construction had reached Aldham Mill at Wombwell and, by 1804, the Worsbrough branch and the main canal to Hoyle Mill were open for business. At Hoyle Mill, the Dearne and Dove Canal met the newly completed Barnsley Canal, thus allowing through traffic between the two navigations systems as well as access to Barnby Basin near Cawthorne with its connecting wagonways to the Silkstone collieries, controlled by the Clarke family of Noblethorpe Hall.

Leaving the River Don at Swinton, the canal rises steeply through a series of six locks to cross the watershed with the River Dearne through a 472-yard tunnel. Level passage was now permitted along a terrace a short distance above the level of the River Dearne to the small town of Wath-upon-Dearne. A further flight of four locks brought the navigation to

Wombwell Junction near Brampton, where the Elsecar branch diverged from the main canal. This passed through six locks raising the formation by 48 feet and travelled two miles to terminate at Elsecar Basin. The main canal continued on the level through the town of Wombwell, now following the tributary valley of the River Dove to Aldham Mill where it crossed the river by a small aqueduct, possibly the most notable engineering feature on the canal. A final flight of eight locks raised the navigation to its highest level at Worsbrough Junction where the Worsbrough branch diverged along the River Dove valley for two miles to terminate at Worsbrough Basin. The main canal continued on the level through Stairfoot, crossing the watershed back into the valley of the River Dearne. Beyond Stairfoot, the Dearne & Dove Canal followed the curving contour high above the river passing Barnsley Oaks Colliery and Barnsley Brewery before joining the Barnsley Canal at Hoyle Mill. Above Elsecar Basin, the Knoll Beck was dammed to form a small reservoir to feed the canal. Similarly, above Worsbrough Basin another reservoir was constructed on the River Dove to supply the canal, this reservoir being significantly larger as it was intended to serve the Barnsley Canal as well as provide a drinking water supply to the town. From Worsbrough Basin to the junction with the Barnsley Canal, the Dearne & Dove was free from locks, a significant engineering achievement at the time.

The opening of the Dearne & Dove Canal in 1804 immediately stimulated trade around the two canal basins. At Elsecar, the various mining operations and iron works owned by Earl Fitzwilliam now had a convenient transport outlet for their products. Small pits further afield were connected to the two basins by wagonways or inclined planes (where coal, contained in small wagons, could be lowered down a fixed course by a steam powered winch by means of a rope attached to the wagons). In 1810, 73,384 tons of coal were carried along the Dearne & Dove Canal. Of this figure 26.462 tons was dispatched from Elsecar Basin, 20,312 tons from Worsbrough basin and 22,395 tons entered the navigation from the Barnsley Canal, much of which was bound for the London market. Tolls levied on the passage of coal enabled the canal company to raise income and, by 1810, the first dividend was paid to shareholders. Coal traffic continued to rapidly increase and, by 1817, over 100,000 tons were carried along the canal; the annual tonnage figure had reached 181,000 tons by 1830.

However, although coal was by far the most important cargo, other goods were transported along the canal. Limestone was imported to Elsecar and Worsbrough Basins for use in the iron industry, with pig iron being exported from the ironworks. Corn was shipped to the various watermills and sand from the Bawtry region was imported for use in the Dearne Valley glassworks. Other shipments included timber and various general merchandise. It must also be noted that during the early operation of the canal, coal traffic was mostly generated from the two canal basins at Elsecar and Worsbrough. These were both located in the west within two tributary valleys where the coal seams were nearest to the surface. The remainder of the Dearne Valley was largely untouched by mining operations during the first half of the 19th century. The most profitable seams - the Barnsley, Parkgate and Silkstone - were too deep to be exploited by the engineering technologies of the day. The arrival of the Dearne & Dove Canal had encouraged the development of the coalfield, particularly along these two branches; however, it would require the arrival of the railways in 1840 to initiate colliery development in the rest of the Dearne Valley.

The arrival of the North Midland Railway in 1840 was initially not considered a major threat to the coal traffic carried on the Dearne & Dove Canal. In fact, the railway brought a small benefit to the canal as during construction of the line near Swinton, a large cutting was made through the watershed between the Don and Dearne Valleys. This enabled the canal company to abandon their 472-yard-long tunnel and divert the canal to share the new cutting with the railway at this point. However, railway mania was now sweeping the country and, in 1845, the proposed South Yorkshire Coal Railway was deemed a significant threat to the canal's trade as it was intended to connect the Silkstone, Elsecar, Worsbrough and Barnsley coalfields with other railways and national markets and obviously steam powered locomotives hauled trains of wagons at much greater speeds than a horse-drawn canal barges. To counteract these threats the canal company could offer lower tolls but this of course had the result of lowering revenue and profits. The South Yorkshire Coal Railway received parliamentary approval by an act of 1847 as the South Yorkshire, Doncaster & Goole Railway Company, and construction commenced immediately under the name of the South Yorkshire Railway.

Perhaps seeing that 'the writing was on the wall' for the canal trade in the Dearne Valley, the River Dun Navigation Company decided to consolidate its interests and purchased the Dearne & Dove Canal Company for £210,000 on 2 January 1847. The enlarged company then proposed a merger with the new South Yorkshire Railway and in 1850, the South Yorkshire Railway & River Dun Company was established; the merger possibly helped by the fact that many of the shareholders of the new railway venture, including Earl Fitzwilliam, Sir Joseph Copley and Charles Bartholomew of Wombwell Main Colliery, were also shareholders in the canal company. The South Yorkshire Railway constructed a line from Doncaster to Swinton to Wath Junction (where a branch line travelled to a terminus adjacent to Elsecar Basin), with the main line continuing via Wombwell to Aldham Junction (where another branch line diverged to Worsbrough Basin) and continuing to Barnsley, thus largely duplicating the canal network. The first sod of the new railway was cut in a field between Warmsworth and Levitt Hagg in 1847 and, by 1849, the railway was open between Doncaster and Swinton, with Elsecar opening in 1850 and finally Barnsley on 1 July 1851, with the Worsbrough branch following in 1852.

By now the Dearne & Dove Canal was just a minor division of a large and ambitious railway company but it still had a small but dedicated following of regular customers, albeit ones who were unhappy with the high tolls and lack of modernisation. Therefore, in 1888, the Sheffield and South Yorkshire Canal Company was formed with the intention of acquiring the canal from the railway company to promote its use and fund improvements, free from the control of a largely uninterested railway company. Following the passing of an Act of Parliament in 1889, the Sheffield and South Yorkshire Navigation Company was established with a capital of £1,000,000 to purchase the following canal companies: River Dun Navigation, Sheffield Canal, Stainforth & Keadby Canal and the Dearne & Dove Canal.

The initial Sheffield & South Yorkshire Navigation board of directors included Earl Fitzwilliam of Wentworth Woodhouse; John Buckingham Pope, chairman of Denaby & Cadeby Main Collieries; Samuel Roberts of Wombwell Main Colliery; Joseph Mitchell of Mitchells Main Colliery; J D Ellis, chairman of John Brown & Company; and Lord Edmund Talbot, the future Viscount Fitzalan and brother to the Duke of Norfolk. Other directors included the agents to the Duke of Norfolk and Earl Fitzwilliam and past and present Mayors of Barnsley, Doncaster and Rotherham. The new concern intended to modernise the waterways which were currently restricted to 110-ton capacity craft and construct larger locks that could handle 400-ton capacity barges, together with the development of compartment boat operations - these were known as 'Tom Puddings' - a well-established method of hauling groups of compartment boats used on the neighbouring Aire & Calder Navigation for coal transport from West Yorkshire Collieries to Goole.

Upper Left: The Dearne & Dove Canal left the South Yorkshire Canal at Swinton and immediately passed through three locks separated by small basins to permit the passing of craft travelling in opposite directions. Barnsley photographers Haigh Brothers have captured a busy scene on this 1905 postcard view taken from the hump backed bridge at Swinton. On the left the boy is about to lead the horse to tow a barge into the lock in the foreground. Swinton bridge was always a favourite picnic spot for the character *Uncle Mort* in the Peter Tinniswood novels – due to it being adjacent to three pubs – the Ship Inn, the Red House and the Canal Tavern! *(Norman Ellis Collection)*

Upper Right: Taken from the same point but turning 180 degrees to look upstream, Haigh Brothers have captured another busy scene on the canal featuring five craft. The canal ran alongside the former Midland Railway at this point and a coal train can be seen on the embankments together with two impressive signal gantries. The canal passed under the railway in the distance by the tall signal box. The premises on the right are Dale Brown & Company's Glass Works which received sand deliveries by barge, using the simple A-framed crane on the right to off-load the material. This section of canal remains in water today as a fishery. *(Norman Ellis Collection)*

Lower Left: The hump backed bridge at Swinton. This was rebuilt in 1906 at the expense of the Mexborough & Swinton Tramway Company to accommodate the weight of the trams which passed over the bridge from 1907. The bridge remained in the ownership of the tramway company until 1966 when it passed to West Riding County Council. Swinton photographer C F Hurst captured this view which was published as a postcard by John Crowther-Cox of Rotherham.

Lower Right: Another Haigh Brothers postcard capturing Bowbroom Bridge, the viaduct carrying the road from Swinton to Roman Terrace at Mexborough. At this point the canal formerly passed through a tunnel, but with the creation of a deep cutting for the Midland Railway, the opportunity was taken to divert the canal to share the new cutting. The barge is being hauled by the horse visible in the distance through the first arch. The viaduct and railway still exist but the canal has been infilled.

However, although the new company managed to raise the finance to purchase the canals from the railway company, it struggled to find enough capital to make significant improvements. The Dearne & Dove Canal was suffering from declining traffic, dwindling revenues and high maintenance costs. The last particularly resulted from allowing coal to be mined from beneath the canal; coal, ultimately the *raison d'etre* for the canal's formation, was now becoming the reason for its ruin, as coal mining subsidence soon had a detrimental effect on maintaining a sufficient level of water.

Above: A superb study of the canal at Wath-upon-Dearne captured by postcard publisher Edgar Scrivens c1910. A barge is waiting to off-load its coal to Whitworth, Son & Nephew's Brewery on the left. This was run by Spedding Whitworth and his son Henry Whitworth and his nephew James Kelly, who was the brewery manager. The Whitworth's constructed a row of 21 cottages nearby known as Brewery Terrace for their workers. The footbridge provided access from the brewery to the town centre and permitted the transfer of the towpath from the northern to the southern side of the canal. The picture is completed with 20 local children on the footbridge, all smiling for the photographer. Behind the photographer, the canal widened to pass along the 'Bay of Biscay', a large embankment which carried the canal over a tributary of the River Dearne, earning its nickname from its exposed and windy nature, as experienced by ships in the Bay of Biscay in Spain. The location today is almost unrecognisable, forming the traffic lights at the road junction with Biscay Way and the access road to a current TESCO supermarket.

In 1884, a 25 yard stretch of the Worsbrough Branch collapsed due to mining subsidence and this had cost £19,000 and taken six months to repair. Due to continuing subsidence leading to breaches and a shallowing of the canal depth, the Worsbrough branch closed completely in 1906, although it was maintained to act as a water feeder into the Barnsley Canal and the rest of the Dearne & Dove system. The Elsecar branch closed due to subsidence in 1928 and in 1934 the company applied for an abandonment order for the remainder of the navigation, apart from a mile at the Barnsley end to supply the Stairfoot glassworks and a mile at the

Swinton end to serve Manvers Main Colliery. In 1934, the *Colliery Guardian* reported that some areas of the canal had dropped by 10 feet due to mining subsidence caused by the removal of three separate seams of coal and they speculated that a new road could be built along the course of the canal.

Above Left: At Wombwell, the canal passed to the north of the town and is depicted in a quiet scene recorded by postcard photographer Edgar Scrivens looking eastwards towards Wath. The buildings on the left form part of the Wombwell Urban District Council Gas Works, with Primrose Cottages on the right. Today both gas works and cottages have disappeared and the Wombwell bypass is situated nearby, yet amazingly the canal survives in water at this point, albeit choked with reeds and vegetation. *(Norman Ellis Collection)*

Above Right: Tingle Bridge was located on the short canal branch to Elsecar where Tingle Bridge Lane joined the Elsecar to Brampton Road. The small settlement of Tingle Bridge was built to house miners at Earl Fitzwilliam's Hemingfield Colliery can be seen to the left of this postcard by F R Haigh, c1905. Most of these cottages were demolished and the bridge has been replaced, but the Elephant & Castle Inn remains today. *(Norman Ellis Collection)*

In 1942, the Stairfoot to Barnsley glassworks sand deliveries by canal ceased and six years later the canals were nationalised with the formation of the British Transport Commission on 1 January 1948. In 1952, the remaining coal and tar shipments from the staithes at Manvers Main Colliery ceased when the NCB transferred them to road transport. In 1961, the British Transport Commission applied to formally abandon the canal, except for a ¼ mile length at the Swinton end to deliver sand to Dale Brown & Company's Glassworks and provide access to Waddington's Boatyard. This sand traffic ceased in 1977 and since then the flight of locks at Swinton have been incorporated into Waddington's Boatyard with the remaining section alongside the former glassworks retained as a fishery.

After closure, the canal land passed into the hands of the local authorities. Several areas between Wath and Swinton were used as landfill sites and the canal was filled in, although most of the remainder of the canal was left to deteriorate, becoming clogged with reeds and vegetation, although several stretches contain water to this day. There has been no working of coal beneath the canal since 1980 and mining subsidence in the area has now settled. Other parts of the canal have been built upon, for example industrial units at the Mitchells Industrial Estate near Wombwell and call centres and offices at Manvers. Some short lengths of the canal were used for new roads; for example, in the 1960s, the A633 Doncaster Road between Wath and Manvers was re-routed along the canal bed and, in 1985, the South Yorkshire County Council opened the Wath Bypass (Biscay Way) along the line of the canal. Many of the locks have been filled in and the picturesque stone built hump-backed bridges have been removed, although Wetmoor Bridge at Wath is a rare survivor and is now a Grade II listed structure.

The two branches have faired rather better than the main canal, as they pass through more rural areas where the pressures on land development are lower. Although some areas have been filled in (particularly along the Worsbrough branch) most of the Elsecar branch and the basins at Worsbrough and Elsecar remain in water. Reflecting the possibility of the waterway re-opening as a pleasure canal, when the new A6195 Dearne Towns Link Road opened on 12 October 1998, a new bridge was constructed over the Elsecar branch at a sufficient height to permit future pleasure craft to pass beneath.

On 1 April 1984, the Barnsley Canal Group was formed with the aim of restoring and re-opening the Barnsley Canal and the Dearne & Dove Canal. In June 2000, the group was reformed as the Barnsley, Dearne & Dove Canals Trust. Initial efforts have been focussed on restoring the Elsecar branch downstream from Elsecar Basin, as this now forms a major tourist attraction as the Elsecar Heritage Centre, complete with a preserved steam railway on a length of the former South Yorkshire Railway parallel to the canal. It is hoped that the aims of the trust come to fruition although the chance of restoring the canal line between Wombwell and Swinton is probably now out of reach due to subsequent development. However, the Trust hope that pleasure craft could use the River Dearne to Wombwell from which the two restored branches can be accessed, together with the remainder of the line to Barnsley, and thus along a restored Barnsley Canal to Wakefield.

In the 1970s, the NCB proposed to construct a new canal from the River Dearne at Manvers to Grimethorpe Colliery. The intention was not to export coal from the pits along the route at Grimethorpe, Houghton, Wath and Manvers, but rather to transport colliery waste material to the Humber estuary. Huge colliery spoil heaps had now accumulated in the area and it was hoped to transport the material for use in land reclamation schemes. However, this project failed to materialise and it remains to be seen whether the Barnsley, Dearne & Dove Canal Trust, hopefully with the support of local authorities and with funding from National Lottery grants, ultimately completes its aim of restoring the canals, which would be a very commendable achievement.

The Arrival of the Railways

Early Wagonways

Prior to the arrival of standard gauge railways with the opening of the Midland Railway through the Dearne Valley in 1840, several horse-drawn wagonways used to transfer goods from landlocked collieries to the canal basins at Elsecar and Worsbrough. These early railway lines were generally referred to as wagonways, plateways, tramways or inclines (the latter where the gradient was too steep for the use of horses). The cast iron rails along these wagonways were usually set upon stone sleepers which enabled the horses' hooves to gain purchase against the sleepers when hauling the wagons. The rails were typically L-shaped in cross section; thus, the flange was set in the rail as opposed to the wheel of the wagon as commonly happened later. Horses would typically haul one or two wagons at a time, these wagons being commonly referred to as tubs or corves and being much smaller than railway wagons and the wagonway was often of narrower gauge than the national railway network. Where the gradient was too steep, the wagons would be unhitched from the horses and attached to a rope linked to a small stationary steam powered engine. The wagons, sometimes several at a time, were gently lowered down the incline under gravity to the canal basin where they were marshalled on to loading staithes for tipping in to waiting barges. Empty wagons were than winched back up the incline by the steam engine or even as a counterbalance to heavier full wagons being lowered down the incline.

At Worsbrough Canal Basin, a lengthy wagonway was in operation by around 1820, extending several miles westwards to Rockley Pit & Furnace, from which it continued to climb to serve small coal pits in the Pilley area. This wagonway ceased operation around 1920, a rare survivor well into the age of the steam locomotive. Another short incline left Park Staithe and climbed steeply to the south to serve the Worsbrough Park Colliery owned by Messrs Cooper & Company. When Barrow Colliery purchased the Worsbrough Park Colliery in 1872 to open a large colliery extracting the deeper seams from beneath the Worsbrough Park estate, the new pit was served by a branch line from the South Yorkshire Railway (diverging from the Sheffield branch at Dovecliffe Station). The Park Staithe incline closed a few years later following the closure of Worsbrough Park Colliery.

At Elsecar a lengthy incline left the canal basin to Milton Ironworks. The incline was used for the import of coal to the blast furnaces and the export of pig iron and was operational by 1840. The incline then continued westwards as a wagonway serving Lidgett Colliery (which later became part of Skiers Spring Colliery) and further westwards to serve ironstone pits in Tankersley Park, before continuing westwards to Tankersley Colliery. In 1850, the rails on this wagonway were replaced with standard gauge rails to enable easier interchanging with the newly opened South Yorkshire Railway at Elsecar Basin. The opening of the Midland Railway in 1897 through Skiers Spring Colliery gradually saw most of the wagonway close from Tankersley to Milton Ironworks, but the incline from Milton Ironworks to Elsecar Basin remained in operation well into the early twentieth century.

From Elsecar Basin a second incline led up a small valley to Earl Fitzwilliam's Jump Pit and this was also operational by 1840. This incline was extended to serve the Hoyland Silkstone Colliery at Platts Common, although this was later served by a short branch line from the South Yorkshire Railway's Sheffield line. When the Midland Railway was under construction through Elsecar in 1895 it bridged the incline via a four-arched viaduct and threw a short branch line to Hoyland Silkstone Colliery, replacing the northern half of the incline, and the lower portion from Jump Pit to Elsecar basin was dismantled shortly afterwards.

Above: The Cobcar Arches were constructed by the Midland Railway in 1895 to carry the Sheffield to Barnsley line across a small valley and the incline to Jump pit and Hoyland Silkstone Colliery. The incline appears to be out of use although the circular guiding wheels for the winch cable remain in position. It may be that standard gauge locomotives were using the incline when this postcard was published c1910, thus removing the need for the winch. The incline closed in 1920. *(Chris Sharp / Old Barnsley)*

However, in 1840 the Midland Railway opened its main line across the Dearne Valley and this was followed by a succession of other railways. By now a railway 'mania' was sweeping the country and various private railway companies competed to take a slice of the coal freight traffic. Numerous plans and proposals were put forward and many fell by the wayside. Nevertheless, several received parliamentary approval and had the capital to construct new lines. Within a few years, the Midland Railway would be joined by the South Yorkshire Railway, the Swinton & Knottingley Joint Railway, the Hull & Barnsley Railway with its branches to Denaby and Wath, the new Midland Railway Sheffield to Barnsley line, with the Dearne Valley Railway finally opening in 1909. In 1864, the South Yorkshire Railway became part of the Manchester Sheffield & Lincolnshire Railway – itself renamed Great Central Railway in 1897. Ten years later, the Great Central Railway constructed a large concentration yard at Wath to marshal its coal trains. The transport of coal was the main priority and although a limited passenger service was provided, this was always secondary to the freight traffic. Coupled with this railway development were internal railways constructed by the colliery companies, the most notably being the private line from Manvers Main Colliery to Barnburgh Main Colliery. A hundred years after the opening of the Dearne & Dove Canal, the Dearne Valley was now the home to a thriving and intensive freight railway network.

Midland Railway.

The arrival of the North Midland Railway in 1840 was initially not considered a major threat to the coal traffic carried on the Dearne & Dove Canal. The North Midland Railway operated from Derby to Leeds, entering the Dearne Valley from Rotherham with stations at Swinton, Wath North, Darfield, and Cudworth, the last designated as the station for Barnsley. However, the North Midland Railway was mainly a passenger line, with its engineer, George Stephenson, choosing the easiest gradients and gentlest of curves to enable high speed from the locomotives. Therefore, due to their location amongst undulating topography, Sheffield and Barnsley were bypassed. In 1844, the North Midland Railway merged with three other railway companies to form the Midland Railway.

The Midland Railway initially considered the South Yorkshire Coal trade as of secondary importance to passenger traffic. However, once the profits to be made from the transport of coal became clear, freight traffic became of increasing importance. Connections were made to Manvers Main Colliery, Wath Main Colliery, Houghton Main Colliery and Dearne Valley Colliery. In 1897, the Midland Railway opened another important freight and passenger line between Sheffield and Barnsley (See later section on Midland Railway Sheffield to Barnsley line).

Above: Wath-upon-Dearne would eventually have three railway stations and the first to open on 1 April 1841 was Wath Station on the Midland Railway. On 1 May 1850, it was renamed Wath & Bolton and is shown here on a postcard by an anonymous photographer c1910. The other stations were Wath Central on the Great Central Railway and Wath (Hull & Barnsley Railway). William Cobbett was station manager and he is shown second from left together with his staff. In 1914, the station was renamed Wath-upon-Dearne and on 25 September 1950 it received its fourth and final name: Wath North. The station finally closed in 1968. *(Norman Ellis Collection)*

Above: On 18 May 1948, a passenger train derailed whilst travelling along the former Midland Railway at Manvers resulting in the deaths of eight people with a further 55 casualties taken to Mexborough Montague Hospital. The London to Bradford express was being pulled by two engines when the first engine ran off the track but remained upright. Unfortunatly the second engine turned over and six carriages piled up behind it in a heap of wreckage. The colliery officials summuned 100 miners and ambulance men to assist in the rescue operations. In 1998 a memorial was placed on Doncaster Road near the site of the disaster. The memorial was dedicated to those who had died whilst also serving as a tribute to those who assisted with the rescue.

South Yorkshire Railway (Great Central Railway from 1897)

Ten years after the opening of the Midland Railway, the country was in the grip of railway mania. In 1849, the Great Northern Railway had opened a line from Doncaster to London, enabling the West Riding and South Yorkshire collieries to have a direct transport link to the booming London market. Looking to tap into this new market, the South Yorkshire Railway proposed building a railway from Doncaster through the Dearne Valley to Barnsley, complete with two branches to Elsecar and Worsbrough, mirroring the two canal branches of the Dearne & Dove Canal. The priority of the South Yorkshire Railway was simply to transport coal, with the operation of a passenger service almost as an afterthought.

Above Left: The original Wombwell Railway Station was opened in 1851 by the South Yorkshire Railway and was rather a primitive wooden building. It was replaced with the structure in the Edgar Scrivens postcard above in the 1880s, built to typical Manchester, Sheffield & Lincolnshire Railway station design of the time and is shown in this c1920 postcard when Frederick Lewis was station master. It was subsequently renamed Wombwell Central to distinguish it from the Midland Railway's new Wombwell Station. Wombwell Central closed with the withdrawal of the Barnsley to Doncaster passenger trains on 29 June 1959.

Above Right: A contrast in transports: A passenger train operated by the Great Central Railway speeds over Rainbow Bridge above the River Don near Conisbrough. Meanwhile a 'humber keel', the traditional wooden craft of the South Yorkshire canal network, takes a leisurely journey. The graceful cast iron Rainbow Bridge was built by the South Yorkshire Railway in 1850 and replaced by the London Midland & Scottish Railway in the 1920s with a stronger bridge, able to bear the weight of heavier freight trains. This postcard view was published in 1905 by an anonymous photographer.

On 10 November 1849, the South Yorkshire Railway opened between Doncaster and Swinton where there was a Rotherham facing junction with the Midland Railway. Construction of the main line continued westwards, passing through a deep cutting to the west of Mexborough and, by 1 February 1850, the railway had reached Elsecar Canal Basin. Following the opening on 1 July 1851 of the full line to Barnsley, a passenger service was instigated between Doncaster and Barnsley with four trains per day in each direction utilising Great Northern Railway locomotives and carriages. Basic stations at Hexthorpe, Warmsworth & Sprotbrough, Conisbrough, Mexborough, Wath, Wombwell and Stairfoot. The two branch lines remained as goods lines, although Earl Fitzwilliam stationed his private railway carriage at Elsecar Rockingham Station which he used to transport himself and his guests to race meetings at Doncaster Race Course.

Above: Stairfoot was once a complicated railway junction. Initially a simple crossing of two turnpike roads, the Dearne & Dove Canal opened in 1804 passing behind the cottages on the left. The first railway on the scene was the South Yorkshire Railway in 1851 which operated over the lowermost bridge in both pictures. Stairfoot became a complicated railway junction with the subsequent opening of the Barnsley Coal Railway, the Hull & Barnsley Railway and the Houghton Main Colliery branch line. Passing overhead on the uppermost bridge is the Midland Railway branch from Cudworth Station to Monk Springs where it joined a new line from Barnsley to Sheffield in 1897. Stairfoot Railway Station opened on 1 July 1851 as Ardsley Station but was then moved to a new site in 1872; it finally closed on 16 September 1957. These late 1920s postcard views are by Bamforth of Holmfirth and feature Wombwell Road (left) and Doncaster Road (right), complete with tram tracks belonging to the Dearne District Light Railway. The former Midland Railway Cudworth to Monks Springs Junction line was removed in the 1960s and the bridge was dismantled. However, the former South Yorkshire Railway bridges remain, now carrying a section of the Trans Pennine Trail. In the 1980s, a new roundabout was constructed at Stairfoot and the houses were demolished, however, the Black Bull pub remains, but is currently closed. Another pub, the Cross keys Inn has been demolished - a third pub named the Keel Inn remains open, its name reflecting its former canal side location adjacent the Dearne & Dove Canal with its 'Humber Keel' barges. *(Paul Fox Collection)*

On April 1852, the freight only branch was completed from Aldham Junction near Wombwell to Worsbrough Canal Basin where it continued a short distance to Moor End to serve pits in the Worsbrough and Silkstone areas, including Wentworth Silkstone Colliery. Finally, in 1854 another goods line opened from Aldham Junction passing through Birdwell and Hoyland Common (to tap collieries in this area) and onwards via Chapeltown to Tinsley where a connection was made with the Midland Railway to Sheffield and a Barnsley to Sheffield passenger service was introduced. On 1 July 1854, the Manchester, Sheffield & Lincolnshire Railway opened a line from Manchester to Penistone and Barnsley. This enabled a Doncaster- Barnsley- Penistone passenger service to be implemented with around a dozen trains running in each direction. Eastwards from Doncaster the South Yorkshire Railway continued to Thorne Waterside, opening in 1855, and along the south bank of the Stainforth & Keadby Canal to Keadby on the River Trent; this section opened in 1859. The full opening of the South Yorkshire Railway stimulated the development of the Dearne Valley collieries, enabling access to London markets via the national rail network and exports from ocean going ships at Keadby on the River Trent and Goole on the River Aire.

The opening of the South Yorkshire Railway stimulated the opening of the first large pits adjacent to the line at Lundhill, Wombwell Main, Mitchell Main, Darfield Main, Wath Main, Manvers Main and Cortonwood. The railway was incredibly successful and in its first full year of operation in 1855, 421,755 tons of coal were transported. This had risen by 1861 to

1,016,659 tons of coal, mostly sourced from the pits of the Dearne Valley. This profitable venture soon came to the attention of larger railway companies, and, in 1874, the South Yorkshire Railway was absorbed by the Manchester Sheffield & Lincolnshire Railway. An important connection was made on 2 August 1880 when the Manchester Sheffield & Lincolnshire Railway filled the gap between Penistone and the western terminus of the Worsbrough Branch at Moor End. This provided an important western outlet for Dearne Valley Coal, however, the extension included two tunnels and a notoriously steep gradient known as the Worsbrough Bank, which fully laden coal trains could only overcome with the assistance from additional banking locomotives.

Following the completion of its line to London Marylebone in 1897, the Manchester Sheffield & Lincolnshire Railway was renamed Great Central Railway. With outlets to the Lancashire and Yorkshire coasts and to London, the Great Central Railway became a very efficient transporter of millions of tons of coal and the line between Mexborough and Stairfoot was quadrupled to handle the sheer number of freight trains. However, a scheme for marshalling the coal trains was increasingly need and on 4 December 1907, the Great Central Railway opened Wath Concentration Yard.

Swinton & Knottingley Joint Railway

Above Left: The Swinton & Knottingley Railway crossed the River Dearne and the Bolton – Mexborough Road on a viaduct of ten arches, constructed from Staffordshire blue bricks. During the Miners' Strike it was daubed with graffiti and formed part of the Manvers Colliery NUM picket line. Note the effigy on the right and the slogan: 'Make thousands happy – hang a yank', presumably a reference to Ian MacGregor, the Scottish-American chairman of the NCB during the 1984/5 Miners' Strike. *(Peter Davies)*
Above Right: Bolton-on-Dearne was the only railway station provided by the Swinton & Knottingley Railway in the Dearne Valley. It is shown here on this postcard by Edgar Scrivens c1910 looking south towards the viaduct over the River Dearne. At the time of the photograph, John Martin was Station Master. The railway station remains operational today with a frequent service to Leeds and Sheffield, although the station buildings have disappeared and have been replaced with simple waiting shelters.

The next railway to appear in the Dearne Valley was the Swinton & Knottingley Railway, a scheme jointly proposed by the Midland Railway and the North Eastern Railway, and authorised by an Act of Parliament on 16 July 1874. Despite its name, the Swinton & Knottingley Railway served neither Swinton nor Knottingley, as it was constructed between Manvers and Ferrybridge, and was around 16 miles in length. The line was promoted out of necessity resulting from the boom in freight and passenger traffic on the Midland Railway which had previously been routed through a bottleneck at Normanton in West Yorkshire. However, another reason for the promotion of the joint line was that the Midland Railway would gain running powers over the North Eastern Railway to York, with the North Eastern similarly gaining running powers over the Midland Railway to Sheffield, bringing benefits to both parties.

The line opened on 1 July 1879 and left Manvers (with an eastwards and a westwards junction with the former South Yorkshire Railway in addition to the Midland Railway) proceeding northwards crossing the River Dearne by a viaduct known as the 'Ten Arches'. A railway station was opened at Bolton-on-Dearne and the line continued via Goldthorpe and Thurnscoe with a second railway station provided at rural Frickley (possibly at the whim of the local landowner, William Wright Aldham of Frickley Hall) before passing into West Yorkshire with a station at Moorthorpe near South Elmsall. Short branch lines were opened to Hickleton Main Colliery in 1892 and Frickley Colliery in 1898 although, despite the growth of Goldthorpe and Thurnscoe, no stations were provided at these locations until the later promotion of passenger services in the 1980s.

Hull & Barnsley Railway and its branches

Another private railway company desiring a piece of the lucrative coal transporting trade was the Hull & Barnsley Railway, originally promoted under the rather cumbersome name of the Hull, Barnsley & West Riding Junction Railway & Dock Company. The main reason for its existence was to break the North Eastern Railway's monopoly on the coal export trade through Hull and the line received its Act of Parliament on 14 August 1880. Despite its name, the railway never reached Barnsley terminating with branches to Cudworth and Stairfoot, having skirted to the north of the Dearne Valley. However, the Hull & Barnsley Railway would be served by two long branch lines, originally promoted by the colliery companies themselves, who were keen to have rival railway companies serving each pit as this would provide competition and keep transport prices down.

The first of these schemes was promoted as The South Yorkshire Junction Railway receiving royal consent by an Act of Parliament dated 14 August 1890. The South Yorkshire Junction Railway was essentially a subsidiary of Denaby and Cadeby Main Collieries Ltd although the line was leased to and operated by the Hull & Barnsley Railway. The South Yorkshire Junction Railway opened on 1 September 1894 leaving the main line at Wrangbrook Junction before heading southwards to terminate at Denaby and Cadeby collieries. Following British Rail rationalisation schemes, the line closed completely on 20 October 1975.

The second colliery company-sponsored line was promoted in 1895 when the Hickleton Main Colliery Company approached the Hull & Barnsley Railway to build a railway to their newly opened pit. This the Hull & Barnsley Railway were reluctant to do, since Hickleton Colliery was already connected to the adjacent Swinton & Knottingley Joint Line and they possibly feared that the colliery company were trying to play one railway off against the other to lower transport prices. Undeterred, the Hickleton Main Colliery Company teamed up with Wath Main and Manvers Main to promote the South Yorkshire Extension Railway by an Act of Parliament granted on 6 August 1897. The Hull & Barnsley Railway decided to join the partnership and operate the line on behalf of the colliery companies. The first directors were

David Davy (a director of Hickleton and Manvers) George Shaw (Chairman of Wath Main), with John Fisher, Charles Poston and George Walker representing the railway company.

The South Yorkshire Extension Railway opened from Wrangbrook Junction to Wath Station on 31 March 1902. From Wrangbrook Junction heading southwards, stations were provided at Moorhouse, Thurnscoe and Wath (H&BR Station). Branch lines were opened to Frickley Colliery, Hickleton Main Colliery, Wath Main Colliery and Manvers Main Colliery. The line also served Wath Main Brickworks at Ingsfield Lane, Bolton-on-Dearne. A passenger service was operated from Wath through to Kirk Smeaton on the Hull & Barnsley Railway although this was short lived ceasing operation in 1929. Today, the railway station building and Stationmaster's house at Wath survive as private residences.

Midland Railway (Sheffield to Barnsley Line)

Above: Wombwell's second railway station was opened by the Midland Railway on 1 July 1897 and was located adjacent to the entrance to Wombwell Woods, over a mile from the town centre. The station is shown in this c1920 postcard by Edgar Scrivens when Thomas Collett was station master. The view is looking towards Sheffield, where a group of local workmen are waiting for the train to Elsecar. The station was sometimes referred to as Wombwell Main after the adjacent colliery and its community and was renamed Wombwell West in 25 September 1950 to distinguish it from Wombwell Central Station. The buildings have since been demolished but the station remains open and popular with commuters to Sheffield and Barnsley and is currently records 225,000 passenger journeys per year. *(Brian Brownsword Collection)*

Prior to 1895, passengers travelling between Sheffield and Barnsley had to take a rather circuitous journey via the former South Yorkshire Railway lines now operated by the Great Central Railway. However, a more direct route opened on 1 July 1897 when the Midland Railway entered the fray, keen to break the monopoly on the coal traffic in the area currently enjoyed by the Great Central Railway. The Midland Railway adapted a pre-existing wagonway from Chapeltown to Thorncliffe Ironworks and converted it to a main gauge railway, linking it up with their line from Chapeltown to Sheffield. From Thorncliffe, the new formation entered Tankersley Tunnel before running parallel to the former Elsecar wagonway, with a station at Wentworth & Hoyland and sidings into Skiers Spring Colliery and Brickworks. The formation continued via Elsecar Station before bridging the old incline at Jump over a fine arched viaduct before entering Wombwell Station, throwing a spur line into Wombwell Main Colliery. The Midland Railway then crossed the Dove Valley over Swaithe viaduct before splitting into two at Monk Spring Junction. The western fork provided access to Barnsley Court House Station whilst the eastern fork crossed the complex of roads, railways and canals at Stairfoot via a high viaduct before linking up with the main Midland Railway at Cudworth.

Near Swaithe Viaduct a branch line threaded up the Dove Valley to serve Barrow, Rockingham and Wharncliffe Silkstone Collieries. This branch line was one of the first lines to close in 1948, following the nationalisation of the railways, as it already duplicated other lines to these pits; the eastern fork from Monk Spring to Cudworth closed in 1968. However, the remaining line from Barnsley to Sheffield now forms an important passenger line with trains running frequently from Sheffield to Barnsley where they continue to either Penistone and Huddersfield or Wakefield and Leeds.

Dearne Valley Railway

The final railway line to enter the fray was the Dearne Valley Railway which received royal assent on 6 August 1897, the same date as the South Yorkshire Extension Railway. The Dearne Valley Railway was another line promoted by various colliery companies and the directors included James Addy of Carlton Main Colliery Company (owner of Grimethorpe Colliery); Robert Armitage (Chairman of Hickleton Main Colliery Company); Ernest Hague, a director of Hickleton Main and Manvers Main; and Charles Edward Hunter (director of Houghton Main and Manvers Main). The partnership proposed to build a railway linking the Hull & Barnsley Railway at Brierley eastwards to Black Carr Junction on the Great Northern Line south of Doncaster. At Black Carr Junction spur lines were proposed to link with the South Yorkshire Joint Railway and the Great Northern & Great Eastern Joint Line to Lincoln and East Anglia, providing access to these additional markets.

The colliery company intended to operate the line in partnership with a railway company and the Lancashire & Yorkshire Railway joined the scheme, the latter constructing a six-mile-long linking line from Crofton Junction near Wakefield to Brierley, under the name of the Dearne Valley Junction Railway thus providing a western outlet to serve the West Riding markets with connections to Manchester and Liverpool. The Dearne Valley Railway opened in stages from 1902 onwards, finally opening entirely on 7 October 1908. A notable engineering feature was the construction of a magnificent viaduct over the River Don near Conisbrough. Over its working life the line successfully transported vast tonnages of coal from Grimethorpe Colliery, Houghton Main, Hickleton Main, Highgate Colliery, Goldthorpe Colliery, Barnburgh Colliery, Denaby Main, Cadeby Main and Yorkshire Main at Edlington.

A passenger service was provided from 3 June 1912 utilising a small Hughes Motorcar, which was a combined railway engine and solitary passenger coach, with a guard issuing tickets and collecting fares en-route. The service commenced at Edlington and called at stations at

Harlington, Goldthorpe, Great Houghton, Grimethorpe and Ryhill before continuing over the Lancashire & Yorkshire line to Wakefield, with around four or five trains operating each way. The stations were referred to as 'halts' and were very primitive affairs, using old dilapidated wooden coaches as waiting rooms; the halts had no platforms, so intending passengers had to simply wait by the side of the railway line.

Above Left: Facilities at stations along the Dearne Valley Railway were practically non-existent. At least passengers at Denaby Halt were provided with two gas lights although the provision of a station platform was deemed unnecessary. The name board rather grandly proclaims DENABY FOR CONISBROUGH AND MEXBOROUGH. The station was positioned in an isolated position by the River Dearne and was probably built to appease the local landowner as a footpath was installed across the fields and up the hill to High Melton Hall. Five maintenance workers are pictured in this postcard from 1905 and the station closed on 10 September 1951. The area now forms Denaby Ings Nature Reserve operated by the Yorkshire Wildlife Trust and a field centre now sits on the station site. *(Norman Ellis Collection)*

Above Right: The most remarkable feat of railway engineering in the district was the construction of the Dearne Valley Railway viaduct across the River Don near Conisbrough. This commenced in 1906 and was aided by an overhead cable suspended between two masts erected at either end of the structure. This enabled the delivery of men and materials to each of the viaduct piers and this delivery contraption can be seen in the upper centre of the postcard. The viaduct was 115 feet high with seven arches on the Conisbrough side and 14 arches on the Cadeby side with a 130-foot-long steel girder bridge spanning the river in the centre. Following withdrawal of trains, the viaduct remained derelict for several years, but it has recently become incorporated into a new cycling and walking footpath from which spectacular views can be obtained.

Wath Concentration Yard.

The Great Central Railway proposed to improve the efficiency of its South Yorkshire coal traffic with the construction of a new marshalling yard known as the Wath Concentration Yard, following the visit of the railway's general manager to view a similar set up in the United States. A site on the level flood plain of the River Dearne was chosen near Wath Colliery, roughly in the centre of the South Yorkshire Coalfield and two blocks of sorting sidings were laid out to serve both directions of the main line with the facility opening in 1907. Each set of 31 sidings totalling 36 miles in length was connected to a shunting hump to allow the swift marshalling of coal wagons from various collieries into trains of coal wagons all bound for the same destination. Wagons arriving from the collieries were handled by two specially built locomotives which pushed the wagons up a short gradient and over the hump at either end of the sidings. Once over the hump, the wagons free-wheeled under the power of gravity into one of the many sidings. A train for Manchester, for example, would therefore be formed of wagons from numerous different collieries, all painted in varied colours and bearing the colliery name on the side. On their return, the assorted wagons were once again pushed over the hump and marshalled into individual trains of common wagons for return to the individual collieries. In connection with the scheme, the line from Wath to Stairfoot received a quadruple set of tracks to accommodate all the freight movements from the western end of the yard.

Many trains of export coal were dispatched eastwards via a newly built bypass railway around Doncaster (the Doncaster Avoiding Line) to Immingham on the River Humber where in 1912 the Great Central Railway opened extensive coal sidings and export terminals. At the time, it was believed that coal from 107 pits passed through Wath Concentration Yard. To operate the yard, powerful locomotives were required and four Beyer & Peacock tank engines were delivered at the end of 1907. These were designated as GCR Class 8H locos and numbered 1170-1173 in the GCR fleet and based at Mexborough shed. They gained the nickname 'Wath Daisies' and were finally withdrawn in the 1950s. At its height in the 1960s, there were approximately 230 trains departing and arriving or passing through Wath Yard every weekday and coal trains were departing every 30 minutes to Manchester.

Above: Edgar Scrivens published this postcard of The Hump, Wath Sidings, from Moor Road bridge looking west following the opening of Wath Concentration Yard. Two of the powerful 'Wath Daisies' tank engines can be identified performing shunting duties whilst in the foreground the solitary wagon belongs to Morten & Storer of Sheffield, Lime & Coal Merchants. Wath Yard eventually handled coal from 107 collieries and in 1950s it was electrified as part the eastern terminus of the Manchester-Woodhead-Wath Electrification Scheme.

Industrial Railways and Private Owner Wagons

The only private industrial railway of note within the Dearne Valley was the line of around one mile in length from the sidings at Manvers Main Colliery to Barnburgh Main Colliery, constructed in 1924. Prior to this, Barnburgh Colliery had dispatched its output via the adjacent Dearne Valley Railway, but it was subsequently decided to transport it overland to Manvers Main Colliery for processing. The line left the Manvers sidings through an arch under the Swinton & Knottingley Joint line, before crossing the Bolton-Mexborough road via a level crossing. It then continued to the north of Adwick-upon-Dearne through an area used for tipping colliery spoil, before crossing the River Dearne. From this point, it passed a particularly unpleasant smelling maggot farm before heading up a steep gradient to the Barnburgh pit yard. At the western end of Manvers Main, certain lines formerly constructed by the Hull & Barnsley (Wath Branch) between Wath and Manvers were also used for internal shunting operations.

Although the railway companies provided the main rail freight network, mention must be made of the contribution made by the colliery companies. When the railways had been constructed, traditions had governed that the transport provider owned the rails and the locomotives, with the wagons, referred to as 'private owner wagons' provided by the customers themselves: whether a coal merchant, colliery company or any other carrier of freight. In 1887, the Railway Clearing House standardised the private owner wagon fleet throughout the railway network. Colliery private owner wagons were typically open-topped wagons with sides of 7 wooden planks, held together with iron brackets. The structure was mounted on a two-axle truck with wheels to standard gauge.

Specialised wagon builders, for example Charles Roberts & Company of Horbury and the Gloucester Railway Carriage & Wagon Company, supplied or leased thousands of private owner wagons to the colliery companies, each one colourfully painted with the colliery name. From 1891-3, Charles Robert supplied 300 wagons to Manvers Main Colliery and, in 1900, they supplied 700 to Hickleton Main Colliery. Both these pits would eventually own over 3,000 private owner wagons. Smaller side-tipping 'jubilee' wagons were often used for colliery spoil, particularly at pits which lacked dirt disposal by means of an aerial ropeway, for example Wath Colliery.

The shunting of empty and full wagons in the colliery yard and railway sidings was often performed by colliery owned locomotives, built to standard gauge, with smaller locos and wagons built to smaller gauges often used for transporting material and supplies around the colliery stock yard. Many colliery companies built up large fleets of steam powered tank engine locomotives, typically to 0-4-0ST or 0-6-0ST (saddle tank) designs. Manvers Main Colliery purchased their first 0-4-0ST in 1872, joined by a more powerful 0-6-0ST in 1875. In the late 1870s, Black Hawthorn & Company of Gateshead supplied four 0-6-0STs to Manvers Main Colliery; these were all named Manvers Main No1 to No4 on the boiler tank. Several of these tank engines survived beyond nationalisation into more recent times, despite the NCB turning to the purchase of diesel locomotives for internal shunting operations. Flameproof diesel locomotives were also used underground for coal transport as mine cars as well as for man-riding purposes, where they were given the name 'paddy trains'.

Upper Left: Many colliery companies purchased their own locomotives for internal shunting operations and this photograph depicts Hickleton Main Colliery 13. This was a Manning Wardle & Company Class 0-6-0 saddle tank locomotive. The date of delivery and the identity of the photographer is unknown, but the locomotive may date to around 1900.

Upper Right: Emerging from the tunnel under the Swinton & Knottingley Railway embankment is a Rolls-Royce Sentinel 0-6-0DH diesel locomotive with works number 10261. The 325hp loco entered service on 20 December 1966 at Manvers Main Colliery and was named *Raymond*, after Raymond Orton, the Assistant Mechanical Engineer. *Raymond* is pictured in 1969 travelling along the NCB internal railway from Manvers Main to Barnburgh Main Colliery and was believed to have been scrapped in 1988. *(John Law)*

Lower Left: In 1911, Henry Lodge & Sons ordered a batch of 28 private owner wagons for Goldthorpe Colliery from the Ince Waggon & Ironworks of Wigan. This example is numbered 256 and is pictured at the manufacturers. By 1912, Goldthorpe colliery owned 146 wagons, painted with white lettering on a red background with black iron work. In 1923, following the takeover by Old Silkstone Collieries, the fleet of wagons were repainted and the legend GOLDTHORPE was applied in large letters. *(Norman Ellis Collection)*

Lower Right: A significant amount of Dearne Valley coal was exported via the Humber ports and this Arjay Productions postcard from c1935 shows Hickleton Main Colliery wagon 2058 being handled by the dock crane, before its contents are loaded into the ocean-going vessel for export – the name of the latter is obscured but it could be *Crania*. This wagon was one of over 3,000 private owner wagons purchased by Hickleton Main Colliery prior to 1937.

Railway Reorganisation in the 1920s.

During the First World War, the railway network had been taken under government control and this revealed several advantages. Nationalisation had been considered but this had been heavily resisted by the private railway companies. As a compromise, the 1921 Railway Act was formed grouping the multitude of private railway companies into the 'Big Four': LMS (London Midland & Scottish Railway), LNER (London & North Eastern Railway), GWR (Great Western Railway) and SR (Southern Railway) which were all established in 1923. Railways in the Dearne Valley, being under the interests of many companies, were grouped into either the LMS or the LNER. The LMS absorbed the Midland Railway, Great Central Railway and Dearne Valley Railway. The LNER absorbed the Great Northern Railway, the North Eastern Railway and the Hull & Barnsley Railway and its branches.

The grouping of the railways into the Big Four brought about efficiencies and enabled investment projects to be undertaken, although there was little in the way of line closures. However, as a sign of things to come, the first passenger service closed during this time, when the provision along the former Hull & Barnsley Railway (Wath Branch) between Wath and Kirk Smeaton ceased in 1929 due to competition from a growing network of bus services. In fact, the entire southern section of this railway between Wath and Thurnscoe closed entirely shortly afterwards on 2 October 1933, one of the first railway closures in the area having, the line having only operated for 31 years. Some of the sidings at the southern terminus near Wath and Manvers Main Collieries were retained by the coal industry for shunting operations between the two pits, especially with the growth of the Manvers Combined Mine in the 1950s.

The LNER introduced the most powerful and longest steam locomotive in the country to the Dearne Valley when the triple articulated Class U1 Garratt 2-8-0+0-8-2 was delivered to Mexborough Shed in 1925. The vehicle was designed by Sir Nigel Gresley and manufactured by Beyer Peacock & Company of Manchester and numbered 2395 in the LNER fleet. Known as the 'Wath Banker', it was designed solely to push coal trains (already consisting of a standard locomotive pulling 60 loaded coal wagons with another banking locomotive pushing from behind) from Wath Concentration Yard up the Worsbrough Bank for onward transport across the Pennines. The Worsbrough Bank was the name given to the stretch of former Great Central Railway between Worsbrough Bridge and Silkstone, which suffered from mining subsidence and a steep gradient of 1 in 40 (2.5%). Once at the top, the Garratt would uncouple and return to Wath yard, before repeating the process with the next coal train.

The huge Garratt was painted black and was particularly unpopular with engine and firemen crews for it was difficult to operate, notoriously unreliable and frequently out of service. Due to boiler problems, it required a water softening plant to be fitted. Crews suffered from smoke inhalation when the engine passed through the Silkstone tunnels and had to be issued with respirators. On nationalisation, the vehicle was renumbered to 69999 and spent some of its time assisting trains up the Lickey Incline near Birmingham. The engine returned to the Dearne Valley and following an unsuccessful attempt to convert it to run on oil, it was withdrawn in 1955 having covered 425,213 miles, mostly spent pushing coal trains up the Worsbrough bank. The locomotive was scrapped and the haulage of coal over the Pennines was replaced with British Rail's Manchester – Woodhead- Wath electrification scheme.

Above: Despite its troublesome life, the LNER Garratt Class U1 locomotive must have been an impressive sight whilst in full steam pushing coal trains up the Worsbrough Bank. Photographs of this huge beast are relatively rare; however, on 18 December 1984, the Caribbean nation of Union Island (Grenadines & St Vincent) issued these two $3.00 stamps in their Leaders of the World Series. Quite ironic that this huge engine from the industrial Dearne Valley would come to be celebrated on the stamps of a tropical island!

British Rail

The nationalisation of the railways and the establishment of the British Railways Board on 1 January 1948 led to further restructuring and efficiencies to the network over the following decades. Within the South Yorkshire Coalfield, major rationalising schemes were introduced as British Rail sought to streamline operations by eliminating duplicate rail outlets from each pit, a policy that had been encouraged by the private colliery companies to stimulate competition between the private railway companies. This rationalising was coupled with the gradual decline of the coalfield with collieries in the western area closing due to the exhaustion of their coal reserves. Output was increasingly concentrated into several large production sites at the larger and younger pits in the central and eastern parts of the Dearne Valley.

The nationalisation of the British coal industry caused all the colourful wooden private owner wagons to be repainted and gradually replaced with a common fleet of new steel wagons. However, different grades of coal were still required by various customers and Wath Concentration Yard continued to prosper. A significant development came in the early 1950s when the yard was designated as the eastern terminus of the new Manchester-Woodhead-Wath Electrification Scheme which travelled over the Pennines through the Woodhead tunnel with electric locomotives having the power to haul the coal trains up the steep gradients to Penistone. British Rail purchased a fleet of 57 Class 76 Electric Locomotives in 1950 which were constructed at the Gorton Locomotive Works in Manchester. The Class 76 locos (sometimes referred to as class EM1) were numbered 26000-26056, then E2600-26056 then 76 001-76 057. They were equipped with two pantographs and painted in a blue livery with yellow fronts and years and several were housed in a new depot at Wath. They were withdrawn and scrapped in 1981 apart from 76 020 which entered the National Railway Museum collection at York, especially chosen because it had been exhibited at the 1951 Festival of Britain.

Above: Four of the new electric locomotives are depicted here parked up at the eastern end of Wath yard and include 26041 and 26048. This view was taken from Moor Road in 1962. *(Colin J Bowes)*

During the 1950s, passenger services were also under threat elsewhere, with the 'push and pull' trains operating along the former Dearne Valley Railway line between Edlington and Wakefield ceasing on 10 September 1951, together with the closure of the station halts at Edlington, Denaby, Harlington, Goldthorpe, Great Houghton and Grimethorpe. At the end of the decade the Doncaster to Barnsley passenger service was withdrawn along the former South Yorkshire Railway and the stations at Stairfoot, Wombwell and Wath were closed in 1959, although those at Mexborough and Conisbrough remained open as they also served passengers travelling to Rotherham and Sheffield.

Throughout the 1960s and 1970s, the domestic and industrial use of coal declined due to the switch to gas-fired central heating in many homes and it was felt necessary to move electricity generating facilities from numerous individual towns to large centralised power stations. This was coupled with the adaptation of the remaining collieries into feeding 'Merry-Go-Round' trains, which conveyed coal to the new power stations in the Aire and Trent valleys. To facilitate the efficient loading of the merry-go-round trains, this period also saw substantial investment by the NCB at the remaining collieries. The increasing use of mechanisation for coal cutting at the face with conveyor transporting to the pit bottom, was coupled with the widespread introduction of skip winding in many of the shafts, where one large capacity skip replaced cages that had previously carried numerous separate 10cwt tubs.

On the surface, the coal output was now processed through newly built coal preparation plants for grading and washing and new railway loading bunkers were constructed. The idea of a combined mine, a common feature on the continent but previously unheard of in the UK, had been started prior to nationalisation by the Manvers Main Colliery Company which intended to process all the output from the two pits at Manvers, plus Barnburgh and Kilnhurst

Collieries. The NCB added the nearby Wath Main Colliery to the plan. Another centralised processing location, named as Barnsley Eastside, focussed on Grimethorpe Colliery, now designed to handle the deep coal output from Darfield Main and Houghton Main plus shallower seams exploited by new drift mines. Although not a combined mine in the strict senses, a third linking scheme was formed from the merging of operations at Hickleton Main with Highgate and Goldthorpe Collieries.

However, during the 1960s more passenger services fell under the axe, although the reorganisation of the railway network under the Beeching Act of 1963 was not as severe in the Dearne Valley as elsewhere in the country. The only station closures during the decade resulted from the removal of Sheffield to Leeds stopping trains along the former Midland Railway, with Darfield Station closing in 1963 and the stations at Cudworth and Wath North closing in 1968. However, the former Midland Railway mainline was still used for long distance express services until 1986 when these were rerouted along adjoining lines because of mining subsidence, causing the line to close between Swinton and Great Houghton in 1988. The remaining section from Cudworth to Grimethorpe Colliery and Houghton Main Collieries was removed following the closure of these two pits in 1993.

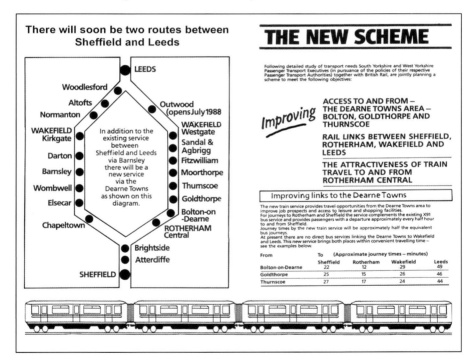

Above: A 1988 publicity flyer issued by British Rail, SYPTE & WYPTE detailing the forthcoming improvements to train services through the Dearne Valley with the proposed re-opening of stations at Bolton-on-Dearne, Goldthorpe and Thurnscoe.

In 1981, the electrified line from Wath to Manchester closed and, although the Wath marshalling yard remained in operation, the closure of many of the local pits after the 1984/5

Miners' Strike caused a sudden decline in traffic and the western outlet to Wombwell and Barnsley was abandoned in 1986. With the closure of Manvers Main Colliery in 1988, the yard finally closed and the remaining tracks were lifted. For several years, the site lay abandoned until the opening of the new A633 from Broomhill to Manvers stimulated the development of new housing, offices and retail parks on the site.

However, there has been a renaissance in passenger traffic albeit operating over a simplified network. In 1974 the South Yorkshire Passenger Transport Executive (SYPTE) took over the promotion of local train services and provided subsidies and service enhancements to the network together with station improvements. During the late 1980s, the rapid decline in coal mining and the changing patterns of employment, together with the lack of passenger stations in the Dearne Valley, were causing concern within the local authorities. In 1988 and 1989, new unstaffed railway stations were opened on the former Swinton & Knottingley Joint Railway line at Goldthorpe and Thurnscoe respectively, served by a new Sheffield – Rotherham – Wakefield – Leeds passenger service promoted by the SYPTE and their West Yorkshire counterpart, the West Yorkshire Passenger Transport Executive (WYPTE). Another unstaffed station opened on 16 May 1990 at Swinton Interchange, together with a Park & Ride facility, ideal for use by commuters to Sheffield, Rotherham, Doncaster and Leeds and for shoppers when the new Meadowhall Shopping Centre opened in September 1990. Swinton Interchange subsequently became a well-used station and gained an extended car park and is now staffed at the busiest times of the day.

Privatised Railways

Between 1994 and 1997, British Rail was privatised in stages and ownership of the track and infrastructure passed to Railtrack on 1 April 1994. Freight services were sold to six private companies and passenger operations were controversially franchised and awarded to 25 private sector operators. The intercity express services passing through the Dearne Valley were awarded to Virgin Cross Country from 5 January 1997 which later sold a 49% stake in the business to Stagecoach Group Ltd. On 11 November 2007, Arriva Cross Country (part of the German state owned Deutsche Bahn Railways) was awarded the franchise.

The local and longer distance train franchise was awarded to MTL Trust Holdings on 2 March 1997 which branded the operation as 'Northern Spirit'. In May 1998, the longer distance trains were rebranded as Trans Pennine Express and in 18 February 2000, MTL Trust Holdings was purchased by Arriva PLC which renamed the remaining Northern Spirit operation as Arriva Trains Northern. On 1 February 2004, the Trans Pennine Express operations were transferred into a separate franchise and awarded to First Trans Pennine Express, a partnership between First Group and the French state-owned transport group Keolis. On 9 September 2015, First Group were awarded the franchise as sole owners. On 1 July 2004, the former Northern Spirit operation was granted to Serco-NED Railways, now Serco-Abellio, a partnership between a British company and the Dutch state-owned railway division. However, on 1 April 2016, the franchise passed back into the hands of Arriva PLC which currently operates it as Northern Rail, serving 462 stations across the north of England.

The current situation in 2017 sees express trains operated by Arriva Cross Country passing through the Dearne Valley travelling along the former Swinton & Knottingley Railway and the former Great Central Railway line to Doncaster and Sheffield, whilst First Trans Pennine Express trains speed through Swinton Interchange and Mexborough Station. However

Northern Rail provide services to the Dearne Valley stations and these are promoted by SYPTE and WYPTE (METRO), the local transport authorities. Between Sheffield and Doncaster, a service operates every 30 minutes calling at Swinton and Mexborough stations. Some of these trains continue beyond Doncaster to Adwick-le-Street or Scunthorpe and from Sheffield to Lincoln. Another hourly stopping service from Sheffield calls at Swinton Interchange, Bolton-on-Dearne, Goldthorpe and Thurnscoe stations before travelling to Wakefield and Leeds. Finally mention must be made of the infrequent service branded as the Dearne Valley Line which provides two trains per day from Swinton to Pontefract and York. The former Midland Railway Sheffield to Barnsley line continues to thrive and Elsecar and Wombwell stations are served by a train every 30 minutes to Sheffield and every 30 minutes to Barnsley - continuing to either Huddersfield or Leeds. Additionally, Northern Rail long distance Nottingham-Sheffield-Barnsley-Leeds trains pass through Elsecar and Wombwell stations without stopping.

Since the last coal train left Goldthorpe Colliery rapid-loading bunker in 1994, most of the former freight lines have been abandoned, the cuttings filled in and embankments and bridges removed - the Dearne Valley railway network is now a shadow of its former self. However, the network that remains is now probably provided with the most frequent passenger service since its formation, and, with passenger numbers projected to increase, its future appears to be secure. Forthcoming railway improvements may be on the cards - a new station at Manvers would be a handy addition - and Swinton Interchange car park has been extended and is now often full on weekdays. Controversial plans to route a new HS2 High Speed Railway from Yorkshire to Birmingham and London may impinge on the Dearne Valley, although at the time of writing, no decisions have been made regarding this scheme.

Above: This modern railway scene shows a Class 144 Pacer DMU (Diesel Multiple Unit) train manufactured in 1986/7 by British Rail Engineering in Derby. Class 144023 heads a three-carriage unit departing from Goldthorpe Railway Station forming the 13:36 Sheffield to Leeds journey on Sunday 28 May 2017.

Public Transport

The creation of a dense network of mining settlements and the rapid increase in population throughout the Dearne Valley created the need for a frequent public transport network to connect the area with the nearby towns of Barnsley, Rotherham and Doncaster. The growth of the railways had been largely governed by the desire to transport coal, and passenger services were deemed an afterthought. Railway stations were often inconveniently situated away from the village centres and passenger services, to a certain extent, were infrequent - and some provided lengthy indirect journeys to the neighbouring towns.

Public transport operators were quick to provide direct and frequent services and, during the 20th century, the area became one of the most fascinating and varied public transport districts in the country, served by trams, trolleybuses and motor buses belonging to numerous operators. The Dearne Valley was principally served by the red and cream buses of the Yorkshire Traction Company, or 'Tracky' as it was affectionately known by the local population, and for over 80 years Tracky became synonymous with public transport in the Dearne valley. However, the motor buses of Yorkshire Traction were not the only provider of public transport; other major contributors include the trams of the Dearne District Light Railway, the trams, trolleybuses and motorbuses of the Mexborough & Swinton Traction Company, and numerous motorbuses provided by a hoard of independent bus operators, all painted in a variety of colourful shades.

Yorkshire Traction

Yorkshire Traction originally started life as a tramway operator trading under the name of The Barnsley & District Electric Traction Company Ltd. The company was registered on 27 March 1902 with a capital of £50,000 with a head office at Donington House on Norfolk Street in London - an operating division of the British Electric Traction Company, the country's paramount private tramway operator. In 1902, a tram depot was opened on Upper Sheffield Road in Barnsley and a fleet of 12 double decker tram cars were purchased from the Brush Electrical Engineering Company of Loughborough. The trams were painted in a maroon and cream livery and they were put into operation on a line from the bridge over the River Dearne at Smithies, southwards through Barnsley town centre to Worsbrough Cutting. Here the line divided into two branches: one to a terminus at Worsbrough Dale whilst the other continued along the main Sheffield Road and Park Road to a terminus at Worsbrough Bridge not far from the canal basin. However, any potential southwards extension was hindered by the refusal of the Great Central Railway to allow tram tracks to cross its rails at the level crossing at Worsbrough Bridge.

Trams were restricted to their line of operation and extensions were expensive to build and very quickly this mode of transport became considered as old fashioned so, in 1913, the company opted to purchase five motorbuses. These were Leyland Motors S8 motor buses with seating capacity for 27 passengers. These vehicles received fleet numbers 1-5 and were registered HE8-HE12, being some of the first vehicles registered with the HE prefixes by the County Borough of Barnsley. Smartly attired in a green and cream livery, with wooden seats and solid rubber tyres, these vehicles were put into service on a network of routes radiating from Barnsley: to Hoyland, Royston, Grimethorpe, Goldthorpe, and West Melton, the last three settlements located in the Dearne Valley.

Above Left: Barnsley & District Tram 6 is shown in this postcard by an anonymous photographer at the Worsbrough Dale terminus at the bottom of High Street. The Masons Arms on the right was sometimes used as the venue for inquests into pit disasters in the area. Out of view along West Street to the left is the Mitchell Memorial Hall, which opened in 1880 following the death of Joseph Mitchell. The Hall later became the Worsbrough Dale Social Club and Institute.
Above Right: The staff of Barnsley & District photographed at the Upper Sheffield depot on a postcard by an anonymous photographer issued c1914. Two of the five new motorbuses are proudly displayed, including number 2 (HE 9) with a Goldthorpe destination and number 4 (HE 11) with a West Melton destination. The nature of the occasion is unknown, but a large silver cup is pictured in front of General Manager Mr P H Marco.

The motor buses were an immediate success and by 23 May 1914, the motor bus fleet numbered 20 vehicles which were employed on an expanding network of 20 routes radiating from Barnsley, and given the following service numbers in the company's first timetable:

Service	Destination	Service	Destination
1	Hoyland Common	11	Shafton Fox & Hounds
2	Dodworth	12	Hoyle Mill Dearne Grove Inn
3	Ardsley Manor	13	Cawthorne
4	Goldthorpe & Doncaster	14	Grimethorpe Hotel
5	Darton	15	Cudworth Star Hotel
6	Staincross	16	Darfield & Goldthorpe Hotel
7	Royston	17	Darfield & Thurnscoe Church
8	Pontefract	18	Wakefield
9	Hemsworth	19	Wombwell Town Hall
10	Brierley Three Horse Shoes	20	West Melton Police Station

After the end of the First World War more services were introduced and a second and third depot opened in Doncaster and Huddersfield in 1920. During the 1920s, new routes were introduced to Huddersfield, Penistone, South Elmsall, Mexborough and Doncaster, with another service announced in 1923 from Barnsley to Thurnscoe via Wath, Bolton-on-Dearne and Goldthorpe, in obvious competition with a forthcoming tramway route under construction by a consortium of local authorities. From 1925, a policy of purchasing independent bus operators was pursued, leading to the acquisition of services to Sheffield and Rotherham and the South Elmsall service was extended to meet the Doncaster trams at the Woodlands Hotel. In 1929, over 20 million passenger journeys were made, compared to two million on the original tram network.

In 1928, to reflect the increasing sphere of influence of the company throughout South and West Yorkshire away from its home territory of Barnsley, the company was renamed Yorkshire Traction and the bus fleet was painted into the now traditional red and cream colours. In 1929, summer holiday motor coaches were introduced on services to Scarborough and Blackpool, and, at the end of the year, a 49% stake in the holding company, British Electric Traction, was jointly acquired by the London Midland & Scottish and London North Eastern Railways. In 1930, the original trams were abandoned and replaced with a fleet of Leyland Titan 48 seater double-deckers, the first double-deckers operated by the company.

Throughout the 1930s the service network continued to grow through a combination of expansion and the acquisition of other bus firms and bus services were now operated across the Pennines to Manchester, from Doncaster to Goole, and from Sheffield to Upton via Wombwell and Darfield. In 1930, long distance coach services were introduced from various Yorkshire towns to London and private coach hire was promoted. This was especially popular with many of the chapel, clubs and organisations of the area, who could hire a whole fleet of buses for the annual children's treat to the seaside.

The 1930 Road Traffic Act introduced a structured market, with services being licensed and regulated by the local authorities and this method of control remained in force until the introduction of a deregulated market on 26 October 1986. Prior to 1930, bus operators were not required to operate to a timetable (although Yorkshire Traction had always done so) and it was often a free-for-all on the busiest routes, with buses from rival firms racing each other for passengers. However, takeovers of rivals were a major way of expanding the influence of the company and, in 1933, the Dearne District Light Railway was purchased, bringing with it the garage at Wombwell, and, in 1934, Lancashire & Yorkshire Motors was acquired, together with depot premises at Shafton.

With the outbreak of the Second World War, 83 staff left the company to join the forces so frequencies were reduced and some services withdrawn, with priority given to the operation of workmen's buses. This resulted in the dismissal of 240 staff and 35 buses were requisitioned by the military, many for use on the continent which were never returned after the end of the war. Other buses were converted to ambulances and to counteract a shortage of petrol, 26 buses were converted to run on gas, produced in apparatus housed in trailers towed by the vehicles. The situation eased shortly afterwards and most of the staff made redundant were re-engaged but a strike in 1943 for three weeks saw the army introduce bus services over some of the key routes but these were only permitted for use by miners travelling to work as well as other classified workmen.

Following the end of hostilities, expansion and acquisitions continued and passenger growth increased until its peak in 1955, after which there was a gradual decline in numbers, hastened by the 1957 Suez Crisis and the increasing ownership of private motor cars. Despite this, Tracky remained a very profitable concern, with healthy passenger numbers, and this was reflected in continued investment in the fleet, both with new vehicles and the re-bodying of older wartime utility vehicles. In 1959, twelve futuristic looking 73 seater rear-engine Leyland Atlanteans were purchased as fleet numbers 1151-1162 (registrations RHE801-RHE812). These vehicles were put to work on Service 22 and 22A, the main trunk route from Barnsley to Doncaster through the Dearne Valley.

The 1960s saw a further decline in passenger numbers but the company remained profitable, reducing overheads through the introduction of higher capacity vehicles. From 1913 to 1966, all vehicles had been numbered sequentially, from fleet number 1 (registration HE 8) reaching fleet number 1343 (registration FHE343D). However, from 1967 a classification for vehicle types was introduced. This was necessary to avoid the allocating of certain vehicle types on routes that passed under one of the many low railway bridges in the area. In 1969, British Electric Traction sold out to the British Government which had inherited the 49% stake held by the LMS and LNER on the formation of British Rail in 1948, and Yorkshire Traction became a division within the state owned National Bus Company.

As part of this re-organisation, the Huddersfield bus operator County Motors became part of Yorkshire Traction, bringing 23 vehicles and premises at Huddersfield Waterloo into the fleet. More importantly was the acquisition of the 40 vehicles operated by Mexborough & Swinton, as well as the depot premises at Rawmarsh; these joined the main Yorkshire Traction fleet, bringing a very profitable network of services into the Tracky fold. The National Bus Company introduced a corporate logo and poppy red livery, which was applied to the fleet, and vehicle purchasing policy was now standardised with other National Bus Company subsidiaries throughout the country, mostly obtaining vehicles from state owned manufacturers.

However, changes to local government in 1974 saw the establishment of West Yorkshire and South Yorkshire County Councils and their transport operating divisions, the Passenger Transport Executives. Both West Yorkshire and South Yorkshire established a county wide service numbering system. The 22 and 22A from Barnsley to Doncaster were renumbered 222/223 and the 23 from Barnsley to Thurnscoe, along the former Dearne District Light Railway route, was renumbered as 226. From 1 April 1974, local authorities no longer handled the issuing of registration numbers and the last County Borough of Barnsley registration applied to a Yorkshire Traction vehicle was 820 (SHE 820M), a Bristol VRT decker with Eastern Coach Works 74 seater bodywork. The HE Barnsley registration, together with ET of Rotherham and DT of Doncaster, joined WA, WB, WE & WJ at the Sheffield office, which also acquired WG from Yorkshire East Riding, plus KU, KY & KW from Bradford. Any of these registration letters were now applied to new Yorkshire Traction vehicles.

The South Yorkshire County Council introduced a cheap fares policy from 1 April 1974, partially subsiding local bus fares through a charge on the rates. Children travelled for 2p and the adult fare from Barnsley to Doncaster was reduced to 10p. This brought about a dramatic increase in loadings with passenger numbers increasing for the first time since 1956. The policy was so successful that the buses became very crowded during the 1970s and 1980s; the author remembers one busy journey as a child, having to stand all the way from Doncaster to Barnsley on service X19. A conductor recalled a time when conducting a 3-hour round trip on service 222 from Doncaster to Barnsley and back, having to issue over 1,000 tickets to passengers.

On 1 April 1986, the national government abolished the South Yorkshire County Council and fares increased by 225% to commercial levels, resulting in a dramatic decline in passenger numbers. The 1985 Transport Act established the privatisation of the National Bus Company, and the introduction of a deregulated market, a day subsequently known as D-Day, was established on 26 October 1986. In preparation for this, Yorkshire Traction began removing all vestiges of the National Bus Company and started to paint its buses in the traditional dark red and white colours. Following the introduction of deregulation, bus operators had to split their services into the profitable ones with the unprofitable services and journeys put up for tender by the South Yorkshire Passenger Transport Executive. This brought outside bus operators into the Dearne Valley for the first time and one service, the 194 Doncaster - Barnburgh - Mexborough passed under contract to East Midland Motor Services of Worksop. With a deregulated market now in effect, anybody could in theory now operate a bus service shadowing the profitable routes of an established operator, the effect of competition hopefully holding fares in check.

In preparation for privatisation the management of Yorkshire Traction led by Chairman Frank Carter acquired an 'off-the-shelf' company called Broomco (187) Ltd with which to purchase Yorkshire Traction from the government and on 28 January 1987, Yorkshire Traction became fully independent for the first time in its life when the 361 buses and six depots were purchased for £1,400,000 by a management buyout. The new team immediately established its own bus purchasing policy and speeded up the application of its new traditional red and cream livery to its fleet, although some buses at Huddersfield and Rawmarsh depots were painted in a stylised colour scheme resembling the old County Motors and Mexborough & Swinton liveries.

Limited stop service X19, X20, X22, X30, X32, X33, X52, X60, X71 & X90, were branded under the FastLink logo and minibus services under the TownLink brand were introduced in greater numbers, although an initial batch of these had been introduced from 26 October 1986 in Doncaster and South Elmsall and these soon spread throughout the area, operating around narrow roads and housing estates on a 'hail and ride' basis. Travel agents were branded under the TravelLink logo, and InfoLink was used for information points in the bus stations, whilst coaching operations were operated as CoachLink. After exactly one year of independent ownership, Yorkshire Traction purchased the 172 vehicles and premises of Lincolnshire Road Car Company from the National Bus Company on 28 January 1988, quickly followed by the purchase of the Newark bus operator, W Gash & Sons, whose operations were absorbed into Lincolnshire Road Car. One thing of note, and reflecting the changing employment patterns of the time, was the cessation of the last Tracky pit bus at the end of 1988 with the forthcoming closure of Barnburgh Colliery.

However, deregulation brought new independent operators on to the scene, keen to take a share of the profits throughout the Tracky network, and independent bus operators made a return to the Dearne Valley for the first time since Larratt Pepper of Thurnscoe sold out to Yorkshire Traction in 1979. New operators appeared almost overnight and included Pride of The Road, Shearing Coaches, Globe Coaches, Tom Jowitt Travel and Aldham Coaches. These eventually sold out to the incumbent operator and with the purchase of Tom Jowitt Coaches in July 1990, a new low-cost subsidiary was established trading under the Barnsley & District name, with a blue and white livery and based at the former Shearing's premises on Wakefield Road, Barnsley.

In 1991, the first move into Scotland was made when Tracky purchased the 164 buses and seven depots of Strathtay Scottish Omnibuses, based in Dundee. Further expansion continued with the acquisition of Lincoln City Transport and Ridings Travel and another foray into Scotland with the purchase of Meffan of Kirriemuir in 1993. Reflecting its status as the largest independent bus operator in the country, the company now traded as Traction Group, with Yorkshire Traction becoming an operating subsidiary and the 90th anniversary of the company was celebrated with an open day at the Barnsley Head Office and unveiled a revised livery and fleet name.

Just as Yorkshire Traction was busy expanding its operations in a deregulated market, so other bus operators were turning their attention to South Yorkshire, resulting in some unusual 'tit for tat' manoeuvres. Chesterfield Transport was awarded the contract to operate Service 8 Barnsley to Barnsley Grove Street by SYPTE, and extended their Service X12 from Chesterfield via Sheffield and Rotherham to Barnsley to link up with their newly awarded route. In retaliation for this Yorkshire Traction introduced a new service 20 from Chesterfield to New Whittington, running directly ahead of the existing Chesterfield Transport service 20, with the buses operating from Rawmarsh depot as 'positioning journeys' on service X20 Rawmarsh to-Chesterfield. However, Tracky was now looking to move into the profitable Sheffield bus market and purchased Andrews of Sheffield in 1992, followed by South Riding in 1994 and Sheffield Omnibus and Yorkshire Terrier in 1995. These four independent operators had all started up following deregulation in 1986 and eventually traded under the Yorkshire Terrier name from premises at Holbrook and Ecclesfield.

The fashion for minibus operations was now declining and in 1997 the company bought its first low floor buses, accessible to buggies and wheel chair users. Yorkshire Traction continued with a policy of new, second hand and re-bodied vehicle purchases for its core fleet. By 1998 the Tracky fleet had reached its highest ever figure of 398 vehicles and the Traction Group operated 1,100 buses throughout the country and a 25% stake in London bus operator Metropolitan Omnibuses Ltd was acquired. However, the turn of a new century saw a decline in the core operations, with maintenance problems and an aging fleet resulting in the operator having to appear before the Yorkshire Traffic Commissioners in 2000 resulting in the replacement of older vehicles with quality second hand purchases and the closure of the depot at Wombwell to secure economies. Despite this, the company celebrated its 100th anniversary in 2002 with all staff treated to a night's entertainment with one day's takings being donated to Barnsley Hospice.

From 2004, all new buses and older low floor vehicles were delivered or repainted into a bold new purple and yellow livery and seven high profile new double-deckers were purchased for use on X19 Barnsley - Doncaster – Robin Hood Airport and 226 Barnsley – Wath – Thurnscoe routes. However, the original directors were looking to retire and on 15 December 2005, Traction Group, the largest independent bus operator in the country, was sold to Stagecoach Holdings for £26,000,000.

The new owners rebranded the operation as Stagecoach Yorkshire and by 2007 all the vehicles had been repainted with corporate Stagecoach livery and renumbered into Stagecoach's national 5-digit fleet numbering scheme. The new owners also undertook major investment in new vehicles and placed their Chesterfield subsidiary and the Sheffield operations directly under control of the Barnsley head office. A new network of buses serving the Dearne Valley was introduced on 20 May 2007 to coincide with the opening of the new Barnsley Interchange. However, since then the operation has reduced to a profitable core network, with Stagecoach closing the Barnsley & District operation in 2006 and disposing of the Huddersfield depot to CentreBus in 2008. Later that year the Doncaster depot was closed followed by the closure of the head office and original Tracky sheds in Barnsley after 106 years of operation. This was coupled with the moving of the head office into the town centre and the Barnsley depot buses into the former Shearings / Barnsley & District premises on Wakefield Road. A final depot closure occurred in 2011 when the Shafton depot was shut.
The Dearne Valley network now appears to have stabilised into a handful of profitable services although other changes have occurred recently to reflect the changing employment patterns, notably with the growth of two new flagship services: the 22X from Rotherham -

Manvers – Barnsley; and Route 66, linking the old canal basins at Elsecar and Worsbrough to Hoyland and Barnsley After 95 years of operation, the famous route 222 from Barnsley to Doncaster was truncated to terminate at Mexborough, although this did coincide with the re-introduction of Service X20 from Doncaster – Manvers – Barnsley. The Yorkshire Traction name may have disappeared from the sides of the buses but the company still exists, albeit with a registered office in Stockport rather than Barnsley. Look closely when boarding one of the Stagecoach Yorkshire buses for the 'small print': the legal lettering applied on the side of the bus by the front wheel arch which still reads Yorkshire Traction, Barnsley trading as Stagecoach Yorkshire.

Above: A film making relic. An amusing part in the 1996 film *Brassed Off* featured a scene in a fish and chip shop named *In Cod We Trust*. This was filmed in Grimethorpe High Street and the mocked-up shop façade remained in situ for several years afterwards, although the derelict property has since been demolished. The bus belongs to Yorkshire Traction and is fleet number 424 (L424 LET) a 41 seater Dennis Dart on route 211 from Doncaster to Barnsley, photographed in 2005.

Mexborough and Swinton

Proposals to connect some of the Dearne towns with Rotherham to the south were first granted by a 1902 parliamentary act promoted by the Mexborough & Rawmarsh Construction Syndicate Ltd. However, this company suffered bankruptcy and the scheme was taken over by the National Electric Construction Company, which established a subsidiary under the name Mexborough & Swinton Tramways with a head office and depot at Dale Road in Rawmarsh. The depot at Rawmarsh was built across the road from a development of 150 houses known as 'Silver City'. These houses were built by John Brown & Company Ltd for their workforce at Aldwarke Colliery and were named after the 1897 silver rush in Yukon Territory, Canada.

In 1905, construction commenced on a street tramway from Rotherham through Parkgate, Rawmarsh, Swinton and Mexborough to Denaby Toll Bar with a proposed branch from Mexborough to Manvers Main Colliery. The new tramway system opened on .6 Feb 1907 from Rotherham to Parkgate with the complete route to Denaby Toll Bar following on 3 August 1907, although the authorised branch from Mexborough to Manvers Main Colliery was not constructed.

To operate the new service, a fleet of 16 double-decker tram cars were ordered from the Bruch Electrical Engineering Company of Leicester. The new trams were painted in a red and cream livery and received fleet numbers 1-16. These vehicles, with seating capacity for 54 and with their upper decks open to the elements, were powered by an unusual and ultimately disastrous system of 'Dolter Stud Contacts', rather than by the traditional overhead wires provided for most tramway systems. Electrical power was fed to a series of contact studs laid in the road surface at frequent intervals between the rails. Trams would activate the studs to receive electrical power to propel them to the next stud and so on, a contact beneath the trams rendering the studs inactive once the tram had passed overhead.

However, serious problems were experienced with this form of electrical supply due to the unreliability of the Dolter system. Trams often came to a halt between the studs, powerless and requiring a push by the tram car behind. Much more serious was the fact that on some instances, several of the studs remained live, leading to several electrical flashes and explosions and to the deaths of two unfortunate horses which had trodden on live studs.

Realising the potential danger to human life, the Government's Board of Trade ordered the Dolter Stud Contact system to cease operation from 30th July 1908. Consequently, the entire system was quickly converted to the traditional overhead power supply wires, supported by a series of tram poles positioned alongside the road. Trams could operate over the Rotherham County Borough owned line from Rawmarsh Road to gain access to Rotherham and consequently Rotherham Corporation Transport became a nominal joint operator on the network. At the same time the open top tram cars received fixed roofs and four new trams numbered 17-20 joined the fleet.

Shortly afterwards, the Company began to investigate the possibilities of operating railless electrical traction vehicles, known as trolleybuses, but commonly known to the people of the Dearne Valley as 'tracklesses'. Like trams, trolleybuses received their power from overhead electrical wiring, but their advantage was that they were not restricted to rails as they had rubber tyres. Several trolleybus lines were promoted by a Parliamentary Act which received approval in 1913 and these routes were:

Route 1: Swinton Woodman Inn to Wath via Quarry Hill Road, Cemetery Road, Stump Cross Road and Fitzwilliam Street to Wath Church Street.
Route 1A: Swinton Woodman Inn to Wath direct via Sandygate.
Route 2: Wath Church Street to West Melton, via High Street, West Street, Barnsley Road, Melton Road to Brampton Christ Church.
Route 3: Wath Church Street to Goldthorpe, via Moor Road (across a swing bridge over the Dearne & Dove Canal), Recreation Road, Station Road, Dearne Road, Ingsfield Lane, Thurnscoe Road, Back Lane, Furlong Road and High Street to Goldthorpe Horse & Groom.
Route 4: Denaby Old Toll Bar tram terminus to Conisbrough Elm Green Lane, via Doncaster Road, Denaby Main Colliery and Station Road.
Route 5: Mexborough Post Office Square to Wath, via Main Street, Wath Road, Manvers Main Colliery, Doncaster Road and High Street to Montgomery Square.

However, when the bill was published, the local councils of Wombwell, Wath, Bolton-on-Dearne and Thurnscoe successfully objected to the scheme as they were promoting the Dearne District Light Railways. Consequently, only Route 4 and Route 5 from Mexborough to Manvers Main Colliery were constructed and these services commenced on 31 August 1915. To operate the new routes, three 26 seater Daimler Railless Electric Traction vehicles numbered 21-23 (registered WT938, WR6823 and WR6824), and painted red and cream were purchased. All Mexborough & Swinton vehicles were issued with West Riding registrations bearing the prefixes WR, WT, WU, WW, WX, WY & YG. The three trolleybus vehicles were housed in a new depot at Denaby Toll Bar, which also accommodated a handful of tram cars. In 1917, the trolleybus fleet was supplemented with a similar second-hand vehicle from Stockport Corporation. War time staff shortages and the lack of spare parts for repairs as well as the state of the roads led to the frequent suspension and sporadic operation of the new services, despite the need to transport men to the collieries along the route, and it wasn't until 1922 that these vehicles, with their solid rubber tyres and bumpy suspension, resumed continuous operation. Three further new vehicles were supplied by AEC of London in 1924-26; these were AEC 602 models with seating capacity for 32 passengers.

However, the Company were obviously impressed with the flexibility of the new trolleybuses and proposed to convert the entire tramway system to trolleybus operation. Between 1928-1930, 30 Garrett trolleybuses with a seating capacity for 32 passengers were delivered to replace the trams, and the entire network was converted by 10 March 1929. As part of these plans, a new branch diverged from the Conisbrough service at the Station Hotel, passing along Low Road to a terminus at Brook Square, known as Conisbrough Low. The main line was extended through Conisbrough town centre to serve a new development of 400 colliery houses at Conanby, this service going by the name Conisbrough High. In 1931, another development was the creation of a branch line to Rawmarsh, along Green Lane and Kilnhurst Road, and a new Mexborough terminus was created by extending alternate trips to a turning circle at Adwick Road Clock. Trolleybuses now operated Rotherham to Adwick Road, Rotherham to Conisbrough Low and Manvers Main to Conisbrough High. As part of these arrangements, larger six wheel Rotherham vehicles now appeared on certain journeys to Adwick Road and Conisbrough Low, roughly in the proportion of 1 Rotherham vehicle to 8 Mexborough vehicles, reflecting the proportion of mileage operated within the two areas.

In 1931, the National Electric Construction Company sold out to British Electric Traction and Mexborough & Swinton became a sister company to the neighbouring Yorkshire Traction, the larger operator frequently loaning motor buses to Mexborough to assist with the operation of a growing motor bus network. From 1943-1950, the Garrett trolleybuses were replaced with an entirely new fleet of 39 Sunbeam trolleybuses numbered 1-39. These vehicles received a striking livery of green and cream which replaced the earlier red and cream colours. The Sunbeams would prove to be a very reliable purchase, each operating over a million miles during their working lives and working an intensive and frequent network, enabling Mexborough & Swinton to become one of the most profitable divisions within British Electric Traction.

Upper Left: Mexborough & Swinton Tram 8 is depicted on this 1907 postcard by an anonymous photographer. The vehicle has passed Pinch Row Cottages and is heading along Warren Vale from Swinton towards Rotherham. On reaching the Rotherham Corporation boundary near Parkgate, power would be drawn from traditional overhead wiring using the tram pole on the top of the vehicle. Warren Vale was remodelled in the late 1920s with the construction of a new road for the A633 and Pinch Row Cottages were subsequently demolished.

Upper Right: The smartly attired driver and conductor of tram 13 pause for the camera lens of C F Hurst at Swinton Common in 1907 and this view was later issued as a postcard by John Crowther Cox of Rotherham. The upper deck passengers appear pleased to be captured by the camera and behind the trees on the right is Swinton Common Colliery in Creighton Woods, a small land sale pit working a shallow seam. In the distance, another tram heads along Rockingham Road towards Swinton.

Lower Left: Tram 12 is depicted in 1907 prior to the introduction of traditional overhead wiring. This postcard was published by John Crowther Cox of Rotherham and titled 'Swinton trams'. The location is in Rowms Lane outside the Swinton Board Schools and looking towards Mexborough. *(Andrew McGarrigle Collection)*

Lower Right: In 1908, the tram fleet was fitted with fixed roofed upper deck covers and the electrical traction was delivered by overhead wiring. Tram 16 is depicted here at 'Journey's End' – outside Denaby Toll Bar at Pastures Road in Mexborough. The houses were named Don View and faced the small sub-depot out of camera to the right. *(Paul Fox Collection)*

Motorbus operation had been first trialled in 1910 with a charabanc operating from Mexborough to Wath and from Denaby Toll Bar to the Denaby Main Hotel; however, this operation was short lived. Motor buses reappeared in 1922 for a new service from Mexborough to Goldthorpe operated by a trio of Daimler vehicles which received fleet numbers 27-29. This service passed to Yorkshire Traction in 1929, although elsewhere motor buses were still serving Upper Haugh, Greasborough, Kilnhurst and Mexborough's Windhill Estate. Additionally, several pit buses operated services to local collieries. In the 1950s, it was decided not to extend the trolleybus network and concentrate on developing the motorbus network. In 1959, the company received parliamentary consent to abandon the trolleybus operations and these were replaced with motor buses from 26 March 1961. Mexborough & Swinton, having been the first non-municipally owned operator of trolleybuses in 1915, became the last company operator to close its trolleybus system. On 25 March 1961, to commemorate the closure of the trolleybus system, a souvenir timetable was issued, and the Rawmarsh Silver Prize band toured the network on an especially cut down open ended trolleybus for the day.

Above: In 1961, Glyn Hague and Geoff Pilkington, engineers at Rawmarsh depot, made a series of six models to commemorate the vehicles operated by the company. Up until the 1980s, these excellent models were on display in the booking office at Rawmarsh depot, fascinating the author as a young boy. Later two of these models were displayed at the Museum of South Yorkshire Life at Cusworth Hall, but sadly their present whereabouts is unknown. It would be a fitting scenario for these models to return to the area and go on public exhibition.
Upper Left: Glyn with trolleybus 37 (JWW 375) in Warren Vale. **Upper Right**: Glyn at work the models. **Lower Left**: The models featured in a '54 years of progress' exhibit in the company's booking office. **Lower Right**: three of the completed models. *(*All: *Paul Fox Collection)*

Above: The Manvers terminus was bleakly situated amongst the colliery headgear, coking plant, brickworks and railway bridges adjacent to the junction of the roads to Swinton, Wath, Bolton and Mexborough. The photographer has captured Mexborough & Swinton Sunbeam trackless 24 (FWX 908) negotiating the turning circle to operate the return journey to Conisbrough High sometime in the 1950s. In the background is Manvers Main No 4 headgear (rebuilt in 1930) and the Simon Carves coal preparation plant. The railway bridge carried the Midland Railway and it appears to have been widened several times over the years, as at this point the formation carries quadruple tracks. Trolleybuses were withdrawn in 1961 and the whole area was landscaped in the 1990s. Today nothing remains from this picture with the new Manvers roundabout on the A6023 occupying this site. *(Norman Ellis Collection).*

New motorbus vehicles introduced to replace the trolleybuses included the company's first new double-deckers, when 11 Leyland Atlanteans entered service, with seating capacity for 72 passengers. These vehicles, with registrations 7001 WU to 7011 WU, received fleet numbers 1-11 and were put to work on the Rotherham to Rawmarsh and Rotherham to Mexborough Adwick Road routes, whilst 14 high capacity single-deckers operated on the remaining system. Coaches had been operated from 1948 and further examples were delivered to the fleet to cater for a growing private hire and excursion trade. An important new route introduced from 1965 was an express service 90 from Mexborough to Sheffield.

The last vehicles delivered to the company were fleet numbers 22-25, registered WWU 922G – WWU 925G, 77 seat Daimler Fleetlines, as from 1 January 1969, British Electric Traction was now owned by the government. Consequently, Mexborough & Swinton became part of the National Bus Company. However, this was short lived as on 1 October 1969, the Company became part of neighbouring Yorkshire Traction and the 40-vehicle fleet and premises at Rawmarsh (the Denaby Toll Bar depot having closed the previous year) passed into Tracky ownership; the buses were repainted red. In 1984, the last former Mexborough & Swinton vehicle operated by Yorkshire Traction (WWU 922G) was withdrawn from service and ended its life in the 'bones yard' next to Wombwell depot, its windows subsequently broken by stones thrown from local kids, before being towed away to be broken up at Wombwell Diesels scrap yard in 1988. To celebrate what would have been the 75th anniversary of the company, in 1982, Yorkshire Traction painted a vehicle, a 1980 Leyland National registered EDT 205V, in Mexborough and Swinton green and cream trolleybus colours. Following privatisation of Yorkshire Traction in 1987, several buses at Rawmarsh depot also received a simplified green and cream colour scheme with Mexborough & Swinton fleet names, but these had all disappeared when Yorkshire Traction introduced a new corporate image in 1992. To celebrate what would have been the 100th anniversary of the company in 2007, new owners Stagecoach Yorkshire painted a former 1995 Yorkshire Terrier Dennis Dart, registered N106 CET, into a green and cream livery, with Mexborough & Swinton fleet names. This vehicle, with fleet number 32930, was transferred to Rawmarsh depot to spend the rest of its working life operating over the former Mexborough & Swinton system.

In the present day, there exist a couple of reminders of the trolleybus era. Until its removal around 2005, one of the old trolleybus poles remained opposite the junction of Welfare Road and Old Road in Conisbrough. Another pole and a nearby truncated stump remain in situ at the time of writing at the Adwick Road Clock terminus. The bus shelter at the Adwick Road terminus originally featured a large Mexborough & Swinton name board. This has been restored and displayed in the Mexborough Heritage Centre in Mexborough Library. Further afield, the National Museum of the Trolleybus at Sandtoft is home to one of the original 1928 trolleybuses (34, WW 4688) which was rescued from a nearby farm and hopefully will one day be fully restored to working order. Is this the end of tram and trolleybus operation in the area? Possibly not for there has always been talk of extending the Sheffield Supertram system to Wath to serve the new employment district of Manvers, although this may have been partially replaced by a new scheme scheduled to open in 2018 to operate 'tram trains' from Sheffield to a new station at Parkgate Shopping Centre.

Above: Motorbuses replaced the trolleybuses in 1961 but Mexborough & Swinton also operated a private hire and excursions business. Pictured in a publicity photograph outside the western façade of Earl Fitzwilliam's Wentworth Woodhouse is fleet number 100 (OWU 660), a 1955 Leyland Leopard coach with Burlingham 41 seat bodywork, lending a stylistic appearance to the vehicle.

Dearne District Light Railways

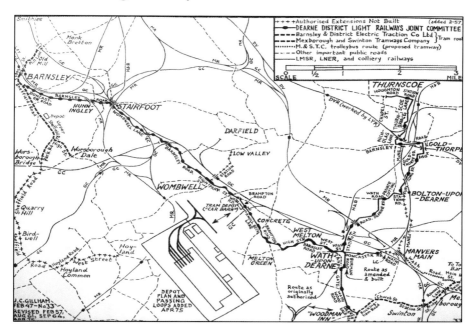

Above: Dearne District Light Railway route map was drawn by J Gillham in 1947. From 1924 to 1930 it was possible to take a tram journey from Worsbrough Bridge to Firth Park (a distance of eight miles as the crow flies), via Barnsley, Swinton, Rotherham and Sheffield, using five different South Yorkshire tram operators.

The Dearne District Light Railway (DDLR) has the distinction of being the last traditional street tramway constructed in the country, and ironically having the shortest operating life - the system opened in 1924 and closed in 1933 after nine fascinating and eccentric years. In November 1913, the four urban district councils of Wombwell, Wath, Thurnscoe and Bolton-on-Dearne prepared plans for a street tramway linking the Dearne Valley with Barnsley, and, in 1915, consent was granted by the Light Railway Commissioners for its construction. An earlier scheme for a street tramway through the Dearne Valley had been put forward by the promoters of the Barnsley & Doncaster Light Railway at a cost of £140,000. However, in 1902 this scheme was abandoned and it would be another 22 years until trams operated through the Dearne towns.

Plans were approved for a tramway nearly 19 miles in length from Barnsley to Thurnscoe, via Stairfoot, Wombwell, Brampton Bierlow, West Melton, Wath, Manvers Main Colliery, Bolton-on-Dearne, Goldthorpe and Highgate. Branches were authorised from Wombwell to Darfield via Low Valley and from Wath to Swinton Common, with a southward facing connection to the Mexborough & Swinton tramways to Rotherham laid at the Woodman Inn. At Barnsley, although the intention was to operate into the town centre, the tramway terminated at Doncaster Road near the Alhambra Theatre, adjacent to the tram tracks belonging to Barnsley & District Tramways running along Sheffield Road. This was because the latter company objected to the new system entering the town centre and refused to grant permission for a junction.

Another objection was raised by the Great Central Railway who opposed the tramway operating over their railway level crossing on Doncaster Road near Manvers Main Colliery. Consequently, the tramway was diverted to operate along a more direct route from Wath to Bolton-on-Dearne. In Bolton, a short private section though an old quarry was laid, thus eliminating a series of narrow stretches and tight corners near Bolton Church. Part of the former main line was incorporated into a new branch line from Wath to the Staithes Public House, terminating adjacent to the Great Central Railway's level crossing. The whole scheme also included proposals for several minor additional routes:

Route 1 Barnsley Alhambra Theatre to Barnsley Eldon Street.
Route 2 Brampton Bulls Head to West Melton Police Station via Pontefract Road and Hollowgate.
Route 3 Thurnscoe Chapel Lane Top along Houghton Road to Clayton Lane Junction.
Route 4 Thurnscoe Brough's Corner via Lidgett Lane to Hickleton Main Colliery.
Route 5 Thurnscoe Station Hotel along Windsor Street to the Fairway Hotel.
Route 6 Thurnscoe Three Lanes End to High Street and Common Road to Clayton Lane Junction.

Above: Laying the tram tracks in Goldthorpe High Street depicted on a postcard published by Edgar Scrivens in 1923. The houses in the background were built c1912 for miners at Goldthorpe and Barnburgh Main Collieries.

Although authorisation had been given to construct the tramway in 1915, the outbreak of the First World War delayed the scheme. Rapid post-war inflation saw the construction costs escalate to £300,000 by the time work finally commenced at Thurnscoe on 11 May 1923 when Councillor Mark Lane Nokes cut the first sod to mark the beginning of construction. Possibly to save costs, the six minor route extensions were abandoned, together with the authorised branch line from Wombwell to Darfield. A minor route deviation was authorised on the Swinton branch which was diverted along Burman Road to serve a new housing estate, delaying the opening on this branch line until 29 September 1924. The remainder of the network opened for service on 10 July 1924 when Councillor Nokes, chairman of the Light Railway Joint Board, presided over the opening ceremony and drove the first tram car from Barnsley to Wombwell.

A depot was constructed on Brampton Road near Wombwell, known as 'Car Barns', - adopting American tramway terminology. This housed the fleet of 30 single decker trams supplied by the English Electric Company Ltd and numbered 1-30. The trams had a capacity for 36 passengers, with seating arranged in two long benches running the length of the interior, with curtained windows behind. The tram cars were of a very smart appearance, finished in a dark red and white colour scheme, with linings in maroon and gold - they were referred to as 'red dragons' by the local population.

Above: A fine study of tram 30 travelling along High Street towards Wath Montgomery Square. The vehicle is probably working on one of the two branches from Manvers Main Colliery to Swinton Woodman Inn. The photograph was issued as a postcard by Edgar Scrivens in 1930.

Most of the staff required to operate the system were not local people. The Paisley & District Tramways Company had recently been absorbed by Glasgow Corporation Tramways, enabling many of the staff to travel south to the new undertaking. Major Frederick Coutts was appointed General Manager of the DDLR, previously having been Engineering & General Manager at Paisley. In 1925 Frederick Coutts was succeeded by his son Ronald Coutts and in 1929, 138 people were employed at the Car Barns, including 43 motormen, 46 conductresses and 4 inspectors. To accommodate some of the staff, a small development of 30 houses was constructed on Broomhead Road near the depot. This development, consisted of 10 semi-detached houses for senior staff and 20 smaller houses, arranged in blocks of four. With its

Paisley accents, the street gained the unofficial name of 'Scotch Porridge Row'. The DDLR also owned two bungalows on Brampton Road, possibly as accommodation for managerial staff.

Above: A spectacular scene of social history captured in Goldthorpe, with the crews of two trams pausing in the passing loop and posing for the photographer together with numerous local children no doubt fascinated by the scene. Tram 10 is bound for Barnsley and tram 17 is heading to Thurnscoe. It may be hard to believe today, but Goldthorpe once supported two cinemas and 'going to the pictures' was a very popular pastime during the interwar years throughout the country. The Empire cinema is visible behind tram 10 whilst the Picture House on the left was showing *The Fighting Adventurer*. This was a 1924 silent movie directed by Tom Forman and starring Pat O'Malley and Mary Astor. When the trams ceased operation the poles and overhead wiring were removed but most of the rails were left in situ and covered in tarmac. In 1974, workman digging a trench outside the picture house uncovered the tram rails, a situation repeated 26 years later during another phase of roadworks – this proved in both cases a considerable hindrance but didn't make the work impossible to complete and the rails were subsequently buried beneath new tarmac again.

Trams operated on frequencies of every 10-15 minutes from Barnsley to Wath, where around half the journeys terminated, with the other half continuing to Thurnscoe on a 20-30-minute frequency, taking up to 90 minutes for the full journey. Occasional journeys operated from Barnsley to Manvers or Swinton Woodman along the two branch lines. However, the branch lines had their own dedicated service, each operated by a single tram shuttling from the outer terminus to Wath, usually continuing onwards to terminate at West Melton Police Station, thus providing a journey frequency of 30 minutes on each of the two branches. The terminus at Manvers Main was separated by a short distance of road from the trolleybus terminus belonging to the Mexborough & Swinton Traction Company which had opened in 1915. Therefore, Manvers Main has the distinction of being the only location in the country to have been served by trolleybuses before being served by trams.

The Dearne District Light Railway was well photographed by Edgar Scrivens who published two series of postcards in 1925 and 1930 featuring the tram cars.

Upper Left: Number 3, a Thurnscoe bound tram passes at speed along Barnsley Road in Wombwell. The car on the right, a Jowett registration WT 2345 belongs to the photographer. The scene is little changed today. *(Paul Fox Collection)*

Upper Right: Tram 13 travels towards Barnsley along Goldthorpe High Street near the junction with Barnburgh Lane in another scene which has changed little in the intervening years. *(Paul Fox Collection)*

Lower Left: A splendid scene of tram 18 passing along Wombwell High Street en route to Thurnscoe. Wombwell was a busy shopping centre as can be seen by the number of people. All the buildings on the right were demolished in the 1960s and 1970s and replaced with a modern shopping parade set back from the road.

Lower Right: Tram 17 heads past Wombwell Town Hall en route to Thurnscoe. Meanwhile a beer wagon is making a delivery to the Prince of Wales public house. This part of High Street is instantly recognisable today.

Almost immediately there was tremendous competition with the local bus operators, with the trams gaining around two thirds of the market share and the local bus operators the remainder. The competition had the effect of keeping a check on tramway revenues, although for the first five years the system recorded a small profit - except in 1926 - the year of the General Strike. However, the changing economic climate had a devastating effect on the local mining industry, following the Wall Street Crash of 1929, with many of the pits working on reduced time; money was in short supply. After sustaining heavy losses, not helped by a cheap fares war with the local bus operators and crippling interest charges on the initial construction loan, in 1932 the Light Railway Joint Board approached Yorkshire Traction to discuss their respective futures.

In 1933, Yorkshire Traction promoted the Dearne District Traction Act, to allow for the abandonment of the tram network and paving the way for the transfer of operations. On 30 September 1933, the tram cars operated for the last time, with Yorkshire Traction paying £75,000 for the business which included the premises at Wombwell which would be maintained as a new bus depot. The assets were not included in the deal and several of the tram cars, being relatively new and of modern design were sold for use elsewhere. Five cars saw further use in Falkirk and four others were sold to Lytham-St-Annes Corporation. However, the remaining 21 trams were acquired by people in the local area for use as summer houses, greenhouses, chicken coops, etc.… One of these survived well into the 2000s as a summer house near Langsett Reservoir but this has recently been dismantled. Other assets were disposed of, including the Broomhead Road housing estate and the tram poles, although the truncated stumps of three of these survive at the time of the writing by the old Gore Hill canal bridge on Doncaster Road in Wath. A modern bungalow near the cutting in Bolton-on-Dearne currently bears the name 'Tramways' in recognition of the trams.

The contract with Yorkshire Traction saw the latter continue to make payments to the local councils until 1966 when the initial construction loan had been paid off. Several of the staff joined Yorkshire Traction although others chose to return north to Scotland. Yorkshire Traction continued to operate from the Car Barns depot until its closure in 2000, when the staff were presented with brass souvenir key rings, engraved Wombwell Car Barns 1924-2000.

Many reasons have been put forward for the failure of the tramways. These include the lengthy running time, the positioning of inconvenient passing loops causing delays, municipal pride, the crippling loan repayments and the aggressive nature of the competing faster bus services. However, with the benefit of hindsight, it is easy to draw these conclusions and it is likely that the economic depression contributed to sustained losses. Perhaps it was a mistake to terminate at Thurnscoe Houghton Road where Thurnscoe Urban District Council had just completed construction of 266 houses. This may have provided plenty of passengers, but potential passengers from the 1,000 newly completed pit houses at Thurnscoe East and the 4,000 workers at Hickleton Main Colliery were ignored and served by rival motor bus operators. Whatever the reasons for its decline, the Dearne District Light Railway was ultimately one of the most fascinating and unusual systems in the country.

Independent Bus Operators.

Despite the appearance of Yorkshire Traction, Mexborough & Swinton, and Dearne District Light Railways, the Dearne Valley was home to numerous independent bus operators. Most of these have now been forgotten and lost to the annals of time, but their contribution to the local bus service network was considerable and a few of the larger concerns are mentioned below.

Burrows of Wombwell

In the early years of the century, Thomas Burrows, or Tommy Burrows as he was known, commenced horse drawn haulage and private hire operations, based from his premises at Jubilee Garage in Wombwell High Street. However, in 1921, he acquired his first bus to operate a colliery service. This bus was a Daimler CK with seating for 26 passengers. The vehicle was registered C 2895, C being the issuing prefix for the West Riding prior to the reorganisation of the West Riding registration prefixes in 1922.

A second new vehicle registered WT 637, a 26 seater Vulcan was purchased in 1923 and operated on a new service from Wombwell to Barnsley. At the time, many independent operators were competing for passengers along this busy route and, in 1924, following the opening of the Dearne District Light Railways, many of these fell by the wayside. However, Tommy Burrows was more robust than most and he extended the service to Wath-upon-Dearne. Further new vehicles were purchased and the route was extended northwards from Barnsley to Wakefield in April 1926. On 1 February 1927, the service was extended again from Wakefield to Leeds, and the lengthy Leeds to Wath service was now operating every two hours. From around this time fleet numbering was introduced and new and second-hand vehicles were numbered sequentially from fleet number 9 upwards.

In 1928, Tommy Burrows had hoped to extend his service southwards from Wath to Rotherham, but Rotherham Corporation had always opposed this. Consequently, the company sought another way around this and thus the service was diverted from Wath towards West Melton to the end of Wentworth village. At this point the bus turned around and returned through Wentworth village before continuing through Upper Haugh, Greasborough and Parkgate and then heading up Rawmarsh Hill and terminating outside Rawmarsh Baths. This created one of the longest bus services in the country at the time, operating 39 miles from Rawmarsh to Leeds. The service was maintained on a daytime hourly frequency and took five hours to operate a round trip from Rawmarsh to Leeds and back. To assist matters, several Leyland Lion motor buses were purchased.

Apart from a few cutbacks to the frequency during the Second World War, this service was reinstated after hostilities ended. In 1945, the first double deckers appeared with the purchase of a pair of Bristol K6A buses with utility low bridge bodywork provided by Strachans, with a seating capacity for 56 passengers. These vehicles were registered EWW 943 & EWW 944 and numbered 50 & 51 in the fleet. There then followed a delivery of several new and second-hand buses and coaches throughout the 1950s and early 1960s, but set against a background of declining passenger numbers, increasing operating costs and an aging fleet.

In 1965 Tommy Burrows died and the company (which had been registered as T Burrows & Sons Ltd in 1950) was managed by his sons, Colin and Fred. Yorkshire Traction had made approaches to purchase the bus service but they had no interest in the coaching operations. Consequently, on 22 October 1966, the Burrows brothers sold the operation and 12 second hand double deckers to Yorkshire Traction, retaining 18 coaches to operate their school contracts, works services, private hire operations and excursions business until final closure in 1974. The last vehicle purchased prior to closure was a second-hand Bedford SB5 coach in 1966, registered GNR 805D and numbered 109 in the fleet. Since operations started in 1921, the company had owned a total of 103 vehicles during its lifetime.

The service from Rawmarsh to Leeds was numbered 99 by Yorkshire Traction who acquired the 12 double deckers. However, these were not operated and were sold; Yorkshire Traction supplied their own vehicles to operate the service from their Wombwell depot. This service was short lived because following the completion of the M1 Motorway, a new network of local and express services was operated between Barnsley and Leeds and the 99 was substantially truncated to only operate between Wombwell and Wentworth in October 1969. This was later incorporated into Wombwell-Hoyland Circular routes 121 & 122, which were renumbered 321 & 322 on 1 April 1974. In April 1983, the former remnant of the original Tommy Burrows service was reduced to a couple of journeys on service 322 from Wentworth to Wombwell before complete withdrawal on 25 October 1986, thus ending the tale of one of the longest bus services in the country. Following closure of the coaching operations in 1974, the old Jubilee Garage and Petrol Station was demolished and the site is now occupied by a 1970s-shopping parade constructed along the northern side of Wombwell High Street.

Camplejohns of Darfield

The Camplejohns were a large family living in the Snape Hill area of Darfield and several of the male members of the family worked at Darfield Main Colliery. Although born near York, William Camplejohn had spent his early life living on Alderney in the Channel Islands, working as a carpenter and wheel wright, before moving to Darfield in the 1870s. Shortly after giving birth to his first son, John, his wife passed away. William then remarried and his second wife bore him six sons and two daughters.

In 1905, William and two of his sons, Walter and Thomas joined together to purchase their first motor vehicle, an Arrol-Johnson charabanc registered C 1229, possibly one of the first motorised vehicles ever to be seen in the area. This vehicle had seating for 18 passengers and had been constructed in Paisley, Scotland. It was delivered to Darfield by an Irishman, presumably in employment with Arrol-Johnson, who lodged with William's son, Anthony Camplejohn, for a week, to give the various brothers tuition on how to drive the new vehicle. This vehicle, with its limited suspension and solid rubber tyres and running on imported petrol, was used chiefly on private hire operations. One of its first duties was to take a party of Darfield Church Bell Ringers on a tour of the churches at Bawtry, Tickhill and Blyth to participate in bell ringing demonstrations. On Saturday evenings, the charabanc was used on a local bus service from Snape Hill through Low Valley to Wombwell Town Hall.

Over the following years further charabancs were purchased including C 1793 in 1907, a Humber 10 seater vehicle; and in 1910, a Durham Churchill 14 seater registered W 1643 was supplied by a Sheffield dealer, hence the W prefix Sheffield registration; C 4085, another 14 seater Dennis arrived in 1910; C 6232, a 19 seater Dennis, followed in 1912, together with C

7020, a much larger 29 seater Karrier charabanc. These vehicles were housed in a new garage constructed on Pitt Street in Low Valley with the company's office at Alderney Cottages on Snape Hill, the name Alderney reflecting the family's connections with the Channel Islands.

In 1909, the Wombwell service was extended to Barnsley and now operated daily. Later that year William Camplejohn died and the new partnership subsequently traded under the name Camplejohn Brothers. At the time, very few people had private cars, relying upon horse drawn wagonettes for transport, or simply walking, and the new bus service to Barnsley had been a tremendous success. One of the few private car owners at the time was Joseph Mitchell, the chairman of Mitchell Main Colliery Company, who lived in Netherwood Hall. One of William's grandsons, Sydney Camplejohn, sometimes assisted in the maintenance of the gardens at Netherwood Hall, guiding a horse drawn lawnmower across the lawns. With a small fleet of several charabancs now owned by the brothers, regular miners' services were started, running from Wombwell and Darfield to Houghton Main Colliery

Showing their entrepreneurial flair, the Camplejohn Brothers commenced a new charabanc service in 1910. However, this operated quite far away from their home area, working from Doncaster to Woodlands Model Village. This was the name given to a new colliery village that had opened to house the miners at Brodsworth Colliery. The Woodlands service continued in operation until 1916 when Doncaster Corporation opened street tramway. Possibly in connection with this new enterprise, two of the other Camplejohn Brothers opened a new cinema in 1912 in Adwick-le-Street and named the Woodlands Picture Palace. In 1915, Thomas Septimius Camplejohn left the partnership to go it alone in the Doncaster area when he established a bus garage at Askern Road in Bentley. From there he operated a bus service to another new Doncaster colliery, this time linking Bullcroft Main Colliery at Carcroft via Bentley to Doncaster. In 1927, this service was extended from Carcroft to Ackworth, serving new colliery villages at Skellow and Upton. Thomas Septimius Camplejohn survived in business for 20 years before selling out to Yorkshire Traction on 1 June 1935.

In 1920, the Barnsley-Wombwell-Darfield service was extended to Great Houghton. Alternative journeys now operated direct from Darfield to Barnsley via Ardsley, to provide quicker journey times. New motor buses were purchased throughout the 1920s. In 1930, the main hourly service was extended from Great Houghton to Thurnscoe, first to the Station Hotel, and then to a new pit housing estate, terminating at Hanover Street. The motor buses were painted in a pleasant maroon, red and cream livery.

In 1928, Walter Camplejohn retired as general manager. However, the family, always keen to explore potential new business opportunities, applied to the Hemsworth Rural District Council for planning permission for a new house, petrol station, and a small transport depot on a site at Darfield Cat Hill cross roads, adjacent to the main A635 road. Planning permission was granted and a rather grand villa was built, together with the petrol station and a two-level depot. This last was used to house the family's Darfield Motor Company haulage business, with the upper floor used as a showroom and for repairs. During the digging out of the foundations of the premises, the Shafton coal seam was discovered beneath the soil.

Deliveries of buses from 1929 onwards now received fleet numbers, commencing with fleet number 6, a new Thornycroft BC motor bus with 32 seater Willowbrook bodywork. Fleet numbering was now applied sequentially upwards to future new and second-hand vehicles, with some of the older buses receiving fleet numbers 1 to 5, on paper at least. In 1936, Sidney Camplejohn was appointed as general manager. Sidney (known as 'Johnny' from his surname) was one of seven sons of Anthony Camplejohn, who in turn was one of seven sons of the company founder William Camplejohn. The Second World War put a temporary halt to the deliveries of new vehicles. However, the first post war delivery received fleet number 19 and was registered EYG 94, an AEC Regal coach with seating for 36 passengers. During the late 1940s and 1950s further vehicles were purchased, both new and second-hand. These included traditional Dennis Lancets and some unusual vehicles manufactured by Atkinson and Sentinel. The last vehicle to be purchased was a 1959 Ford 470E coach with Plaxton 41 seater bodywork. This vehicle received fleet number 36 and was registered XWX 376.

By the end of the 1950s, the remaining brothers in the partnership were all nearing retirement age and on 31 December 1960 they sold the bus business to Yorkshire Traction which thus acquired their nine-vehicle fleet. Yorkshire Traction disposed of three vehicles and retained the other six, painting them into corporate colours. At the time of sale, the Camplejohn brothers had owned a total at least 48 vehicles since its formation in 1907, although this figure may be incorrect as many of the early records detailing the early charabancs are incomplete. The Camplejohn family remained in business as haulage contractors until 1997.

The two Barnsley to Thurnscoe routes were numbered by Yorkshire Traction as service 2 (via Wombwell) and service 3 (via Ardsley). Service 2 was subsequently withdrawn and incorporated into another Yorkshire Traction service whilst Service 3 was extended from Thurnscoe to Goldthorpe and renumbered to 373 on 1 April 1974. On 21 May 1978 Yorkshire Traction recast the service network in the Dearne Valley and service 373 was withdrawn, being replaced with services 212 and 273. Post-deregulation brought considerable changes and the former Camplejohn's service is now incorporated into Stagecoach Yorkshire's 219 Barnsley – Thurnscoe – Doncaster. The rather grand villa was demolished around 1995 to make way for the new Cat Hill roundabout, forming the intersection of the of the A635 and A6195. However, several artefacts commemorating the company are on display in the Maurice Dobson Museum & Heritage Centre in Darfield.

Above Left: Number 22 in the Camplejohn fleet was registered GWW 532, a 1948 Bedford OB with Duple Vista coachwork for 29 passengers. It is seen here in Low Valley outside the depot. Although used on private hire duties, the vehicle also saw service work too, as evidenced by its destination blind which reads Houghton via Ardsley. *(Photographer unknown)*

Above Right: This timetable flyer for the Wombwell to Darfield service must have been issued between 1948-1952 when Hargreaves & Bibbing were members of the Darfield Road Bus Operators Association *(Paul Fox Collection)*

Darfield Road Bus Owners Association

The Low Valley area was dominated by terraced housing constructed for miners at Darfield Main Colliery and they looked towards the nearby town of Wombwell for their shopping and leisure facilities. Consequently, several independent bus services began to operate along the busy corridor between Darfield, Snape Hill, Low Valley and Wombwell, all competing for passengers. Saturdays became particularly busy with shoppers and evening customers travelling to the various pubs and clubs in Wombwell or to the cinema.

In the mid-1920s four of the independent bus operators formalised an arrangement to trade as the Darfield Road Bus Owners Association, on a jointly operated timetable, and sharing proceeds, handling paperwork, license applications and lobbying local authorities. The original four members were Greenhow & Sons of Darfield, William Pickerill of Low Valley, Dan Smith of Darfield and Linley & Spencer. The latter sold out to Horace Hargreaves & Thomas Bibbing in 1948 which in turn passed into the ownership of G Hardman of Low Valley in 1952. The co-ordinated service was operated on a rota with each member operating two days per week, and, as eight days doesn't fit into a single week, two members operated on Saturdays on an enhanced frequency.

Thomas Greenhow of Darfield commenced operations with a horse drawn wagonette, which he used to transport miners from Wombwell and Darfield to Houghton Main Colliery. In 1908, he purchased his first motor vehicle and, by 1912, he was operating a bus service from Darfield to Barnsley. This was changed in 1915 to operate between Darfield and Wombwell. Details of the early fleet are sketchy, although as each member required only two vehicles to operate their share of the service, it is unlikely that vehicles were owned in significant quantities. He was later joined by his sons Herbert and Joseph and the business traded as Greenhow Brothers. Post war additions to the fleet were typically purchased second-hand from other bus operators. These included two second hand Leyland Lions purchased from Yorkshire Traction, one registered HE 4756 and another from the batch registered HE 5999 – HE 6001. Further acquisitions of second-hand vehicles followed throughout the 1950s. When the older generation of the Greenhow family reached retirement age in 1960, the company of their final two vehicles and their share in the Darfield Road Bus Operators Association was distributed between the remaining three members.

William Pickerill of Hope Street, Low Valley purchased his first motorbus in 1924 registered WT 5434, a brand-new Morris convertible, which could either operate as a flat-bed lorry, a van or a 14-seat bus. In 1928, another new vehicle was purchased, registered WW 4537. This was a 20 seater Dennis G with fixed bus bodywork. Further new and second-hand vehicles were acquired in the 1930s including WX 9009, a Bedford bus with a seating capacity for 20 passengers, acquired from fellow Darfield Road Bus Operators Association member Linley & Spencer. Post war vehicle purchases continued with a handful of new and second-hand vehicles and by now the business was trading as William Pickerill & Son, the son being William J Pickerill who joined the firm together with his wife and his sister Ivy Cadwallader (nee Pickerill). The last vehicle delivered was in 1962. This was registered 404 CWW, a Bedford SB5 with 41 seat coachwork by Duple. In 1964, the Pickerill family, by now the last surviving member of the Darfield Road Bus Operators Association, sold the business to Yorkshire Traction, having operated at least 22 vehicles during its lifetime. Three vehicles passed into Yorkshire Traction ownership; one was disposed of but the remaining two saw further service at the Wombwell Car Barns depot.

Dan Smith, based at 13 Barnsley Road, Darfield, started operations in the early years of the 20th century with a horse drawn wagonette plying for trade along the Darfield to Wombwell route. In 1921, he purchased a brand-new Ford Model T registered WY 1059 with seating for 14 passengers, which replaced the wagonette. He then bought a series of second-hand vehicles throughout the remainder of his membership of the Darfield Road Bus Operators Association, the only exception being a new coach purchased in 1938. This was registered CWU 581, a Bedford WTB with Plaxton 26 seat coachwork. In March 1955, Dan Smith's son, Brian, became a partner in the business which was now trading from 164 Barnsley Road, Darfield. Further second-hand vehicles followed during the 1950s until 1962 when Dan Smith decided to retire, offering his business to fellow member William Pickerill & Son. However, the Pickerill family refused to purchase the business so Yorkshire Traction stepped in and acquired the remaining three vehicles, two of which saw further service. Records show that Dan Smith operated 26 vehicles between 1921 and 1962.

The fourth member of the Darfield Road Bus Operators Association was J Linley & E Spencer of Darfield. Early records detailing this operator are unclear, although it was operating from Darfield to Wombwell in the early 1920s. In 1931, it purchased a new vehicle registered WX 9009. This was a Bedford WLB 20-seater bus which was sold in 1938 to William Pickerill. In 1948 Linley & Spencer sold their share in the Darfield Road Bus Operators Association to Hargreaves & Bibbing, along with their final vehicle, a 20-seater Dennis Ace. Four years later Hargreaves & Bibbing sold out to G Hardman of Low Valley. Hardman's first vehicles were a pair of coaches, a 1937 Bedford WTB 26 seater registered BWW 577 and a 1938 Bedford WLB 20 seater registered HE 8535. The company also operated private hire work but by 1954, a single vehicle was being used for the bus service on two days per week and was used on private hire duties on the remaining days. This was a brand new 1951 Bedford SB coach registered KWY 40. In 1958 the coach was sold and the business distributed between the other remaining members of the Association.

The former Darfield to Wombwell route was incorporated as a 30-minute frequency Yorkshire Traction services 125 and 126, both interworking with new routes 123 and 124 between Wombwell and Aldham House, worked by crews from Yorkshire Traction's Wombwell depot. For many years, this group of routes were referred to as "Danny's" by the drivers, a legacy of Dan Smith, the last member of the Darfield Road Bus Operators Association. On 1 April 1974, the services were renumbered 318 and 319 as part of the countywide renumbering policy. They survived in various guises and now form part of a longer distance Stagecoach Yorkshire route 67 from Wombwell – Darfield – Grimethorpe – Barnsley.

Dearneways of Goldthorpe

Dearneways was a relative late comer to the transport scene in the Dearne Valley when in 1949 Percy Philipson and his son, Maurice Philipson, commenced operations. Prior to 1949, the Phillipson's had traded as funeral directors but the growing trade in NCB colliery contract work caused them to change their career. In 1949, they purchased their first coach, an Albion CX9 with 35 seat bodywork. This vehicle was registered CS 7968 and subsequently received fleet number 1. The Phillipson's traded from new premises on High Street, Goldthorpe, adjacent to the former Dearne Valley Railway cutting. They officially traded as Dearneways Coaches but were frequently referred to as Dearneways. Further second-hand vehicles were acquired throughout the 1950s to operate additional NCB contracts. In 1958, the first double deckers were purchased. These were Guy Arab models new in 1945 and 1943, numbered 12 and 13 and registered JNU 558 and DCR 869 respectively. However, they only lasted for a brief time and were replaced in 1960 with a batch of five second hand Bristol K5G 53 seat double deckers which lasted until 1964.

In 1960 the local Goldthorpe firm of Harold Oscroft, trading as Irene Motors, was acquired. Although two vehicles were included in the deal, neither of these operated with Dearneways. The real reason for the acquisition of Irene Motors had been to acquire the firm's tours and excursions licence. To operate these an assortment of seven second-hand Leyland Leopard coaches were acquired becoming fleet numbers 40-46. These vehicles replaced some of the older coaches in the fleet as well as well as six vehicles damaged in a storm in 1962 which had caused the depot roof to collapse. A new bus depot was constructed on the old site in Goldthorpe High Street.

The company were looking to secure a regular revenue stream from operating a local bus service and proposed a long-distance route from the Dearne Valley to Rotherham and Sheffield. Following a lengthy battle with Sheffield Corporation, Rotherham Corporation, Mexborough & Swinton, Yorkshire Traction & British Rail, who all objected to the plan, to their surprise, Dearneways were granted the application for a limited stop service from Thurnscoe Big Lamp to Sheffield Castlegate, via Goldthorpe, Bolton-on-Dearne, Wath, Swinton, Rawmarsh, Rotherham and Attercliffe. The new hourly service commenced on 5 October 1964 with a fleet of four second hand Leyland Leopard buses numbered 47-50. The service began to prosper with local folk keen to undertake shopping trips to the city of Sheffield. On 1 April 1974, the Sheffield terminus was moved into the City Bus Station and the service was numbered X91 under the countywide service numbering policy.

An unusual long-distance coach service commenced in 1967, running from Kiveton Park near Worksop and picking up at many of the South Yorkshire pit villages before operating nonstop to Glenrothes in Fife. In the 1960s many Scottish pits were facing the exhaustion of their coal reserves and thus closure. The NCB encouraged Scottish mining families to move to the South Yorkshire Coalfield and the new service, operating at pit holidays, Christmas and New Year was ideal for Scottish miners wishing to return to Fife to visit friends and relatives. The Miner's express lasted until 1980.

In 1969 Percy Philipson left the partnership leaving Maurice Philipson in charge, and the first brand new vehicle arrived in 1971 with the delivery of a Leyland Leopard coach with 45 seater Plaxton bodywork. This vehicle was numbered 69 and registered GWT 235J. In 1974 the coaching company Fretwell's of Bentley, was acquired bringing four vehicles into the fleet, together with additional tours and excursions licences. Throughout the 1970s a succession of Leyland Leopards coaches was purchased but the last vehicles delivered new were in 1979 when 91-93 (AWJ291-293T) joined the fleet with the final second-hand purchases occurring in 1981 with the delivery of 94-95 (MWJ468-469P). The fleet was painted in a very smart royal blue and cream livery and the coaches certainly made an impression as they speeded through the Dearne Valley carrying shoppers to Sheffield.

On 6 December 1981, the South Yorkshire Passenger Transport Executive, which had been pursuing a policy of purchasing the remaining independent bus operators in the county, acquired Dearneways Ltd for £235,000. A total of 15 coaches and 18 staff transferred to the SYPTE's depot at Rotherham and the Goldthorpe premises were closed. SYPTE continued to operate the hourly service X91 with a peak hour duplicate operating as X92 and omitting

Rotherham. On 25 November 1985, three unique articulated Leyland-DAB vehicles were purchased to operate the service; these were known locally as 'bendy buses'. They were spectacular vehicles with 67 seats and two entry doors were unique in the country at the time and were numbered 2011-2013 in the SYPTE fleet with registrations C111-113 HDT. They were a certainly a favourite of the author as a child who was fascinated with the flexible bending portion in the middle! At Thurnscoe, the route was extended to loop round the 'Reema' and 'Whin Wood' estates to the Big Lamp, returning along Houghton Road, thus removing the need to perform a three-point reversing manoeuvre at the Big Lamp, a particularly difficult movement in an articulated bus.

With the opening of Meadowhall Shopping Centre on 4 September 1990, the bendy buses were transferred to operate new services between the shopping centre and Rotherham and Sheffield. However, the opening of new railway stations at Goldthorpe and Thurnscoe now provided much faster journeys to Rotherham, Meadowhall and Sheffield, and the X91 service was subsequently cut back to operate Sheffield to Wath only displaying route number 67. Ironically, where the growth of bus services had led to railway station closures in the 1920s and 1930s, the reverse was now happening and the 67 was quickly withdrawn and replaced by a short-lived Yorkshire Traction service 225 from Rotherham to Thurnscoe. This has also been withdrawn and the former Dearneways depot and house has been demolished, with a new Netto supermarket built on the site in 1998.

Larratt Pepper of Thurnscoe

Larratt Pepper was born in 1893 in Thurnscoe and, by 1907, at the age of 14 was operating a horse drawn wagon delivering meat from local butchers' shops and farms in the area. In 1914 at the age of 21 he purchased his first motorised vehicle. This was a Ford Model T to undertake his meat delivering business. This was replaced in 1921 when he purchased another Ford Model T registered WR 4032. This vehicle was licensed to carry eight passengers. A larger 25-seater Daimler CK charabanc registered WR 9453 also joined the fleet the same year. With these two vehicles, Larratt Pepper gave up the meat delivery side of his business and chose to operate a bus service, based from his premises on Clayton Lane. Surprisingly, his first service wasn't in Thurnscoe but operated from Doncaster to the large colliery village of Woodlands built to house the miners at Brodsworth Colliery a few miles away. This service, operated in competition with Doncaster Corporation trams which had begun in 1916. Interestingly, and probably not by coincidence, the Woodlands route had been the first route chosen by Camplejohns of Darfield from 1910-1916. Larratt Pepper's Woodlands route struggled to compete with the frequent trams so was it was diverted to operate from Carcroft to Doncaster instead. Two more vehicles followed in 1925 and 1927 and were used on another service some distance from his Thurnscoe base. This was from Barnsley to Grimethorpe along Pontefract Road. This route was subject to intense and aggressive competition from a multitude of other independent operators together with Yorkshire Traction.

In 1930, the establishment of the Road Traffic Act sought to eliminate the previously unregulated system and bus operators had to apply to the local Traffic Commissioners for licences to operate local bus services, preferably being of good standing and with a good reputation. In preparation for this, Larratt Pepper decided to cease his services to Carcroft and Grimethorpe and concentrate on providing a quality service from Barnsley to Thurnscoe via Darfield and Great Houghton. This service ran every two hours and took two hours to operate a round trip; however, most trips were duplicated, hence the need for two buses.

A co-ordinated timetable was introduced with the other operators on the route. These were Sydney McAdoo trading as Pioneer Motors based at Cudworth and Camplejohn Brothers of Darfield. The co-ordinated regulated timetable provided a bus every 30 minutes and impressed the Traffic Commissioners. Larratt Pepper operated this service for the following 50 years, providing them a regular source of income. In 1933, fleet numbering was introduced with the delivery of fleet number 7 (AWT 743) a brand-new Dennis Lancet with Fielding & Bottomley bodywork. Older vehicles in the fleet received fleet numbers 6, 5 & 4, whilst much earlier vehicles, long since disposed of, were posthumously numbered 3, 2 and 1, the last being applied to the 1921 Ford Model T.

Following the war further new vehicles were delivered commencing with vehicle number 8 (CWT 993), with the fleet continuing to grow during the 1950s and 1960s to serve an expanding private hire and excursions market. Buses and coaches were smartly presented in a maroon and cream livery bearing the LP logo, with the company now trading as Larratt Pepper & Sons Ltd. Following the takeover of Sydney McAdoo in 1940 and Camplejohns in 1960, both by Yorkshire Traction, Larratt Pepper remained with a ¼ share of the service from Thurnscoe to Barnsley. Delivery of buses and coaches continued with the last bus purchased being 36 (HWU 939J), a Bedford YRQ with 49 bus seats in 1971. The last coach delivered was in 1977 when 49 (TWA 553S), a Bedford YMT with Duple bodywork accommodating 53 passengers joined the fleet.

In May 1978, Yorkshire Traction purchased Larratt Pepper's bus service, but the firm retained four of its newest coaches to continue operations in the private hire business. This continued until November 1998 when the company ceased trading and the assets were sold off. For a few years afterwards, the Clayton Lane depot was used by coach operator National Holidays but the premises have since been demolished. Yorkshire Traction allocated service 372 to the former Larratt Pepper service but this was short lived as on 21 May 1978 the Dearne Valley network was reorganised and the services to Thurnscoe operated as 212 (Barnsley – Thurnscoe – Doncaster) and 273 (Barnsley – Thurnscoe – Mexborough). At the time of writing, the former Larratt Pepper service had been incorporated into Stagecoach Yorkshire service 219, operating every 30 minutes from Barnsley to Doncaster via Thurnscoe.

Above Left: The Mexborough Motor Omnibus Company Ltd was registered with a capital of £5,000 and traded as *The Pioneer*. It operated this charabanc with registration C3420 on a service between Wath and the Woodman Inn at Swinton. The vehicle is shown decorated for the coronation of King George V and is pictured on Sandygate in Wath-upon-Dearne. *(Brian Brownsword Collection)*
Above Right: Greenhow Brothers Durham Churchill Motorbus W2898 is shown outside Middlewood Hall Lodge in Darfield in 1914. In the 1920s the company became a member of the Darfield Bus Operators Association which co-ordinated its operations along the busy Darfield to Wombwell route. *(Maurice Dobson Museum & Heritage Centre)*

Above: During its lifetime, Yorkshire Traction purchased numerous other Dearne Valley bus companies including G S T Deverew whose staff and fleet are shown above at their Thurnscoe premises. From left to right are Thornycroft WU4226, Thornycroft DT445, Leyland Lion WE3134, Thornycroft WW505 and a new Leyland Tiger WE4584. The Deverew fleet was immaculately maintained and were "in much better condition than any vehicles which have been purchased so far", according to the Yorkshire Traction manager when the company was acquired on 1 June 1929. The depot was possibly located on Common Road or High Street in Thurnscoe.

The Deregulated Market

In addition to Burrows, Camplejohn Brothers, the Darfield Road Bus Operators Association, Dearneways and Larratt Pepper, the Dearne Valley once hosted numerous other minor bus operators. Additionally, the road from Barnsley to Shafton and Grimethorpe was the scene of intense competition and a survey in 1930 revealed that 40 buses per hour passed beneath Cudworth Railway Bridge. Some of these operators continued to trade into the 1970s, but they all eventually sold out to Yorkshire Traction or withdrew from the provision of passenger services in favour of concentrating on their coaching and private hire operations.

This purchase of all the independent operators cemented Yorkshire Traction's monopoly across the Dearne Valley, a situation it enjoyed until the introduction of a deregulation on 26 October 1986. This date, known in the transport industry as D-Day, was the result of the 1985 Transport Act and saw the introduction of a deregulated market and most of the state owned and local authority owned bus companies have since been privatised.

Since D-Day, new independent bus operators have returned to the area with, for example, Pride of the Road, Headlight Bus Company, Tom Jowitt Travel and Aldham Coaches registering new bus services in direct competition with Yorkshire Traction. Other routes, where bus fares were insufficient to cover operating costs, were awarded on a contract basis to local and outside operators, for example Wilfreda Beehive of Doncaster and TM Travel of Sheffield. However, most of these new independent bus companies have since ceased operating or have withdrawn from the area. Yorkshire Traction, which became Stagecoach Yorkshire in 2005, currently enjoys a monopoly across the Dearne Valley, although the recent appearance of First South Yorkshire operating from Rotherham to Wath and a contract network awarded to Yorkshire Tiger in 2017 brings a certain variety to the local transport scene. Whatever, a deregulated market can bring frequent changes with the entitlement that any bus operator with the appropriate insurance and facilities can commence a commercial bus service, set their own fares and bid for contracted bus services, so it is likely that future changes will continue.

The transport networks of the Dearne Valley have substantially changed in recent years. The roads are now busier than ever, especially at peak times or when there are shift changes at the many new businesses constructed on the former colliery sites. The railway network will continue to go from strength to strength, mirroring national trends, and the current service pattern is probably the most frequent passenger provision ever experienced. The potential for service enhancements and new station openings is considerable, although the once discussed reinstatement of the railway line from Mexborough to Barnsley now looks unlikely to happen. The bus network has shrunk down to a profitable core of routes provided by Stagecoach Yorkshire and a group of contracted routes provided by other 'low cost' operators, the latter routes possibly under threat from funding cuts in the future, however, the core commercial routes look assured, and some of these are experiencing gradually increasing passenger numbers.

Part 4 Conclusion

For most people, Friday 21 April 2017 was probably just another Friday, but this date marked a significant milestone in the history of energy generation in the UK because it was the first day since the Industrial Revolution that the burning of coal was no longer required to generate electricity. Yet, during the 1940s, coal provided over 90% of the country's electrical generating capacity as well as fuelling the nation's industries - a sizable proportion of this output was contributed from the pits of the Dearne Valley. During a period of 150 years from 1850-2000, the region experienced rapid development and exploitation of its coal reserves, which had been followed by an equally rapid contraction since the 1984/5 Miners' Strike, with the last deep coal mine closing in 1994 at Goldthorpe. Open cast coal mining continued for a few years; however, since the start of the new century, coal has no longer been mined in the Dearne Valley and the last pits in Yorkshire closed at Maltby (2013) and Hatfield and Kellingley (2015).

The Dearne Valley as a 21st century tourist destination? **Upper Left:** Elsecar Heritage Centre. **Upper Right:** Elsecar Newcomen Beam Engine. **Lower Left:** Hoober Stand on the Wentworth Woodhouse estate. **Lower Right:** The RSPB's Dearne Valley Nature Reserve at Old Moor.

The exploitation of the Dearne Valley's coal reserves saw the growth of numerous colliery communities and a dramatic population explosion as people migrated to the area to live in the new settlements and work in the new pits. The coal needed transporting to market and an extensive road, rail and canal network was developed. The new population also needed transporting to work and leisure, and tram, trolleybus and motorbus networks spread throughout the valley. The pits have now all closed and the transport systems have been reduced; nevertheless, the former colliery communities remain and face an uncertain future. Some have suffered from terrible deprivation, hardship and unemployment. However, new industries and employment opportunities have been brought to the area, and, whereas many of their fathers and grandfathers once worked in the mining industry, some of the younger generation are now employed in businesses that have opened on the former colliery sites. Most of the signs of coal mining have been removed from the landscape and, together with the demolition of some of the pit housing, some smaller colliery communities have now entirely disappeared from the map. The only signs of the coal industry to be seen today are the mining memorials and the grassed over spoil heaps - even the latter are now beginning to blend into the landscape. The Dearne Valley has now become the greenest and tree covered that it has ever been since the start of the industrial revolution.

However, other positive aspects have been recently developed and the tourist potential of Elsecar Heritage Centre and the Wentworth Woodhouse area is likely to be fully unlocked in the future. It would be pleasing to see the restoration of the Dearne & Dove Canal and the full development of the Elsecar Heritage Railway. Elsewhere in the Dearne Valley, the establishment of the RSPB's Old Moor visitor centre has been a remarkable success as has the opening of the Trans-Pennine Trail. Other heritage attractions have also helped to increase visitor numbers, including Brodsworth Hall, Conisbrough Castle, the Maurice Dobson Museum at Darfield and Worsbrough Watermill & Country Park, although at the time of the writing, the closure of Wentworth Castle & Gardens is a significant setback. Perhaps the future lies in developing the tourist potential of the region as it reverts to its pre-industrial landscape - one studded with traditional villages, former colliery communities, retail parks and new offices and industries. Whatever the future may hold, it would be a shame if the legacy of the mining industry is eventually forgotten, although I am sure this will not and should not happen. The Dearne Valley, once described to the author as forming the centre of a 'golden triangle', may yet experience another golden age. And on that note, I raise a glass to that thought! Good luck Dearne Valley.

Table of Colliery Openings and Closures.

Colliery	First Sod Cut	Barnsley Seam Reached	Depth (yards)	Closure
Lundhill	22 March 1853	1855	217	1895
Wombwell	8 December 1853	28 October 1854	224	23 May 1989
Darfield	1856	1860	330	31 July 1989
Manvers No 1	21 May 1867	1869	276	25 March 1988
Mitchells	August 1871	September 1875	307	26 July 1956
Wath	1873	1876	346	23 January 1987
Houghton	1873	1 February 1878	516	30 April 1993
Cortonwood	October 1873	March 1875	212	28 October 1985
Manvers No 2	1875	1877	280	25 March 1988
Hickleton	December 1892	28 June 1894	542	31 March 1988
Grimethorpe	8 October 1894	1897	581	14 May 1993
Elsecar	17 July 1905	20 September 1906	344	28 October 1983
Barnburgh	June 1912	28 May 1914	508	16 June 1989
		Shafton Seam		
Brierley	1910	23 April 1912	220	1947
Ferrymoor	1915	1916	70	1980
Dearne Valley	1900	1901	200	5 April 1981
Billingley Drift	1951	1951	33	1956
Highgate	May 1916	1917	c100	1985
Goldthorpe	27 June 1901	January 1910	63	4 February 1994

Table of Mining Memorials and Pit Wheels

Colliery	Memorial/Pit Wheel
Lundhill Colliery	Memorial to 1857 Explosion in Darfield Churchyard
	Memorial at Hillies Golf Course, Wombwell
Manvers Main Colliery	No 2 and No 3 shaft caps decorated with artwork, Manvers Way
	Manvers First World War Memorial, Golden Smithies Lane
Wath Main Colliery	Pit Wheel at Manvers Lake & Waterfront Park
Houghton Main Colliery	Memorial to 1886 Winding Disaster in Darfield Churchyard
	Pit Wheel at Little Houghton Middlecliffe Lane
	Memorial Garden at Great Houghton Welfare
Cortonwood Colliery	Pit Wheel on Knoll Beck Lane, Brampton Bierlow
	Proposed Memorial at Cortonwood Railway Station
Hickleton Main Colliery	Small wheel on Lidgett Lane, Thurnscoe
	Stained Glass Window in Goldthorpe Church
	Memorial in Thurnscoe Park
Grimethorpe Colliery	Pit Wheel outside Willowgarth School and Milefield Primary School
	Memorial outside Grimethorpe Church
Elsecar Main Colliery	Plaque on site of Simon Wood Colliery
	Pit Wheel in Elsecar Heritage Centre
Barnburgh Main Colliery	Pit Wheel on Hollowgate, Harlington
	Artwork at Goldthorpe Welfare Hall
	Stained Glass Window in Goldthorpe Church
Dearne Valley Colliery	1901 Datestone on Middlecliffe Lane, Little Houghton
Highgate Colliery	Artwork at Goldthorpe Welfare Hall
	Stained Glass Window in Goldthorpe Church
Goldthorpe Colliery	Artwork at Goldthorpe Welfare Hall
	Stained Glass Window in Goldthorpe Church

Glossary

Aerial Ropeway or Aerial Flight. A steel rope with buckets attached, supported on pylons and used to convey coal or waste material to a tipping site.

Barnsley Seam. A highly-prized seam of coal up to 10 feet thick within the Coal Measures of South Yorkshire which is only found at the surface near the town of Barnsley but lies buried at depth in the Doncaster area.

Bunker. A large container used for the storage of coal.

Cage. A steel structure used to transport men or tubs up and down the shafts. Some cages had two or three decks. The cage was attached by a steel rope to the winding engine.

Coal Measures. A thick sequence of rocks and strata which consists of sandstones, shales, clays and coal seams. The coal measures of Yorkshire contain around 30 different coal seams.

Coal Preparation Plant. A building where the treatment of coal is undertaken prior to dispatch, usually containing screens, washery and a conveyor leading to a rapid loading bunker.

Coalfield (Exposed & Concealed). An area of land above coal measure rocks. A coalfield may be "exposed", i.e. the coal measures are found at the surface, or "concealed" where they are hidden at greater depths beneath younger rocks. Barnsley and the Dearne Valley are located on the exposed coalfield whilst Doncaster is situated on a concealed coalfield where the coal measures are buried beneath younger Magnesian Limestone and Bunter Sandstones.

Cupola Shaft. A shaft with a furnace at the base to aid the ventilation of underground workings.

Drift. A sloping tunnel connecting coal seams to the base of the shafts or to the surface.

Endless Rope Haulage. A continuous rope used to haul coal tubs to the bottom of the shafts.

Electrical Ring. A scheme whereby surplus electrical power was distributed from one pit to neighbouring collieries. Carlton Main Collieries and Doncaster Collieries Association each operated an electrical ring.

Fault. A geological fracture resulting from the upward or downward movement of rock strata.

Gin Pit. A small colliery with a horse powered winding apparatus.

Gob. The area left following removal of a coal seam. The roof above was supported with waste material or allowed to collapse in a controlled way.

Headgear. A structure of wooden, steel or reinforced concrete situated above the shafts and used to support the winding wheels from which the cage was attached by a rope.

Heapstead. A structure located beneath the headgear providing a covered means of transport for coal exiting the shafts via filled tubs enabling transport to the nearby screens buildings.

Land Sale. A yard at the pit where coal could be purchased by individuals or tradesmen and usually transported away for local use by horse and cart or lorry.

Longwall Mining. A method of coal working in which coal is mined from a long coal face. The coal face connects two tunnels which lead back to the base of the shafts. The coalface thus advances away from the shafts leaving an area of gob behind. This method was later replaced by retreat mining.

Main. A suffix used mainly in South Yorkshire to denote those collieries which mined the largest or main seam from the coal measures, i.e. the Barnsley Seam

Merry-Go-Round. A scheme for the continuous loading and transport of coal by train from pit to power station.

Pillar and Stall Mining. A method of coal working where coal was extracted from areas known as stalls leaving pillars of coal to support the surface. Typically used when the coal seams lie at shallow depths and largely replaced with longwall mining due to the advance in technology in the 19th century.

Pit. A local term for a coal mine or colliery.

Private Owner Wagons. Railway wagons owned by private coal producers and merchants used on the national railway network.

Rapid Loading Bunker. A large bunker containing many tons of coal which is deposited into railway Merry-Go-Round wagons passing beneath the structure.

Retreat Mining. The most economical method in mining in which roadways are driven out to the extremity of the royalty so that a coal face can then be worked back towards the shaft bottom. Largely superseded longwall mining in the 1960s.

Rake. A group of railway coaches or wagons all coupled together.

Roadways. Underground tunnels leading from the bottom of the shaft to the coal faces.

Royalty. An area of land beneath which coal can be extracted by paying a fee or royalty to the landowner on every ton produced.

Screens. A building containing numerous devices for sorting individual lumps of coal by size or weight.

Shaft. A vertical tunnel from the surface to the coal seam through which the coal is raised and men and materials can access the workings. Following a mining disaster at Hartley Colliery in County Durham each colliery was required to have two shafts, downcast and upcast, to aid escape in the event of an accident. Typically, air was sucked through the downcast shaft to ventilate the workings and then drawn out of the colliery via the upcast shaft.

Shaft Pillar. An area of coal left intact to support the colliery's surface buildings and thus protect them from the effects of subsidence. Some coal was removed from the shaft pillar to form roadways or tunnels to access the underground workings.

Sinking. The process of tunnelling vertically downwards from the surface to the coal seam to construct a shaft, usually undertaken by workers called sinkers who specialised in this highly skilled but dangerous work.

Skip Winding. A method of winding coal up a shaft by using a large capacity metal container or skip. A more economical way of transport than that previously used when individual coal filled tubs were brought to the surface in a cage.

Staple Shaft. A shaft that doesn't reach the surface, usually sunk underground from a coal seam to a deeper seam.

Staithes. A landing stage for the loading of cargo into boats.

Tubbing. A waterproof casing, usually of iron, inserted into a shaft as it was sunk to keep back water and soft sediments.

Tubs. Small wagons used to transport coal underground, usually hauled by pit ponies or endless rope haulage.

Tumblers. Machinery for screening and sorting coal.

Vesting Day. 1 January 1947, the day when the privately-owned mining industry was nationalised,

Washery. A surface plant building for dealing with the cleaning and washing of coal.

Wayleave. A royalty paid to the owner of the land on which the colliery is situated.

Winding Engine. An engine, initially steam driven but later powered by electricity, used to raise the cages up and down the colliery shafts.

Bibliography

Abell, P H (1977) **Transport and Industry in South Yorkshire**. Eastwood Press, Rotherham.
Bailey, C (2007) **Black Diamonds: The Rise and Fall of an English Dynasty**. Penguin Books.
Barker, C (2008) **Mexborough & Swinton Trolleybuses**. Middleton Press.
Barnsley Canal Group (1991) **Dearne and Dove Canal – the vital link**. Barnsley Canal Group.
Barnett, A L (1984) **The Railways of the South Yorkshire Coalfield from 1880**. RCTS Publishing.
Benson, J & Neville, R G (Eds, 1976) **Studies in the Yorkshire Coal Industry**. Manchester University Press.
Benson, R (2014) **The Valley**. Bloomsbury.
Benton, R (2012/3) **Dearne District Light Railways Tram Services**. Published in 8 parts in Sheffield Transport Study Group Journal Issues 68-75.
Booth, A J (1996) **Industrial Railways of Manvers Main and Barnburgh Main**. Industrial Railway Society.
Booth, A J & Chapman S (2009) **Railway Memories 21: Rotherham, Mexborough & Wath**. Bellcode Books.
Brearley, M (2008) Mexborough, **A Railway Junction to Anywhere and its Steam Locomotive Depot**. Shadowline Publishing Ltd.
Buckley, K W (1956) **A Geographical Account of the Village of Darfield**. Thesis, University of London Institute of Education
Buckley, R J (1987) **A study in the decline of the British Street Tramway Industry in the twentieth century with special reference to South Yorkshire**. Thesis, University of Hull.
Burgin, F (1999) **Historical South Yorkshire**. People & Mining, Bolton-on-Dearne.
Cockshott, J (1983) **Yorkshire Traction Company Limited Part 1 1902-1960 – Fleet History PB20**. PSV Circle/Omnibus Society.
Cockshott, J (1984) **Yorkshire Traction Company Limited Part 2 1961-1984 – Fleet History PB21**. PSV Circle/Omnibus Society.
Colliery Guardian (1927) **The Colliery Year Book & Coal Trades Directory**. Louis Cassier Publishing.
Darfield Area Amenity Society (2006) **Wheels: The early life of Sydney (Johnny) Camplejohn of Darfield**.
Dearne Local History Group (1993) **The Lane Enders: A History of Goldthorpe 1894-1904**.
Dearne Local History Group & Young, M (1996) **Goldthorpe Thurnscoe & Bolton-upon-Dearne**. Chalford Publishing.

Denton, A S (1980) **DDLR: The Story of The Dearne District Light Railways and Competitors**. Omnibus Society Publications.
Doncaster Amalgamated Collieries Limited (1944). (Souvenir Brochure published on the occasion of the visit of a delegation of American Mining Engineers).
Downes, E (2016) **Yorkshire Collieries 1947-1994**. Think Pit Publications.
Ellis, N (1992) **Coal – its cost and its cards**. In Picture Postcard Monthly Magazine 164, p16-18.
Ellis, N (1995) **South Yorkshire Collieries on old picture postcards**. Reflections of a Bygone Age.
Elliott, B (2001) **Darfield & Wombwell**, Sutton Publishing.
Elliott, B (2003) **Darfield & Wombwell**: A Second Selection, Sutton Publishing.
Elliott, B (2006) **South Yorkshire Mining Disasters Vol I: The Nineteenth Century**. Wharncliffe Publishing.
Elliott, B. (2009). **South Yorkshire Mining Disasters Vol II: The Twentieth Century**. Wharncliffe Publishing.
Edwards, D G (2001) **A Historical Gazetteer and Bibliography of By-Product Coking Plants in the United Kingdom**, Merton Priory Press.
Evison, J (1972) **The opening up of the central region of the South Yorkshire Coalfield and the development of its townships as colliery communities**. M Phil Thesis, University of Leeds.
Fordham, D (2016) **Denaby and Cadeby Main Collieries: the development of a Mining Community**, Fedj-el-Adoum Publishing.
Fox D (1935) **Coal Combines in Yorkshire**. The Labour Research Department.
Fox, P (2004) **The Dearne District**. Notes to accompany a talk presented to the Doncaster Omnibus & Light Railway Society, Privately Printed.
Franks, D L (1971) **South Yorkshire Railway**. Turntable Enterprises.
Franks, D L (1979) **Swinton and Knottingley Railway**. Dalesman Publishing Company.
Glister, R (2004) **The Forgotten Canals of Yorkshire**. Wharncliffe Books.
Godfrey, A (Various) **Godfrey Edition Reproduction Maps (with notes by contributors)**. Alan Godfrey
Goode, C T (1975) **Railways in South Yorkshire**. Dalesman Publishing Company.
Goode, C T (1986) **The Dearne Valley Railway**. Anlaby, Hull.
Grudgings, S (2015) **The last years of coal mining in Yorkshire**. Folly Books.
Hadfield, C (1972) **The Canals of Yorkshire and North East England Volume 1 & 2**. David & Charles.
Hay, H & Fordham, D (2017) **New Coalfields New Housing: Reviewing the Achievements of The Industrial Housing Association**. Fedj-el-Adoum Publishing.
Heal, E F (1951) **The History of Thurnscoe**. Doncaster Chronicle.
Jones, M (2000) **The Making of the South Yorkshire Landscape**. Wharncliffe Books.
Kelly (1912**) Kelly's Directory of the West Riding of Yorkshire**. Kelly's Directories Ltd.
Kennedy R (no date) **Mining Memories**. Thurnscoe Local History Group.
Malpass, J (1991) **The Building and Development of Hickleton Main Colliery 1892-1988**. Dearne Local History Group.
Mercer, N (2015) **Independent Bus Operators in Western Yorkshire**. Venture Publications Ltd.
Mitchel, G H (1947) **Geology of the Country Around Barnsley** HMSO, London.
Nott-Bower, G & Walkerdine R H (1957) **National Coal Board: the first ten years**. Colliery Guardian Company Ltd.
People and Mining (no date) **A brief history of the "Concrete Cottages" Brampton Bierlow**.
Quarrell, H W (1954) **A History of Swinton**. Times Printing Co Ltd, Mexborough.
Spaven, P J (1978) **Accommodating the Miners. A comparative study of industrial relations and community involvement in some South Yorkshire coalmining townships 1955-1894**. PhD Theses, University of Warwick.
Sharp, C & P (1994) **Old Wombwell and Hemingfield**. Richard Stenlake Publishing
Sykes, J A (1982) **Yorkshire Traction Early Development**. Published by Yorkshire Traction.

Smith, H. (1992) **A History of Rotherham's Roads & Transport**. Rotherham Metropolitan Borough Council Department of Libraries, Museums & Arts.
Smith S (1995) **The Cinemas of Mexborough and the Dearne Valley**. Mercia Cinema Society.
Taylor, M (1996) **Dearne Valley Memories**. In Picture Postcard Monthly Magazine 210, p34-35.
Tefler, B (2008) **Yorkshire Traction Glory Days**. Ian Allan Publishing.
Tomlinson, J (1879) **From Doncaster into Hallamshire**. Brook White & Hatfield.
Tuffrey, P (2011) **South Yorkshire Railway Stations**. Amberley Publishing.
Wain, K (2014) **The Coal Mining Industry of Barnsley, Rotherham and** Worksop. Amberley Publishing.
Walters, Sir J Tudor (1927) **The Building of Twelve Thousand Houses**. Ernest Benn Publishing Ltd.
Walker, A G (1993) **Social and Cultural Construction of Communities in South Yorkshire Colliery Settlements: the mining households of the Darfield and Wombwell District c1851-1900**. PhD Thesis, University of Sheffield.
Ward, G (2007) **Burrows Motor Coach Service**. Privately printed, Hoyland Common.
Ward, J T (1976) **West Riding landowners and mining in the nineteenth century**. In Benson & Neville (1976) qv, p45-65.
Whitehouse, A (2016) **Rails through Barnsley: A Photographic Journey**. Pen & Sword Transport.
Williams, P (2005) **Images of Yorkshire Coal**. Landmark Publishing Ltd.

MAURICE DOBSON MUSEUM & HERITAGE CENTRE

2 Vicar Road, Darfield, Barnsley, S73 9JZ

A restored Georgian yeoman's residence where Darfield's long history is brought to life

Open Easter to October
Saturdays 10am-4pm, Sundays 2-5pm & Wednesdays 1-4pm
Winter Opening times:
Saturdays 10am-2pm & Wednesdays 1-4pm

01226 754593 www.darfieldmuseum.co.uk

Researching South Yorkshire's Transport History

I am always looking for photos, information, and recollections of Sheffield / Rotherham / Mexborough & Swinton / Dearne District Light Railway buses, trams and trolleybuses and of the people who operated them?

...likewise transport related memorabilia?

...collections bought where local material included!

Paul Fox
113 Tinker Lane, Walkley, Sheffield, S6 5EA   0114 266 3173